JAMES MADISON
On
RELIGIOUS LIBERTY

*edited, with introductions
and interpretations by*
Robert S. Alley

PROMETHEUS BOOKS
Buffalo, New York

Published 1985 by Prometheus Books
700 East Amherst Stree, Buffalo, New York 14215

Copyright © 1985 by Robert S. Alley
All Rights Reserved

Library of Congress Catalog Card Number: 85-62743
ISBN 0-87975-298-X
Printed in the United States of America

To

Horton Davies
Princeton University
A Gifted Teacher

The structure of our government has, for the preservation of civil liberty, rescued the temporal institutions from religious interference. On the other hand, it has secured religious liberty from the invasion of the civil authority.

—*Watson v. Jones* (1871).

There remains no medium, either a liberty of conscience must be permitted us to enjoy our owne opinions in matters of religion, or else there is a necessity of being liable and subject against conscience, whensoever the civil powers which surely are no more infallible than ecclesiasticall, shall happen to enact or stablish any thing else.

—Henry Robinson (1643)

Religious *freedom* in an open society has the best prospects of flourishing to the extent that it expresses itself as freedom of religious *inquiry*.

—Sidney Hook (1963)

On consideration of the bill establishing religious freedom, agreed: That the said bill, in our opinion, puts religious freedom upon its proper basis; prescribes the just limits of the power of the state, with regard to religion; and properly guards against partiality towards any religious denomination; we, therefore, heartily approve of the same, and wish it to pass into a law.

—Virginia Baptist General Association
(October 9, 1779)

Freedoms vindicated anew are more precious than those achieved without effort, and only those who are required to justify freedom can fully understand it.

—Henry Steele Commager (1954)

Among those I call the great men of the world are Thomas Jefferson, James Madison, and various others who participated in formulating the ideas behind the First Amendment for this country and in writing it. . . . The First Amendment is truly the heart of the Bill of Rights. The Framers balanced its freedoms of religion, speech, press, assembly, and petition against the needs of a powerful central government, and decided that in those freedoms lies this nation's only true security. They were not afraid for men to be free. We should not be.

—Hugo Black (1960–1962)

Contents

Preface

The year 1985 marks the two-hundredth anniversary of the writing of James Madison's *A Memorial and Remonstrance*, and in some sense this volume may be understood as a commemoration of that publication. Indeed, woven through these pages the reader will discover the thread of the *Memorial* constantly in evidence. The scholar-commentators represented here are all aware of the central importance of that single slim document. But they are equally aware that Madison's contributions to religious freedom in America span his entire adult life, from his early days at Princeton to those productive years of retirement at Montpelier. Indeed, as the Madison writings in this book make clear, religious liberty was a burning issue for him from 1772 to 1833.

Thus, this present collection is intended to honor Madison as America's premier exponent *and* practitioner of the principle of freedom of conscience. The essays make it evident that such is the opinion of those contributing to this volume. In addressing the life and work of Madison, attention has been given to his own religious views as a means of understanding his existential commitments. And in every instance, it is intended that the historical events, far from being blueprints for modern times, should provide the context in which to comprehend the principles of natural rights and freedom. If James Madision is significant for modern America it is because his ideas have merit, his insights a timeless quality that confound those who would incarcerate the man in the past glory of the nation.

In the preparation of this monument to Madison I have been aided by all those who have graciously consented to participate in the project. In particular, there are individuals who have devoted time and energy absolutely essential to achieving the final results. Paul Kurtz, whose thoughtful ideas led to the conception of the work, has lent constant support. He is dedicated to every effort that will enlighten the American public concerning Madison. Robert Rutland, whose scholarly efforts continue to expand our knowledge of the "Father of the Constitution," has been ready with assistance and guidance from the beginning. Donald Drakeman has been an effective critic, offering valuable suggestions over many months. A. E. Dick Howard, who along with Kurtz and me serves on a steering committee for the James Madison Memorial Committee, has been a colleague and advisor, as well as major contributor to the final product. To these friends and the many others whose assistance and help made this book a reality, thank you.

For me the last word in such acknowledgments always relates to my family. My wife Norma, along with Bob, John, and Vickie have not only understood the long hours, they have been eager listeners concerning the progress of an undertaking in which they all believed.

University of Richmond   ROBERT S. ALLEY

PART I

Introduction

To know what ultimate position James Madison will hold in his country's history one must know what that country's future will be. If the American people abandon the rights and liberties he worked so hard to establish, he will be forgotten along with them. Should those rights and liberties be taken away by force or deception, they and he will continue to live in hope and aspiration. If they are maintained and cherished, the memory of James Madison will be as enduring as the mountains at which he looked so often across field and forest from his Virginia home.

—Irving Brant

It would not be surprising to find most Americans jaded by the ten years of bombardment from the media, particularly television, concerning our nation's bicentennial. When citizens were first enjoined to celebrate the country's two-hundredth anniversary, Watergate and Vietnam were vivid images from our immediate past. From Bunker Hill to Philadelphia to Valley Forge to Yorktown, the population was reminded of our heritage as a nation as "Bicentennial Minutes" vied with dog food commercials as they recalled the myriad of events that combined to create the Union. We were, in all this, celebrating valor and victory. We were seldom reminded that having established colonial independence from England, the leadership stumbled into a government coalition, under the Articles of Confederation, that provided only limited latitude for the spirit of freedom manifest in those grinding years

13

of conflict. The promise of Jefferson's Declaration lay beyond the grasp of those first representatives who sought to fulfill their responsibilities as lawmakers.

In truth, the fundamental principles that would eventually establish that "more perfect union" were still awaiting *The Federalist* to find expression. Fortunately, Americans had time for failure in their isolated, eighteenth-century world, time to allow the "Spirit of '76" to work its will in the cherished words of the Constitution and the Bill of Rights. Thus, Americans begin, in 1985, to celebrate that second bicentennial, the birth of those pragmatic documents, grounded in principles of freedom and justice, that would make the American Revolution genuinely unique in world history. And when all contributors have been honored, one name alone lays claim to peculiar recognition. For the second wave of the bicentennial is most particularly the story of James Madison.

As the pages in this volume will amply attest, the years 1785 to 1791 belong preeminently to the gentleman from Orange County, Virginia. From *Memorial and Remonstrance* (1785) through the Constitutional Convention (1787) to *The Federalist* (1788) to the ratification convention in Virginia (1788) to the United States Congress (1789) to the ratification of the Bill of Rights (1791), the thinking of Madison so consistently dominated that historians easily refer to him as "Father of the Constitution." In this present undertaking we identify those contributions of Madison's that relate most directly to religious freedom, beginning with his successful effort to strengthen George Mason's Bill of Rights (1776), progressing to his victory in the struggle for the passage of the Virginia Bill to Establish Religious Freedom (1786), and concluding with his role in the construction of the First Amendment. And while the essays to follow may be construed as an elaborate panegyric of James Madison, something far more substantial is intended.

In 1607 the Jamestown settlers quickly established the Church of England in the Virginia colony, making life intolerable for Catholics and Quakers and uncomfortable for Protestant dissent. These conditions prevailed for more than a century. By 1630 Puritans in Massachusetts had covenanted together to establish "God's New Israel." Their "city upon a hill" was a beacon of intolerance of all dissent, a theocracy that made life impossible for Quakers, Catholics, separatists, and freethinkers. This government, with the Bible for a text, was slowly tempered, but not until the nineteenth century was a coalition of 'sectarian-pietists' and rationalists able to secure religious liberty. In 1656 Roger Williams began the Providence settlement, which "admitted no reservations" respecting religious liberty. Williams's concept of government was not biblical, but rational, based upon his understanding of the nature of religion. A devout man, he was convinced that his theological convictions gave him no right to impose upon others his own definitions. Combining reason and piety Williams effected a system of church/state separation that was and remains the sterling example of a principle brought to practical fruition.

As these examples demonstrate, we were, and remain, a nation of distinctly different traditions, some of which have been tested and found wanting in the democratic crucible. Historian Sidney Mead observed: "The struggle for religious freedom during the last quarter of the eighteenth century provided the kind of practical issue on which rationalists, and sectarian-pietists could and did unite, in spite of underlying theological differences, in opposition to 'right wing' traditionalists."[1]

The richness of America's philosophical heritage includes profound religious thinkers, brilliant humanists, and dedicated rationalists. As the eighteenth century drew to a close a fortuitous coalition of events and ideas resulted in a free church and a secular republic. It offered an exciting environment in which religious leaders were proffered the unhindered opportunity, all too often ignored, to exercise a prophetic voice on matters of justice and peace and freedom. By the same token, the politician was encouraged to seek rational justification for policies, rather than retreat into pious pronouncements and national messianism. The purpose of this volume is to explore how and why the founders chose from among the various traditions available that peculiar form of church/state relationship we possess. This is all the more important because there are those in 1985 who would prefer to view the Constitution and the Bill of Rights through the prism of seventeenth-century Virginia establishment and Puritan New England. In a 1985 dissenting opinion, Justice William Rehnquist gave expression to the sentiment that the First Amendment was intended only to prohibit the federal government from showing partiality toward any particular sect. The evidence from Madison's life and work, set forth in this volume, completely vitiates such an interpretation.

Americans are at present in the midst of a shouting match about the founding fathers. Some say Madison was unconcerned about establishment of religion in the states.[2] Others seek to uncover flaws of inconsistency in the historical records related to Madison and Jefferson.[3] They miss the point. When the founders are discussed herein, it is not intended that heroes be created as ideological models. One should not embrace religious freedom in 1985 merely because two prominent Virginians did so two centuries ago. Rather we develop respect for those individuals and their associates because they espoused principles considered essential to true democracy. This is no game in which each side seeks to uncover old quotes favorable to their cause; it is a confrontation over basic presuppositions, a conflict between democracy and theocracy, both of which have deep roots in our past.

Writing just as the Supreme Court began its post-World War II series of cases focused on the religion clause of the First Amendment, Joseph L. Blau offered an effective definition of the task set before those who would seek to reinforce the principles enunciated by Madison and Jefferson:

The true history of the struggle for religious freedom is to be found after the principle of the wall of separation had been formulated. The struggle of the past century and three quarters to give substance to the formula of religious freedom is the true history of religious freedom. It is an unending struggle; it has not been finally determined by the McCollum decision, nor will any future decision determine the meaning of the principle once and for all. Each generation must fight the battles of freedom anew in terms of the problems and powers of its time. To use unchanged the arms of tradition is to invite defeat; to see in the past a guide and instrument in the development of unfolding values and meanings is to be on the road to victory.[4]

The current generation is faced with a new challenge. Most of the Supreme Court cases since 1947 have been concerned with testing the limits of the First Amendment. The question was posed as to how far that document would stretch in response to new situations. In short, what would it allow? Justices Black and Rutledge set the tone for this national discussion when both used Madison in their opposite opinions in the *Everson* case. The underlying assumption in the following years was that all sides believed in the First Amendment principles. It was then a matter of deciding how modern problems might be addressed while adhering to the separation of church and state. People discussed the nature of Jefferson's "wall," seldom if ever its appropriateness.

Today the challenge is distinctly different. The First Amendment is now under threat from persons who find fault with its premise, or refuse to accept the historic line from Madison and Jefferson through the Amendment to modern Supreme Court decisions on church and state. Advocates of various forms of a "Christian America" argue against the Jeffersonian wall. This is a fundamental shift to which citizens should be alerted. And it makes the words of Blau even more pertinent.

Those who espouse unconditioned religious liberty with its broad implications are inclined to understand the nation in terms of human rights, freedom, and social justice rather than in dogmatic and Armageddon phrases. Our historical sense allows us to identify past political leadership that exhibited those same concerns. Hence certain eighteenth-century figures become important because they share a common experience with us.

Our pride in them is a reflection of our pride in our national character. There were voices of other patriots reflecting a different spirit in the colonial period, committed to oligarchy and theocracy, church establishment and religious intolerance. We are a nation with a diverse quilt of political and religious traditions: Some of those traditions do not translate well or inspire emulation today.

The distinction between human rights and right beliefs is at the heart of this discussion. Beginning with Roger Williams the tradition of a nation committed to emancipation, human dignity, justice, and liberty developed. The Williams model languished only to be revived in the second half of the eighteenth century by his successors, who, inspired by the Enlightenment, issued the clarion call for religious liberty. And as a result of the prodigious efforts of James Madison and his compatriots the American republic came to practice a secular morality influenced by many philosophies. As Henry Steele Commager notes in his closing essay, "Its testaments, moral, philosophical, or political, celebrated virtue, happiness, equality in the sight of God and the law, justice, and life here rather than hereafter. It believed in one form of immortality—the immortality of *fame*—which was the spur: 'Take care of me when I am dead,' Jefferson wrote Madison; it was in a sense the *cri de coeur* of their generation."[5] The fame has to do with ideas, not dogma from the past. The recognition of a spirit of equality and justice in Madison causes us to honor him. The quality of his political thought and actions makes him a giant. We know he was, for all that, a man, and we may anticipate inconsistencies, errors of judgment, and moral blindnesses similar to our own. Indeed it was Madison himself who observed "men are not angels."

One does not need to evoke Madison or any person in order to justify an unswerving dedication to the principles of justice and liberty; *but* we will always require women and men to espouse those rights and freedoms if they are to be secured for posterity. To such persons, as to Madison, we owe a debt that can only be paid in the currency of continued vigilance regarding the first experiment on our liberties.

Daniel Boorstin phrases it well in his essay: "The courage to doubt, on which American pluralism, federalism, and religious liberty are founded, is a special brand of courage, a more selfless brand of courage, than the courage of orthodoxy. A brand that has been far rarer and more precious in the history of the West than the courage of the crusaders or the true believer who has so little respect for his fellow man and for his thoughts and feelings that he makes himself the court of last resort on the most difficult matters on which wise men have disagreed for millennia."[6]

In the following pages there is no dogma, no one way to view the First Amendment. The single constant, running through all the contributions, is the assumption that freedom and justice are best secured through the continued implementation of that amendment according to living principles.

The scholars assembled for this current volume encompass a broad range of disciplines—history, philosophy, religion, political science—and their approaches offer a panoramic view of Madison and the First Amendment. A historical chronology has been utilized in order to guide the reader from the early colonial experiments through the life of Madison to the application of his principles in modern America. Many of the essays have appeared in other publicatons over the past few decades, but until now no single collection has attempted to examine the subject of religious freedom through the life and legacy of James Madison. Together they provide the reader with a means of understanding a tradition that may only be possessed as it is lived. Thus, Blau's observation provides an appropriate context in which to begin: "There are many brave words here of continuing vitality, rich in suggestive power—but the most stirring words are those yet to be spoken."[7]

NOTES

1. Sidney Mead, "American Protestantism during the Revolutionary Epoch," in *Religion in American History*, eds. John M. Mulder and John F. Wilson (Englewood Cliffs, N.J.: Prentice Hall, 1978), page 165-66.

2. *Jaffree* v. *James*, U.S. District Court decision.

3. Phyllis Schlafly, "Court Establishes Prayer in Schools," February 23, 1983, syndicated by Copley News Service.

4. Joseph L. Blau, ed., *Cornerstones of Religious Freedom in America* (Boston: Beacon Press, 1950), p. 30.

5. Henry Steele Commager, "Take Care of Me When I am Dead," *Free Inquiry* 3 (1983). This quote appears on page 332 of this volume.

6. Daniel J. Boorstin, "The Founding Fathers and the Courage to Doubt," *Free Inquiry* 3 (1983). This quote appears on page 211 of this volume.

7. Blau, p. 30.

PART II

A Historical Analysis

The subject of religious freedom was central to the thought of James Madison from his earliest involvement in government. Yet it is important to understand that his philosophy of freedom respecting the conscience was developed against a rich tapestry of political and social ideas. Understanding Madison first in relation to the founding of the republic provides the reader with a far more satisfying context for interpreting his profound ideas about religious liberty. Indeed, because of Madison's dominating role in the writing of the Constitution, those ideas become a basic guideline for understanding what the Constitution means. With this in mind Professor Howard provides a thoroughly engaging essay on Madison as "Father of the Constitution."

A. E. Dick Howard

James Madison and
The Founding of the Republic

James Madison—by common consent, the Father of the nation's Constitution—was in many ways an unlikely candidate for the historic role he played in the founding of our republic. Madison was not what we today would call "charismatic"; indeed, for strong personality, it is Dolley, not James, that history remembers.

Unprepossessing in appearance—he stood only five feet six inches tall—and often in ill health during his early years, Madison lacked the majestic bearing, physical prowess, and martial skills of George Washington. His prose, while copious and competent, missed the bite of Paine or the elegance and lucidity of Jefferson. In an age when public speaking was a highly prized political tool, Madison was plagued by a weak voice and hobbled by self-consciousness. Madison was so unimpressive a public speaker that he felt suited neither for the ministry nor the law as a profession (either of which would have been a natural vocation for a person of Madison's intellectual interests).

Madison more than made up for his shortcomings, however, with his rigorously logical mind, appetite for reading, and indefatigable industry. As he matured, he drew around him a circle of important friends who recognized in him a quiet but keen sense of humor, a potential for iconoclasm, and unshakable integrity and convictions.

History can appreciate how Madison's strengths came to outweigh, by any measure, whatever may have been his limitations. For it is Madison who, more than any other founder, shaped our constitutional system of government. How this came to be—how Madison's ideas of politics and government were formed, and how he put those ideas to work—makes a fascinating story.

Madison was born to James Madison, Senior, and Nelly Conway Madison, both from Virginia's landed gentry, on March 16, 1751, at the home of his maternal grandmother at Port Conway on the Rappahannock River. Shortly after his birth, the family moved west to the Rapidan River, in Orange County. The trip was only fifty miles or so, but it took the Madisons from the Tidewater to the Virginia Piedmont at the foot of the Blue Ridge Mountains. Both in Madison's day, and for decades after the revolution, life and politics in Virginia were heavily colored by differences in outlook conditioned by living in the east (where established power lay) and in the more westerly regions.

James Madison thus grew up, as did Thomas Jefferson (who lived only thirty miles away), with that strange blend of rustic life and cultivated social and intellectual discourse that marked plantation life in the Piedmont. At the same time, growing up at the family seat at Montpelier, young James Madison enjoyed the leisure purchased by slavery—a leisure employed in the education of a young Virginia gentleman.

After early education at home and at Donald Robertson's school on the Mattapony, Madison entered the College of New Jersey (now Princeton University) in 1769. Madison's choice of Princeton was distinctly unusual; a young Virginia gentleman was likely to attend the College of William and Mary at Williamsburg. It seems that Madison was swayed by his admiration for Thomas Martin, a tutor recently graduated from Princeton. Moreover, Madison (and his father) may also have been drawn by Princeton's eighteenth-century reputation for religious strictness and staunch patriotism. These qualities were exemplified in John Witherspoon, the Edinburgh-educated President, an active Presbyterian, who had come to Nassau Hall shortly before Madison became a student there.

The decision to go to Princeton was a momentous one for Madison, for it brought him directly under the influence of the ideas of the Scottish Enlightenment. At the college, Madison encountered an early experiment with what would become a staple of American education in the late eighteenth and early nineteenth centuries—a curriculum heavily influenced by the Scottish school. Edinburgh, which produced many of the intellectual leaders of Madison's younger years, had emerged as the most progressive English-speaking university. While the figures associated with the Scottish Enlightenment varied considerably in their views, the general thrust was an appeal to "common sense," a belief that all men possess an innate sense that enables them to distinguish between good and bad, truth and falsehood, beauty and ugliness. The Scottish philosophers, especially Thomas Reid and Francis Hutcheson, combined their belief in "common sense" with Whiggish patriotism, a "plain" rhetorical style, a plea for empirical investigation of nature (including human nature and political institutions), and a program for a more practical education.

John Witherspoon's Princeton was not friendly to all Scottish thinkers (certainly not free-thinking skeptics like David Hume), and many vestiges of an earlier educational model remained. But Madison eagerly entered into a remarkable political education. He was active in the newly founded American Whig Society, a political club that included Hugh Henry Brackenridge, the gifted writer and jurist; Phillip Freneau, soon to become America's leading poet; William Bradford, later attorney general under Washington; and John Henry of Maryland, later a senator and governor. Above all, Madison devoted himself to an intense study of "The Law of Nature and of Nations." With what he recalled as the "minimum of sleep and the maximum of application," he finished his bachelor studies in less than three years.

Madison was a diligent student, especially in history and government. Following his graduation, he spent several more months studying Hebrew, law, and ethics under Witherspoon. Madison's Princeton years brought him tutelage in such works as those of Locke, Montesquieu, Harrington, Grotius, and Hobbes. Through his grounding in Scottish intellectual attitudes, Madison came to appreciate the notion—a fundamental assumption among Enlightenment writers—that the study of history yielded generalizations about human nature and thus furnished guidelines for the governance of human affairs. Thus the stirrings of empiricism (part political theory, part embryonic sociology) played an important part in shaping Madison's thinking about laws and constitutions.

Some years later, therefore, when Madison argued in *The Federalist* for the ratification of the new Constitution, he stressed an appeal to "experience . . . that last best oracle of wisdom." Madison's appeal was no submission to the fetters of the past. Quite the contrary, Madison looked to experience to illuminate a progressive future. As he said in *Federalist* No. 14: "Is it not the glory of the people of America, that, whilst they have paid a decent regard to the opinions of former times and other nations, they have not suffered a blind veneration for antiquity, for custom, or for names to overrule the suggestions of their own good sense, the knowledge of their own situation, and the lessons of their own experience?"

When Madison returned to Montpelier in 1772, he continued his studies and tutored his younger siblings while pondering his own future. Plagued with ill health and depressed by the death of a close friend from Princeton, Madison brooded over his prospects. "I am too dull and infirm now," he wrote, "to look out for any extraordinary things in this world for I think my sensations for many months past have intimated to me not to expect a long or healthy life."

Melancholia soon gave way to a passionate interest in public events, nurtured by his inquiring mind. One of the earliest controversies to engage Madison's attention—emblematic of his overarching concern for the freedom of the human spirit—concerned religious liberty. Local persecutions of Baptists and other dissenters moved Madison to write to a friend that "well meaning men" were in jail for publishing their religious sentiments. He prayed "for Liberty of Conscience to revive among us." Correspondence about political events led to more active roles for Madison, including a seat on Orange County's committee of safety.

In May 1774 Lord Dunmore dissolved Virginia's assembly. The burgesses simply repaired to a nearby tavern and proceeded to form the first of a series of conventions that functioned as the effective government of the colony. In 1776 Madison was elected to the Virginia Convention, representing Orange County. At twenty-five he was one of the youngest members. In May 1776 the convention took the momentous step of instructing Virginia's delegates to the Continental Congress, then meeting in Philadelphia, to introduce a resolution calling for independence from Great Britain.

In moving for independence, the convention also created a committee to draft a declaration of rights and a frame of government for Virginia. The principal draftsman of Virginia's new constitution was George Mason, a well-read and politically active planter from Fairfax County. In the debates over the new charter, Madison's chief contribution came when the delegates took up the question of religious freedom. Mason's draft provided that "all Men should enjoy the fullest Toleration in the Exercise of Religion, according to the Dictates of Conscience . . . ." This approach, grounded in John Locke's *Letter on Toleration*, ensured only a limited form of religious freedom—toleration of dissenters in a state where there was an established church. Madison, however, wanted stronger language. He drafted a substitute declaring that "all men are equally entitled to the full and free exercise of religion"—language sounding of natural right rather than toleration.

Madison's resolution also declared that "no man or class of men ought, on account of religion to be invested with any peculiar emoluments or privileges . . . ." In the course of debate, however, Madison was obliged to drop this clause, which would surely have disestablished the Anglican Church in Virginia and probably also have barred state support of religious sects generally. The question of disestablishment remained to be settled in 1786, with the passage of Jefferson's Statute for Religious Freedom.

In 1777 Madison suffered the only defeat of his electoral career. It was customary at that time for candidates for public office to ply the voters at the polls with some rum or hard cider. Madison (perhaps with the shade of Witherspoon looking over his shoulder) thought it "inconsistent with the purity of moral and of republican principles" to sully an election with the "corrupting influence of spirituous liquors." The voters of Orange County seem to have been offended by this display of virtue. (They may well have decided Madison was being arrogant or perhaps simply being tightfisted with his money.)

Madison was not out of public office long. Remembering the impression he had made at the Virginia convention in Williamsburg, the leadership of the new state government chose Madison as one of the eight members of the

Council of State, a body that worked closely with the governor in carrying out the Commonwealth's executive business.

Three years later, he served as a delegate to the Continental Congress. Between 1780 and 1783, when the Peace Treaty was signed with Great Britain, Madison was immersed in national rather than merely regional politics. In 1780 he wrote the instructions to John Jay, American minister to the court of Spain, supplying Jay with arguments supporting free navigation of the Mississippi by the United States. Spain claimed a monopoly on navigation of the lower Mississippi, while the United States claimed the lands between the mountains and the Mississippi, as well as navigation rights, derived from England's 1763 treaty ending the last French and Indian War.

In another "national" matter of great urgency, Madison took the leading role in fashioning the compromise over western lands. Virginia, under its colonial charter, had vast territorial claims, asserting dominion over what are now the states of Kentucky, Ohio, Indiana, Michigan, Illinois, Wisconsin, and parts of Pennsylvania and Minnesota. Other states likewise claimed western lands, and frequently these claims overlapped one another. Land companies, liberally doling out rum to Indian tribes, speculated with millions of acres of land. It was Madison who, with parliamentary skill, steered through Congress the terms by which the eastern states would cede land for the common benefit of the American nation. The settlement fashioned by Madison and his colleagues formed the basis for national land policy under which state after state would be added to a union that ultimately would stretch from ocean to ocean.

Returning to his home at Montpelier in December 1783, Madison carried on his intellectual pursuits, including the study of law. As if in training for the task ahead of him in Philadelphia four years later, Madison made a particular study of confederations, ancient and modern. He wrote to Thomas Jefferson, then in Paris, asking his friend to buy him books, especially those throwing light on the "general constitution and droit public of the several confederacies which have existed"—leagues such as those of ancient Greece and Switzerland.

Jefferson, with his characteristic energy, saw to it that a stream of books flowed westward to Madison—nearly 200 volumes in all. Madison's reading ranged from Plutarch and Polybius to Mably and Montesquieu. In the historians he found repeated confirmation of what was becoming a favorite Madisonian thesis: a confederacy could not hold together without a strong federal center. One by one, Madison considered the strengths and weaknesses of the confederacies, ancient and modern—the Lycian, the Amphictyonic, the Achaean, the Helvetic, the Belgic, the Germanic. Out of these musings came a manuscript of forty-one pages, describing these confederacies, analyzing their federal nature, and summing up each section with conclusions on "The Vices of the Constitution." Much of this essay, even to its actual language, Madison later carried forward into Nos. 18, 19, and 20 of The Federalist.

Elected in 1784 to the Virginia House of Delegates, Madison quickly became a leader in the General Assembly. He had a hand in virtually every major project between 1784 and 1786—development of the state's resources, improvement in its commerce, and modernization of its laws. Looking to the western regions, he inaugurated a series of surveys to improve transmontane communications. Less successful—though unquestionably forward-looking—were Madison's efforts on behalf of public education; he was unable to persuade the Assembly to establish a general system of common schools as proposed by Jefferson's Bill for the More General Diffusion of Knowledge. (It took another century for a statewide system of public education to be established, by the Constitution of 1870).

A landmark of this period was Madison's role in helping define the proper boundaries between church and state in a free society. In 1784 Patrick Henry and others proposed a general assessment to support ministers of religion. Madison, in reply, wrote his famous A *Memorial and Remonstrance against Religious Assessments*—a document that furnished the intellectual roots of the First Amendment's ban on an establishment of religion.

Religion, said Madison, "must be left to the conviction and conscience of every man," religious freedom being an "unalienable right." Government support of religion, he argued, is not necessary for the health of religion; to the contrary, its legacy has been "superstition, bigotry, and persecution." Moreover, aiding religion at public expense would "destroy that moderation and harmony which the forebearance of our laws to intermeddle with Religion has produced among its several sects."

Government's role, Madison concluded, is simple: "protecting every Citizen in the enjoyment of his Religion with the same equal hand which protects his person and his property; by neither invading the equal rights of any Sect, nor suffering any Sect to invade those of another." Madison's spirited defense of religious freedom and of the separation of church and state helped defeat Henry's bill. In its place the General Assembly enacted Jefferson's Bill for Religious Freedom.

On the national scene, the mid-eighties were a time of discouragement for those who cared about the health of the American nation. The defects of the Articles of Confederation were increasingly apparent. Under the Articles, Congress had neither the power to tax nor to regulate commerce. The Articles declared that "each state retains its sovereignty, freedom, and independence," and the states were ever quick to assert and promote their own interests, at the expense of the national welfare.

Commercial rivalries were especially sharp. Concerned with building its own prosperity, a state was inclined to treat a sister state as it would a foreign nation. States without seaports were especially hard hit. New Jersey, finding itself between the ports of New York and Philadelphia, was, said Madison, like a "cask tapped at both ends." North Carolina, between Virginia and South

Carolina, resembled a "patient bleeding at both arms." Indeed, Madison believed, most of the new nation's "political evils may be traced to our commercial ones."

The answer to these problems, Madison concluded, was to give Congress power to regulate commerce. As he told James Monroe, the states could no more exercise this power separately "than they could separately carry on war, or separately form treaties of alliance or commerce." After the Virginia legislature emasculated a bill calling for an enlargement of Congress's commercial powers, Madison drafted a resolution that called for the states to appoint commissioners to meet and consider "how far a uniform system in their commercial regulations may be necessary to their common interest and their permanent harmony . . . ."

Thinking it prudent to avoid intimations of influence by either Congress or commercial interests, Virginia proposed the meeting take place at Annapolis, in September 1786. Attendance was spotty; only five states were represented. Finding that they could accomplish little, the delegates at Annapolis decided that stronger measures were necessitated. They resolved that the states should appoint commissioners to meet at Philadelphia the following year "to devise such further provisions as shall appear to them necessary to render the constitution of the federal government adequate to the exigencies of the Union" and to report such proposed changes to Congress.

No one who attended the great gathering at Philadelphia in 1787 was better prepared for the job of constitution-making than Madison, who came as a member of the Virginia delegation. His years of study paid rich dividends. Before arriving at Philadelphia, Madison wrote "Notes on Ancient and Modern Confederacies" and a paper on the "Vices of the Political System of the United States." In "Vices," Madison noted that, lacking coercive power, the federal system under the Articles lacked "the great vital principles of a Political Constitution" and was in fact "nothing more than a treaty of amity" between so many independent and sovereign states. Anticipating objections to centralized power—indeed, rehearsing the arguments he later used in *Federalist* No. 10—Madison argued that enlarging the sphere of government should lessen the insecurity of private rights, as society would become "broken into a greater variety of interests, of pursuits, and of passions, which check each other . . . ."

In letters to Jefferson, Edmund Randolph, and George Washington, Madison set out his thinking about the nation's constitutional needs. The larger states should have fairer representation, and the national government needed adequate authority to act in those areas requiring uniformity. In particular, Madison thought there should be national power, including authority in the federal courts, to override state laws in conflict with national legislation. To Washington, Madison summed up his middle ground: "Conceiving that an individual independence of the States is utterly irreconcilable with their aggregate sovereignty; and that a consolidation of the whole into one simple republic would be as inexpedient as it is unattainable, I have sought for some middle ground, which may at once support a due supremacy of the national authority, and not exclude the local authorities whenever they can be subordinately useful."

Although called merely to draft amendments to the Articles of Confederation, the Philadelphia convention soon moved to more ambitious business—the writing of a new constitution. Advocates of reform had a head start. A caucus of Virginians produced the "Virginia Plan," which Madison played the major role in shaping. Introduced by Randolph four days after the convention opened, the Virginia Plan proposed a national executive, a national judiciary, and a national legislature of two houses, apportioned according to population and empowered to legislate "in all cases to which the separate States are incompetent." Madison's scheme also included a Council of Revision, drawn from the national executive and judiciary, which could veto laws passed by Congress or by the state legislatures.

All in all, the thirty-six-year-old Madison was the dominating spirit of the Philadelphia convention. Certainly his influence on the convention was such that he has been aptly described as the "master-builder of the Constitution." His winning ways, persuasive powers, and command of constitutional principles deeply impressed the other delegates. South Carolina's Pierce Butler later wrote that Madison blended "the profound politician, with the Scholar" and that in the "management of every great question he evidently took the lead in the Convention."

Many of Madison's specific ideas, for example, the revisionary council to veto state and congressional legislation, failed to be adopted. Yet, in addition to furnishing the basis for discussion, his plan laid down the basic features that distinguished the Constitution as finally agreed to by the convention—three branches in the federal government (thus institutionalizing Montesquieu's notions of the separation of powers) and sufficient authority in the central government to provide national solutions for national problems.

As if his intellectual contributions were not enough, Madison was also the convention's main, if unofficial, recorder. Using a self-invented shorthand to speed his note taking, Madison carefully transcribed each speech. As he reported later, "It happened, also, that I was not absent a single day, nor more than a casual fraction of an hour in any day, so that I could not have lost a single speech, unless a very short one."

His account of the convention was not published until 1840, four years after his death, because Madison scrupulously observed the secrecy imposed on convention delegates. Once published, however, his notes provided a remarkably detailed account of the proceedings, adding, as Madison foresaw, an essential "contribution to the fund of materials for the History of a Constitution on which would be staked the happiness of a people great even in its infancy, and possibly the cause of Liberty throughout the world."

As the country turned to the debate over ratification of the proposed Constitution, Madison once again was a leader. Together with Alexander Hamilton and John Jay, Madison wrote essays for New York newspapers. The series of essays was introduced by Alexander Hamilton in the *New York Independent Journal* on October 27, 1787. Madison's first contribution, *Federalist* No. 10, appeared on November 23. Of the eighty-five essays—published in 1788 as *The Federlaist*—Madison wrote twenty-nine.

The Federalist has few competitors as America's single most important contribution to political theory and to the art of governance. In *Federalist* No. 10, Madison saw a central problem of government—in terms that are uncannily prescient—as being to reconcile rivalries among competing economic groups. Madison looked to the new Constitution to control the excesses of "faction"—factions being those groups which, united by some common interest (such as landed or mercantile interests), pursue ends adverse to the rights of others or to the greater good. "The regulation of these various and interfering interests," says Madison, "forms the principal task of modern legislation"; left to their own devices the most powerful factions must prevail. The variety of interests likely to be represented in the national legislature would furnish a safeguard: "The influence of factious leaders may kindle a flame within their particular States, but will be unable to spread a general conflagration through the other States."

As *Federalist* No. 10 reveals, Madison was under no illusions about the nature of man, even within the salubrious environment of a republic. "What is government itself," he asked in *Federalist* No. 51, "but the greatest of all reflections on human nature? If men were angels, no government would be necessary." Heir to Enlightenment notions of natural rights and limited government, Madison realized that a popular government can be as tyrannical as a monarchy. His pragmatic ideas about government, rooted in a Lockean empirical tradition, furnish a striking contrast to French revolutionary thought, which, combining the imperatives of Rousseau's General Will and the politics of popular sovereignty, ultimately propelled France into the Napoleonic era.

Throughout Madison's *Federalist* essays are found devices for addressing the practical problems of government. In *Federalist* No. 39, Madison emphasizes the dual nature of the new government: "The proposed Constitution therefore is in strictness neither a national nor a federal constitution; but a composition of both. In its foundation, it is federal, not national; in the sources from which the ordinary powers of the Government are drawn, it is partly federal, and partly national: in the operation of these powers, it is national, not federal: In the extent of them again, it is federal, not national: And finally, in the authoritative mode of introducing amendments, it is neither wholly federal, nor wholly national."

Turning, in *Federalist* No. 48, to the relations among the several branches of the federal government, Madison pointed to the benefits of having checks and balances among those branches. Mere "parchment barriers"—Madison's reference is obviously to the original state constitutions—are not enough to halt "the encroaching spirit of power." As a total separation of powers is unworkable, the only way to avoid an undue concentration of powers in one branch of government is to have the several branches "so far connected and blended as to give each a constitutional control over the others . . . ."

The new Constitution, all in all, was one of balance—of states and the central government protected in their respective interests, of power distributed among the branches of the federal government, of limits upon the opportunities of individuals or factions to work their way in derogation of the common good or of the inalienable rights of the citizen.

As Madison and Hamilton added essay after essay to the New York debate, they did more than help ensure ratification of the new Constitution. They gave American constitutionalism its first coherent base in political theory. The Constitution owed much to the give and take of the Philadelphia convention, but Madison was able to make a virtue of that necessity. At first he had resisted efforts to retain powers in the states; now he became an advocate for blended state and federal power.

So elegantly and thoroughly was Madison's defense of the proposed charter marshalled in The Federalist that the essays quickly became, and have remained, essential glosses on the Constitution. Jefferson prescribed The Federalist as a part of the curriculum at his University of Virginia. Chancellor Kent, in his great Commentaries, praised the treatise, saying: "There is no work on the subject of the constitution, and on republican and federal government generally, that deserved to be more thoroughly studied." More than simply a tract on American government, The Federalist is the first significant analysis of modern federalism. Hence it has attracted the attention of intellectuals in other countries, for example, in England, Sir Henry Maine, James Bryce, and John Stuart Mill.

In the contest between Federalists and Antifederalists over ratification of the Constitution, no state's vote was more crucial than that of Virginia. In that commonwealth's ratifying convention, Patrick Henry and George Mason led a spirited opposition to approval of the new document. Madison was also a member of the convention, and his quiet cogent reasoning contrasted with Henry's rococo oratory. The final vote was a close one, 89-79 in favor of ratification. Had the vote gone the other way, it is hard to say what might have become of the Constitution, in light of Virginia's crucial place in terms of wealth, population, and influence in the nation.

An implicit condition of ratification in Virginia and in some other states was the Federalists' undertaking to see that a bill of rights was added to the Constitution. Madison was at first apprehensive about such amendments, fearing that they might imply the existence of powers never meant to be delegated to the central government. Moreover, he was concerned that any attempt to list the rights of the citizen would be incomplete.

As he explained to Jefferson, however, Madison saw that a bill of rights could serve two powerful objectives. First, "the political truths declared in that solemn manner acquire by degrees the character of fundamental maxims of free Government, and as they become incorporated with the national sentiment, counteract the impulses of interest and passion." Second, there might be occasions when a bill of rights "will be a good ground for an appeal to the sense of the community."

When the first Congress met, Madison put aside any doubts he may have felt and led the battle for the Bill of Rights. On June 8, 1789, he initiated discussion of the issue by moving for a Committee of the Whole to receive the proposed amendments. Facing considerable opposition, he then brilliantly engineered passage of the bill, drafting the propositions, answering objections, and adroitly avoiding efforts by opponents to delay the votes or weaken the proposals.

In the course of the debate, Madison responded to the argument that the Bill of Rights would be ineffectual. If the amendments were incorporated into the Constitution, he submitted, "independent tribunals of justice will consider themselves in a peculiar manner the guardian of those rights; they [the courts] will be an impenetrable bulwark against every assumption of power in the Legislative or Executive . . . ." This explicit forecast of the courts' power of judicial review bore fruit in 1803, when Chief Justice John Marshall, in *Marbury* v. *Madison,* declared the Supreme Court's power to refuse to enforce an act of Congress that it found to be unconstitutional.

In framing the amendments, Madison winnowed the lists of proposals submitted by eight of the ratifying conventions. He largely ignored proposals (the work of Henry) that would have restricted federal power. Madison looked instead for inspiration to the twenty libertarian proposals drafted at the Virginia ratifying convention by Mason. As Madison's language wended its way through Congress, some provisions were revised, others dropped altogether (in particular, a proposal that would have forbidden the states to violate rights of conscience or press). But, in the end, Madison's propositions were the basis for nearly all the provisions embodied in the amendments ultimately adopted by Congress. Madison had won perhaps his most successful legislative battle—and all in the service of a cause that he had originally doubted.

In 1797 Madison voluntarily left public life, expecting to devote his time to farming his Montpelier estate. He also expected to devote more time to his new bride. Dolley Payne Todd was a twenty-six-year-old widow of a Philadelphia lawyer when Madison married her in September 1794, just four months after they were introduced. She was a vivacious and charming woman, whose social grace, beauty, and wit made her a political asset as well as a beloved and inseparable companion. Now Madison looked forward to a respite from the political conflict of Philadelphia—and to an opportunity to monopolize his wife's company.

The Federalists were now in full control of the national government. Madison, who had contributed so much to achieving a federal government, by now had become a recognized leader of the opposition, the Jeffersonian party. A dark chapter in Federalist rule was their enactment of the Alien and Sedition Acts, which outlawed "any false, scandalous and malicious writing" against the government, and under which opposition newspaper editors went to jail. The first victim was Congressman Matthew Lyon, of Vermont, who was jailed for publishing in his newspaper a letter charging President John Adams with a grasp for power and a thirst for adulation.

Federalist judges who tried cases under the Sedition Act, especially Justice Samuel Chase, displayed violent partisan bias against the accused. Madison's belief in "independent tribunals of justice" as an "impenetrable bulwark" of the Bill of Rights was gravely undermined. Accordingly, Jefferson and Madison turned to another breastwork—the states. From Jefferson's pen came the Kentucky Resolutions, from Madison's, the Virginia Resolutions. Both denounced the Alien and Sedition Acts as unconstitutional.

Jefferson's resolution was the more forceful, declaring the two laws to be "altogether void and of no force." Madison's language, though more muted, still called upon the states as the ultimate judges of the federal compact: "In case of a deliberate, palpable and dangerous exercise of other powers, not granted by the said compact, the States who are parties thereto, have the right, and are in duty bound, to interpose for arresting the progress of the evil . . . ." The doctrine of "interposition"—appealed to by South Carolinians in 1828—appeared to call for state nullification of federal legislation. But in 1800, as a member of the Virginia legislature, Madison wrote a 20,000-word report on the 1798 resolutions, in which he explained that those declarations were simply "expressions of opinion," for the purpose of "exciting reflection" on objectionable federal actions. However strongly understood, the Virginia Resolutions strikingly reflect Madison's sense of the need for balance wheels in the federal system. The man who in 1787 saw greater central authority as one of the ways to ensure the common good in 1798 looked to the states to resist federal encroachment on individual rights.

The elections of 1800 brought Jefferson to the presidency, and Madison appeared once again in the national spotlight. In his autobiography, Madison rushed over his eight years of service under Jefferson in a single sentence: "In 1801 he was appointed Secretary of State and remained such until 1809." These eight years, however, played a profound role in Madison's later political fortunes, for during this period he not only cemented his political and personal ties with Jefferson but also identified himself with policies of the Jefferson administration.

In 1808 Madison was swept to the presidency by an electoral margin of 122 to 47. His years in office were dominated by the country's difficult relations with Great Britain. Angry at the impressment of American sailors, the plunder of American ships on the high seas, and threats by both England and France against neutrals venturing into a port of either nation's enemy, Jefferson's administration had secured enactment of embargo and non-importation measures. Committed to maintaining these economic pressures, Madison found himself dealing with strong opposition from Federalists in the Northeast (where American ships and sailors were idled by the economic warfare) as well as dissidents within the Jeffersonian Republican ranks.

For a short time it appeared as if negotiations might provide a solution. An agreement in 1809 seemed to respond to American grievances, but it collapsed when Britain's foreign secretary, George Canning, repudiated the negotiations of the British minister in Washington. By 1812 the diplomatic impasse seemed hopeless. With deep misgivings, Madison called upon Congress to declare war. The House supported him 79 to 49, the Senate by a more modest margin of 19 to 13.

The War of 1812 was an indecisive tragi-comedy of errors. Ironically, five days after war had been declared, the British cabinet revoked the Orders in Council (the proclamation threatening neutral ships entering French ports). But news traveled slowly in those days, and the message came too late to avert hostilities. The United States proved ill prepared for war. An invasion of Canada proved a fiasco; Detroit fell to the British with hardly a shot being fired. Only some fine seamanship, especially the Constitution's capture of the Guerriere in late summer, brightened the early war news.

By 1813 the Americans were shown some significant military successes by Captain Oliver Perry on Lake Erie and General William Henry Harrison at Detroit. But even though Madison had been reelected president in a race against "peace candidate" De Witt Clinton of New York, Madison's opponents in Congress frustrated the war effort. When in August 1814, the British invaded Washington and burned the Capitol and the White House—with first Dolley, then the president, fleeing before them—a symbolic low point in the war was reached.

Despite the mixed successes of British troops, Great Britain was not anxious to continue with the war. Good news reached Washington on February 14, 1815, that a treaty of peace had been signed at Ghent. Days before, the nation's spirits had been buoyed as word spread of the Americans' greatest military victory of the war, General Andrew Jackson's decisive defeat of the British at New Orleans (a battle that had taken place after the peace treaty had been signed but before report of that event had reached America).

Although neither side conceded much in the treaty, the war had produced new American heroes (and a national anthem) and had demonstrated American resolve against British might in a "Second War of Independence." The Federalists, who had met in a convention in Hartford amid talk of national disunity, saw their efforts to derail Madison's policies swallowed up in the national surge of patriotic feeling. Peace brought renewed prosperity, and Madison could feel vindicated. Perhaps the most gracious assessment of Madison's presidency came from an old Federalist, John Adams. "Notwithstanding a thousand Faults and blunders," Adams wrote to Jefferson, Madison's administration "has acquired more glory, and established more union; than all his three predecessors put together"—one of those presidents, of course, being Adams himself.

In 1817 Madison left office, returning to Montpelier. His last public appearance was in 1829, at the Virginia Constitutional Convention of 1829-30. For all the dignitaries present—Madison, James Monroe, John Tyler, and John Marshall were among its members—the convention must have struck Madison as a pale shadow of the Philadelphia gathering of 1787. While the convention's debates make compelling reading—they have been called "the last gasp of Jeffersonian America's passion for political disputation"—it accomplished little of the constitutional reform (of the franchise, legislative apportionment, and the self-perpetuating county court system) for which Jefferson and others had been calling for years.

The last two decades of Madison's life, from 1817 to 1836, were devoted largely to private pursuits. An apostle of scientific agriculture, Madison urged his fellow farmers to forego old practices that were exhausting the soil. Concerned about the problem of slavery—an issue he and his fellow delegates at Philadelphia had left as unfinished business—he accepted the presidency of the American Colonization Society, which encouraged the manumission and return of slaves to Africa. For the most part, Madison spent his final years at Montpelier corresponding with friends, entertaining travelers who passed his way, and generally overseeing his plantation. His last public message, dictated to Dolley, showed concern about rising sectional tensions; it called upon his fellow countrymen to ensure that "the Union of the States be cherished and perpetuated."

PART III

Selected Madison Papers

Included in the following pages are those public documents and private papers of Madison that offer insight into his thoughts on the subjects addressed in this volume. While the inclusion of every single reference to religion and religious liberty would have been beyond the bounds of this book, the materials offered here include all significant observations on the topics at hand. Texts dating before 1790 are taken from *The Papers of James Madison*, edited by Robert Rutland. Texts after that date come from Gaillard Hunt, *The Writings of James Madison*, unless otherwise noted. Original spellings, style, and punctuation have normally been preserved in order not to bend Mr. Madison's intentions by inadvertent interpretations.

Notes on William Burkitt's
Expository Notes

These entries are quoted from Burkitt. This volume, first published in 1724, provided a source for Madison to extract what most likely were, in his opinion, the most striking and important portions of the New Testament. Rutland dates this collection in the early 1770s, perhaps while Madison was at Princeton. The most that we may conjecture from these notes is that Madison found particular passages in the Bible of peculiar interest to him. In themselves they offer no clue as to how he might have interpreted them.

Acts

Ch. 18.　Rulers & great Men are like looking Glasses in the places where they live, by which many dress themselves. v. 8 &c.

St. Paul went to the Feast at Jerusalem, not to observe the Ceremony but to Preach to a larger Multitude that he knew would be there v. 21. &c.

Apollos, though mighty in the Scriptures, yet disdained not to be instructed farther by Aquila & Priscilla, for he knew only the Baptism of John. 24 &c

Learned Men, it was a custom among the Jews to allow them a liberty, tho' no Priests, to teach in their Synagogues. ib [id]

Ch. 19　Holy Ghost. have ye recd, the Holy Ghost since ye Believed. the Apostle does not mean in its Sanctifying operations, but in its miraculous Gifts v. 2d.

Spirit of Prophecy, departed (as the Jews believe) from Israel after the Death of Haggai, Zachariah & Malachi. v. 2d.

Baptizm, Christ's & John's were the same for Substance 2d.

Apostles did greater Miracles than Christ, in the matter, not manner, of them v. 11

Evil Spirits, none were, that we read of in the Old Testament, bodily possessed of, but many in the New, v. 13

Conjuring Books burnt by the believing Jews & Greeks at Ephesus amounted to 50,000 pcs. of Silver; £800

Saints fall, intimated by Alexander the Copper Smith turning Apostate. v 33

Ch. 20. Sunday, why kept by the Christians, for the Sabbath v. 7

Sleepers under Gods word (at a Sermon), their wretched contempt of it. v. 9

St. Paul's travelling on foot from Troas to Assos: an happy example for all the Ministers of Christ. v. 13. &c

Tempt. to neglect the means for our own preservation is to Tempt God: and to trust to them is to neglect him v. 3 &c. Ch. 27. v. 31

Humility, the better any man is, the lower thoughts he has of himself v. 19

Ministers to take heed to themselves & their flock. v. 28

Believers who are in a State of Grace, have need of the word of God for their Edification & Building up therefore implies a possibility of falling v. 32.

Grace, it is the free gift of God. Luke. 12. 32—v. 32

Giver more blessed than the Receiver. v 35

Ch. 21. Affections, Spiritual, are stronger than the natural. v. 1.

Clouds governed by Providence. v. 3d &c.

Sins, or Faults, committed before conversion should not be related to the prejudice of the late Sinner v. 8

Isaiah, going barefoot, the reason of it. v. 11. Isa 20

Ezekiel, packing up his Stuff to remove. v. 11. Ezek. 12

Agedness, how Honourable. v. 16.

Jews, 1000ds & 10 000ds of them believed in St. Pauls days, so, not a few, in the litteral sence, but probably many more saved. v. 20.

Turky & Spaniards alluded to. v. 37 &c.

St. Paul, a Jew by Birth, & a Roman by immunity & privilege v. 39

Ch. 22. Baptism necessary to be complyed with. v. 16

Carnal Reason, when against the command of God, should be laid by. v. 19

Ch. 23 Conscience[:] it should be inform'd as well as followed. v. 1.

Herod mentioned ib.

Magistrates, are not to be treated with ill words, nor flattered v. 4

Sadducees, deny the Resurrection & the existence of Angel or Spirit v. 8

Titles of civil Honour & Respect given to persons in place & power, are agreable to the Mind & will of God. v. 25 Ch. 26. v. 25

Magistrates must do nothing blindfold or blindly. Should know a Cause before they give sentence or Judgment about it. v. 35.

Ch. 24. Persecution, a persecuting Spirit claps Wings to a Person [.] it makes him swift in his Motions & Zealous in his application & Endeavours. v. 1.

Flattery. Tis Hell and Death to flatter Sinners, or suffer ourselves to be flattered by them v. 2 &c.

Judgments & Plagues are staved off for the sakes of God's holy & faithful Servants v. 5 &c.

Sedition may be committed three ways; by the Head, by the Tongue, and by the Hand. v. 10 &c.

Church of Rome mentioned. v. 14

Ch. 25. Politicians (Carnal) do not so much consider what is Just & Righteous in it's own nature as what is of use & Advantage to themselves be it Right or wrong v. 9 &c.

Dung-hill Cocks of the World know not the Worth of the pearl of Price v. 19 &c.

Ch. 26. Hope is the great excitor of Industry and Endeavor $\Big\}$ v. 6 &c.
Expectations puts it upon Action

Power[:] there is a compelling power and constraining Force in Example v. 11.

Ministers[:] great is the dignity of Gospel Ministers they are God's Messengers v. 16. &c.

Unconverted has little reason to expect to convert others by their Ministry.

Ch. 27. St. Paul's hazardous voyage to Rome, alluded to the Church in her Militant State here on Earth. v. 12. &c. and the danger of spending our youthful days in folly &c.

Ch. 28. Sinful inferrences are drawn from sorrowful premises. v. 4

Charity[:] no duty more certainly rewarded in another World; so is it frequently rewarded in this, as was Publius, by the miraculous cure perform'd on his Father for his Charity to Paul. v. 8.

Ministers of the Gospel[:] it is the great Duty of them, prudently to prevent, if possible, or presently to remove all Prejudices which may be taken up by their People against their Persons, knowing that, if they have a prejudice against their persons, they will never relish their Doctrine, nor be benefitted by their Ministry. v. 20.

Hope (for the) [sake?] of Israel I am bound: That is; for the Object of Israel's Hope, or the Messiah which they so long expected, & so much hoped for. v. 20.

Sun, the same that softens the Wax hardens the Clay v. 24 See St. Mark. Ch. 14 V. 66 &c.

Gospel stiled the Salvation of God v. 28. & why.

Inquisition & Rome, mentioned, at the end.

Gospels.

Mat. Ch   Jesus is an Hebrew name and signifies a Savior v. 1.
   1st   Christ is a Greek name and signifies Anointed. v. 1.

Pollution[:] Christ did by the power of his Godhead purify our nature from all the pollution of our Ancestors v. 5. & c.

Until signifies in Scripture as much as never. v 25.

Virgin Mary had no other Child (probably) but our Saviour. v. 25.

Ch. 2   Bethlehem signifies the House of Bread v. 4 &c.

Rachel is not here the name of a Person but a place v. 18.

Ch. 3   Ministers, none to assume the Office before they are sent v. 1.

Papists mentioned v 3. & concerning Auricular confession v. 6.

Hermits lives not supported from the instance of John the Baptist preaching in the Wilderness.

Sacrament. bad persons upon a profession of Repentance & promise of Amendment may be admitted to the Sacrament. v. 6.

Sins of Omission as Damnable as Sins of Commission v. 10. neglects of Duty as Damnable as Acts of Sin.

Grace, where there is most, there is the greatest sense of the want of it. v. 14.

Ch. 4.   Adoption[:] Satans grand design is first to tempt the children of God to doubt of it. v. 3.

Ch. 5.   Christians who allows themselves in the least Transgression, either of omission, or commission is in a Damnable State. v. 19.

Ch. 6.   Prayer, a form o[b]served by our Saviour & which ought to be used by us. v. 9.

Forgiveness, an indispensable Duty. v. 14

Ch. 7.   Gifts, distinguished from Grace. v. 21 &c.

Ch. [8.]   Marriage not censured nor condemned in Ministers of the Gospel nor the Apostles v. 14.

St: Matt.   Souls, departed are under the conduct of Angels, good or bad
Ch. 9.   to their places of Bliss or Misery. perhaps at their separation they are not, immediately fi[xed in?] their eternal Mansions v. 24.

Shepherds, or Labourers in Christs Harvest; the idle & lazy, are not so in his Acct. 3[6 &c.]

He who doth not instruct his Flock & feed them with the sincere Milk of the Word, from an Heart full of Love to God, & compassion to Souls, deserves not the Name of a true Shepherd.

Dr. Whitby.[1]

Ch. 10.   Apostles, they were Disciples, before they were Apostles. v. 1

Grace, the want of it doth not disannul a Ministers Office, nor hinder the Lawfulness of his Ministry. Judas, though a Traitor, was yet a Lawful Minister. V. 4.

Lost Sheep, the Israelites so call'd because they were lost in themselves & were in great Danger of being eventually & finally lost, by the Ignorance & Wickedness of their spiritual Guides v. 6.

Preachers, must not be strikers v. 10.

Soul, dies not with the Body. 28 V.

Christ's coming. We must distinguish betwixt his intentional Aim, & the accidental Event of it. v. 34.

Reward, There is some special & eminent Reward due to the faithful Prophets of God above other Men. v. 41.

Ch. 11.   Teaching is in order to the Conversion of Sinners: ⎫ v. 1.
Preaching in order to the Edification of Saints.   ⎬
Punishment, there are Degrees of it among the Damned. v. 24

Ch. 12.   Idle words are such as savour nothing of Wisdom nor Piety v. 38 36.

Ch. 13.   Unbelief obstructs Christs gracious works in Heaven. v. 58

Ch. 21.   All reformation of manners must begin first at the House of God. v. 13

St. Luke, Ch. 2d.—the idle are fit for nothing but Temptation to work on v. 8 &c.

—Such Women whom God has blessed with safety of deliverance should make their first visit to the Temple of God to offer up their Praises & thanksgivings there v. 22d. &c.

It is said of some *Turks* that after they have seen *Mahomets* Tomb, the[y] put out their Eyes, that they may never defile them after they have seen so glorious an object. v. 29.

Parts & abilities for the ministerial function are not sufficient to warrant our undertaking of it without a regular Call.

Some Proverbs of Solomon.[2]

Ch. 9.   V. 7. He that reproveth a scorner getteth to himself Shame &c.

8. Reprove not a Scorner, lest he hate thee.

Ch. 10.   .17————; but he that refuseth reproof, erreth

26 As Vinegar to the Teeth, and smoke to the Eyes, so is the Sluggard to them that send him.

XI.   13. A Tale-bearer revealeth Secrets: but he that is of a faithful Spirit concealeth the Matter 12: v. 23

15. He that is surety for a Stranger shall smart for it: & he that hateth suretyship, is Sure. VI. 1. XVII:18.

25. The liberal Soul shall be made Fat. &c.

XII.   22. Lying Lips are abomination to the Lord: but they that deal truly are his delight.

XIII.   12 Hope deferred maketh the Heart Sick &c.
        24. He that Spareth his Rod hateth his Son: But he that loveth
        him chasteneth him betimes
XIV.   29 He that is Slow to wrath is of great understanding: but
        he that is hasty of Spirit exalteth folly.
XV.   Argumt. Ceremonies to be retained for 3 Reasons from
        Melancthon[3]
        1. A Soft Answer Turneth away wrath: but grievous words
        stir up anger
        3. The Eyes of the Lord are in every Place, beholding the
        evil and the Good.
        5. A Fool despiseth his Father's Instruction: but he &c.
XVI   5. Every one that is pround in heart, is an abomination to
        the Lord. &c.
        11 A Just weight & balance are the Lord's: all the weights of
        the bag are his work
        16 How much better is it to get Wisdom than Gold: & to
        get understanding rather to be chosen than Silver
        24. Pleasant Words are as an Honey-comb, sweet to the Soul
        & health to the Bones.
        25. There is a way that seemeth right unto a Man, but the end
        thereof are the ways of Death—XIV. 12.
        28. ———; a Whisperer seperateth chief Friends
        32. He that is Slow to anger, is better than the Mighty; &c.
XVIII   8. The Words of a Tale-bearer are as Wounds, & they go
        down into the innermost parts of the Belly
        13. He that Answereth a Matter before he heareth it, it is folly
        & shame unto him.
        21. Death & Life are in the Power of the Tongue; & they that
        love it, shall eat the fruit thereof.
        22 Whoso findeth a Wife findeth a good thing, & obtaineth
        favour of the Lord.
XX   3 'Tis an honour for a Man to cease from strife: but a fool
        will be medling;
        9 Who can say I have made my Heart clean; I am pure from
        my sin.
        10 Divers weights and measures are abomination to the Lord.
        v. 23.
        14 It is naught, it is naught, saith the buyer: but when he is
        gone his way then he boasteth.

*The following Madison remarks are found only as reprinted in Cabell Rives' Life
and Times of James Madison, 1859.*

In one of these notes, referring to a chapter of the Acts of the Apostles,
where the Bereans' are mentioned as "more noble than those in Thessalonica,

in that they received the word with all readiness of mind, and searched the Scriptures daily whether these things were so," he commends their conduct "as a noble example for all succeeding Christians to imitate and follow. . . ."[4]

In a paraphrase on the Gospel of St. John, referring to the passage in which Mary Magdalene is represented as looking into the Holy Sepulchre and seeing two angels in white, one sitting at the head and the other at the feet, where the body of the Saviour had lain, he makes the following reflection:

"Angels to be desired at our feet as well as at our head—not an angelical understanding and a diabolical conversation—not all our religion in our brains and tongue, and nothing in our heart and life."[5]

In the same spirit, commenting on the chapter of Acts, where Jesus says to St. Paul, who had fallen to the earth under the light which shined round about him from heaven, "*Arise*, and *go* into the city, and it shall be told thee what thou shalt *do*," he subjoins this as the proper deduction from the passage: "It is not the *talking*, but the *walking* and *working* person that is the true Christian."[6]

On doctrinal points, the following brief memoranda[7] and references taken from many others of a like character, may serve to show both his orthodoxy and his penetration:

"Omnisciency—God's foreknowledge doth not compel, but permits to be done." Acts, ch. II. v. 23.

"Christ's divinity appears by St. John, ch. XX. v. 28."

"Resurrection testified and witnessed by the Apostles, Acts, ch. IV. v. 33."

NOTES

1. Daniel Whitby, *A Paraphrase and Commentary on the New Testament*, 1703.
2. Clearly, Madison took these quotes directly from Proverbs rather than from Burkitt.
3. Philip Melanchthon, described by historian Williston Walker as "timid and retiring," was a superior scholar who first provided a systematic presentation of Lutheran theology.
4. William Burkitt, *Expository Notes*.
5. Ibid.
6. Ibid.
7. Ibid.

Madison's Correspondence
with William Bradford

Between 1772 and 1775 Madison carried on an extensive correspondence with William Bradford, a classmate at Princeton, then living in Philadelphia. The letters reflect a concern for career on the part of both young men. Reprinted here are those portions of the letters that have most directly to do with religion and freedom of conscience.

Orange Virginia Novr. 9th. 1772

My dear Billey,

You moralize so prettily that if I were to judge from some parts of your letter of October 13 I should take you for an old Philosopher that had experienced the emptiness of Earthly Happiness. And I am very glad that you have so early seen through the romantic paintings with which the World is sometimes set off by the sprightly imaginations of the Ingenious. You have happily supplied by reading and observation the want of experiment and therefore I hope you are sufficiently guarded against the allurements and vanities that beset us on our first entrance on the Theatre of Life. Yet however nice and cautious we may be in detecting the follies of mankind and framing our Oeconomy according to the precepts of Wisdom and Religion I fancy there will commonly remain with us some latent expectation of obtaining more than ordinary Happiness and prosperity till we feel the convincing argument of actual disappointment. Tho I will not determine whether we shall be much the worse for it if we do not allow it to intercept our views towards a future State, because strong desires and great Hopes instigate us to arduous enterprizes fortitude and perseverance. Nevertheless a watchful eye must be kept on ourselves lest while we are building ideal monuments of Renown and Bliss here we neglect to have our names enrolled in the annals of Heaven. These thoughts come into my

44

mind because I am writing to you and thinking of you. As to myself I am too dull and infirm now to look out for any extraordinary things in this world for I think my sensations for many months past have intimated to me not to expect a long or healthy life, yet it may be better with me after some time tho I hardly dare expect it and therefore have little spirit and alacrity to set about any thing that is difficult in acquiring and useless in possessing after one has exchanged Time for Eternity. But you have Health Youth Fire and Genius to bear you along through the high tract of public Life and so may be more interested and delighted in improving on hints that respect the temporal though momentous concerns of man.

I think you made a judicious choice of History and the Science of Morals for your winter's study. They seem to be of the most universal benefit to men of sense and taste in every post and must certainly be of great use to youth in settling the principles and refining the Judgment as well as in enlarging Knowledge & correcting the imagination. I doubt not but you design to season them with a little divinity now and then, which like the philospher's stone, in hands of good man will turn them and every lawful acquirement into the nature of himself, and make them more precious than fine gold. . . .

James Madison Junr.

Septr. 25th 1773.

MY DEAR FRIEND

I received yours of the 12 August and give you this repeated Testimony of my punctuality. I got your letter to Mr Wallace at the same time much worn and abused. I have given it a new coat & shall forward it as soon as a safe Opportunity serves.

Since you first hinted to me your suspence as to the settled business of your life, I have partook of your anxiety & [though it] has been often in my thoughts I feel a backwardness to offer my opinion in so critical a matter and the more so for the weight you are pleased to give it. I have too much esteem and affection for you and am too conscious of my want of capacity and experience to direct in so important an Affair. I must therefore premise that it is my earnest request that you would act the candid open friend as well as in rejecting as in asking advice; for I consult nothing but your real interest, and am sensible of my insufficiency to be a counsellor much more a preceptor. You forbid any recommendation of Divinity by suggesting that you have insuperable objections therefore I can only condole with the Church on the loss of a fine Genius and persuasive Orator. I cannot however suppress thus much of my advice on that head that you would always keep the Ministry obliquely in View whatever your profession be. This will lead you to cultivate an acquaintance occasionally with the most sublime of all Sciences and will qualify you for a change of public character if you should hereafter desire it. I have sometimes thought there could not be a stronger testimony in favor of Religion or against temporal Enjoyments even the most rational and manly than for men who occupy the most honorable and gainful departments and are rising in reputation and wealth, publicly to declare their unsatisfatoriness by becoming fervent Advocates in the cause of Christ, & I wish you may give in your Evidence in this way. Such Instances have seldom occurred, therefore they would be more striking and would be instead of a "Cloud of Witnesses." If I am to speak my Sentiments of Merchandize, Physic and Law I must say they are all honorable and usefull professions and think you ought to *have* more regard to their Suitableness to your Genius than to their comparative Excellence. As far as I know your endowments I should prounounce Law the most eligeble. *It* alone can bring into use many parts of knowledge you have acquired and will still have a taste for, & pay you for cultivating the Arts of Eloquence. It is a sort of General Lover that wooes all the Muses and Graces. This cannot be said so truly of commerce and Physic & therefore less Learning & smaller understanding will do for them. The objection founded on the number of Lawyers should stimulate to Assiduity rather than discourage the Attempt. I greatly commend your determined adherence to probity and Truth in the Character of a Lawyer but fear it would be impracticable. Misrepresentation from a client or intricacy in a cause must often occasion doubt and ignorance till the matter has been considerably debated at the bar; Though it must be allowed there are a thousand cases in which your rule would be safe and highly commendable. I must add after all that if you should enter on a mercantile State (to which peculiar reasons for ought I know may advise) I should be loth to disapprove. . . .

JM Jnr.

Dec. 1. 1773.

MY KIND FRIEND

. . . I am glad you have rescued yourself from your anxiety and suspence and have come to a determination to engage in the study of the Law, which I hope you had better reasons for chusing than I could suggest. I intend myself to read Law occasionally and have procured books for that purpose so that you need not fear offending me by Allusions to that science. Indeed any of your remarks as you go along would afford me entertainment and instruction. The principles & Modes of Government are too important to be disregarded by an Inquisitive mind and I think are well worthy a critical examination by all students that have health & Leisure. I should be well pleased with a scetch of the plan you have fixed upon for your studies, the books & the order you intend to read them in; and when you have obtained sufficient insight into the Constitution of your Country and can make it an amusement to yourself send me a draught of its Origin & fundamental principals of Legislation; particularly the extent of your religious Toleration. Here allow me to propose the following Queries. Is an Ecclesiastical Establishment absolutely necessary to support civil society in a supream Government? & how far is it hurtful to a dependent State? I do not ask for an immediate answer but mention them as worth attending to in the course of your reading and consulting experienced Lawyers & Politicians upon. When you have satisfied yourself in these points I should listen with pleasure to the Result of your reserches. . . .

JM JUNR.

Jan. 24. 1774

MY WORTHY FRIEND,

Yours of the 25 of last month came into my hands a few days past. It gave singular pleasure not only because of the kindness expressed in it but because I had reason to apprehend the letter you recd. last from me had miscarried and I should fail in procuring the intelligence I wanted before the Trip I design in the Spring.

I congratulate you on your heroic proceedings in Philada. with regard to the Tea. I wish Boston may conduct matters with as much discretion as they seem to do with boldness: They seem to have great Tryals and difficulties by reasons of the obduracy and *ministerialism* of their Governour. However, Political Contests are necessary sometimes as well as military to afford excercise and practise and to instruct in the Art of defending Liberty and property. I verily believe the frequent Assaults that have been made in America, Boston especially, will in the end prove of real advantage. If the Church of England had been the established and general Religion in all the Northern Colonies as it has been among us here and uninterrupted tranquility had prevailed throughout the Continent, It is clear to me that slavery and Subjection might and would have been gradually insinuated among us. Union of Religious Sentiments begets a surprizing confidence and Ecclesiastical Establishments tend to great ignorance and Corruption all of which facilitate the Execution of mischievous Projects. But away with Politicks! Let me address you as a Student and Philosopher & not as a Patriot now. I am pleased that you are going to converse with the Edwards and Henry's & Charles &c&c who have swayed the British Sceptre though I believe you will find some of them dirty and unprofitable Companions unless you will glean Instruction from their follies and fall more in love with Liberty by beholding such detestable pictures of Tyranny and Cruelty. I was afraid you would not easily have loosened your Affections from the Belles Lettres. A Delicate Taste and warm imagination like yours must find it hard to give up such refined & exquisite enjoyments for the coarse and dry study of the Law: It is like leaving a pleasant flourishing field for a barren desert; perhaps I should not say barren either because the Law does bear fruit but it is sour fruit that must be gathered and presssed and distilled before it can bring pleasure or profit. I perceive I have made a very awkward Comparison but I got the thought by the end and had gone to[o] far to quit it before I perceived that it was too much entangled in my brain to run it through. And so you must forgive it. I myself use to have too great a hankering after those amusing Studies. Poetry wit and Criticism Romances Plays &c captivated me much: but I begin [to] discover that they deserve but a moderate portion of a *mortal's* Time. and that something more substantial more durable more profitable befits a riper Age. It would be exceeding improper for a labouring man to have nothing but flowers in his Garden or to determine to eat nothing but sweet-meats and Confections. Equally absurd would it be for a Scholar and man of Business to make up his whole Library with Books of Fancy and feed his Mind with nothing but such Luscious performances.

When you have an Opportunity and write to Mr. Brackinridge pray tell him I often think of him and long to see him and am resolved to do so in the Spring. George Luckey was with me at Christmas and we talked so much about old Affairs & Old Friends that I have a most insatiable desire to see you all. Luckey will accompany me and we are to set off on the 10th. of April if no disa[s]ter befalls either of us. I want again to breathe your free Air. I expect it will mend my Constitution & confirm my principles. I have indeed as good an Atmosphere at home as the Climate will allow: but have nothing to brag of as to the State and Liberty of my Country. Poverty and Luxury prevail among all sorts: Pride ignorance and Knavery among the Priesthood and Vice and Wickedness among the Laity. This is bad enough But It is not the worst I have to tell you. That diabolical Hell conceived principle of persecution rages among some and to their eternal Infamy the Clergy can furnish their quota of Imps for such business. This vexes me the most of any thing whatever. There are at this [time?] in the adjacent County not less than 5 or 6 well meaning men in close Goal for publishing their religious Sentiments which in the main are very orthodox. I have neither patience to hear talk or think any thing relative to this matter, for I have squabbled and scolded abused and ridiculed so long about it, [to so lit]tle purpose that I am without common patience. So I [leave you] to pity me and pray for Liberty of Conscience [to revive among us.].

I expect to hear from you once more before I see you if time will admit: and want to know when the Synod meets & where: What the Exhcange is at and as much about my friends and other Matters as you can and think worth notice. Till I see you Adieu.

JM

March 4. 1774. Philada.

Dear Sir

I am sorry to hear that Persecution has got so much footing among you. The discription you give of your Country makes me more in love with mine. Indeed I have ever looked on America as the land of freedom when compared with the rest of the world, but compared with the rest of america Tis Pennsylvania that is so. Persecution is a weed that grows not in our happy soil: and I do not remember that any Person was ever imprisoned here for his religious sentiments however heritical or unepiscopal they might be. Liberty (As Caspipina says in his Letters) [is] the Genius of Pennsylvania; and it[s] inhabitants think speak and act with a freedom unknow—I do indeed pity you; & long to see you according to your expression, "breathing our purer air." The

Synod will meet here about the middle of may. You will then have an opportunity of seeing most of your Nassovian friends, and higthing the felicity that
friends long seperated enjoy when they meet. . . .

WB JUNR.

April 1st. 1774. Virginia Orange Cy.

MY WORTHY FRIEND

I have another favour to acknowledge in the receipt of your kind Letter of
March the 4th. I did not intend to have written to you before I obtained a
nearer communication with you but you have too much interest in my inclinations ever to be denied a request.

Mr. Brackinridge's illness gives me great uneasiness: I think he would be a
loss to *America:* His merit js rated so high by me that I confess if he were gone,
I could almost say with the Poet That His Country could furnish such a Pomp
for Death no more. But I solace myself from Finley's ludicrous description as
you do.

I agree with you that the World needs to be peopled but I should be sorry
it should be peopled with bastards as my old friend Dod and —— —— seem
to incline. Who could have thought the old monk had been so letcherous.
I hope his Religion, like that of some enthusiasts, was not of such a nature as
to fan the amorous fire.

Our Assembly is to meet the first of May When It is expected something
will be done in behalf of the Dissenters: Petitions I hear are already forming
among the Persecuted Baptists and I fancy it is in the thoughts of the Presbyterians also to intercede for greater liberty in matters of Religion. For my part I
can not help being very doubtful of their succeeding in the Attempt. The Affair
was on the Carpet during the last Session; but such incredible and extravagant
stories were told in the House of the monstrous effects of the Enthusiasm
prevalent among the Sectaries and so greedily swallowed by their Enemies that
I believe they lost footing by it and the bad name they still have with those
who pretend too much contempt to examine into their principles and Conduct
and are too much devoted to the ecclesiastical establishment to hear of the
Toleration of Dissentients, I am apprehensive, will be again made a pretext for
rejecting their requests. The Sentiments of our people of Fortune & fashion on
this subject are vastly different from what you have been used to. That liberal
catholic and equitable way of thinking as to the rights of Conscience, which is
one of the Characteristics of a free people and so strongly marks the People of
your province is but little known among the Zealous adherents to our
Hierarchy. We have it is true some persons in the Legislature of generous
Principles both in Religion & Politicks but number not merit you know is
necessary to carry points there. Besides[,] the Clergy are a numerous and
powerful body[,] have great influence at home by reason of their connection
with & dependence on the Bishops and Crown and will naturally employ all
their art & Interest to depress their rising Adversaries; for such they must

consider dissenters who rob them of the good will of the people and may in time endanger their livings & security.

You are happy in dwelling in a Land where those inestimable privileges are fully enjoyed and public has long felt the good effects of their religious as well as Civil Liberty. Foreigners have been encouraged to settle amg. you. Industry and Virtue have been promoted by mutual emualtion and mutual Inspection, Commerce and the Arts have flourished and I can not help attributing those continual exertions of Gen[i]us which appear among you to the inspiration of Liberty and that love of Fame and Knowledge which always accompany it. Religous bondage shackles and debilitates the mind and unfits it for every noble enterprize every expanded prospect. How far this is the case with Virginia will more clearly appear when the ensuing Trial is made. . . .

JM

Virginia Declaration of Rights

Madison was elected as a delegate from Orange County to the Revolutionary Convention in Virginia, which began meeting on May 6, 1776. On May 16th Madison was added to a committee "to prepare a declaration of rights." George Mason was the primary author of that Declaration. Madison found difficulty with the concept of "toleration" and offered an amendment (A) to change the wording on that subject, and at the same time call for disestablishment of the Church of England. It became obvious to him that the second goal could not be achieved at the time and so Madison offered a second amendment (B). The final version, as adopted, was dated June 12, 1776.

GEORGE MASON'S PROPOSAL

[9] That as Religion, or the Duty which we owe to our divine and omnipotent Creator, and the Manner of discharging it, can be governed only by Reason and Conviction, not by Force or Violence; and therefore that all Men shou'd enjoy the fullest Toleration in the Exercise of Religion, according to the Dictates of Conscience, unpunished and unrestrained by the Magistrate, unless, under Colour of Religion, any Man disturb the Peace, the Happiness, or Safety of Society, or of Individuals. And that it is the mutual Duty of all, to practice Christian Forbearance, Love and Charity towards Each other.

COMMITTEE'S PROPOSAL

18. That religion, or the duty which we owe to our CREATOR, and the

51

manner of discharging it, can be directed only by reason and conviction, not by force or violence; and therefore, that all men should enjoy the fullest toleration in the exercise of religion, according to the dictates of conscience, unpunished and unrestrained by the magistrate unless, under colour of religion, any man disturb the peace, the happiness, or safety of society. And that it is the mutual duty of all to practice Christian forbearance, love and charity, towards each other.

MADISON'S TWO PROPOSALS

A

That Religion or the duty we owe to our Creator, and the manner of discharging it, being under the direction of reason and conviction only, not of violence or compulsion, all men are equally entitled to the full and free exercise of it accordg to the dictates of Conscience; and therefore that no man or class of men ought, on account of religion to be invested with peculiar emoluments or privileges; nor subjected to any penalties or disabilities unless under &c

B

18. That religion, or the duty which we owe to our CREATOR, and the manner of discharging it, can be directed only by reason and conviction, not by force or violence; and therefore, that all men are equally entitled to enjoy the free exercise of religion, according to the dictates of conscience, unpunished and unrestrained by the magistrate, Unless the preservation of equal liberty and the existence of the State are manifestly endangered; And that it is the mutual duty of all to practice Christian forbearance, love, and charity towards each other.

ARTICLE ON RELIGION ADOPTED BY CONVENTION

16. That religion, or the duty which we owe to our CREATOR, and the manner of discharging it, can be directed only by reason and conviction, not by force or violence; and therefore, all men are equally entitled to the free exercise of religion, according to the dictates of conscience; and that it is the mutual duty of all to practise Christian forbearance, love, and charity, towards each other.

Virginia Religious Freedom Debate: 1784-86

As noted in the essay on "Assessment and Incorporation," several documents of primary importance emerged during the debate in the Virginia General Assembly. The second document here consists of two versions of Madison's notes on the debate over assessment that occurred in December 1784. Irving Brant has reconstructed that debate in the second volume of his biography James Madison. *Madison's notes are followed by the text of* A Memorial and Remonstrance, *written by Madison at the urging of friends, including Mason, during the spring of 1785. The third document is the* Act for Establishing Religious Freedom, *written by Thomas Jefferson and introduced into the assembly by him in 1779. It was finally signed into law on January 19, 1786. The last item on this subject is an excerpt from Madison's letter to Jefferson dated January 22, 1786.*

TO RICHARD HENRY LEE FROM MADISON
NOVEMBER 14, 1784

I did not get to this place till the fourteenth day after that fixed for the meeting of the Assembly, but was two days only after a H. of D was actually made. You will infer therefore that little business of moment has yet been done. Excepting a few Resolutions for the Delegation urging a Treaty with the Southern Indians, and negociations with the Spaniards touching the Mississippi, our time has been cheifly taken up with the scheme of a Genl. Assessment. The one proposed & supported, comprehends Christians alone and obliges other sects to contribute to its maintenance. It was opposed not only on the general principle that no Religious Estabts. was within the purview of Civil authority, but on th[e . . .] ground on which it was placed; and the infraction [. . .] the last article of the Decl: of Rights. On the question 47 w[er]e f[or the] proposition, 32 against it. The majority was produced by a Coalition between the Episcopal & Presbyterian Sects. A Memorial presented since the vote by the Clergy of the latter shews that a Schism will take place. They do not deny but rather betray a desire that an Assessment may be estabt. but protest agst. any which does not embrace all Religions, and will not coincide with the Decl: of Rights. It is probable that the Foundation of the scheme will finally be enlarged, & that an experiment at least of its practicability will be made.[1]

MADISON'S NOTES ON DEBATE

A.

Debate on Bill for Relig. Estabt proposed by Mr Henry
1. limited
2. in particular
3. What is Christianity? Courts of law to Judge
4. What edition, Hebrew, Septuagint, or vulgate? What copy—what translation?
5. What books canonical, what apochryphal? the papists holding to be the former what protestants the latter, the Lutherans the latter what other protestants & papists the former
6. In What light are they to be viewed, as dictated every letter by inspiration, or the essential parts only? or the matter in generall not the words?
7. What sense the true one, for if some doctrines be essential to *Christianity*, those who reject these, whatever name they take are no *Christian* Society?
8. Is it Trinitarianism, arianism, Socinianism? Is it salvation by faith or works also—by free grace, or free will—&c &c &c—
9. What clue is to guide Judge thro' this labyrinth? When the question comes before them whether any particular Society is a Christian society?
10. Ends in what is orthodoxy, what heresy?

B.

I. *Rel:* not within purview of Civil Authority.
   tendency of Estabg. Christianity

                     1. to project of Uniformity
                     2. to penal laws for supportg. it.

Progres[s] of Gen: Assest. proves this tendency

difference between estbg. & tolerating errour—

II. True question not—Is Rel: neccsy.?
   are Religs. Estabts. neccsy. for Religion? no.

1. propensity of man to Religion.
2. Experience shews Relig: corrupted by Estabt.
3. downfall of States, mentioned by Mr. H[enry], happened where there was Estabts.
4. Experience gives no model of Gel. Asst?
5. Case of Pa. explained—not solitary. N.J.
   See Const.: of it. R. I. N. Y. D.

   factions greater in S. C.
6. Case of primitive Christianity.
   of Reformation
   of Dissenters formerly.

III. Decl: Rig[hts]. 7. Progress of Religious Liberty

IV. Policy.
   1. promote emigrations from State
   2. prevent [immgration]into it as *asylum*

V. Necessity of Estabts. inferred from State of Conty.

true causes of war
1. War   ⎫ common to other States &
2. bad laws   ⎬ produce same complts. in N. E.
3. pretext from taxes
4. State of Administration of Justice.
5. transition from old to new plan.
6. policy & hopes of friends to G. Asst.

---

true remedies not Estabt. but being out war
1. laws cherish virtue
2. Adminst: justice
3. personal example—Association for R.
4. By present vote cut off hope of G. Asst.
5. Education of youth

Probable defects of Bill
   dishonor Christianity

4. panegyrie on it on our side

4. Decl: Rights

TO THE HONORABLE GENERAL ASSEMBLY OF THE COMMONWEALTH OF VIRGINIA A MEMORIAL AND REMONSTRANCE

We the subscribers, citizens of the said Commonwealth, having taken into serious consideration, a Bill printed by order of the last Session of General Assembly, entitled "A Bill establishing a provision for Teachers of the Christian Religion," and conceiving that the same if finally armed with the sanctions of a law, will be a dangerous abuse of power, are bound as faithful members of a free State to remonstrate against it, and to declare the reasons by which we are determined. We remonstrate against the said Bill,

1. Because we hold it for a fundamental and undeniable truth, "that Religion or the duty which we owe to our Creator and the manner of discharging it, can be directed only by reason and conviction, not by force or violence."[2] The Religion then of every man must be left to the conviction and conscience of every man; and it is the right of every man to exercise it as these may dictate. This right is in its nature an unalienable right. It is unalienable, because the opinions of men, depending only on the evidence contemplated by their own minds cannot follow the dictates of other men: It is unalieniable also, because what is here a right towards men, is a duty towards the Creator. It is the duty of every man to render to the Creator such homage and such only as he believes to be acceptable to him. This duty is precedent, both in order of time and in degree of obligation, to the claims of Civil Society. Before any man can be considered as a member of Civil Society, he must be considered as a subject of the Governour of the Universe: And if a member of Civil Society, who enters into any subordinate Association, must always do it with a reservation of his duty to the General Authority; much more must every man who becomes a member of any particular Civil Society, do it with a saving of his allegiance to the Universal Sovereign. We maintain therefore that in matters of Religion, no mans right is abridged by the institution of Civil Society and that Religion is wholly exempt from its cognizance. True it is, that no other rule exists, by which any question which may divide a Society, can be ultimately determined, but the will of the majority; but it is also true that the majority may trespass on the rights of the minority.

2. Because if Religion be exempt from the authority of the Society at large, still less can it be subject to that of the Legislative Body. The latter are but the creatures and vicegerents of the former. Their jurisdiction is both derivative and limited: it is limited with regard to the co-ordinate departments, more necessarily is it limited with regard to the constituents. The preservation of a free Government requires not merely, that the metes and bounds which separate each department of power be invariably maintained; but more especially that neither of them be suffered to overleap the great Barrier which defends the rights of the people. The Rulers who are guilty of such an encroachment exceed the commission from which they derive their authority, and are Tyrants. The People who submit to it are governed by laws made neither by themselves nor by an authority derived from them, and are slaves.

3. Because it is proper to take alarm at the first experiment on our liberties. We hold this prudent jealousy to be the first duty of Citizens, and one of the noblest characteristics of the late Revolution. The free men of

America did not wait till usurped power had strengthened itself by exercise, and entangled the question in precedents. They saw all the consequences in the principle, and they avoided the consequences by denying the principle. We revere this lesson too much soon to forget it. Who does not see that the same authority which can establish Christianity, in exclusion of all other Religions, may establish with the same ease any particular sect of Christians, in exclusion of all other Sects? that the same authority which can force a citizen to contribute three pence only of his property for the support of any one establishment, may force him to conform to any other establishment in all cases whatsoever?

4. Because the Bill violates that equality which ought to be the basis of every law, and which is more indispensible, in proportion as the validity or expediency of any law is more liable to be impeached. If "all men are by nature equally free and independent,"[3] all men are to be considered as entering into Society on equal conditions; as relinquishing no more, and therefore retaining no less, one than another, of their natural rights. Above all are they to be considered as retaining an "*equal* title to the free exercise of Religion according to the dictates of Conscience."[4] Whilst we assert for ourselves a freedom to embrace, to profess and to observe the Religion which we believe to be of divine origin, we cannot deny an equal freedom to those whose minds have not yet yielded to the evidence which has convinced us. If this freedom be abused, it is an offence against God, not against man: To God, therefore, not to man, must an account of it be rendered. As the Bill violates equality by subjecting some to peculiar burdens, so it violates the same principle, by granting to others peculiar exemptions. Are the Quakers and Menonists the only sects who think a compulsive support of their Religions unnecessary and unwarrantable? Can their piety alone be entrusted with the care of public worship? Ought their Religions to be endowed above all others with extraordinary privileges by which proselytes may be enticed from all others? We think too favorably of the justice and good sense of these denominations to believe that they either covet pre-eminences over their fellow citizens or that they will be seduced by them from the common opposition to the measure.

5. Because the Bill implies either that the Civil Magistrate is a competent Judge of Religious Truth; or that he may employ Religion as an engine of Civil policy. The first is an arrogant pretension falsified by the contradictory opinions of all Rulers in all ages, and throughout the world: the second an unhallowed perversion of the means of salvation.

6. Because the establishment proposed by the Bill is not requisite for the support of the Christian Religion. To say that it is, is a contradiction to the Christian Religion itself, for every page of it disavows a dependence on the powers of this world: it is a contradiction to fact; for it is known that this Religion both existed and flourished, not only without the support of human laws, but in spite of every opposition from them, and not only during the period of miraculous aid, but long after it had been left to its own evidence and the ordinary care of Providence. Nay, it is a contradiction in terms; for a Religion not invented by human policy, must have pre-existed and been supported, before it was established by human policy. It is moreover to weaken in those who profess this Religion a pious confidence in its innate excellence and

the patronage of its Author; and to foster in those who still reject it, a suspicion that its friends are too conscious of its fallacies to trust it to its own merits.

7. Because experience witnesseth that ecclesiastical establishments, instead of maintaining the purity and efficacy of Religion, have had a contrary operation. During almost fifteen centuries has the legal establishment of Christianity been on trial. What have been its fruits? More or less in all places, pride and indolence in the Clergy, ignorance and servility in the laity, in both, superstition, bigotry and persecution. Enquire of the Teachers of Christianity for the ages in which it appeared in its greatest lustre; those of every sect, point to the ages prior to its incorporation with Civil policy. Propose a restoration of this primitive State in which its Teachers depended on the voluntary rewards of their flocks, many of them predict its downfall. On which Side ought their testimony to have greatest weight, when for or when against their interest?

8. Because the establishment in question is not necessary for the support of Civil Government. If it be urged as necessary for the support of Civil Government only as it is a means of supporting Religion, and it be not necessary for the latter purpose, it cannot be necessary for the former. If Religion be not within the cognizance of the Civil Government how can its legal establishment be necessary to Civil Government? What influence in fact have ecclesiastical establishments had on Civil Society? In some instances they have been seen to erect a spiritual tyranny on the ruins of the Civil authority; in many instances they have been seen upholding the thrones of political tyranny: in no instance have they been seen the guardians of the liberties of the people. Rulers who wished to subvert the public liberty, may have found an established Clergy convenient auxiliaries. A just Government instituted to secure & perpetuate it needs them not. Such a Government will be best supported by protecting every Citizen in the enjoyment of his Religion with the same equal hand which protects his person and his property; by neither invading the equal rights of any Sect, nor suffering any Sect to invade those of another.

9. Because the proposed establishment is a departure from that generous policy, which, offering an Asylum to the persecuted and oppressed of every Nation and Religion, promised a lustre to our country, and an accession to the number of its citizens. What a melancholy mark is the Bill of sudden degeneracy? Instead of holding forth an Asylum to the persecuted, it is itself a signal of persecution. It degrades from the equal rank of Citizens all those whose opinions in Religion do not bend to those of the Legislative authority. Distant as it may be in its present form from the Inquisition, it differs from it only in degree. The one is the first step, the other the last in the career of intolerance. The magnanimous sufferer under this cruel scourge in foreign Regions, must view the Bill as a Beacon on our Coast, warning him to seek some other haven, where liberty and philanthropy in their due extent, may offer a more certain repose from his Troubles.

10. Because it will have a like tendency to banish our Citizens. The allurements presented by other situations are every day thinning their number. To superadd a fresh motive to emigration by revoking the liberty which they now enjoy, would be the same species of folly which has dishonoured and depopulated flourishing kingdoms.

11. Because it will destroy that moderation and harmony which the for-

bearance of our laws to intermeddle with Religion has produced among its several sects. Torrents of blood have been spilt in the old world, by vain attempts of the secular arm, to extinguish Religious discord, by proscribing all difference in Religious opinion. Time has at length revealed the true remedy. Every relaxation of narrow and rigorous policy, wherever it has been tried, has been found to assuage the disease. The American Theatre has exhibited proofs that equal and compleat liberty, if it does not wholly eradicate it, sufficiently destroys its malignant influence on the health and prosperity of the State. If with the salutary effects of this system under our own eyes, we begin to contract the bounds of Religious freedom, we know no name that will too severely reproach our folly. At least let warning be taken at the first fruits of the threatened innovation. The very appearance of the Bill has transformed "that Christian forbearance, love and charity,"[5] which of late mutually prevailed, into animosities and jealousies, which may not soon be appeased. What mischiefs may not be dreaded, should this enemy to the public quiet be armed with the force of a law?

12. Because the policy of the Bill is adverse to the diffusion of the light of Christianity. The first wish of those who enjoy this precious gift ought to be that it may be imparted to the whole race of mankind. Compare the number of those who have as yet received it with the number still remaining under the dominion of false Religions; and how small is the former! Does the policy of the Bill tend to lessen the disproportion? No; it at once discourages those who are strangers to the light of revelation from coming into the Region of it; and countenances by example the nations who continue in darkness, in shutting out those who might convey it to them. Instead of Levelling as far as possible, every obstacle to the victorious progress of Truth, the Bill with an ignoble and unchristian timidity would circumscribe it with a wall of defence agianst the encroachments of error.

13. Because attempts to enforce by legal sanctions, acts obnoxious to so great a proportion of Citizens, tend to enervate the laws in general, and to slacken the bands of Society. If it be difficult to execute any law which is not generally deemed necessary or salutary, what must be the case, where it is deemed invalid and dangerous? And what may be the effect of so striking an example of impotency in the Government, on its general authority?

14. Because a measure of such singular magnitude and delicacy ought not to be imposed, without the clearest evidence that it is called for by a majority of citizens, and no satisfactory method is yet proposed by which the voice of the majority in this case may be determined, or its influence secured. "The people of the respective counties are indeed requested to signify their opinion respecting the adoption of the Bill to the next Session of Assembly."[6] But the representation must be made equal, before the voice either of the Representatives or of the Counties will be that of the people. Our hope is that neither of the former will, after due consideration, espouse the dangerous principle of the Bill. Should the event disappoint us, it will still leave us in full confidence, that a fair appeal to the latter will reverse the sentence against our liberties.

15. Because finally, "the equal right of every citizen to the free exercise of his Religion according to the dictates of conscience" is held by the same tenure with all our other rights. If we recur to its origin, it is equally the gift of nature;

if we weigh its importance, it cannot be less dear to us; if we consult the "Declaration of those rights which pertain to the good people of Virginia, as the basis and foundation of Government," it is enumerated with equal solemnity, or rather studied emphasis. Either then, we must say, that the Will of the Legislature is the only measure of their authority; and that in the plenitude of this authority, they may sweep away all our fundamental rights; or, that they are bound to leave this particular right untouched and sacred: Either we must say, that they may controul the freedom of the press, may abolish the Trial by Jury, may swallow up the Executive and Judiciary Powers of the State; nay that they may despoil us of our very right of suffrage, and erect themselves into an independent and hereditary Assembly or, we must say, that they have no authority to enact into law the Bill under consideration. We the Subscribers say, that the General Assembly of this Commonwealth have no such authority: And that no effort may be omitted on our part against so dangerous an usurpation, we oppose to it, this remonstrance; earnestly praying, as we are in duty bound, that the Supreme Lawgiver of the Universe, by illuminating those to whom it is addressed, may on the one hand, turn their Councils from every act which would affront his holy prerogative, or violate the trust committed to them: and on the other, guide them into every measure which may be worthy of his [blessing, may re]dound to their own praise, and may establish more firmly the liberties, the prosperity and the happiness of the Commonwealth.

ACT FOR ESTABLISHING RELIGIOUS FREEDOM

I. WHEREAS Almighty God hath created the mind free; that all attempts to influence it by temporal punishments or burthens, or by civil incapacitations, tend only to beget habits of hypocrisy and meanness, and are a departure from the plan of the Holy author of our religion,[7] who being Lord both of body and mind, yet chose not to propagate it by coercions on either, as was in his Almighty power to do; that the impious presumption of legislators and rulers, civil as well as ecclesiastical, who being themselves but fallible and uninspired men, have assumed dominion over the faith of others, setting up their own opinions and modes of thinking as the only true and infallible, and as such endeavouring to impose them on others, hath established and maintained false religions over the greatest part of the world, and through all time; that to compel a man to furnish contributions of money for the propagation of opinions which he disbelieves, is sinful and tyrannical; that even the forcing him to support this or that teacher of his own religious persuasion, is depriving him of the comfortable liberty of giving his contributions to the particular pastor, whose morals he would make his pattern, and whose powers he feels most persuasive to righteousness, and is withdrawing from the ministry those temporary rewards, which proceeding from an approbation of their personal conduct, are an additional incitement to earnest and unremitting labours for the instruction of mankind; that our civil rights have no dependence on our religious opinions, any more than our opinions in physics or geometry; that therefore the proscribing any citizen as unworthy the public confidence by laying upon him an incapacity of being called to offices of trust and emolument, unless he profess or renounce this or that religious opinion, is depriving him injuriously of those privileges and advantages to which in common with his fellow-citizens he has a natural right; that it tends only to corrupt the principles of that religion it is meant to encourage, by bribing with a monopoly of wor[l]dly honours and emoluments, those who will externally profess and confirm to it; that though indeed these are criminal who do not withstand such temptation, yet neither are those innocent who lay the bait in their way; that to suffer the civil magistrate to intrude his powers into the field of opinion, and to restrain the profession or propagation of principles on supposition of their ill tendency, is a dangerous fallacy, which at once destroys all religious liberty, because he being of course judge of that tendency will make his opinions the rule of judgment; and approve or condemn the sentiments of others only as they shall square with or differ from his own; that it is time enough for the rightful purposes of civil government, for its officers to interfere when principles break out into overt acts against peace and good order; and finally, that truth is great and will prevail if left to herself, that she is the proper and sufficient antagonist to error, and has nothing to fear from the conflict, unless by human interposition disarmed of her natural weapons, free argument and debate, errors ceasing to be dangerous when it is permitted freely to contradict them:

II. *Be it enacted by the General Assembly,* That no man shall be compelled to frequent or support any religious worship, place, or ministry whatsoever, nor shall be enforced restrained, molested, or burthened in his body or goods, nor shall otherwise suffer on account of his religious opinions or belief; but that all men shall be free to profess, and by argument to maintain, their opinion in matters of religion, and that the same shall in no wise diminish, enlarge, or affect their civil capacities.

III. And though we well know that this assembly elected by the people for the ordinary purposes of legislation only, have no power to restrain the acts of succeeding assemblies, constituted with powers equal to our own, and that therefore to declare this act to be irrevocable would be of no effect in law; yet we are free to declare, and do declare, that the rights hereby asserted are of the natural rights of mankind, and that if any act shall be hereafter passed to repeal the present, or to narrow its operation such act will be an infringement of natural right.

MADISON TO JEFFERSON — JANUARY 22, 1786

Dear Sir

. . . The only one of these which was pursued into an Act is the Bill concerning Religious freedom. The steps taken throughout the Country to defeat the Genl. Assessment, had produced all the effect that could have been wished.

The table was loaded with petitions & remonstrances from all parts against the interposition of the Legislature in matters of Religion. A General convention of the Presbyterian church prayed expressly that the bill in the Revisal might be passed into a law, as the best safeguard short of a constitutional one, for their religious rights. The bill was carried thro' the H of Delegates, without alteration. The Senate objected to the preamble, and sent down a proposed substitution of the 16th. art: of the Declaration of Rights. The H. of D. disagreed. The Senate insisted and asked a Conference. Their objections were frivolous indeed. In order to remove them as they were understood by the Managers of the H. of D. The preamble was sent up again from the H. of D. with one or two verbal alterations. As an amendment to these the Senate sent down a few others; which as they did not affect the substance though they somewhat defaced the composition, it was thought better to agree to than to run further risks, especially as it was getting late in the Session and the House growing thin. The enacting clauses past without a single alteration, and I flatter myself have in this Country extinguished for ever the ambitious hope of making laws for the human mind. . . .

Adieu affectly —

NOTES

1. JM wrote circumspectly of the General Assessment bill and probably was reluctant to explain his own position until Lee's attitude was known. From Lee's reply of 26 November 1784 it was clear that they were in opposite camps on the religious issue.

2. Article XVI of the Virignia Declaration of Rights, 1776.

3. Article I, Virginia Declaration of Rights.

4. Article XVI, Virginia Declaration of Rights.

5. Ibid.

6. General Assembly Resolution, October 1784.

7. In his autobiography Jefferson states that an effort was made to alter this phrase to read, "a departure from the plan of Jesus Christ, the holy author of our religion." Jefferson contended that in defeating the suggested change the legislators "meant to comprehend, within the mantle of it's protection, the Jew and the Gentile, the Christian and Mahomatan, the Hindoo, and infidel of every denomination."

There was considerable debate over the preamble, particularly concerning some of the more sweeping statements about reason. Responding to Madison's letter of January 22, explaining the minor changes in language, Jefferson replied that he was satisfied to see "the standard of reason at length erected."

Selected Excerpts from Madison Papers:
1784–1787

The following notations from various letters and papers reflect the tone of the debate over assessment and establishment. Only those portions of the documents relating to the subjects under consideration are included.

TO MADISON FROM JOHN BLAIR SMITH
JUNE 21, 1784

Since my arrival at home, I have seen a part of your Journals, & by them have learned the objects of the Petition from the Episcopal Clergy, which in one or two instances, appear to me very exceptionable. The first part of their prayer is necessary & proper; & the whole of it might pass without much animadversion to its disadvantage, 'till you hear them requesting that "they, the Clergy, may be incorporated by law;" & then an attentive mind must revolt against it as very unjustifiable, & very insulting to the members of their communion in general. Had they requested that an incorporating act should pass, in favour of that Church as a party of Christians, whereby the *people* might have had a share in the direction of ecclesiastical regulations, & the appointment of Church officers for that purpose, it would have been extremely proper. But as the matter now stands, the Clergy seem desirous to exclud[e] *them* from any share in such a privilege & willing to oblige the members of their Churches to sit down patiently, under such regulations as an incorporated body of Clergymen, who wish to be peculiarly considered as ministers in the view of the law, shall chuse to make, without a legal right to interfere in any manner, but such as these spiritual leaders may think fit to allow. I should expect that such an Idea of spiritual domination, would be resented & opposed by every adherent to that Society. I should suppose that every one of them who felt the spirit of his station would regard the attempt as an indefensible remain of Star-chamber tyranny, & resist it accordingly. However, if the Gentlemen, of the communion are so used to Dictators, that they either have not observed the Jure divino pretension to domineer over them, or have not inclination of Spirit to oppose it, perhaps it may be thought proper for one so little interested in the matter as myself to be Silent. I confess that I have less reason to interfere than many others: but as a Citizen of a free State I am interested in the Spirit which my Countrymen discover, & am sorry that there is room to suppose them too insensible of their own importance in any instance whatever.

But that part of the petition, which concerns me most, as well as every Non-Episcopalian in the state, is, where these Clergymen pray for an act of the Assembly to *Enable*, them to regulate all the spiritual concerns of that Church &c. This is an express attempt to draw the State into an illicit connexion & commerce with them, which is already the ground of that uneasiness which at present prevails thro' a great part of the State. According to the spirit of that prayer, the Legislature is to consider itself as the head of that Party, & consequently they as Members are to be fostered with particular care. This is unreasonable & highly improper, as well as dangerous. It ought therefore to [be] treated by the assembly as an ill-digested Scheme of policy in the present State of affairs. I am sorry that Christian Ministers should virtually declare their Church a mere political machine, which the State may regulate at pleasure; but I shall be surprised if the Assembly shall assume the improper office. The interference of the Legislature is always dangerous, where it is unnecessary. And I am sure it is plainly so in this case. It would be to decide upon a matter which a Superior power, I mean the Convention in the Bill of Rights, has already determined. It would be to give leave to do what every class of Citizens has a natural, unalienable right to do without any such leave; for surely every religious society in the State possesses full power to regulate their internal police; without depending upon the Assembly for leave to do so. Surely we are not again to be irritated & harassed with the heavy weight of a State-Church, that is to sit as sovereign over the rest, by depending in a more particular manner for direction in Spirituals, upon that antiquated fountain head of influences, the secular power.

I have here hastily throw together the very first thoughts which occurred to me upon reading the Journals; & as you certainly have taken notice of the same improprieties in the petition which I have now done, I hope you will use your extensive influence to prevent the consequences intended to flow from it.

MADISON TO JEFFERSON — JULY 3, 1784

Several Petitions came forward in behalf of a Genl. Assessmt which was reported by the Come. of Religion to be reasonable. The friends of the measure did not chuse to try their strength in the House. The Episcopal Clergy introduced a notable project for re-establishing their independence of the laity. The foundation of it was that the whole body should be legally incorporated, invested with the present property of the Church, made capable of acquiring indefinitely—empowered to make canons & by laws not contrary to the law of the land, and incumbents when once chosen by Vestries to be immovable otherwise than by sentence of the Convocation. Extraordinary as such a project was, it was preserved from a dishonorable death by the talents of Mr. Henry. It lies over for another Session.

FROM RICHARD HENRY LEE TO MADISON
NOVEMBER 26, 1784

I received your agreeable letter the day after mine of the 28th. instant had been dispatched. I thank you Sir for the very particular and satisfactory information that you have favord me with. It is certainly comfortable to know that the Legislature of our country is engaged in beneficial pursuits—for I conceive that the Gen. Assessment, and a wise digest of our militia laws are very important concerns: the one to secure our peace, and the other our morals. Refiners may weave as fine a web of reason as they please, but the experience of all times shows Religon to be the guardian of morals—and he must be a very inattentive observer in our Country, who does not see that avarice is accomplishing the destruction of religion, for want of a legal obligation to contribute something to its support. The declaration of Rights, it seems to me, rather contends against forcing modes of faith and forms of worship, than against compelling contribution for the suport of religion in general. I fully agree with the presbyterians, that true freedom embraces the Mahomitan and the Gentoo as well as the Christian religion. And upon this liberal ground I hope our Assembly will conduct themselves.

FROM JEFFERSON TO MADISON — DECEMBER 8, 1784

The proposition for a Convention has had the result I expected. If one could be obtained I do not know whether it would not do more harm than good. *While Mr. Henry lives* another bad constitution would be formed, & saddled for ever on us. What we have to do I think is *devo*[u]*tly* to *pray for his death*, in the mean time to *keep alive* the *idea* that the present is *but* an *ordinance* & to *prepar*[e] the *minds* of the *young men*. I am glad the *Episcopalians* have again shewn their teeth & fangs. The *dissenters* had almost forgotten them.

TO JAMES MONROE FROM MADISON
DECEMBER 24, 1784

The Genl. Assest. on the question for engrossing it, was yesterday carried by

44 agst. 42. Today its third reading was put off till Novr. next by 45 agst. 37 or thereabouts, and is to be printed for consideration of the people.

MADISON TO HIS FATHER
JANUARY 6, 1785

The Genl. Assesst. has been put off till next Session & is to be published in the mean time. Mr. Porter has a number of printed copies for our County. The inclosed Act for incorporating the Episcopal Church is the result of much altercation on the subject. In its original form it was wholly inadmissible. In its present form into which it has been trimmed, I assented to it with reluctance at the time, and with disatisfaction on a review of it. There has been some error in the case too, for it was unquestionably voted in the House that *two* laymen should be deputed from each Parish to the Convention spoken of. I had taken it for granted also that the Clergy were hereafter to be elected by the Vestries, and was much surprised on examining the Act since it was printed to find that the mode in which vacant parishes are to be filled, is left to be provided for by the Convention: I consider the passage of this Act however as having been so far useful as to have parried for the present the Genl. Assesst. which would otherwise have certainly been saddled upon us: & If it be unpopular among the laity it will be soon repealed, and will be a standing lesson to them of the danger of referring religious matters to the legislature.

TO JEFFERSON FROM MADISON
JANUARY 9, 1785

An act for incorporating the Protestant Episcopal Church   This act declares the ministers & vestries who are to be trienially chosen, in each period a body corporate, enables them to hold property not exceeding the value of £800 per per annum, and gives sanction to a Convention which is to be composed of the Clergy and a lay deputy from each parish, and is to regulate the affairs of the Church. It was understood by the House of Delegates that the Convention was to consist of two laymen for each clergyman, and an amendment was received for that express purpose. It so happened that the insertion of the amendment did not produce that effect, and the mistake was never discovered till the bill had passed and was in print. Another circumstance still more singular is that the act is so constructed as to deprive the Vestries of the uncontrouled right of electing clergymen, unless it be referred to them by the canons of the Convention, and that this usurpation actually escaped the eye both of the friends and adversaries of the measure, both parties taking the contrary for granted throughout the whole progress of it. The former as well as the latter appear now to be dissatisfied with what has been done, and will probably concur in a revision if not a repeal of the law. Independently of those oversights the law is in various points of view exceptionable. But the necessity of some sort of incorporation for the purpose of holding & managing the property of the Church could not well be denied, nor a more harmless modification of it now obtained. A negative of the bill too would have doubled the eagerness and the pretexts for a much greater evil, a General Assessment, which there is good ground to believe was parried by ths partial gratification of its warmest votaries. A Resolution for a legal provision for the "teachers of Christian Religion" had early in the Session been proposed by Mr. Henry, and in spite of all the opposition that could be mustered, carried by 47 agst. 32 votes. Many Petitions from below the blue ridge had prayed for such a law; and though several from the presbyterian laity beyond it were in a contrary Stile, the Clergy of that Sect favoured it. The other Sects Seemed to be passive. The Resolution lay some weeks before a bill was brought in, and the bill some weeks before it was called for; after the passage of the incorporating act it was taken up, and on the third reading, ordered by a small majority to be printed for consideration. The bill in its present dress proposes a tax of blank per Ct. on all taxable property for support of Teachers of the Christian Religion. Each person when he pays his tax is to name the society to which he dedicates it, and in case of refusal to do so, the tax is to be applied to the maintenance of a school in the County. As the bill stood for some time, the application in such cases was to be made by the Legislature to pious uses. In a committee of the whole it was determined by a Majority of 7 or 8 that the word "christian" should be exchanged for the word "Religious". On the report to the House the *pathetic zeal of the late governor Harrison* gained a like majority for reinstating discrimination. Should the bill ever pass into a law in its present form it may & will be easily eluded. It is chiefly obnoxious on account of its dishonorable principle and dangerous tendency.

TO JAMES MONROE FROM MADISON
APRIL 12, 1785

The only proceeding of the late Session of Assembly which makes a noise thro' the Country is that which relates to a Genl. Assessmt. The Episcopal people are generally for it, tho' I think the zeal of some of them has cooled. The laity of the other Sects are equally unanimous on the other side. So are all the Clergy except the Presbyterian who seem as ready to set up an establishmt. which is to take them in as they were to pull down that which shut them out. I do not know a more shameful contrast than might be formed between their Memorials on the latter & former occasion.

FROM GEORGE NICHOLAS TO MADISON
APRIL 22, 1785

My brother informs me that he conversed with you on the propriety of remonstrating against certain measures of the last session of Assembly and that you seemed to think it would be best that the counties opposed to the measures should be silent. I fear this would be construed into an assent especially to the law for establishing a certain provision for the clergy: for as the Assembly only postponed the passing of it that they might know whether it was disagreeable to the people, I think they may justly conclude that all are for it who do not say to the contrary. A majority of the counties are in favor of the measure but I believe a great majority of the people against it; but if this majority should not appear by petition the fact will be denied. Another reason why all should petition is that some will certainly do it and those who support the bills will insist that those who petition are all the opposition. Would it not add greatly to the weight of the petitions if they all hold the same language? by discovering an exact uniformity of sentiment in a majority of the country it would certainly deter the majority of the Assembly from proceeding. All my expectations are from their fears and not their justice. I have been through a considerable part of the country and am well assured that it would be impossible to carry such laws into execution and that the attempt would bring about a revolution. If you think with me that it will be proper to say something to the Assembly will you commit it to paper. I wish this because, I know you are most capable of doing it properly and because it will be most likely to be generally adopted. I can get it sent to Amherst Buckingham, Albemarle. Fluvanna, Augusta, Botetourt, Rock Bridge and Rockingham and I have no doubt that Bedford and the counties southward of it will readily join in the measure. I will also send it [to] Frederick and Berkeley and if it goes from your county to Fauquier, Culpeper and Loudoun it will be adopted by the most populous part of the country. I shall be glad to hear from you on this subject and am With esteem and respect Dr: Sir, Yr. obdt. servt.

G: Nicholas

The bill for supporting the clergy, the act for incorporating the Episcopal church and the faithful adherency to the treaty are the subjects on which the people have wish to demonstrate. It being supposed that Mr. Carter was against the latter lost him his election in this county.

TO JEFFERSON FROM MADISON
APRIL 27, 1785

The Bill for a Genl. Assesst. has produced some fermentation below the Mountains & a violent one beyond them. The contest at the next Session on this question will be a warm & precarious one. The port bill will also undergo a fiery trial. I wish the Assize Courts may not partake of the danger. The elections as far as they have come to my knowledge are likely to produce a great proportion of new members.

TO EDMUND RANDOLPH FROM MADISON
JULY 26, 1785

Your favour of the 17th. inst: inclosing a letter from Mr. Jones and a copy of the ecclesiastical Journal, came safe to hand. If I do not dislike the contents of the latter, it is because they furnish as I conceive fresh and forcible arguments against the Genl. Assesment. It may be of little consequence what tribunal is to judge of Clerical misdemesnors or how firmly the incumbent may be fastened on the parish, whilst the Vestry & people may hear & pay him or not as they like. But should a legal salary be annexed to the title, this phantom of power would be substantiated into a real monster of oppression. Indeed it appears to be so at present as far as the Glebes & donations extend. I had seen some prints of these proceedings before I recd. your letter, and had remarked the sprinklings of liberality to which you allude. My conjectures I believe did not err as to the quarter from which they came.

TO JEFFERSON FROM MADISON
AUGUST 20, 1785

The opposition to the general assessment gains ground. At the *instance of some of its adversaries I drew up the remonstrance* herewith inclosed. It has been *sent thro' the medium of confidential persons in a member of the upper county*[s] and I am told will be pretty extensively signed. The presbyterian clergy have at length espoused the side of the opposition, being moved either by *a fear of their laity* or *a jealousy of the episcopalians*. The mutual hatred of these sects has been much inflamed by the late act incorporating the latter. *I am far from* being *sorry for it* as *a coalition between them* could *alone endanger our religious rights* and a tendency to *such an event had been suspected.*

JEFFERSON TO MADISON
DECEMBER 16, 1786

The Virginia Act for religious freedom has been received with infinite approbation in Europe and propagated with enthusiasm. I do not mean by the governments, but by the individuals which compose them. It has been translated into French and Italian, has been sent to most of the courts of Europe, and has been the best evidence of the falsehood of those reports which stated us to be in anarchy. It is inserted in the new Encyclopedie and is appearing in most of the publications respecting America. In fact it is comfortable to see the standard of reason at length erected, after so many ages during which the human mind has been held in vassalage by kings, priests and nobles: and it is honorable for us to have produced the first legislature who has had the courage to declare that the reason of man may be trusted with the formation of his own opinions.

TO EDMUND PENDLETON FROM MADISON
OCTOBER 28, 1787

I have recd. and acknowledge with great pleasure your favor of the 8th. instt. The remarks which you make on the Act of the Convention appear to me to be in general extremely well founded. Your criticism on the clause exempting vessels bound to or from a State from being obliged to enter &c in another is particularly so. This provision was dictated by the jealousy of some particular States, and was inserted pretty late in the Session. The object of it was what you conjecture. The expression is certainly not accurate. Is not a religious test as far as it is necessary, or would operate, involved in the oath itself? If the person swearing believes in the supreme Being who is invoked, and in the penal consequences of offending him, either in this or a future world or both, he will be under the same restraint from perjury as if he had previously subscribed a test requiring this belief. If the person in question be an unbeliever in these points and would notwithstanding take the oath, a previous test could have no effect. He would subscribe it as he would take the oath, without any principle that could be affected by either.

Defense of the Constitution
Virginia Ratification Convention: June 12, 1788

Among those issues addressed at this critical gathering was that of religious freedom. Here Madison referred to the subject in his response to Patrick Henry entitled *General Defense of the Constitution.*

The honorable member has introduced the subject of religion. Religion is not guarded—there is no bill of rights declaring that religion should be secure. Is a bill of rights a security for religion? Would the bill of rights in this state exempt the people from paying for the support of one particular sect, if such sect were exclusively established by law? If there were a majority of one sect, a bill of rights would be a poor protection for liberty. Happily for the states, they enjoy the utmost freedom of religion. This freedom arises from that multiplicity of sects, which pervades America, and which is the best and only security for religious liberty in any society. For where there is such a variety of sects, there cannot be a majority of any one sect to oppress and persecute the rest. Fortunately for this commonwealth, a majority of the people are decidedly against any exclusive establishment—I believe it to be so in the other states. There is not a shadow of right in the general government to intermeddle with religion. Its least interference with it would be a most flagrant usurpation. I can appeal to my uniform conduct on this subject, that I have warmly supported religious freedom. It is better that this security should be depended upon from the general legislature, than from one particular state. A particular state might concur in one religious project. But the United States abound in such a variety of sects, that it is a strong security against religious persecution, and is sufficient to authorise a conclusion, that no one sect will ever be able to out-number or depress the rest.

TO JEFFERSON FROM MADISON —
OCTOBER 17, 1788

[This section deals with the proposed Bill of Rights for the Constitution.]

The little pamphlet herewith inclosed will give you a collective view of the alterations which have been proposed for the new Constitution. Various and numerous as they appear they certainly omit many of the true grounds of opposition. The articles relating to Treaties—to paper money, and to contracts, created more enemies than all the errors in the System positive & negative put together. It is true nevertheless that not a few, particularly in Virginia have contended for the proposed alterations from the most honorable & patriotic motives; and that among the advocates for the Constitution, there are some who wish for further guards to public liberty & individual rights. As far as these may consist of a constitutional declaration of the most essential rights, it is probable they will be added; though there are many who think such addition unnecessary, and not a few who think it misplaced in such a Constitution. There is scarce any point on which the party in opposition is so much divided as to its importance and its propriety. My own opinion has always been in favor of a bill of rights; provided it be so framed as not to imply powers not meant to be included in the enumeration. At the same time I have never thought the omission a material defect, nor been anxious to supply it even by *subsequent* amendment, for any other reason than that it is anxiously desired by others. I have favored it because I supposed it might be of use, and if properly executed could not be of disservice. I have not viewed it in an important light I. because I conceive that in a certain degree, though not in the extent argued by Mr. Wilson, the rights in question are reserved by the manner in which the federal powers are granted. 2 because there is great reason to fear that a positive declaration of some of the most essential rights could not be obtained in the requisite latitude. I am sure that the rights of Conscience in particular, if submitted to public definition would be narrowed much more than they are likely ever to be by an assumed power. One of the objections in New England was that the Constitution by prohibiting religious tests opened a door for Jews Turks & infidels. 3. because the limited powers of the federal Government and the jealousy of the subordinate Governments, afford a security which has not existed in the case of the State Governments, and exists in no other. 4 because experience proves the inefficacy of a bill of rights on those ocasions when its controul is most needed. Repeated violations of these parchment barriers have been committed by overbearing majorities in every State. In Virginia I have seen the bill of rights violated in every instance where it has been opposed to a popular current. Notwithstanding the explicit provision contained in that instrument for the rights of Conscience it is well known that a religious establishment wd. have taken place in that State, if the legislative majority had found as they expected, a majority of the people in favor of the measure; and I am persuaded that if a majority of the people were now of one sect, the measure would still take place and on narrower ground than was then proposed, notwithstanding the additional obstacle which the law has since created.

Wherever the real power in a Government lies, there is the danger of oppression. In our Governments the real power lies in the majority of the Community, and the invasion of private rights is *chiefly* to be apprehended, not from acts of Government contrary to the sense of its constituents, but from acts in which the Government is the mere instrument of the major number of the constituents. This is a truth of great importance, but not yet sufficiently attended to: and is probably more strongly impressed on my mind by facts, and reflections suggested by them, than on yours which has contemplated abuses of power issuing from a very different quarter. Wherever there is an interest and power to do wrong, wrong will generally be done, and not less readily by a powerful & interested party than by a powerful and interested prince. The difference, so far as it relates to the superiority of republics over monarchies, lies in the less degree of probability that interest may prompt abuses of power in the former than in the latter; and in the security in the former agst. oppression of more than the smaller part of the society, whereas in the former it may be extended in a manner to the whole. The difference so far as it relates to the point in question—the efficacy of a bill of rights in controuling abuses of power—lies in this, that in a monarchy the latent force of the nation is superior to that of the sovereign, and a solemn charter of popular rights must have a great effect, as a standard for trying the validity of public acts, and a signal for rousing & uniting the superior force of the community; whereas in a popular Government, the political and physical power may be considered as vested in the same hands, that is in a majority of the people, and consequently the tyrannical will of the sovereign is not [to] be controuled by the dread of an appeal to any other force within the community. What use then it may be asked can a bill of rights serve in popular Governments? I answer the two following which though less essential than in other Governments, sufficiently recommend the precaution. I. The political truths declared in that solemn manner acquire by degrees the character of fundamental maxims of free Government, and as they become incorporated with the national sentiment, counteract the impulses of interest and passion. 2. Altho' it be generally true as above stated that the danger of oppression lies in the interested majorities of the people rather than in usurped acts of the Government, yet there may be occasions on which the evil may spring from the latter sources; and on such, a bill of rights will be a good ground for an appeal to the sense of the community. Perhaps too there may be a certain degree of danger, that a succession of artful and ambitious rulers, may by gradual & well-timed advances, finally erect an independent Government on the subversion of liberty. Should this danger exist at all, it is prudent to guard agst. it, especially when the precaution can do no injury. At the same time I must own that I see no tendency in our governments to danger on that side. It has been remarked that there is a tendency in all Governments to an augmentation of power at the expense of liberty. But the remark as usually understood does not appear to me well founded. Power when it has attained a certain degree of energy and independence goes on generally to further degrees. But when below that degree, the direct tendency is to further degrees of relaxation, until the abuses of liberty beget a sudden transition to an undue degree of power. With this explanation the remark may be true; and in the latter sense only is it in my opinion applicable to the Governments in America. It is a melancholy reflection that liberty should be equally exposed to danger whether the Government have too much or too little power, and that the line which divides these extremes should be so inaccurately defined by experience.

TO GEORGE EVE FROM MADISON
JANUARY 2, 1789

[*Eve was a Baptist minister in Virginia.*]

Being informed that reports prevail not only that I am opposed to any amend-mends whatever to the new federal Constitution; but that I have ceased to be a friend to the rights of Conscience; and inferring from a conversation with my brother William, that you are disposed to contradict such reports as far as your knowledge of my sentiments may justify, I am led to trouble you with this communication of them. As a private Citizen it could not be my wish that erroneous opinions should be entertained, with respect to either of those points, particularly, with respect to religious liberty. But having been induced to offer my services to this district as its representative in the federal Legis-lature, considerations of a public nature make it proper that, with respect to both, my principles and views should be rightly understood.

I freely own that I have never seen in the Constitution as it now stands those serious dangers which have alarmed many respectable Citizens. Accord-ingly whilst it remained unratified, and it was necessary to unite the States in some one plan, I opposed all previous alterations as calculated to throw the States into dangerous contentions, and to furnish the secret enemies of the Union with an opportunity of promoting its dissolution. Circumstances are now changed: The Constitution is established on the ratifications of eleven States and a very great majority of the people of America; and amendments, if pursued with a proper moderation and in a proper mode, will be not only safe, but may serve the double purpose of satisfying the minds of well meaning opponents, and of providing additional guards in favour of liberty. Under this change of circumstances, it is my sincere opinion that the Constitution ought to be revised, and that the first Congress meeting under it, ought to prepare and recommend to the States for ratification, the most satisfactory provisions for all essential rights, particularly the rights of Conscience in the fullest latitude, the freedom of the press, trials by jury, security against general warrants &c. I think it will be proper also to provide expressly in the Constitution, for the periodical increase of the number of Representatives until the amount shall be entirely satisfactory; and to put the judiciary department into such a form as will render vexatious appeals impossible. There are sundry other alterations which are either eligible in themselves, or being at least safe, are recommended by the respect due to such as wish for them.

I have intimated that the amendments ought to be proposed by the first Congress. I prefer this mode to that of a General Convention, Ist. because it is the most expeditious mode. A convention must be delayed, until 2/3 of the State Legislatures shall have applied for one; and afterwards the amendments must be submitted to the States; whereas if the business be undertaken by Congress the amendments may be prepared and submitted in March next. 2dly. because it is the most certain mode. There are not a few States who will absolutely reject the proposal of a Convention, and yet not be averse to amendments in the other mode. Lastly, it is the safest mode. The Congress, who will be appointed to execute as well as to amend the Government, will probably be careful not to destroy or endanger it. A convention, on the other hand, meeting in the present ferment of parties, and containing perhaps insidious characters from different parts of America, would at least spread a general alarm, and be but too likely to turn every thing into confusion and uncertainty. It is to be observed however that the question concerning a General Convention, will not belong to the federal Legislature. If 2/3 of the States apply for one, Congress can not refuse to call it: if not, the other mode of amendments must be pursued. I am Sir with due respect your friend & Obedt. servant

CONGRESSIONAL RECORD OF MADISON'S REMARKS ON CONSTITUTIONAL AMENDMENTS

August 15, 1789

The committee took up the fourth amendment (containing a bill of rights) proposed by the select committee. The first clause, "No religion shall be established by Law, nor shall the equal rights of conscience be infringed," was under discussion.

MR. MADISON Said he apprehended the meaning of the words to be, that congress should not establish a religion, and enforce the legal observation of it by law, nor compel men to worship God in any manner contrary to their conscience; whether the words were necessary or not he did not mean to say, but they had been required by some of the state conventions, who seemed to entertain an opinion that under the clause of the constitution, which gave power to congress to make all laws necessary and proper to carry into execution the constitution, and the laws made under it, enabled them to make laws of such a nature as might infringe the rights of conscience, or establish a national religion. To prevent these effects he presumed the amendment was intended, and he thought it as well expressed as the nature of the language would admit.

Cong. Register, II, 195. The committee changed the wording to read, "congress shall make no laws touching religion, or infringing the rights of conscience."

August 17, 1789

Tucker moved to strike out, "No state shall infringe the equal rights of conscience, nor the freedom of speech, or of the press, nor of the right of trial by jury in criminal cases."

MR. MADISON Conceived this to be the most valuable amendment on the whole list; if there was any reason to restrain the government of the United States from infringing upon these essential rights, it was equally necessary that they should be secured against the state governments; he thought that if they provided against the one, it was an necessary to provide against the other, and was satisfied that it would be equally grateful to the people.

MADISON ESSAY IN *NATIONAL GAZETTE*
MARCH 27, 1792

PROPERTY

THIS term in its particular application means "that dominion which one man claims and exercises over the external things of the world, in exclusion of every other individual."

In its larger and juster mening, it embraces every thing to which a man may attach a value and have a right; and *which leaves to every one else the like advantage.*

In the former sense, a man's land, or merchandize, or money is called his property.

In the latter sense, a man has a property in his opinions and the free communication of them.

He has a property of peculiar value in his religious opinions, and in the profession and practice dictated by them.

He has a property very dear to him in the safety and liberty of his person.

He has an equal property in the free use of his faculties and free choice of the objects on which to employ them.

In a word, as a man is said to have a right to his property, he may be equally said to have a property in his rights.

Where an excess of power prevails, property of no sort is duly respected. No man is safe in his opinions, his person, his faculties, or his possessions.

Where there is an excess of liberty, the effect is the same, tho' from an opposite cause.

Government is instituted to protect property of every sort; as well that which lies in the various rights of individuals, as that which the term particularly expresses. This being the end of government, that alone is a *just* government, which *impartially* secures to every man, whatever is his *own*.

According to this standard of merit, the praise of affording a just security to property, should be sparingly bestowed on a government which, however scrupulously guarding the possessions of individuals, does not protect them in the enjoyment and communication of their opinions, in which they have an equal, and in the estimation of some, a more valuable property.

More sparingly should this praise be allowed to a government, where a man's religious rights are violated by penalties, or fettered by tests, or taxed by a hierarchy. Conscience is the most sacred of all property; other property depending in part on positive law, the exercise of that, being a natural and unalienable right. To guard a man's house as his castle, to pay public and enforce private debts with the most exact faith, can give no title to invade a man's conscience which is more sacred than his castle, or to withhold from it that debt of protection, for which the public faith is pledged, by the very nature and original conditions of the social pact.

That is not a just government, nor is property secure under it, where the property which a man has in his personal safety and personal liberty, is violated by arbitrary seizures of one class of citizens for the service of the rest. A magistrate issuing his warrants to a press gang, would be in his proper functions in Turkey or Indostan, under appellations proverbial of the most compleat despotism.

That is not a just government, nor is property secure under it, where arbitrary restrictions, exemptions, and monopolies deny to part of its citizens that free use of their faculties, and free choice of their occupations, which not only constitute their property in the general sense of the word; but are the means of acquiring property strictly so called. What must be the spirit of legislation where a manufacturer of linen cloth is forbidden to bury his own child in a linen shroud, in order to favour his neighbour who manufactures woolen cloth; where the manufacturer and wearer of woolen cloth are again forbidden the œconomical use of buttons of that material, in favor of the manufacturer of buttons of other materials!

A just security to property is not afforded by that government, under which unequal taxes oppress one species of property and reward another species: where arbitrary taxes invade the domestic sanctuaries of the rich, and excessive taxes grind the faces of the poor; where the keenness and competitions of want are deemed an insufficent spur to labor, and taxes are again applied, by an unfeeling policy, as another spur; in violation of that sacred property, which Heaven, in decreeing man to earn his bread by the sweat of his brow, kindly reserved to him, in the small repose that could be spared from the supply of his necessities.

If there be a government then which prides itself in maintaining the inviolability of property; which provides that none shall be taken *directly* even for public use without indemnification to the owner, and yet *directly* violates the property which individuals have in their opinions, their religion, their persons, and their faculties; nay more, which *indirectly* violates their property, in their actual possessions, in the labor that acquires their daily subsistence, and in the hallowed remnant of time which ought to relieve their fatigues and soothe their cares, the influence will have been anticipated, that such a government is not a pattern for the United States.

If the United States mean to obtain or deseve the full praise due to wise and just governments, they will equally respect the rights of property, and the property in rights: they will rival the government that most sacredly guards the former; and by repelling its example in violating the latter, will make themselves a pattern to that and all other governments.

Selected Writings after 1799

On a number of occasions during his public life and later in retirement at Montpelier, Madison addressed the issues of religion and religious freedom in letters to various individuals. Included here are excerpts from the most informative parts of that correspondence.

MADISON'S ADDRESS TO VIRGINIA
GENERAL ASSEMBLY—JANUARY 1799

So insatiable is a love of power that it has resorted to a distinction between the freedom and licentiousness of the press for the purpose of converting the third amendment of the Constitution, which was dictated by the most lively anxiety to preserve that freedom, into an instrument for abridging it. Thus usurpation even justifies itself by a precaution against usurpation; and thus an amendment universally designed to quiet every fear is adduced as the source of an act which has produced general terror and alarm.

The distinction between liberty and licentiousness is still a repetition of the Protean doctrine of implication, which is ever ready to work its ends by varying its shape. By its help, the judge as to what is licentious may escape through any constitutional restriction. Under it men of a particular religious opinion might be excluded from office, because such exclusion would not amount to an establishment of religion, and because it might be said that their opinions are licentious. And under it Congress might denominate a religion to be heretical and licentious, and proceed to its suppression. Remember that precedents once established are so much positive power; and that the nation which reposes on the pillow of political confidence, will sooner or later end its political existence in a deadly lethargy. Remember, also that it is to the press mankind are indebted for having dispelled the clouds which long encompassed religion, for disclosing her genuine lustre, and disseminating her salutary doctrines.

VETO MESSAGES TO CONGRESS — FEBRUARY 21 AND 28, 1811

Veto message, February 21, 1811

To the House of Representatives of the United States:
Having examined and considered the bill entitled "An Act incorporating the Protestant Episcopal Church in the town of Alexandria, in the District of Columbia," I now return the bill to the House of Representatives, in which it originated, with the following objections:

Because the bill exceeds the rightful authority to which governments are limited by the essential distinction between civil and religious functions, and violates in particular the article of the Constitution of the United States which declares that "Congress shall make no law respecting a religious establishment." The bill enacts into and establishes by law sundry rules and proceedings relative purely to the organization and polity of the church incorporated, and comprehending even the election and removal of the minister of the same, so that no change could be made therein by the particular society or by the general church of which it is a member, and whose authority it recognizes. This particular church, therefore, would so far be a religious establishment by law, a legal force and sanction being given to certain articles in its constitution and administration. Nor can it be considered that the articles thus established are to be taken as the descriptive criteria only of the corporate identity of the society, inasmuch as this identity must depend on other characteristics, as the regulations established are in general unessential and alterable according to the principles and canons by which churches of that denomination govern themselves, and as the injunctions and prohibitions contained in the regulations would be enforced by the penal consequences applicable to a violation of them according to the local law.

Because the bill vests in the said incorporated church an authority to provide for the support of the poor and the education of poor children of the same, an authority which, being altogether superfluous if the provision is to be the result of pious charity, would be a percedent for giving to religious societies as such a legal agency in carrying into effect a public and civil duty.

Veto message, February 28, 1811

To the House of Representatives of the United States:
Having examined and considered the bill entitled "An act for the relief of Richard Tervin, William Coleman, Edwin Lewis, Samuel Mims, Joseph Wilson, and the Baptist Church at Salem Meeting House, in the Mississippi Territory," I now return the same to the House of Representatives, in which it originated,

with the following objection:

Because the bill in reserving a certain parcel of land of the United States for the use of said Baptist Church comprises a principle and precedent for the appropriation of funds of the United States for the use and support of religious societies, contrary to the article of the Constitution which declares that "Congress shall make no law respecting a religious establishment."

MADISON TO MORDICAI NOAH — MAY 15, 1818

NOTE: A letter from Noah to Madison stated that Jews in America owed many of the blessings they enjoyed to him.

Sir, — I have rec.^{d} your letter of the 6th with the eloquent discourse delivered at the Consecration of the Jewish Synagogue. Having ever regarded the freedom of religious opinions & worship as equally belonging to every sect, & the secure enjoyment of it as the best human provision for bringing all either into the same way of thinking, or into that mutual charity which is the only substitute, I observe with pleasure the view you give of the spirit in which your Sect partake of the blessings offered by our Govr and Laws.

As your foreign Mission took place whilst I was in the Administration, it cannot but be agreeable to me to learn that your acc.^{ts} have been closed in a manner so favorable to you. And I know too well the justice & candor of the present Executive to doubt, that an official [illegible] will be readily allowed to explanations necessary to protect your character against the effect of any impressions whatever ascertained to be erroneous. It is certain that your religious profession was well known at the time you rec.^{d} your Commission; and that in itself could not be a motive for your recall.

TO ROBERT WALSH FROM MADISON — MARCH 2, 1819

That there has been an increase of religious instruction since the revolution can admit of no question. The English church was originally the established religion; the character of the clergy that above described. Of other sects there were but few adherents, except the Presbyterians who predominated on the W. side of the Blue Mountains. A little time previous to the Revolutionary struggle the Baptists sprang up, and made a very rapid progress. Among the early acts of the Republican Legislature, were those abolishing the Religious establishment, and putting all Sects at full liberty and on a perfect level. At present the population is divided, with small exceptions, among the Protestant Episcopalians, the Presbyterians, the Baptists & the Methodists. Of their comparative numbers I can command no sources of information. I conjecture the Presbyterians & Baptists to form each ab.^{t} a third, & the two other sects together third. The Old churches, built under the establish.ᵗ at the public expence, have in many instances gone to ruin, or are in a very dilapidated state, owing chiefly to a transition desertion of the flocks to other worships. A few new ones have latterly been built particularly in the towns. Among the other sects, Meeting Houses, have multiplied & continue to multiply; tho' in general they are of the of which the Methodists are much the smallest, to make up the remaining plainest and cheapest sort. But neither the number nor the style of the Religious edifices is a true measure of the state of religion. Religious instruction is now diffused throughout the Community by preachers of every sect with almost equal zeal, tho' with very unequal acquirements; and at private houses & open stations and occasionally in such as are appropriated to Civil use, as well as buildings appropriated to that use. The qualifications of the Preachers, too among the new sects where there was the greatest deficiency, are understood to be improving. On a general comparison of the present & former times, the balance is certainly & vastly on the side of the present, as to the number of religious teachers the zeal which actuates them, the purity of their lives, and the attendance of the people on their instructions. It was the Universal opinion of the Century preceding the last, that Civil Gov.ᵗ could not stand without the prop of a Religious establishment, & that the Xⁿ religion itself, would perish if not supported by a legal provision for its Clergy. The experience of Virginia conspicuously corroborates the disproof of both opinions. The Civil Gov.ᵗ tho' bereft of everything like an associated hierarchy possesses the requisite stability and performs its functions with complete success; Whilst the number, the industry, and the morality of the Priesthood, & the devotion of the people have been manifestly increased by the total separation of the Church from the State.

TO JACOB DE LA MOTTA FROM MADISON — AUGUST 1820

NOTE: de la Motta had written concerning his congregation in Savannah.

The history of the Jews must forever be interesting. The modern part of it is, at the same time so little generally known, that every ray of light on the subject has its value.

Among the features peculiar to the Political system of the U. States, is the perfect equality of rights which it secures to every religious Sect. And it is particularly pleasing to observe in the good citizenship of such as have been most distrusted and oppressed elsewhere, a happy illustration of the safety & success of this experiment of a just & benignant policy. Equal laws protecting equal rights, are found as they ought to be presumed, the best guarantee of loyalty & love of country; as well as best calculated to cherish that mutual respect & good will among Citizens of every religious denomination which are necessary to social harmony and most favorable to the advancement of truth. The account you give of the Jews of your Congregation brings them fully within the scope of these observations.

TO F. L. SCHAEFFER FROM MADISON —
DECEMBER 3, 1821

NOTE: *Madison is replying to the receipt of a sermon sent by Schaeffer, a New York clergyman.*

It is a pleasing and persuasive example of pious zeal, united with pure benevolence and of a cordial attachment to a particular creed, untinctured with sectarian illiberality. It illustrates the excellence of a system which, by a due distinction, to which the genius and courage of Luther led the way, between what is due to Caesar and what is due God, best promotes the discharge of *both* obligations.

. . . The experience of the United States is a happy disproof of the error so long rooted in the unenlightened minds of well-meaning Christians, as well as in the corrupt hearts of persecuting usurpers, that without a legal incorporation of religious and civil polity, neither could be supported. A mutual independence is found most friendly to practical Religion, to social harmony, and to political prosperity.

TO EDWARD LIVINGSTON FROM MADISON —
JULY 10, 1822

I observe with particular pleasure the view you have taken of the immunity of Religion from civil jurisdiction, in every case where it does not trespass on private rights or the public peace. This has always been a favorite principle with me; and it was not with my approbation, that the deviation from it took place in Cong.^{s} when they appointed Chaplains, to be paid from the Nat.^{l} Treasury. It would have been a much better proof to their Constituents of their pious feeling if the members had contributed for the purpose, a pittance from their own pockets. As the precedent is not likely to be rescinded, the best that can now be done, may be to apply to the Const.^{n} the maxim of the law, de minimis non curat.

There has beeen another deviation from the strict principle in the Executive Proclamations of fasts & festivals, so far, at least, as they have spoken the language of *injunction*, or have lost sight of the equality of *all* religious sects in the eye of the Constitution.

Whilst I was honored with the Executive Trust I found it necessary on more than one occasion to follow the example of predecessors. But I was always careful to make the Proclamations absolutely indiscriminate, and merely recommendatory; or rather mere *designations* of a day, on which all who thought proper might *unite* in consecrating it to religious purposes, according to their own faith & forms. In this sense, I presume you reserve to the Gov^t a right to *appoint* particular days for religious worship throughout the State, without any penal sanction *enforcing* the worship.

I know not what may be the way of thinking on this subject in Louisiana. I should suppose the Catholic portion of the people, at least, as a small & even unpopular sect in the U.S., would rally, as they did in Virg^a when religious liberty was a Legislative topic, to its broadest principle.

Nothwithstanding the general progress made within the two last centuries in favour of this branch of liberty, & the full establishment of it, in some parts of our Country, there remains in others a strong bias towards the old error, that without some sort of alliance or coalition between Gov^t & Religion neither can be duly supported. Such indeed is the tendency to such a coalition, and such its corrupting influence on both the parties, that the danger cannot be too carefully guarded agst. And in a Gov^t of opinion, like ours, the only effectual guard must be found in the soundness and stability of the general opinion on the subject. Every new & successful example therefore of a perfect separation between ecclesiastical and civil matters, is of importance. And I have no doubt that every new example, will succeed, as every past one has done, in shewing that religion & Gov^t will both exist in greater purity, the less they are mixed together.

It was the belief of all sects at one time that the establishment of Religion by law, was right & necessary; that the true religion ought to be established in exclusion of every other; and that the only question to be decided was which was the true religion. The example of Holland proved that a toleration of sects, dissenting from the established sect, was safe & even useful. The example of the Colonies, now States, which rejected religious establishments altogether, proved that all Sects might be safely & advantageously put on a footing of equal & entire freedom. . . . We are teaching the world the great truth that Gov^{ts} do better without Kings & Nobles than with them. The merit will be doubled by the other lesson that Religion flourishes in greater purity, without than with the aid of Gov^t.

TO EDWARD EVERETT FROM MADISON — MARCH 19, 1823

NOTE: Everett was a professor at Harvard University. He complained in his letter to Madison about one sect monopolizing theological positions in his school.

Our University has lately rec^d a further loan from the Legislature which will prepare the Buildings for ten Professors and about 200 Students. Should all the loans be converted into donations, at the next Session, as is generally expected, but for which no pledge has been given, the Visitors, with an annuity of $15,000 settled on the Institution, will turn their thoughts towards opening it, and to the preliminary engagement of Professors.

I am not surprised at the dilemma produced at your University by making theological professorships an integral part of the System. The anticipation of such an one led to the omission in ours; the Visitors being merely authorized to open a public Hall for religious occasions, under *impartial* regulations; with the opportunity to the different sects to establish Theological schools so near that the Students of the University may respectively attend the religious exercises in them. The village of Charlottesville also, where different religious worships will be held, is also so near, that resort may conveniently be had to them.

A University with sectarian professorships, becomes, of course, a Sectarian Monopoly: with professorships of rival sects, it would be an Arena of Theological Gladiators. Without any such professorships, it may incur for a time at least, the imputation of irreligious tendencies, if not designs. The last difficulty was thought more manageable than either of the others.

On this view of the subject, there seems to be no alternative but between a public University without a theological professorship, and sectarian Seminaries without a University.

I recollect to have seen, many years ago, a project of a prayer, by Govr Livingston father of the present Judge, intended to comprehend & conciliate College Students of every X^n denomination, by a Form composed wholly of texts & phrases of scripture. If a trial of the expendient was ever made, it must have failed, notwithstanding its winning aspect from the single cause that many sects reject all set forms of Worship.

The difficulty of reconciling the X^n mind to the absence of a religious tuition from a University established by law and at the common expence, is probably less with us than with you. The settled opinion here is that religion is essentially distinct from Civil Gov.^{t} and exempt from its cognizance; that a connexion between them is injurious to both; that there are causes in the human breast, which ensure the perpetuity of religion without the aid of the law; that rival sects, with equal rights, exercise mutual censorships in favor of good morals; that if new sects arise with absurd opinions or overheated maginations, the proper remedies lie in time, forbearance and example; that a legal establishment of religion without a toleration could not be thought of, and with a toleration, is no security for public quiet & harmony, but rather a source itself of discord & animosity; and finally that these opinions are supported by experience, which has shewn that every relaxation of the alliance between Law & religion, from the partial example of Holland, to its consummation in Pennsylvania Delaware N.J., &c, has been found as safe in practice as it is sound in theory. Prior to the Revolution, the Episcopal Church was established by law in this State. On the Declaration of independence it was left with all other sects, to a self-support. And no doubt exists that there is much more of religion among us now than there ever was before the change; and particularly in the Sect which enjoyed the legal patronage. This proves rather more than, that the law is not necessary to the support of religion.

With such a public opinion, it may be expected that a University with the feature peculiar to ours will succeed here if anywhere. Some of the Clergy did not fail to arraign the peculiarity; but it is not improbable that they had an eye to the chance of introducing their own creed into the professor's chair. A late resolution for establishing an Episcopal school within the College of William & Mary, tho' in a very guarded manner, drew immediate animadversions from the press, which if they have not put an end to the project, are a proof of what would follow such an experiment in the University of the State, endowed and supported as this will be, altogether by the Public authority and at the common expense.

TO FREDERICK BEASLEY FROM MADISON —
NOVEMBER 20, 1825

NOTE: Beasley had written to Madison requesting that he offer his opinion on a pamphlet, Vindication of the Argument a prior in Proof of the Being and Attributes of God.

DEAR SIR I have duly rec^d the copy of your little tract on the proofs of the Being & Attributes of God. To do full justice to it, would require not only a more critical attention than I have been able to bestow on it, but a resort to the celebrated work of Dr. Clarke, which I read fifty years ago only, and to that of Dr Waterland also which I never read.

The reasoning that could satisfy such a mind as that of Clarke, ought certainly not to be slighted in the discussion. And the belief in a God All Powerful wise & good, is so essential to the moral order of the World & to the happiness of man, that arguments which enforce it cannot be drawn from too many sources nor adapted with too much solicitude to the different characters & capacities to be impressed with it.

But whatever effect may be produced on some minds by the more abstract train of ideas which you so strongly support, it will probably always be found that the course of reasoning from the effect to the cause, "from Nature to Nature's God," Will be the more universal & more persuasive application.

The finiteness of the human understanding betrays itself on all subjects, but more especially when it contemplates such as involve infinity. What may safely be said seems to be, that the infinity of time & space forces itself on our conception, a limitation of either being inconceivable; that the mind prefers at once the idea of a self-existing cause to that of an infinite series of cause & effect, which augments, instead of avoiding difficulty; and that it finds more facility in assenting to the self-existence of an invisible cause possessing infinite power, wisdom & goodness, than to the self-existence of the universe, visibly destitute of those attributes, and which may be the effect of them. In this comparative facility of conception & belief, all philosophical Reasoning on the subject must perhaps terminate. But that I may not get farther beyond my depth, and without the resources which bear you up in fathoming efforts, I hasten to thank you for the favour which has made me your debtor, and to assure you of my esteem & my respectful regards. . . .

TO GEORGE MASON FROM MADISON —
JULY 14, 1826

I have received, Sir, your letter of the 6th inst. requesting such information as I may be able to give as to the origin of the document, a copy of which was inclosed in it. The motive and manner of the request would entitle it to respect if less easily complied with than by the following statement.

During the session of the General Assembly 1784-5 a bill was introduced into the House of Delegates providing for the legal support of Teachers of the Christian Religion, and being patronized by the most popular talents in the House, seemed likely to obtain a majority of votes. In order to arrest its progress it was insisted with sucess that the bill should be postponed till the evening session, and in the meantime be printed for public consideration. That the sense of the people might be the better called forth, your highly distinguished ancestor Col. Geo. Mason, Col. Geo. Nicholas also possessing much public weight and some others thought it advisable that a remonstrance against the bill should be prepared for general circulation and signature and imposed on me the task of drawing up such a paper. The draught having received their sanction, a large number of printed copies were distributed, and so extensively signed by the people of every religious denomination that at the ensuing session the projected measure was entirely frustrated; and under the influence of the public sentiment thus manifested the celebrated bill "Establishing Religious Freedom" enacted into a permanent barrier against Future attempts on the rights of conscience as declared in the Great Charter prefixed to the Constitution of the State. Be pleased to accept my friendly respects.

TO GENERAL LAFAYETTE FROM MADISON — NOVEMBER 24, 1826

The Anglican hierarchy existing in Virginia prior to the Revolution was abolished by an early act of the Independent Legislature. In the year 1875, a bill was introduced under the auspices of Mr. Henry, imposing a general tax for the support of 'Teachers of the Christian Religion.' It made a progress threatening a majority in its favor. As an expedient to defeat it, we proposed that it should be postponed to another session, and printed in the mean time for public consideration. Such an appeal in a case so important and so unforeseen could not be resisted. With a view to arouse the people, it was thought proper that a memorial should be drawn up, the task being assigned to me, to be printed and circulated through the State for a general signature. The experiment succeeded. The memorial was so extensively signed by the various religious sects, including a considerable portion of the old hierarchy, that the projected innovation was crushed, and under the influence of the popular sentiment thus called forth, the well-known Bill prepared by Mr. Jefferson, for 'Establishing Religious freedom," passed into a law, as it now stands in our code of statutes.

TO JASPER ADAMS FROM MADISON — SPRING 1833

NOTE: *Adams was president of the College of Charleston. He had sent Madison a copy of his pamphlet,* The Relations of Christianity to Civil Government in the United States, *and requested Madison's comments. Adams contested the view*

*"that Christianity had no connection with our civil constitutions of government."
Rather, he argued, "the people of the United States have retained the Christian
religion as the foundation of their civil, legal, and political institutions." Adams
contended that the nation had a national religion. In addition to Madison, Adams
sent the pamphlet to numerous other statesmen, including John Marshall and Justice
Joseph Story. Marshall replied, "The American population is entirely Christian,
and with us, Christianity and religion are identified." Story went further, writing, "I
have read it with uncommon satisfaction. I think its tone and spirit excellent. My
own private judgment has long been (and every day's experience more and more
confirms me in it) that government can not long exist without an alliance with
religion; and that Christianity is indispensable to the true interests and solid
foundations of free government."*

I rec^d in due time the printed copy of your Convention sermon on the
relation of Xnity to Civil Gov^t with a manuscript request of my opinion on the
subject.

There appears to be in the nature of man what insures his belief in an
invisible cause of his present existence, and anticipation of his future existence.
Hence the propensities & susceptibilities in that case of religion which with a
few doubtful or individual exceptions have prevailed throughout the world.

Waiving the rights of Conscience, not included in the surrender implied by
the social State, and more or less invaded by all religious Establishments, the
simple question to be decided is whether a support of the best & purest
religion, the Xn religion itself ought not so far at least as pecuniary means are
involved, to be provided for by the Gov^t rather than be left to the voluntary
provisions of those who profess it. And on this question experience will be an
admitted Umpire, the more adequate as the connection betwen Gov^{ts} &
Religion have existed in such various degrees & forms, and now can be compared with examples where connection has been entirely dissolved.

In the Papal System, Government and Religion are in a manner consolidated, & that is found to be the worst of Gov^{ts}.

In most the Gov^{ts} of the old world, the legal establishment of a particular
religion and without or with very little toleration of others makes a part of the
Political and Civil organization and there are few of the most enlightened judges
who will maintain that the system has been favorable either to Religion or to
Gov^t.

Until Holland ventured on the experiment of combining a liberal toleration
with the establishment of a particular creed, it was taken for granted, that an
exclusive & intolerant establishment was essential, and notwithstanding the
light thrown on the subject by that experiment, the prevailing opinion in
Europe, England not excepted, has been that Religion could not be preserved
without the support of Gov^t. nor Gov^t. be supported with^t. an established religion that there must be at least an alliance of some sort between them.

It remained for North America to bring the great & interesting subject to a
fair, and finally to a decisive test.

In the Colonial State of the Country, there were four examples, R. I. N. J.
Penn^a and Delaware, & the greater part of N.Y. where there were no religious

Establishments the support of Religion being left to the voluntary associations & contributions of individuals; and certainly the religious conditions of those Colonies, will well bear a comparison with that where establishments existed.

As it may be suggested that experiments made in Colonies more or less under the Controul of a foreign Government, had not the full scope necessary to display their tendency, it is fortunate that the appeal can now be made to their effects under a compleat exemption from any such controul.

Detached Memoranda

This document was discovered in 1946 among the papers of William Cabell Rives, biographer of Madison. Scholars date these observations in Madison's hand sometime between 1817 and 1832. They offer glimpses of Madison's opinions on several topics and personalities. What follows is that part of the "Memoranda" devoted to the subjects addressed in this volume. The entire document was published by Elizabeth Fleet in the William and Mary Quarterly *of October 1946.*

The danger of silent accumulations & encroachments by Ecclesiastical Bodies have not sufficiently engaged attention in the U.S. They have the noble merit of first unshackling the conscience from persecuting laws, and of establishing among religious Sects a legal equality. If some of the States have not embraced this just and this truly Xn principle in its proper latitude, all of them present examples by which the most enlightened States of the old world may be instructed; and there is one State at least, Virginia, where religious liberty is placed on its true foundation and is defined in its full latitude. The general principle is contained in her declaration of rights, prefixed to her Constitution: but it is unfolded and defined, in its precise extent, in the act of the Legislature, usually named the Religious Bill, which passed into a law in the year 1786. Here the separation between the authority of human laws, and the natural rights of Man excepted from the grant on which all political authority is founded, is traced as distinctly as words can admit, and the limits to this authority established with as much solemnity as the forms of legislation can express. The law has the further advantage of having been the result of a formal appeal to the sense of the Community and a deliberate santion of a vast majority, comprizing every sect of Christians in the State. This act is a true standard of Religious liberty: its principle the great barrier agst usurpations on the rights of conscience. As long as it is respected & no longer, these will be safe. Every provision for them short of this principle, will be found to leave crevices at least thro' which bigotry may introduce persecution; a monster, that feeding & thriving on its own venom, gradually¹ swells to a size and strength overwhelming all laws divine & human.

Ye States of America, which retain in your Constitutions or Codes, any aberration from the sacred principle of religious liberty, by giving to Caesar what belongs to God, or joining together what God has put asunder, hasten to revise & purify your systems, and make the example of your Country as pure & compleat, in what relates to the freedom of the mind and its allegiance to its maker, as in what belongs to the legitimate objects of political & civil institutions.

Strongly guarded as is the separation between Religion & Govt in the Constitution of the United States the danger of encroachment by Ecclesiastical Bodies, may be illustrated by precedents already furnished in their short history. (See the cases in which negatives were put by J. M. on two bills passed by Congs and his signature withheld from another. See also attempt in Kentucky for example, where it was proposed to exempt Houses of Worship from taxes.)

The most notable attempt was that in Virga to establish a Gen assessment for the support of all Xn sects. This was proposed in the year (1784) by P. H. and supported by all his eloquence, aided by the remaining prejudices of the Sect which before the Revolution had been established by law. The progress of the measure was arrested by urging that the respect due to the people required in so extraordinary a case an appeal to their deliberate will. The bill was accordingly printed & published with that view. At the instance of Col: George Nicholas, Col: George Mason & others, the memorial & remonstrance agst it was drawn up, (which see) and printed Copies of it circulated thro' the State, to be signed by the people at large. It met with the approbation of the Baptists, the Presbyterians, the Quakers, and the few Roman Catholics, universally; of the Methodists in part; and even of not a few of the Sect formerly established by law. When the Legislature assembled, the number of Copies & signatures prescribed displayed such an overwhelming opposition of the people, that the proposed plan of a genl assessmt was crushed under it: and advantage taken of the crisis to carry thro' the Legisl: the Bill above referred to, establishing religious liberty. In the course of the opposition to the bill in the House of Delegates, which was warm & strenuous from some of the minority, an experiment was made on the reverence entertained for the name & sanctity of the Saviour, by proposing to insert the words "Jesus Christ" after the words "our lord" in the preamble, the object of which would have been, to imply a restriction of the liberty defined in the Bill, to those professing his religion only. The amendment was discussed, and rejected by a vote of   agst (See letter of J. M. to Mr. Jefferson dated   )¹ The opponents of the amendment having turned the feeling as well as judgment of the House agst it, by successfully contending that the better proof of reverence for that holy name wd be not to profane it by making it a topic of legisl. discussion, & particularly by making his religion the means of abridging the natural and equal rights of all men, in defiance of his own declaration that his Kingdom was not of this world. This view of the subject was much enforced by the circumstance that it was espoused by some members who were particularly distinguished by their reputed piety and Christian zeal.

But besides the danger of a direct mixture of Religion & civil Government, there is an evil which ought to be guarded agst in the indefinite accumulation of property from the capacity of holding it in perpetuity by ecclesiastical corporations. The power of all corporations, ought to be limited in this respect. The growing wealth acquired by them never fails to be a source of abuses. A warning on this subject is emphatically given in the example of the various Charitable establishments in G. B. the management of which has been lately scrutinized. The excessive wealth of ecclesiastical Corporations and the misuse of it in many Countries of Europe has long been a topic of complaint. In some of them the Church has amassed half perhaps the property of the nation. When the reformation took place, an event promoted if not caused, by that disordered state of things, how enormous were the treasures of religious societies, and how gross the corruptions engendered by them; so enormous & so gross as to produce in the Cabinets & Councils of the Protestant states a disregard, of all the pleas of the interested party drawn from the sanctions of the law, and the sacredness of property held in religious trust. The history of England during the period of the reformation offers a sufficient illustration for the present purpose.

Are the U. S. duly awake to the tendency of the precedents they are establishing, in the multiplied incorporations of Religious Congregations with the faculty of acquiring & holding property real as well as personal? Do not many of these acts give this faculty, without limit either as to time or as to amount? And must not bodies, perpetual in their existence, and which may be always gaining without ever losing, speedily gain more than is useful, and in time more than is safe? Are there not already examples in the U. S. of ecclesiastical wealth equally beyond its object and the foresight of those who laid the foundation of it? In the U. S. there is a double motive for fixing limits in this case, because wealth may increase not only from additional gifts, but from exorbitant advances in the value of the primitive one. In grants of vacant lands, and of lands in the vicinity of growing towns & Cities the increase of value is often such as if foreseen, would essentially controul the liberality confirming them. The people of the U. S. owe their Independence & their liberty, to the wisdom of descrying in the minute tax of 3 pence on tea, the magnitude of the evil comprized in the precedent. Let them exert the same wisdom, in watching agst every evil lurking under plausible disguises, and growing up from small beginnings. Obsta principiis.

see the Treatise of Father Paul on beneficiary matters.[2]

Is the appointment of Chaplains to the two Houses of Congress consistent with the Constitution, and with the pure principle of religious freedom?

In strictness the answer on both points must be in the negative. The Constitution of the U. S. forbids everything like an establishment of a national religion. The law appointing Chaplains establishes a religious worship for the national representatives, to be performed by Ministers of religion, elected by a majority of them; and these are to be paid out of the national taxes. Does not this involve the principle of a national establishment, applicable to a provision for a religious worship for the Constituent as well as of the representative Body, approved by the majority, and conducted by Ministers of religion paid by the entire nation.

The establishment of the chaplainship to Congs is a palpable violation of equal rights, as well as of Constitutional principles: The tenets of the chaplains elected [by the majority] shut the door of worship agst the members whose creeds & consciences forbid a participation in that of the majority. To say nothing of other sects, this is the case with that of Roman Catholics & Quakers who have always had members in one or both of the Legislative branches. Could a Catholic clergyman ever hope to be appointed a Chaplain? To say that his religious principles are obnoxious or that his sect is small, is to lift the evil at once and exhibit in its naked deformity the doctrine that religious truth is to be tested by numbers. or that the major sects have a right to govern the minor.

If Religion consist in voluntary acts of individuals, singly, or voluntarily associated, and it be proper that public functionaries, as well as their Constituents shd discharge their religious duties, let them like their Constituents, do so at their own expense. How small a contribution from each member of Cong wd suffice for the purpose? How just wd it be in its principle? How noble in its exemplary sacrifice to the genius of the Constitution; and the divine right of conscience? Why should the expence of a religious worship be allowed for the Legislature, be paid by the public, more than that for the Ex. or Judiciary branch of the Gov

Were the establishment to be tried by its fruits, are not the daily devotions conducted by these legal Ecclesiastics, already degenerating into a scanty attendance, and a tiresome formality?

Rather than let this step beyond the landmarks of power have the effect of a legitimate precedent, it will be better to apply to it the legal aphorism de minimis non curat lex: or to class it cum "maculis quas aut incuria fudit, aut humana parum cavit natura."

Better also to disarm in the same way, the precedent of Chaplainships for the army and navy, than erect them into a political authority in matters of religion. The object of this establishment is seducing; the motive to it is laudable. But is it not safer to adhere to a right principle, and trust to its consequences, than confide in the reasoning however specious in favor of a wrong one. Look thro' the armies & navies of the world, and say whether in the appointment of their ministers of religion, the spiritual interest of the flocks or the temporal interest of the Shepherds, be most in view: whether here, as elsewhere the political care of religion is not a nominal more than a real aid. If the spirit of armies be devout, the spirit out of the armies will never be less so; and a failure of religious instruction & exhortation from a voluntary source within or without, will rarely happen: if such be not the spirit of armies, the official services of their Teachers are not likely to produce it. It is more likely to flow from the labours of a spontaneous zeal. The armies of the Puritans had their appointed Chaplains; but without these there would have been no lack of public devotion in that devout age.

The case of navies with insulated crews may be less within the scope of these reflections. But it is not entirely so. The chance of a devout officer, might be of as much worth to religion, as the service of an ordinary chaplain. [were it admitted that religion has a real interest in the latter.] But we are always to keep in mind that it is safer to trust the consequences of a right principle, than reasonings in support of a bad one.

Religious proclamations by the Executive recommending thanksgivings & fasts are shoots from the same root with the legislative acts reviewed.

Altho' recommendations only, they imply a religious agency, making no part of the trust delegated to political rulers.

The objections to them are 1. that Govts ought not to interpose in relation to those subject to their authority but in cases where they can do it with effect. An *advisory* Govt is a contradiction in terms. 2. The members of a Govt as such can in no sense, be regarded as possessing an advisory trust from their Constituents in their religious capacities. They cannot form an ecclesiastical Assembly, Convocation, Council, or Synod, and as such issue decrees or injunctions addressed to the faith or the Consciences of the people. In their individual capacities, as distinct from their official station, they might unite in recommendations of any sort whatever, in the same manner as any other individuals might do. But then their recommendations ought to express the true character from which they emanate. 3. They seem to imply and certainly nourish the erronious idea of a *national* religion. The idea just as it related to the Jewish nation under a theocracy, having been improperly adopted by so many nations which have embraced Xnity, is too apt to lurk in the bosoms even of Americans, who in general are aware of the distinction between religious & political societies. The idea also of a union of all to form one nation under one Govt in acts of devotion to the God of all is an imposing idea. But reason and the principles of the Xn religion require that all the individuals composing a nation even of the same precise creed & wished to unite in a universal act of religion at the same time, the union ought to be effected thro' the intervention of their religious not of their political representatives. In a nation composed of various sects, some alienated widely from others, and where no agreement could take place thro' the former, the interposition of the latter is doubly wrong: 4. The tendency of the practice, to narrow the recommendation to the standard of the predominant sect. The 1st proclamation of Genl Washington dated Jany 1. 1795 (see if this was the 1st) recommending a day of thanksgiving, embraced all who believed in a supreme ruler of the Universe.[3] That of Mr. Adams called for a Xn worship. Many private letters reproached the Proclamations issued by J. M. for using general terms, used in that of Presit W--n; and some of them for not inserting particulars according with the faith of certain Xn sects. The practice if not strictly guarded naturally terminates in a conformity to the creed of the majority and a single sect, if amounting to a majority. 5. The last & not the least objection is the liability of the practice to a subserviency to political views; to the scandal of religion, as well as the increase of party animosities. Candid or incautious politicians will not always disown such views. In truth it is difficult to frame such a religious Proclamation generally suggested by a political State of things, without referring to them in terms having some bearing on party questions. The Proclamation of Pres: W. which was issued just after the suppression of the Insurrection in Penna and at a time when the public mind was divided on several topics, was so construed by many. Of this the Secretary of State himself, E. Randolph seems to have had an anticipation.

The original draught of that Instrument filed in the Dept. of State (see copies of these papers on the files of J. M.) in the hand writing of Mr Hamilton the Secretary of the Treasury. It appears that several slight alterations only had been made at the suggestion of the Secretary of State; and in a marginal note in his hand, it is remarked that "In short this proclamation ought to savour as much as possible of religion, & not too much of having a political object." In a subjoined note in the hand of Mr. Hamilton, this remark is answered by the counter-remark that "A proclamation of a Government which is a national act, naturally embraces objects which are political" so *naturally*, is the idea of policy associated with religion, whatever be the mode or the occasion, when a function of the latter is assumed by those in power.

During the administration of Mr Jefferson no religious proclamation was issued. It being understood that his successor was disinclined to such inter- positions of the Executive and by some supposed moreover that they might originate with more propriety with the Legislative Body, a resolution was passed requesting him to issue a proclamation. (see the resolution in the Journals of Congress.)

It was thought not proper to refuse a compliance altogether; but a form & language were employed, which were meant to deaden as much as possible any claim of political right to enjoin religious observances by resting these expressly on the voluntary compliance of individuals, and even by limiting the recom- mendation to such as wished simultaneous as well as voluntary performance of a religious act on the occasion. The following is a copy of the proclamation: (see it in——[4]).

NOTES

1. Madison is probably referring to his January 9, 1785 letter to Jefferson.
2. This appears to be a reference to Paolo Sarpi (1552-1623), an anti-papal reformer.
3. Actually, the first was October 3, 1789.
4. Probably *Niles Register* for March 11, 1815.

PART IV

Religion in American History

While this volume is devoted to the study of James Madison and his legacy, genuine understanding of the founder can be achieved only against the background of American religious traditions. Therefore, this chapter presents a delineation of various American church-state traditions and an examination of the specific religious roots of the Republic by John Wilson, an interpretation of interaction between church and state by Richard Morris, and two historical studies that highlight the diversity of prerevolutionary attitudes regarding religion and the state. We have selected Roger Williams as the champion of religious freedom in the seventeenth century. Through W. K. Jordan's masterful treatment of the Rhode Island divine, one can sense the tension between Williams and those who supported theocracy. In spite of his remarkable career in New England, which ended in 1681, Williams had little direct impact upon eighteenth-century American thought.

Sentiments supporting religious freedom were emerging during and after the Revolution, but establishment remained the practice in most colonies even beyond the victory at Yorktown in 1783. The colony/state of Virginia has become the focus of most scholarly inquiry on the emergence of new attitudes about both establishment and free exercise of religion. Thus, we have elected to examine the work of Samuel Davies, Presbyterian advocate of toleration in Virginia during the 1750s, as a means of setting the stage for those events that followed.

John Wilson

Church and State in America

"Church and state" currently designates a certain kind of tension implicit in our religiously plural soceity. Aid to parochial schools, public school prayer, tax exemption for religious institutions, religious beliefs of political candidates, abortion, and the nuclear arms race—all these issues (and many others as well) are thought to involve questions of "church and state." Some were first widely recognized in post–World War II America. Others have been long established on the American social scene.

Even when used to describe recently recognized problems, however, "church and state" as a classification should suggest that the issue is an expression of an ancient differentiation between two kinds of institutions that have defined the life of Western men and women. One sort of authority structure has been primarily concerned with temporal life as an end in itself; the other has been concerned with temporal life as a means to "spiritual" ends. To identify certain points of tension in our common life under the rubric "church and state" is to say that the spheres of temporal and spiritual authorities here intersect, or that in the exercise of temporal and spiritual powers, conflicting claims arise.

In one respect the phrase "church and state" is unfortunate because its connotations are excessively formalistic. It suggests that there is one spiritual authority structure confronting a single temporary authority structure. There have been periods in Western history when such a model would have been a plausible description of the existing pattern. In fact the colonial period of

American history exhibits attempts to realize classical kinds of relationships between a single spiritual authority structure—the church—and a single temporal authority structure—the colonial state. But our colonial period also illustrates how different ingredients in American society, for example, ethnic diversity and evangelical separatism, worked to outmode classical church-state patterns. At least on the religious side of the equation, one church could not embody the manifold spiritual life of the American people.

Consequently, desirable or not, the federal government was erected on the assumption that there should be no national establishment of religion. Although largely nominal state establishments continued, ine one case until 1833, it was clear that generally a single spiritual authority structure was not a realistic alternative, even on that level. This pattern, which has subsequently characterized American society, has often been described as "the separation of church and state."

Some interpreters believe that with the formal disengagement of these authority structures the ancient problems of their relationship were dissolved. If there is no one church recognized by the state, the argument runs, how can there by an church-state problems? If difficulties exist, the argument continues, it is only because the separation of the two has not been sufficiently rigorous. The confusion embodied in this position is produced, obviously, by the misleadingly formal character of the church-state formula. Empirically there is no single authority structure—or combination of them—that could presume to embody the "religious" or "spiritual" life of America. In short-hand fashion this situation is usually designated as "religious pluralism"; that is, many different religious movements exist in America and they pursue relatively autonomous courses. Therefore the classical term "church"—in denotation as well as connotation—is alien to the American scene. It is this increasingly diverse religious pluralism that has created such a burden on the American people in their efforts to resolve the church-state question.

It is equally obvious that there is no single authority structure that embodies the temporal life of America—i.e., a single state is no more an empirical reality than a single church. Like religious pluralism, governmental pluralism involves the multiplicity of authorities that possess overlapping jurisdictions within American society. Thus federal, state, county, and local governments are juxtaposed, and all contribute to the structuring of the common life. Sometimes they are mutually reinforcing; on other occasions they counterbalance each other. Although the federal government has precedence, and national power can overwhelm the other orders of government in a way not paralleled among the plural religious institutions, in practice there is considerable deference toward the more local authorities.

The federal constitution was framed with the intent that there should not be an American "state" in the classical sense. Powers were divided at the national level, and manifold governments were fostered at other levels as well. In addition, the development of semiautonomous bureaucratic structures and quasi-judicial commissions (not continuously subordinated to explicit political review) has further "pluralized" the process of governing American society. Also large corporate entities exercise powers in our society that any formal "state" would reserve to itself. There simply is no classical "state" in American experience that corresponds either to the medieval or modern European uses of this term. Accordingly the term "church and state" breaks down completely if the attempt is made to use it in a traditional fashion.

Is "church and state" at all useful, then, in reference to the American scene? Clearly, plural spiritual authority structures interact with each other and with temporal authority structures, which have complex interrelationships. We have in America not "church" and "state" but religions and governments—all interacting within our society.

It might appear desirable, therefore, to give up this rubric altogether and seek one more in accord with American experience. To do so, however, would be to accept only the most formalistic definition of the term. It is as wrong to suggest that the tensions between temporal life and spiritual life in America are wholly unprecedented as it is to argue that church-state problems disappeared with the adoption of the First Amendment, especially as applied to the states through the "due process clause" of the Fourteenth Amendment. The substance of the church-state tradition is still with us but in new forms. The rubric per se is inexact but the tradition designated by that rubric is very much to the point in comprehending America's past and present. By analyzing the historical development of the conception "church and state" it may be possible, on the one hand, to modify its formalistic connotations, and, on the other, to denote more precisely what it has meant in the past and may legitimately signify now.

Consequently this essay will address the following problems: first, the origin, development, and content of the traditional church-state distinction in Western history; second, the range of patterns that has existed in the historical relationships between church and state; and third, the relatively distinctive pattern of church-state relations in America, its sources and significance.

I

The distinction between "church" and "state" in Western history inevitably refers back to the classic New Testament texts recurrently cited in any discussion of the issue. Perhaps the chief text is Jesus' response (as reported in the synoptic gospels: Matthew 22:15-22, Mark 12:13-17, Luke 20:20-26) to the question about rendering tribute to Caesar: "Is it lawful to pay taxes to Caesar or not?" (Mark 12:14). Jesus' injunction was, of course, "Render to Caesar the things that are Caesar's, and to God the things that are God's"

(Mark 12:17). Another text, scarcely less significant, is Saint Paul's Letter to the Romans. As a whole the section runs to seven verses (Romans 13:1-7), but its principle is expressed classically in the first verse alone: "Let every person be subject to the governing authorities. For there is no authority except from God, and those that exist have been instituted by God." Other subordinate texts are much less important than these two. Neither these nor any others refer directly to "church and state." Rather both—and here they correctly represent New Testament teaching as a whole—presuppose that faithfulness to God requires also appropriate obedience to worldly authorities since such are instituted by God. In early Christianity this might even have demanded "obediene unto death."

The early Christian canonical writings did not explore the church-state relationship in a fashion relevant to later needs because, among other reasons, the "state" did not acknowledge the legitimacy of the "church" as a separate authority structure. To recognize such an authority structure as the Church was in principle to introduce the claim that the state should be limited to activities relating to temporal ends. Thus the possibility of a formal church-state pattern emerged only after the emperor Constantine was converted to Christianity in the early part of the fourth century.

As a result of the Constantinian settlement, the Christian movement was at first accepted and then favored over alternative (and generally more syncretistic) religious movements with which it had been competing. The Christian church gained recognition from Caesar because of its persistent obedience to God (and thus to Caesar); it came to possess an authority structure in some measure independent from the state. In the eastern half of the empire the church remained closely associated with the state—even wholly subordinated to it. It was in western Christendom that the distinction between "church" and "state" developed its particular significance.

At the end of the fifth century Pope Gelasius I articulated the fundamental premise concerning "church and state" that has characterized Western history. The premise was simple: "There are two." "Two swords" or "two authority structures" meant a single society under two jurisdictions—one temporal and the other spiritual. From the theological point of view, the coming of Christ and the establishment of the Church had made it unlawful for both authorities to be administered by one figure. King and priest, or church and state, each needed the other, but both were to be separate aspects of the same society.

This separated double authority structure is what differentiated western from eastern Christendom, and it properly locates the significance of "church and state." A universal Christian society with a twofold government or rule was presupposed. While the Church embodied the spiritual order of that society, the empire organized the same society in temporal terms. The persistent problem concerned the relationship between the ecclesiastical and civil authority structures of the common society. What should be the relationship of these two jurisdictions to each other?

From the ninth until roughly the middle of the eleventh century, the Carolingian pattern was taken for granted. Generally the pope was subordinated to the emperor, and thus the Church to the empire. In the person of Pope Gregory VII, the papacy challenged the emperor (Henry IV), however, and on the immediate question at issue—lay investiture of bishops— a moderate papal victory was won in the Concordat of Worms (1122). The Gregorian ambition was to assert at once the spiritual autonomy of the Church and the monarchical rule of the Church by the pope: "If kings are to be judged by priests for their sins, by whom can they be judged with better right than by the Roman Pontiff?" By the end of the twelfth century, Innocent III made further claims, likening the papal church to the sun and the imperial dominion to the moon, which derived its light from the former.

The maximum claim for papal authority in the Church and ecclesiastical authority over the empire was made by Boniface VIII, however, in his *Unam Sanctum*, 1302. It called for the subordination of the temporal to the spiritual, reversing completely the earlier Carolingian pattern: "Both the spiritual sword and the material sword are in the power of the church. The latter should be used for the church and the former by the church; the former by the priest, and the latter by kings and captains (but at the will and by the permission of the priest). Therefore the one sword should be under the other, and temporal authority subject to spiritual."

Even as Boniface was making such claims, however, the papacy was humiliated in its captivity at Avignon, and stirrings from England and France marked the beginnings of new nation-states that would sustain their own national churches in place of that Latin Christendom ordered in a twofold pattern. Concurrently Aristotelian naturalists, such as Marsilius of Padua, argued for the restriction of spiritual authority in the name of an autonomous secular realm. "Church and state" as two swords or authorities no longer meant pope and emperor as jointly quarreling trustees of a universal Christian society. The Church was no longer the spiritual structure of a universal society, but instead was either the religious expression of a national entity or an association of like-minded individuals more often than not in conflict with a repressive state. The ground was present for the growth of the secular states of modern Europe.

From this perspective the "Protestant Reformation" was an ambiguous event, at once allied with the centrifugal national forces that were destroying what remained of universal society and concurrently attempting to repristinate the two-authority doctrine that had been so characteristic of western Christendom. Thus it was neither wholly modern nor wholly reactionary but a curious combination of both. The Lutheran branch of the Reformation identified the two authorities as two realms each dependent directly upon God so that both the faithless prince and the faithful believer had a vocation in the divine economy. The Calvinist branch, by contrast, usually sought to locate temporal authority in the hands of those saints who were responsive to the spiritual authority of the church. In either case the recovery of universalism was impossible as Protestant (and Catholic also) discovered in the bloody religious wars.

This brief review of the developing church-state pattern indicates that it was never a static relationship in Western history, at least through the sixteenth century. Nor was its essence embodied, for instance, in the relationship of emperor and pope in the thirteenth century. On the contrary, the common substance of the church-state relationship was the recognition of two authority structures in the corporate life of humanity—one essentially temporal and the other primarily spiritual. In shorthand form these were designated as "state" and "church," but there were manifold expressions of the phenomena long before the terms and the rubric were introduced into American history. Therefore "church and state in American history" is properly a consideration of the relationship(s) between temporal and spiritual authority structures—or religious institutions and civil governments. These relationships did not end with the adoption of either the First or Fifth Amendments.

II

Another type of analysis of "church and state" may help to suggest the range of phenomena properly classified under this heading. This should establish in another way why the church-state rubric must not be identified with a particular form of that relationship, e.g., papal church and imperial magistracy within a single and inclusive Christian society. What have been the chief alternative patterns of the relationship between the temporal and spiritual authority structures? Answers to this question may be arranged schematically.

One sort of answer curiously brackets bitter antagonists. The antagonists both deny that there should be two authority structures, i.e., that human life is to be comprehended under the dual aspect of temporal and spiritual concerns. The parties to this strange consensus disagree, of course, as to which of the two authority structures should absorb the other. On the one hand a "hierocratic" regime authorizes the priests to hold all power—spiritual and temporal both—in their hands. By contrast a "statist" or consistent "totalitarian" position refuses to recognize an independent spiritual authority structure, and may not only create a subservient temporal religion but also proscribe and persecute traditional religious faith. While the latter position has been a common one in the modern West (and is in some respects a return to paganism), "hierocracies" have been uncommon since the destruction of ancient Israel. Priest-king and commissar both deny the traditional Western consensus on church and state—that an independence of the two authority structures is fundamental.

Another categorization of the relationship between church and state allows a certain independence of the two institutions but it ultimately subordinates one to the other. Like the previous position it may also be resolved into clearly differentiated alternatives. One option involves the subordination of spiritual authority to temporal authority—at the extreme the utilization and manipulation of the church by the state. Usually this alternative is designated as 'Erastianism' after a sixteenth-century Swiss theologian, Thomas Erastus, who argued that where there is unformity of religion, ecclesiastical jurisdiction is to be exercised under the review of the civil authorities. Although the label is usually applied only to nation-states from the sixteenth century on, the principle involved (subordination of spiritual to temporal authority) expresses no less exactly the pretensions of many emperors, beginning with Charlemagne.

The other form of subordination argues that spiritual ends take precedence over temporal ones. Such were the classical papal claims. It was also characteristic of Calvinism as it pursued the ideal of the holy community. It is appropriate to label such an alternative "theocratic" as long as it is distinguished from the "hierocratic" pattern, which grants full autonomy to the spiritual authority. This broader theocratic tradition, whether in Rome, Geneva, or Massachusetts Bay, was not essentially the rule of "priests" (or preachers for that matter) over temporal matters. Rather it presupposed that the consciences of the lay civil authorities—autonomous in temporal matters—should be formed by, and their outward practice conformed to, the Christian faith. The whole society—in its dual aspect—was created by God, and both authorities were to be appropriately conformed to the divine intention. The "medievalism" of early Protestant ideals is apparent once again.

A third approach to church-state patterns recognizes that there are separate authority structures and proposes that they should be disengaged from each other. Again, however, there are different ways in which this independence can be construed. One alternative is the segregation of the spiritual authority structure from the temporal authority structure, which is close to the sectarian Anabaptist ideal. In another way this would seem to be implied in the Jeffersonian "wall of separation" metaphor, and it is the substantial meaning intended in a great deal of contemporary rhetoric about the "separation of church and state." Another kind of independence between church and state is a recognition of mutually supportive roles. While the spiritual authority structure or structures ought to lend their power to the civil order, the temporal authorities should recognize and assist religious institutions.

It is clear that such a typology as the foregoing has a certain artificiality, although it is sufficiently flexible to comprehend reasonably well most concrete instances of church-state relationships. Its chief significance, however, ought to be the weight it lends to the argument of this essay—that if "church and state" is to be a useful phrase it must be construed with a sufficiently broad scope to include a wide variety of historical relationships between spiritual and temporal authority structures. The rubric is relatively useless if it is primarily identified with one particular pattern that is considered normative—most frequently the papal version of the relationship between empire and papacy within the universal Christian society of the Middle Ages.

III

For the purpose of this study of church and state in American history, seven different periods may be identified: before 1700, 1700-1760, 1760-1820, 1820-1860, 1860-1920, 1920-1960, and 1960 to the present. Each is distinctive because it represents a new phase in the relationship between religious institutions and civil governments in light of the changing patterns of religious pluralism in America. Through these stages ideological resources have been joined with social circumstances to produce a series of experimental resolutions of the tensions between spiritual and temporal authority structures.

Before briefly surveying these periods it is important to recognize that the American experiments in church-state relations have almost universally assumed that the dual authority pattern was appropriate. The United States has not provided congenial soil for the anticlerical sentiment that was so widespread in Europe during the nineteenth century and understandably resulted in a defensive posture on the part of religious institutions there. It might be argued that the more militant forms of modern secularism effectively deny this presumption of two "realms." But, characteristically, American secularism is little more than indifferent toward the claim that the spiritual dimension of life has an authority of its own. Again— contrary to many interpretations of New England Puritanism—the U.S. has not witnessed many attempts at a hierocratic melding of spiritual and temporal authorities. Perhaps the most interesting, and certainly the only significant, experiment with this kind of order was the early Mormon venture. In the person of Joseph Smith, Jr., the offices of prophet, priest, and king were once again united. Brigham Young and his associates received this mantle and structured the Salt Lake Valley community on this pattern. The mainstream of American experience, however, has taken for granted that there should be two authority structures—although a significant variety of interpretations has been offered.

The seventeenth-century Atlantic colonies represent a useful first period in the present study. There we find the traditional church-state terms very much present. We are introduced to that language of establishment, which was simply taken for granted. For even the likes of Roger Williams, although denying the propriety of established religion, could make his case only in those same terms. It is important to grasp that—aside from the "lively experiment" of Rhode Island—all of the colonies erected "establishments" of some sort. No one would deny the vastly different rigor (both in the conception and execution of their establishments) that characterized, for example, Massachusetts Bay and Pennsylvania. But it is entirely wrong to emphasize the relative latitude of the latter and thus overlook the common language used by both.

Contrary to popular misconception, the New England Puritan colonies were not hierocratic regimes. John Cotton was neither a latter-day Sadduccee nor an early Joseph Smith, Jr. The New England Puritan assumptions were far more akin to the ideals of Innocent III. Their colony was to be a commonwealth, ruled in temporal affairs by Christian laymen whose consciences were formed by the preaching of the Word (if not nourished by the administration of the Eucharist).

Not all the colonies aspired to such a formally theocratic constitution of the relationship between church and state. By virtue of economic necessity, if not ideological programs, some represented more nearly the Erastian position that the religious institution should be subordinated to (though not absorbed in) the temporal regime and its needs. Nevertheless the language of establishment was universal.

During the first six decades of the eighteenth century that language, which previously had been taken for granted, was challenged by the diversification of religious life in the colonies. The overwhelming number of colonists were Protestant in sympathy—if not allowed or willing to become active church members. But different kinds of Protestant families and groups relentlessly immigrated; even the relatively homogeneous New England settlements yielded, first on the fringes and then at the center as well: Scottish-Irish Presbyterians in Anglican Virginia, "German" Mennonites in Quaker Pennsylvania, Anglicans in Congregational Connecticut and Massachusetts. In addition, the upheavals of the "Great Awakening" split asunder the Presbyterians and Congregationalists, and served to expand the slim Baptist ranks. Altogether this proliferation of Protestant groups, given the circumstances of colonial development, made necessary the policy of toleration.

Toleration of dissent is perfectly compatible with a pattern of establishment. It does not, however, make credible the theocratic subordination of state to church, nor on the other hand does it render society religiously uniform (which is the great strength in the Erastian subordination of church to state). Therefore the first six decades of the eighteenth century represent a transitional period during which the language of establishment became outdated. In no sense was the fundamental assumption of dualism denied—there were two realms, each with its appropriate institutional expressions. But the radical competition among the churches made it inevitable (though the illusion died hard) that a single spiritual authority structure on the traditional model would be out of the question.

During the third period of our study, which runs between 1760 and approximately 1820, direct confrontations with the problem of establishment took place. A basic reevaluation of the traditional pattern had become necessary. As the colonies were drawn into a closer network the multiplicity of Protestant groups was all the more evident. Continuing feeble efforts to regularize if not prefer the Church of England in the colonies dramatized for the proto-Americans the desirable latitude present in their religious life.

Religious liberty as an ideal began to be discussed. The "enlightenment" estimate of religion exerted an effect. The net result of these and other factors can be seen with particular clarity in the public newspaper debate during the 1760s over the scheme to appoint Church of England bishops in America. The colonial critics of this proposal did everything in their power to marshal public antipathy toward it through belittlement and ridicule. In the course of this argument they articulated notions about religion that would have been unthinkable a century earlier, for example, that plural religious institutions were desirable, or that clergymen should be meagerly paid so that their pretension and power would not corrupt their exercise of spiritual functions. Such sentiments indicate how tenuous the traditional language of establishment had become.

In the Virginia struggle for religious freedom and disestablishment, however, we find the first consistent political argument toward the "independence" of church and state. Jefferson's passion for religious freedom is well known, and he later bequeathed that attractive if confusing metaphor of a "wall of separation" between church and state, which continues to echo throughout the common life. But James Madison is probably the more significant figure, both in the Virginia struggle and in the adoption of the First Amendment, which guarantees religious freedom and prohibits congressional legislation "respecting an establishment of religion." With the debate over the bishops and with Madison's contribution, the issue of church-state relations in the United States seemed clearly to have been settled on the side of an independence between spiritual and temporal authority structures.

This "revolution" in the position of the churches makes the next period— roughly extending to the Civil War—significant. Many relevant events were taking place that would in their own time influence church-state relationships in America, e.g., the influx of large contingents of Catholic immigrants and significant numbers of German Jews. While these trends were quietly setting the stage for the post–Civil War period, however, the most fascinating development was the attempt by the evangelical forces in the United States to recover in an informal way what had been their legal position before disestablishment. During this "era of republican Protestantism" interdenominational agencies developed a great "united front" that aspired to make the U.S. a Protestant Christian republic, in substance if not in form.

This enterprise profoundly shaped and formed the common life, so that even more than a century after its zenith our political, social, and economic— as well as religious—languages testify to its vital impact. The effort had its critics, and many of its coveted projects failed; but the conception of making effective an indirect relationship between religious and political authority structures presupposed an independence of church from state, construed in the terms of mutual support. Madison's theory had not allowed for the cooperation among the evangelical denominations any more than it had anticipated the development of political parties (not altogether dissimilar entities). One of the broader questions concerns the degree to which this was an indigenous American movement and how much it was part of the con-servative Anglo-American response to the French Revolution.

After the Civil War the ethnic multiplication and religious diversifica-tion that had begun in the previous era could no longer remain unrecognized and unacknowledged. As might be expected, public schools became a battle-ground (even before the Civil War) over the interrelationship of temporal and spiritual authority structures. This anticipated, of course, more modern discussions. It is interesting that where the "burden of religious pluralism" was explicitly recognized, a position favoring a neutral relationship between church and state emerged that clearly repudiated the assumptions underlying "republican protestantism."

For Roman Catholics this interpretation required dissent from European interpretations of the normative relationships between the two authority structures and led to the advocacy of "Americanism," which appeared almost heretical to Europeans. Protestants faced a more difficult task; beneath and behind that sense of national mission and anti-Roman animus nourished by the evangelical tradition, the Protestants had to locate more ancient resources that would equip them to comprehend other church-state alternatives than the one so dear to them. As the eighteenth century had been a transitional period during which formal disestablishment became necessary, so this period (1860-1920) was also a time of both transition and "disestablishment"—not of state-recognized churches but of a Protestant religious consensus.

During the period from the First World War until the election of a Roman Catholic president in 1960, the ancient problem of the relationship of temporal and spiritual authority structures was widely discussed in the context of an American religious pluralism encompassing the three major religions: Protestantism, Judaism, and Roman Catholicism. The church-state relationship was viewed from three perspectives: first, as a theological-religious problem; second, as a guise for political struggles within a pluralist society; and third, as a constitutional and legal issue. A responsible consensus seemed to ensue: that the United States, as a matter of necessity if not choice, must develop its particular pattern on the basis of independence between church and state. The existence of two authority structures seems to have been recognized in principle if not always honored in practice, and the historical alternatives of subordinating one to the other were not widely viewed as plausible formal options. There was, however, no agreement in the consensus on whether the independence of church and state should be one of segregation, neutrality, or mutual support.

In the most recent period, commencing in the early 1960s, the meaning of the term 'pluralism' has been expanded to include yet other, and very diverse, groups. This era has been marked by a willingness within American institutions to give unprecedented recognition to claims for equal treatment made by a variety of ethnic, racial, religious, and minority bodies. But not all Americans have welcomed the new radical religious pluralism, which extends well beyond the Judeo-Christian mainstream. As a result, a deep struggle is underway about the place of religion in society. The essential question is: Should the government disregard or take formal account of those Western values thought by many to be at the foundation of American national culture? More broadly speaking, the church-state issue in the contemporary era separates those who think that government should accommodate and encourage religion, which they see as intrinsic to our culture, and those who think that government should not extend aid or support to religion in any way. In short, this is a battle between believers in benevolent neutrality and proponents of strict separation.

Richard B. Morris

The Judeo-Christian Foundation
of the American Political System

We do not know just what James Madison would have done had he been in Philadelphia when the First Continental Congress convened; for, as John Adams reported the incident to his wife, Abigail: "When the Congress first met, Mr. Cushing [of Massachusetts] made a motion that it should be opened with Prayer. It was opposed by Mr. Jay of New York and Mr. Rutledge of South Carolina, because we were so divided in religious sentiments, some Episcopalians, some Quakers, some Anabaptists, some Presbyterians and some Congregationalists. So that we could not join in the same Act of Worship. Mr. Sam Adams arose and said he was no Bigot, and could hear a Prayer from a Gentleman of Piety and Virtue, who was at the same time a friend to his country." He then recommended the Reverend Duché, an Episcopal clergyman, to whose eloquence John Adams was to attest. That was done and thereafter a chaplain was regularly employed in opening the Congress. In fact, and I could be wrong, there is no record of Mr. Madison ever objecting to a chaplain when he himself sat in Congress.

So, instead of a moment of silence, Congress heard a preacher read the thirty-fifth Psalm.

There is another incident that comes to mind on the division of the Founding Fathers over this question.

Let us pass ahead some thirteen years, when at the Constitutional Convention, as a result of intensified debate over the suffrage for the lower house, Benjamin Franklin urged that a clergyman be invited to offer prayers at the beginning of each session. Hamilton objected on the ground that it was late in the day to start the sessions with prayer and that it might give the public the

From *Free Inquiry* 3: no. 3 (Summer 1983). Copyright © 1983 by *Free Inquiry*. Reprinted by permission.

impression of dissension at the convention. A later version had Hamilton express his confidence that the convention could transact the business entrusted to its care "without the necessity of calling in foreign aid."

Now what are we to make of a government that started a revolution with daily invocation to God by an ordained churchman who turned out to be a defector and included God in the Declaration of Independence and then drew up a constitution being scrupulously careful to keep God out of it.

No statistics would confirm a decline of piety between 1774 and 1787— quite the contrary so far as church attendance would suggest. What seems clear is that if one sees origins through the eyes of a Jefferson, a Madison, a Tom Paine, or an Ethan Allen one will find one point of view; a Patrick Henry, a John Adams, or a John Jay, yet another.

The depth and degree of religious conviction was controversial then and remains so today. The Founding Fathers varied in the degree to which they paid obeisance to rational currents and in their display of outward piety. True, they were united in their devotion to the principles of religious toleration, but one can detect subtle shadings of difference in their attitude toward the separation of church and state.

In the main the Founding Fathers would hardly have labeled themselves orthodox Christian thinkers, but they were Christian, dues-paying, if not orthodox. One of the least orthodox, Thomas Jefferson, once remarked, "I never told my own religion, nor scrutinized that of another" and added that he had "ever judged the religion of others by their lives" rather than their words. Yet Jefferson resented the charge that he was irreligious. He was assailed by more pious New Englanders when, at the end of his first term, he offered Tom Paine free passage to America on a sloop-of-war. Yet, by expressing the hope that Paine's "useful labors" would continue, he really meant to show that he was not anti-Christian, but rather antisectarian, whether toward Calvinism, which he loathed, or Unitarianism. In 1803, while he was president, he began to pick out of the Gospels selections that he felt came from Jesus. Then toward the end of his life he wrote the "Morals of Jesus," which proved, he felt, that he was, in his own words, "a real Christian," that is to say a disciple of the doctrines of Jesus.

Like Jefferson and Franklin, George Washington did not adhere to the dogmas of any single denomination. He attended church without formal affiliation, accepted Christianity in the sense that he did not question the teachings of Jesus, which he commended to the Indians, but fitted into the deistic pattern to which so many of the Founding Fathers conformed. The fact that he took no communion once the American Revolution began may have larger political than religious significance, considering the tight bonds of the Church of England to the Crown. As he eloquently expressed his liberal sentiments in a communication to the members of the New Church of Baltimore: "In the enlightened Age and in this Land of equal liberty it is our boast, that a man's religious tenets will not forfeit the protection of the Law, nor deprive him of the right of attaining and holding the highest Offices that are known in the United States." To date the very highest office in the land still eludes non-Christians as well as women of any sect.

The religious convictions of the Founding Fathers cover a broad spectrum. At one end, range the deistic provisions of a Washington (who preferred "Providence" when speaking of God), a Franklin, a Jefferson, or a Madison; at the other end, the orthodox piety of John Jay; and, somewhere in between, the religious views of John Adams and Alexander Hamilton. His later years found John Jay absorbed in the propagation of the Bible, whose literal truths he accepted without question. There is every ground to doubt that Jay would have agreed with his prestigious chief about eligibility of non-Christians for the highest office. In the closing years he questioned whether "our religion" permits Christians to vote for "infidel rulers." As for Jay himself, he reminded his correspondents of what the prophet had said to Jehosophat about the attachment to Ahab: "Shouldst thou help the ungodly and love them that hate the Lord?" In truth, the deistic positions of a Franklin, a Washington, a Jefferson, or a Madison would seem quite at variance with the orthodox piety of our first chief justice.

Nor could John Adams by any stretch of definition have been categorized as a deist. While he did not subscribe to Calvinist dogma, he was a Puritan through and through, the author of the Constitution of 1780, which continued the Congregational as the established church of Massachusetts, and a vigorous defender of that establishment whenever it was challenged.

I cannot stay the urge to point out that, like all great men, James Madison had the virtue of inconsistency. Thus, while in general he stood for the separation of church and state, he had not the slightest concern for due process so far as Tories and enemies of the state were concerned during the Revolution. He only wished he could get his hands on the Tory printer of New York, James Rivington, which New York Whigs managed to do. We would have had a wonderful example of *prior restraint* in the absence of the First Amendment, which he had not yet written. When a Scottish parson in Virginia refused to observe the fast designated for July 20, 1775, by the Continental Congress, Madison applauded the committee's ordering his church door closed and gleefully anticipated that he would "get ducked in a coat of tar and surplus of feathers."

With Madison, this vindictiveness toward Tories and other dissidents—of which there are numerous examples—passed, as it did in the case of Jefferson, Jay, and the other fair-minded men of that generation. The champion of liberty of conscience and the Bill of Rights, and a principal rallier of public opinion against the hated Alien and Sedition Acts, Madison found out in time that without civil rights and due process no republican system can survive.

Before we leave James Madison, I should point out that the latter's campaign against the Virginia assessment bill evoked an extraordinary popular response, and figures like George Washington hoped that the assessment bill would never even come up for a vote. Washington, recognizing the division of opinion, feared that agitation over the bill might "convulse the state" and expressed the hope that "the bill could die an easy death." In point of fact, it is believed that the assessment bill lost by a *bare majority of only three votes*. It would be fair to say that few private papers framed in the Revolutionary Era have had as momentous an impact on American constitutional law as did Madison's "Memorial and Remonstrance." It was the principal authority for the scholarly dissenting opinion of Justice Wiley Rutledge in a 1947 decision of the Supreme Court.

Thus, what we had in seventeenth-century New England was a set of theocracies modeled on that of Massachusetts and set up in Connecticut, New Haven, and Plymouth. In the celebrated foreword to the 1658 revision of the laws, Plymouth's founders confessed their indebtedness to the Scriptures and stated that the test of good laws was the extent to which they were agreeable "to the antient platform of God's laws," particularly singling out the legal code enjoyed by the Jews "as grounded on principles of moral equity, to which Christians especially ought alwaies to have an eye thereunto."

Aside from the rhetorical excursions into the fundamentalism of the law of God, one can show a direct relation between the Puritan concept of a covenant between God and the people—a view, distinctive I believe, to Judaism as adapted by Christianity to its own theological needs. The Pilgrims and Puritans placed special status in a covenant theology, sometimes called "federal theology." Just as the church was created by covenantors, so, too, the political order comes into existence as a voluntary creation of the convenanting members of society—the "We the People" of the Preamble to the Constitution. One can trace a direct movement from biblical covenant to church covenant (Congregationalism) to constitutions, whether state or federal.

Other factors would in the course of time have a more immediate weight. Certainly by the mid-eighteenth century, when New England was being transformed from a simple agrarian and fishing community to a more secular society, a nascent merchant capitalistic society, it began to rely more heavily for its defense, both civil and political, upon common lawyers and the common law, which Sir William Blackstone would one day insist was based on Christianity. Hence, by the time of the Revolution the lawyers, while great Bible readers, studied and practiced the English common-law system, and biblical precedents largely disappeared from the judicial-legal system.

The Founding Fathers were a product of covenant theology, common-law teaching, of a belief in the supremacy of parliament over the king, mixed with radical commonwealth thought, plus a heavy dose of Enlightenment thinking, leavened with Hume and Scottish Enlightenment thought, and some unique constitutional ideas of their own.

Yet the Founding Fathers, we should remember, took almost daily inspiration from the Old Testament. John Jay, in his famous Address to the Convention of the State of New York in late 1776, argued that the presecution suffered by the American colonists at the hands of British was worse than that suffered by the Jews from the tyrants of Egypt. Washington urged that the "most atrocious" war profiteers by hung on gallows "five times as high as Haman's," and innumerable like quotations from the revolutionary years can be easily culled.

Ezra Stiles, that learned Yale Hebraist, envisioned America as the new Israel, and saw that out of the American Revolution would come a vast increase in communications in men, manners, and trade. "That prophecy of Daniel is now literally fulfilling—there shall be a universal traveling to and fro, and knowledge shall be increased," he wrote, as the War of the Revolution came to an end.

The more the savants stressed the Judeo-Christian heritage, the more did scholarly physicians like Dr. Benjamin Rush advocate education in the Christian way. And as for Alexander Hamilton, as an embittered politician he proposed the creation of a "Christian Constitutional Society," which died aborning. The Founding Fathers at the Philadelphia convention heard the pleas of dissenting groups and Jews and made provision in the Constitution that "no religious test shall ever be required as a qualification to any office of public trust under the authority of the United States."

Despite their diversity of religious outlook and the pronounced anti-Catholic bias of several of their number, the Founding Fathers stood united on the issue of religious toleration. Still, it is by no means clear that they would have been united in agreement on how the First Amendment to the Constitution should be interpreted, that they would have regarded the federal government as neutral in matters of religion, or upheld the notion of a wall of separation between church and state, a phrase attributed to Jefferson and reviewed in the historic *Everson* case. Certainly John Adams, for one, would have dissented to the more recent Supreme Court's imposition upon the states as well as the federal government of the restrictions laid down in the establishment-of-religion clause. But then even today Americans stand sharply divided on how the First Amendment affects religion.

Before concluding, I should like to utter a word of caution about using history as a guide to contemporary problems. The theocratic Puritans, their more tolerant Founding Fathers, and even the less than infallible Supreme Court drew their experiences and decisions from a far more homogeneous society than we have today. Our present variety and abundance of religious beliefs and nonbeliefs would astonish the Founding Fathers. Hence, we today cannot ignore the concerns of groups who view the sudden upthrust of interest on the part of the government in matters like prayer in school, books in school libraries, and other areas of intrusion into privacy, as evidence of a new style of thought control. These intrusive efforts arouse fear in many persons that the whole spectrum of the Bill of Rights is being systematically chipped away. If the Founding Fathers offer ambiguous answers, the American people of the present day must maintain that vigilant scrutiny that the situation warrants.

W. K. Jordan

Roger Williams

A. INTRODUCTION

One of the greatest of the sectarian writers of the period was Roger Williams, who for our purposes may be considered as a Baptist, though he was more closely associated during his two sojourns in England with the political leaders of Independency. Williams was in England during two critical periods of religious liberty (1643-1644 and 1651-1654), and his most important works were written in the highly charged atmosphere of the English religious scene. His books were published in England and enjoyed a wider circulation and a more decisive contemporary influence in the mother country than in the colonies, where his notable experiment in religious liberty was testing the principles formulated by liberal thinkers. His courageous discussion of the perplexing questions of persecution and toleration was to exercise a considerable influence on the powerful body of opinion in England which had embraced the principles of religious toleration as the only solution to the bitter sectarian strife which engulfed the land.

Williams was not a great creative writer, nor can he be considered as an important contributor to the philosophical foundations of religious liberty. It is evident in all of his writings that he drew heavily from the earlier Baptist theorists, who had performed such notable services to religious toleration by undergirding it with a positive theory which they maintained was implicit in religion itself.[1] Williams expanded this theory only in particulars. It is also apparent that he owed much to the more radical Independents with whom he was intimately associated and to whom he rendered such militant support.

This essay is taken from W. K. Jordan, *The Development of Religious Toleration in England*, Vol. III (Cambridge, Mass.: Harvard University Press, 1938), pp. 472-506.

And, finally, Williams's thought had been moulded by a decade of earnest controversy with intolerant ecclesiastics in America and by the remarkable experiment in religious liberty in Rhode Island which had been conceived in the fire of this controversy.[2] Certainly, few living Englishmen were equipped to render more telling contributions to the development of religious toleration, and no contemporary figure could command such attention as this remarkable and accomplished leader. This obligation to religious liberty in England Roger Williams discharged faithfully and effectively.

Williams was a Baptist only in the sense that he stood nearer to that sect in his religious philosophy than to any other contemporary religious communion. He may more properly be regarded as a wholly emancipated individualist whose religious philosophy never settled into a rigid dogmatic pattern; as a free thinker whose spirit roamed with daring recklessness through the full range of religious speculation.[3] In his writings is to be found a substratum of Baptist teachings shot through with wandering veins of speculation which betoken mystical and Puritan influences.[4] Dominating his thought is a warm mysticism and an anxious yearning for a complete apprehension of the fulness of God's truth.[5] His religious philosophy was fluid and restless, gaining consistency and direction from the steady devotion which he lent to the principle of religious liberty as a religious right.[6] His persistent and unequivocal advocacy of religious toleration may be regarded as the foundation of a religious philosophy upon which an elaborate and somewhat fantastic structure of belief was erected. Williams's own thought demonstrates the axiom that from religious liberty there flows a complete spiritual individualism and a rich and luxuriant freedom of speculation which an ordered religious society can only regard as anarchistic. He was wholly contemptuous of the claims of all organized religious communions, holding "that no Christian Church since Apostolic times had had adequate evidence of its divine origin." He was content with the authority and doctrinal pretensions of no church and plainly hoped that a revelation from God might shortly enlighten men further.[7] But until such time as God's will and truth were clearly and infallibly understood by all men, no authority could legitimately restrict the complete freedom of speculation and belief necessary to the further discovery of truth and essential to the attainment of salvation.

Williams's style reflects the tempestuous freedom of his thought. Masson has admirably said of the Bloody Tenent, "there is a dash in the book, the keenest earnestness and evidence of a mind made up, and every now and then a mystic softness and richness of pity, yearning towards a voluptuous imagery like that of the Song of Solomon."[8] Williams wrote with rich poetry, with passionate conviction, and with an eloquent pleading which left its impress upon the seventeenth century mind. So intense was his zeal for religious liberty that he lifts up the mind troubled with the preoccupations of orthodoxy to view the as yet uncharted vistas which religious freedom opens up to the enquiring and courageous spirit. He argued his case with almost reckless boldness, sweeping away with utter abandon the view of the Church and of organized religion to which ordered and disciplined minds still clung in obedience to the traditions of centuries of Christian history.

At the same time, Williams's works are marred by the very ardour of his spirit. All of his writings suffer from an almost complete want of organization and coherence. There are long arid stretches in which he flounders for the thread of his thought and not infrequently his mystical passages are, at least to the lay mind, simply incomprehensible. He evidently wrote with hot haste and his works are marked by passion and not by reflection. Characteristically, his thought wanders in a maze of subjective rambling, to be broken at last by a passage which glows with an almost transcendent luminosity. His thought must be regarded as unsystematic, eccentric, undisciplined, and occasionally tedious. But supporting and ennobling it at all times was a passionate and unreserved devotion to the cause of religious liberty.

Williams made a notable contribution to the development of religious toleration in England. He defended the cause of complete spiritual freedom, basing his philosophy upon the nobler grounds of liberty of conscience rather than upon the more expedient grounds of religious toleration. His carefully reasoned argument for the complete dissociation of Church and State, resting upon his own experience in America, may be regarded as the most important contribution made during the century in this significant area of political thought. But Williams's contribution to the theory and development of toleration in England was far more limited. His thought cannot be regarded as original, his defence of toleration was neither systematic nor complete, while the radicalism of his doctrinal position robbed him of decisive influence on the political and religious groups which were then founding a tolerant ecclesiastical Establishment in England.[9]

Williams's most significant contribution to the theory of toleration is to be found in his masterly argument against the interference of the State in religious life. The spheres of the Church and the State are sharply dissociated in his theory, which displays no Calvinistic nostalgia for an ordered National Establishment. Indeed, this argument occupies a disproportionate importance in Williams's thought, since it was evolved during his momentous controversy with an embattled Puritan orthodoxy in New England. A full examination of John Cotton's thought would disclose a philosophy almost precisely identical with that examined in our consideration of Puritan theory, though there were, of course, important differences, particularly in Cotton's own estimation. It will be necessary, therefore, to consider briefly the premises of Cotton's thought in order to discover the reasons for Williams's preoccupation with the problem of the relations of the civil State to religion.

Williams held, correctly, that in his opponent's theory the Church and State were inextricably joined.[10] Cotton shared the normal Puritan (Calvinistic) view that the will of God, which is infallibly revealed in the Bible, must engage the attention of both Church and State. Both must labour to protect the purity of faith and to exterminate error from the garden of the Church. Church and State flourish or decline together; their connection is intimate and organic.[11] The Church, which the State shores up with its power, is the Church of God which can brook no rivals and no falsity lest it be ruined, the State consumed, and the fury of God's wrath provoked. Cotton urged this view with such vigour as to arouse his great antagonist to charge that he "publickly taught, and teacheth . . . that body-killing, soule-killing, and State-killing doctrine of not permitting, but persecuting all other consciences and wayes of worship but his own in the civill state, and so consequently in the whole world, if the power or empire thereof were in his hand."[12] Cotton would extirpate by means of force errors which undermined the fundamentals of faith, as defined by the Church, and would extend to circumstantial errors only a very limited toleration.[13] The virtue of such repressive measures is, Cotton admits, largely negative and preventative, but it is at least possible that the fear of corporal punishment may reform those who are not restrained by the certainty of external torment.[14] An heretic is damned in the next world and none but good effects can result from his punishment in this world. The Christian Church must endeavour to create in this world the kingdom which Christ has commanded, seeking to avert the ruin which destroys the Commonwealth that despises His word and will.[15] Cotton's thought reflects and indeed amplifies the Calvinistic conception of the spotless Church. The group of which he was the intellectual leader had sought to plant in the New World such a godly community and it frantically endeavoured to rear up a massive dam against the subtle and insidious forces which eddied against the New England shores as a backwash from the titanic struggle then being waged in England. Heroic measures were taken by the colonial theocracy to isolate itself against the doctrinal and ecclesiastical decay which had set in so morbidly in England. Roger Williams was the Arminius of New England orthodoxy.

B. THE PROBLEM OF CHURCH AND STATE

i. The Role of the Magistrate

Williams dealt at great length with the difficult problem of the relations of Church and State. Since he denied categorically that the magistrate enjoyed any power in the Church he was obliged to frame carefully a new conception of the nature and capacity of the State. Above all, it must establish its power upon foundations unrelated to religious uniformity.

He denounced without reservation the power and influence of the ruler in the Christian State. "All civil states," he wrote, "with their officers of justice in their respective constitutions and administrations are proved essentially civill, and therefore not judges, governours or defendours of the spirituall or Christian state and worship."[16] No power in the Church can be sustained for the magistrate, whether he be Christian or pagan.[17] The power which princes have exercised in religious affairs has been usurped, impious, and uniformly destructive to both Church and State.[18] The orthodox have claimed with one breath that the prince has been set to rule over the Church and with the next that he must "lick the dust of the churches feet."[19] Dominion over men's consciences has been arrogated by selfish factions which have steadily sought their own aggrandizement while destroying the religion of Christ.

That philsophy which grants to the magistrate the direction of the Church and control over conscience is grounded neither in Christian truth nor in natural reason. Again and again Williams drives this barb deep into the theory of an enforced uniformity. Such a view of faith and of the Church makes salvation depend entirely upon the whim of the ruler.[20] The orthodox applaud Elizabeth's persecution of the Catholics, forgetting that by an authority equally valid James persecuted the Puritans. Both sovereigns ruled by an equal right and even the orthodox can be driven to admit that "all magistrates must persecute such whom in their conscience they judge worthy to be persecuted."[21] God has not meant His truth to be subject to the gauge of war and circumstance. Truth is not seen clearly either by the magistrate or by the godly and cannot be ordered by the formula of prescription. Even amongst those who fear and follow God in England there are lamentable and profound differences, and, Williams ironically remarked, these differences have not been cured by the sea passage to New England.[22] In these circumstances it would be madness to deliver the power to define and enforce faith into the fallible hands of the magistrate.

The orthodox have persistently and ruinously confused the functions of the Church and State.[23] They have defined the power of the magistrate in the Church with evasive and deceptive phrases which cannot conceal their disposition to entrust to him the capacity to order doctrine and worship.[24] They have bestowed upon him a power over men's souls equivalent to his just powers over their bodies. "Upon his judgement must the people rest, as upon the minde and judgement of Christ. . . ."[25] They have sought to deliver religion up as a sacrifice to the caprice of the ruler.[26]

Actually, however, the orthodox have sought to conceal the iron chains of dominion which they propose to fasten upon conscience by the prostitution of the ruler's proper authority. When such men talk of the godly magistrate they envisage one prepared to do their bidding. Thus Williams prods Cotton with the awful charge of requiring the ruler to frame religion according to the Cottonian conception of orthodoxy. The orthodox deny the very title of magistracy to those who are not the pawns of their will.[27] These men seek to conceal their own imperious and ruinous intolerance in the power which the ruler wields at their command. They would reduce religion to formulae of their contrivance and stretch the human conscience to the frame of their own arrogant definitions. They seek not the unity of Christ but the dead and formal uniformity of the antichrist.

All of the great Churches have been guilty of delegating to the civil magistrate a power in the Church which Christ has expressly reserved to Himself. The Catholics and prelatists have been the worst offenders, but the Presbyterians seem quite as disposed to make the magistrate "the judge of the true and false church, judge of what is truth, and what error."[28] On the other hand, the true separatists desire the sanction of no civil power in the exercise of their faith, preferring the "two-edged sword of Gods spirit to try out the matter by."[29] They adhere firmly to the conviction that the function of the civil ruler is strictly confined to the exercise of his temporal duties. They recall that Christ consciously and deliberately refrained from mingling the affairs of this world with the problems of faith.[30] They take warning from the annals of history which disclose that the Church has been most injured by those rulers who have sought to reform and direct its spiritual life.[31] The persecuting zeal of a godly Constantine did the Church far graver injury than "the raging fury of the most bloody Neroes."[32] The godly rulers of the past perhaps intended to exalt Christ, but the fruit of their interference was a toll of blood and horrible persecutions which for centuries have wasted the Church.[33] These men may have done their utmost to exalt the Kingdom of Christ, but they accomplished nothing more than the binding of men to an arbitrary and fallible definition of truth.[34] Their policy bred a purge of ruin, division, and bloodshed. The civil magistrate must be scrupulously excluded from any interference in religious affairs. In his public capacity the ruler owes no more to the Church than the protection of his subjects in absolute freedom of worship, whether they worship truly or falsely.[35]

ii. Denunciation of the National Church Ideal and of Enforced Uniformity

The denial of spiritual authority to the magistrate led Williams to a clear and forceful denunciation of a National Church ideal which the Presbyterians were then propounding with such persistent energy. Williams shared the normal Baptist view that the true Church was composed by the voluntary association of men who had experienced personal regeneration. To men who thus conceived the Church the ideal of a National Establishment based upon an enforced uniformity was at once repellent and impious. Williams declared that the attempt to force all men, saints and sinners alike, into a National Church was one of the greatest of the evils threatening England.[36] This constitution of the Church "confounds the civill and religious" and destroys the principles of Christianity and of civil government.[37] A National Establishment delivers spiritual power into the hands of the civil magistrate, making faith rest on no surer foundations than the caprice of his will.[38]

No thoughtful man can possibly hold that a National Church fulfils the will of Christ for His saints. Historically, such establishments have developed in consequene of a tragic confusion between the civil and spiritual orders. They have been constituted by "a racking and tormenting of the soules, as well as of the bodies of persons," since they have endeavoured to compel all men into a common frame of belief.[39] The National Church has been defended exclusively by texts drawn from the Old Testament, despite the fact that the State-Church of the Jews came to an end with the advent of Christ. The Jews were a united people led directly by the hand of God. But no modern nation can claim either such uniformity or such leadership. The Christian age is one of revolution, change, and variety.[40] If we bind the Church of Christ irrevocably to the will of the State, we render it liable to the cyclic changes in political organization which are wholly unconnected with the absolute character of Christ's eternal truth. The tragedy of this error has been abundantly exemplified in England since the days of the Henrician Reformation.[41] "What sober man stands not amazed at these revolutions? and yet like mother like daughter: and how zealous are we their off-spring for another impression and better edition of a nationall Canaan . . . which if attained, who knowes how soone succeeding kings or parliaments will quite pull downe and abrogate."[42]

The Church, then, gains freedom and can attain true organization only when it is completely dissociated from the civil State. The National Church has arisen from a confusion with the civil State and its history has been an unbroken annal of persecution of conscience and perversion of purpose. Both the State and the Church have suffered grievously from the unnatural alliance into which wilful men have forced them. This false identity has to recommend it nothing more than tradition and has to condemn it the manifest Word of God and the blood of countless saints who have been sacrificed to its wicked ends. Men have come to believe that the security of the State is to be found in a religious uniformity which is identical with their religious loyalty. Magistrates have been falsely persuaded that the interests of political stability are somehow linked with the maintenance of religious uniformity. This dangerous and impious conception, which has been foisted on the civil authority by an arrogant and factious clergy, has wrought irreparable harm to both State and Church during the history of Christendom.

iii. The True Nature of Good Citizenship

Williams made a notable contribution to the essentially *politique* view which sought to discover other foundations for civil loyalty than religious uniformity. He had proved that the Church was infinitely harmed when it was bound to the wheel of the secular State. This position had been argued so persistently and successfully by various lay and sectarian groups that it may be regarded as having been established by 1644. Williams undertook, in addition, the more novel and difficult task of demonstrating that the State itself gained strength and stability when it freed itself from the burden of maintaining an enforced uniformity.

The State may attain its highest end only when it can devote itself with singleness of purpose to its proper secular activities. Both Church and State achieve perfection when they develop in a condition of mutual independence. "Divers ages of temporal prosperity to the anti-christian kingdom, prove that common assumption and maxime false, to wit, that the church and commonweale are like Hipocrates twins, weep and laugh, flourish and fade, live and die together." The great prosperity and accomplishments of many heathen states may be said to prove that the roots of civil power do not depend on religious orthodoxy.[43] And history has likewise demonstrated that "true civility and Christianity" may both flourish in a State though the two spheres are completely dissociated.[44] No State burdened with duties which belong properly to religion can be a perfect State. The civil Commonwealth has been weakened and endangered by its unwarranted assumption of the "soul-killing" and "state-killing" doctrine of persecution. The problems and the ills of State and Church are wholly different in quality and in kind, calling for administration and cure by wholly independent agencies. Thus "the straining of mens consciences by civil power, is so far from making men faithful to God or man, that it is the ready way to render men false to both." Intolerance and persecution are ruinous to the State. The attempt of the magistrate to extirpate any group which orthodoxy denominates as heretical can have no other effect than the provocation of civil war. If such a policy is prosecuted to its logical end, the State will be dissolved in war, anarchy, and utter ruin.

Williams seems to argue not only that religious persecution is the gravest enemy to the stability of the State but that its practice almost invalidates the legality of its sovereignty. For persecution destroys the very roots of magistracy and the essential ends of the civil State.[45] The English Revolution gains its chief validity in the resolution which has inspired it to destroy the tyranny over conscience. Persecution lays waste the very foundations of the civil order, and just men may then take up arms for the establishment of a more righteous society.

The civil State, then, can gain security and can command the complete loyalty of its subjects when it reposes its sovereignty upon bases that have no relation to the spiritual life of its citizens. The Christian State evidently rests upon foundations precisely similar to those enjoyed by heathen commonwealths.[46] Nor has diversity of religion produced any impairment in the strength or prosperity of the civil commonwealth.[47] Christianity adds nothing to the legality of the State's power since by its very nature it exercises no influence upon natural things.[48] The State is a voluntary association of human beings whose legitimacy resides in roots that are implicit in the political relationship; in origins that penetrate far beyond the Christian era into the dim mists of pagan antiquity. Moreover, just as the validity of the State has no connection with its Christianity, so the religion of the subject bears no relation to his citizenship. He is bound to the State by ties of loyalty which are explicitly civil, just as his membership in the Church embraces purely spiritual obligations. The subject's social capacity is not affected by his religion. Hence Jews, Turks, or Anti-Christians may be fully as loyal and eminent subjects of the State as its Christian members.[49] The State must cultivate the instinct of loyalty and good citizenship by emphasizing the secular basis upon which it rests. Moral virtue, fidelity, and honesty may be inculcated by the discipline of the State in men who are not saints of God.[50] And above all else, the civil magistrate will not confound moral goodness with religious sanctity.[51] He will perceive that spiritual error presumes no danger to the civil order and that it must be corrected and cured by the Church whose unity it lays waste. The civil ruler will rest content in the assurance that men totally devoid of religion may be possessed of a civic morality which makes them good and valuable members of society.

Williams's argument mounted steadily to a revolutionary plea for the absolute dissociation of Church and State. Utilizing the sectarian conception of religious organization, he had denounced with effective and persuasive logic the very concept of the National Church and had demonstrated that religion is best served when it is left free. He had shown, moreover, that the civil State exists independent of the religious complexion of its citizenry; that it in fact acquires strength and permanency only when it ignores the religious preoccupations which they may have. Good citizenship is entirely unconnected with religious orthodoxy and may, indeed, be found in men who are irreligious. This view repudiated completely a conception of the State which was almost as old as Christianity and renounced without reserve a noble ideal of the interrelations of the temporal and spiritual spheres which had absorbed the attention of wise and pious men through the long and tragic centuries of the Middle Ages. It declared that the social architecture of the past must be adjusted to the living necessities of the present. It opened up a vast area of speculation and experiment in both civil and religious life which human society is still exploring.

iv. *The Argument for the Complete Separation of the Two Spheres*

Williams sought to emphasize the natural origins of the State in order to establish more firmly its dissociation from the religious life of the saints who in part comprise it. The State and the civil society are creations of nature. The family constitutes a prototype of the State which in an historical sense is but an enlargement of its intimate relationship. Men evolved the social contracts which undergird the State long before the knowledge of religion unfolded before them. Its origin is to be found in the free association of a people formed for the attainment of a more stable and prosperous community life. Religious differences amongst its citizens bear no more relation to the sources of its authority or to the sphere of its influence than the complexion or dress of its members. It can be argued neither from divine nor from natural law that it possesses any authority or interest in religious affairs.

The State has been led by crafty and intolerant men into interference in the affairs of the Church in order to secure the aggrandizement of their own position. It has been weakened and perverted by men who would waken Moses from his grave, and who ignore the gospel of Christ.[52] The orthodox have deliberately confounded the civil power with the Church by seeking to order the Christian community on the pattern of the Jewish Common- wealth.[53] They imply in their insidious teaching that the magistrate enjoys valid power only when he yields to their own interpretation and enforces their own glosses.[54] The effect of this philosophy has been to raise up a persecution which has been the chief cause of misery and the disruption of civil peace,[55] while the effect upon religion has been even more invidious. The orthodox have sought to break down the wall of conscience, not with admonition and excommunication, but with powder and shot. They have ignored the patent fact that none but spiritual remedies can prevail against spiritual ills.[56] When the Church is left free to employ its peculiar resources it can prevail over error. But the weapons of man and the weapons of God cannot be joined.[57] Christ was decisive in dissolving the National Church of the Jews and explicit in His establishment of a spiritual worship ordered by a spiritual government.[58] The magistrate shares neither responsibility nor au- thority in that Church.

Williams concluded his discussion of the absolute separation between the civil and spiritual spheres by a famous comparison to a ship at sea. Christ has appointed His ministers to be unquestioned masters of the ship which is the Church. The pilot may not steer a false course or change his course at the command of the prince, who is no more than a passenger in the vessel whose sails are set towards the attainment of divine truth. And, Williams solemnly continued, if the prince persists in his attempt to handle the ship to the peril of its company, the crew may "resist and suppresse these dangerous practices of the prince and his followers, and so save the ship."[59] Similarly, the ship of State is governed absolutely by its master, the magistrate, who steers it towards safety and prosperity. He can brook no interference from the mem- bers of the Church, his passengers, in the sailing of his course. Whether the master of the civil State be pagan or Christian, his civil authority is complete. Neither enjoys authority over the souls on board, but each enjoys complete capacity to enforce order and to govern the course which the State has set.[60]

Protestantism shed the medieval conception of the relations of the Church and State only gradually and painfully. We have observed in England an Anglican philosophy which presumed a regional catholicity and which sought to cement the ties linking the Church with the State by means of a frankly Erastian administration of the National Establishment by an enlightened and undogmatic government. This theory contained rich promise of enlarged religious toleration because the leadership which disciplined the Church was secular and was resolved upon a comprehensive definition of the religious structure. The Elizabethan ideal was perverted and gravely misinterpreted by the small but powerful Anglo-Catholic party which utilized the vast power of government under a weak and unenlightened sovereign to raise up a definition of the Church which did violence both to English history and to English religious opinion. The Anglican thesis concerning the relations of Church and State brought the nation to the brink of war.

Nor did Calvinism, in its various forms, propose a more satisfactory solution. It may be argued that the Presbyterians desired to found in England a religious system which was precisely the reverse of the Anglican. They demanded a national and an exclusive Church; they remained passionately convinced that the magistrate had large and positive capacities in the Church; and they desired an intimate union between the functions of the secular and spiritual spheres. They differed from Anglicanism in their insistence that, in the last analysis, the civil State must rule the Church as the agent of the ministry. The conservative Independents, too, were entrapped by the fatal attractions which the conception of a National Church has for the pious and traditional mind. A national religious order appeared to many thoughtful Englishmen to afford the only preventative against the complete dissolution of Protestant thought and unity. In a desperate effort to check the steady erosion of the theological structure of Protestantism these men reached into the armoury of the past for weapons which had long since lost their efficacy. It was the peculiar role of Roger Williams to denouce the panaceas of orthodoxy as inimical to religion and fatal to civil peace, and to call men to face courageously the problems of the present in an atmosphere of liberty and free enquiry.

C. "THE BLOUDY TENENT OF PERSECUTION"

The weight of Williams's argument was addressed to the destruction of the "Bloudy Tenent of Persecution," which the great sectary regarded as a malignant growth in the body of religion and as a hideous blemish in the structure of Christian civilization. As an astute critic has indicated, he undertook to trace the grim history of persecution in the effort to prove that it had been the chief cause of human misery and wrong.[61] Williams pursued the dark spectre of persecution with wrathful invective and with a passionate logic which laid bare its origins and demanded its destruction. He was so utterly absorbed in the assault upon intolerance that, as we shall notice later, he failed to undertake a systematic exposition of the doctrine of toleration which he desired to replace it. Religious liberty is the inferential by-product of Williams's epical holy war against the evils of persecution.

Williams makes it clear in the early pages of the *Bloudy Tenent of Persecution* that he has undertaken a classical denunciation of a doctrine which has become engrafted in the Christian philosophy. The blood of thousands of innocent souls, Protestants and Catholics alike, has been spilled upon altars which have not been reared to Christ. He sought to prove by "pregnant Scripture and arguments" that the positions which the orthodox had raised to fortify their intolerance have no place in the religion of Christ.[62] England, he wrote in 1644, stands at the cross-roads. A great war has been waged to free the human spirit, the Parliament must secure the liberty of men to walk freely in the way of peace and freedom of conscience. Previous Parliaments have changed the yoke of spiritual oppression but the revolutionary body must destroy it.[63] England must be brought to realize that persecution is the most heinous sin and wrong in the modern world. The wisdom and experience of all the ages testify that no "long liv'd fruit of peace or righteousnesse" ever grew "upon that fatall tree."[64] Christ denounced no wrong with such scathing indictments as the coercion of the human conscience, which should rest free and receptive before His gospel. Yet the Church has been the prey of narrow and rigid sectarian groups which have endeavoured to force all men into churches of their own creation.

Righteous men have grown weary and gloomy before the failure of Christendom to understand the essential meaning of Christ's teachings. Even England in the midst of a war to destroy one species of intolerance seems disposed to embrace the cross of another. "Who can now but expect that after so many scores of yeares preaching and professing of more truth, and amongst so many great contentions amongst the very best of Protestants, a fierie furnace should be heat, and who sees not now the fires kindling?"[65] The liberty which is implicit in the Protestant Reformation will turn to vinegar in men's mouths if it is not implemented by freedom of enquiry and absolute freedom of worship. The Church, indeed Christianity, can be conceived in no larger terms than the individual with whose salvation it is exclusively concerned. Every man must be invested with liberty to seek his salvation in his own way. "In vain have English parliaments permitted English Bibles in the poorest English houses, and the simplest man or woman to search the Scriptures, if they should be forced (as if they lived in Spaine or Rome it selfe without the sight of a Bible) to beleeve as the church beleeves."[66] Protestantism can claim no advance over Catholicism until it vindicates without reservation the liberty upon which it is presumed to rest.

Williams's definition of persecution is clear and unequivocal. There is none of the subtle evasion concerning heresy and blasphemy which normally hedged the pronouncements of orthodoxy. He stated simply: "I acknowledge that to molest any person, Jew or gentile, for either professing doctrine, or practising worship meerly religious or spirituall, it is to persecute him," even if his doctrine or worship is false, or is presumed to be false.[67] This definition includes with considered care both religious toleration and freedom of worship within the province of Christian liberty. It adds to the momentous Elizabethan recognition of liberty of belief the final logical conclusion of liberty of worship. It denouces the inteference by any authority with man's spiritual beliefs as a persecution unwarranted by natural reason or by divine truth. Williams states the case of toleration without reservation.

With this revolutionary definition always threading through his thought, Williams proceeded to an examination and denunciation of the philosophy and fruits of religious repression. In all ages those who have pleaded the cause of truth have been trampled down by the engines of intolerance. They hae been destroyed by men who pleaded Moses, and not Christ, in warrant for their tyranny.[68] These imperious spirits have customarily wrapped their own consciences in tender cloths while outraging the consciences of others. All men have been their prey, all truth has stood still before their awful presumption of infallibility. "Are all the thousands of millions . . . of consciences, at home and abroad, fuel only for a prison, for a whip, for a stake, for a gallows?"[69] The persecutors have persisted in their satanic zeal despite the fact that Christ has armed His truth with none other than spiritual weapons.[30] The blood of those who have stood steadfast for Christ "hath beene spilt like water upon the earth, and that because they have held fast the truth and witnesse of Jesus, against the worship of the state and times, compelling to an uniformity of state religion."[71] The earth has been "made drunk with the bloud of its inhabitants" slaughtering each other with indiscriminate zeal in the effort of each sect to aggrandize itself at the expense of all others. Unless reason and charity intervene, this holocaust can have no other consequence than the ruin of the Church and the devastation of the civil society. The future both of the Church and of civilization depends upon the immediate destruction of the beast of persecution.

No Christian would deny that religious error and seduction to error are hideous sins beside which the worst civil offences stand pale. But we are not given remedy for these ills. We must stay our hands with scrupulous care since God has reserved judgment in these cases to Himself alone. "Such a sentence no civill judge can passe, such a death no civill sword can inflict."[72] The erroneous conscience cannot be rectified by human agencies, and we stand ignorant and naïve when we attempt to assay with exactness the ore of heresy.[73] Those who persecute, therefore, not only do so against the explicit command of Almighty God, but they incur the awful risk of persecuting truth which they conceive to be error. Every man who is tempted by intolerance must enquire of himself, "Is it possible . . . that since I hunt, I hunt not the life of my Saviour, and the bloud of the Lamb of God: I have fought against many severall sorts of consciences, is it beyond all possibilitie and hazard, that I have not fought against God, that I have not persecuted Jesus in some of them?"[74]

In fine and impassioned rhetoric Williams cut away the very foundations of the persecuting logic. He sought to dissuade men from coercion by the warning that persecution enjoyed no sanction in the teachings of Christ and by invoking the realization that when men, who are fallible and limited in their knowledge of truth, persecute they outrage conscience and assail the majesty of God. At the same time, he endeavoured to demonstrate that the coercive sanction implicit in a National Establishment, which orthodoxy had sought to distinguish from persecution, could not in fact be so differentiated.

God has invested His Church with remedies which insulate it against the ravages of heresy, but He has not appointed the civil sword as its preservative.[75] Persecution can be avoided only when the magistrate withdraws unreservedly from jurisdiction in religion. The Christian ruler will scrupulously refrain from the exercise of that coercive jurisdiction which has no other issue than the destruction of souls.[76] He will be stayed by the reflection that while the sword of his authority may make "a whole nation of hypocrites," it is powerless to recover a single soul from error.[77] The intrusion of the secular power into religion beclouds God's purposes and delays the ultimate triumph of truth. The persecution which ensues endangers the security of the State,[78] and provokes the most bitter and dangerous wars to which its existence can be exposed.[79] When religious truth is confined to the frame of a National Establishment it whirls aimlessly with political circumstance without relation to the lodestone of God's truth. In no other country should this be as apparent as in England, for it "hath been Englands sinfull shame, to fashion and change their garments and religions with wondrous ease and lightnesse, as a higher power, a stronger sword hath prevailed."[80] Religion must be emancipated from the paralysing pressure of the civil sword. The hand of God is alone capable of brushing away the scales of untruth which blind men's eyes and of restoring them to their heritage which is the Kingdom of God. This delicate and precious benefit can never be attained unless men are left free. We thwart the very means of God's redeeming mercy when we fasten men irrevocably in their errors through the brutal rage and pressure of persecution.[81] No man can be convinced that a religion is true which requires such instruments of violence to uphold it.[82]

The evil tentacles of the persecuting philosophy have gripped the minds and spirits of the arrogant and wilful with such tenacity that Williams despaired of their release. The heresies of today become the enforced orthodoxies of tomorrow.[83] The roots of persecution are to be found deep in the psychology of all men who seek to clothe their own human ambitions and selfish plans with the faultless mantle of Christ. All who differ from this self-constituted orthodoxy are denominated heretics and blasphemers. "This is the outcry of the pope and prelates, and of the Scotch Presbyterians, who would fire all the world, to be avenged on the sectarian heretics, the blasphemous heretics, the seducing heretics." The sword of Cromwell, Williams wrote in 1651, alone stood between England and a rage of ferocious persecution and bitter war between rival orthodoxies.[84] Men will not learn; persecution itself has not dissolved the hard kernel of malice and pride in men, once under the yoke, who have gained freedom.

Yet, Williams concluded with awful strictures which mount up in a fine cadence of eloquence, persecution must be destroyed if religion itself is not to perish. It is the most iniquitous of all human evils. It is blasphemy against the God of Peace, "who hath of one bloud, made all mankinde, to dwell upon the face of the earth."[85] It wars on Christ, who would have men saved by gentleness and persuasion. It has crucified Christ anew and has raised up a scourge "which no uncleannes, no adulterie, incest, sodomie, or beastialitie can equall, this ravishing and forcing . . . the very soules and consciences of all the nations and inhabitants of the world."[86] It has burdened the consciences of the pious and has forced the weak into hypocrisy. It withdraws from men the means through which Christ may be gained; it "burnes up the holy Scriptures, and forbids them . . . to be read in English, or that any tryall or search, or (truly) free disquisition be made by them: when the most able, diligent and conscionable readers must pluck forth their own eyes, and be forced to reade by the . . . cleargies spectacles."[87] It kindles wars and confusion; it debases the civil ruler to the execution of the will of the clergy; and it lays waste the consciences of the regenerate and the lost alike. It destroys the most flourishing commonwealths, drives resolute men into exile, and despoils the essence not only of religious truth but of common justice.[88]

Williams's rhetoric swept with the force of a clean, strong wind through the ruined halls of the once fair structure which persecution had laid waste. He wrote with the heat of a man moved by a relentless and indomitable conviction. We have observed that he had encumbered his renunciation of religious coercion by no reservations. Civilization, he argued, must choose, and that quickly, between persecution and absolute liberty. Persecution has long been a chronic cancer gnawing at the vitals both of the civil society and of the Church, but it had attained a malignancy in the English Wars and in the Thirty Years' War which threatened the very continuation of civilized life. Williams called his readers to a relentless crusade against the iniquity which religious coercion had wrought in their own and former ages, and summoned them to face the uncertainties of an unplotted and revolutionary future with the steady conviction that religious liberty enjoyed the sanction not only of divine prescription but of common sense and political necessity. From the fires which had devastated Western Europe for a full century, he mused not too optimistically, there might emerge a cleaner, a purer, and a more enlightened civil and religious order. Christendom, he clearly felt, faced with uncertain balance and decision the immediate necessity of a choice between toleration and destruction. It can be said of Williams that he added not inconsiderable weight in that balance which was to incline before his life was out in the direction of a nobler and a more spacious freedom.

D. THE PROBLEM OF HERESY AND ERROR

The refusal of the Christian to employ the arms of persecution does not mean that he is insensitive to the existence of error or unaware of its hideous nature. It means rather that he has resolved to treat it with the spiritual remedies at his disposal, to approach its cure with humility and charity, and to eschew all methods likely to harden the heretic in his error or to destroy him. Even the heathen peoples understood that conscience must be left inviolate.[89] The human mind is staggered and sickened by the implications of the doctrine of persecution. Ideally, those who persecute would destroy all those who differ in faith from the self-appointed prescriptions of the ortho- dox, "and then what heapes upon heapes in the slaughter houses and shambles of civill warres must the world come to."[90] Human wisdom can draw no exact line between truth and error. Even God's own people have erred in the fundamentals of faith with every assurance of resolved con- sciences. The errors which afflict the human spirit can be cured by the revealing light of God's truth, which can persuade and revive men only when they are left free and undisturbed.

The orthodox theorists had frequently sought to distinguish between error passively held, which might be tolerated, and error which men sought to disseminate.[91] Williams alleged hotly that the distinction was without meaning and masked a persecuting disposition in the garb of charity. For the persecuting mind will accuse all who disagree with it of wilful arrogance and heretical zeal. God's saints have commonly been persecuted under this very indictment. The impact of truth upon error will inevitably create dissensions and divisions, but these temporary evils cannot be alleviated by the interven- tion of civil power.[92] Religious dissension flames up into civil commotion when the illegitimate weapon of persecution is grasped to extinguish "such doctrines or practices by weapons of wrath and blood, whips, stockes, im- prisonment, banishment, death." It is then that "the towne is in an uproare, and the country takes the alarum to expell that fog or mist of errour, heresie, blasphemy . . . with swords and guns; whereas tis light alone, even light from the bright shining sunne of righteousnesse, which is able, in the soules and consciences of men to dispell and scatter such fogges and darknesse."[93] The Christian world must be brought to realize that persecution entrenches and solidifies irremediably the very evil which it undertakes to extirpate. Not only is it criminal and impious; it is without efficacy.

We can proceed with violent means against heresy and error only when we labour under the fatal delusion that the foundations of our own faith are infallible. All men agree that Christ's truth must not be persecuted. The persecutors have commonly claimed so clear and certain a knowledge of Christian faith that they need not hesitate for fear they mistake differences of judgment for heresy. This has been the "pretended bulwark" of the "bloudy wolves."[94] No human being possesses such transcendent knowledge of God's truth. But if he did—and here Williams cuts deep—he would know first that Christ has invested His Church with none but spiritual weapons and has explicitly declared excommunication to be the ultimate remedy against heresy.[95] We must confine the heretic to the spiritual prison of excommunication, but we may not proceed against him physically. Those who have arrogated to themselves the claim of infallible knowledge have not only borrowed prisons from the magistrate but have "wrung the keyes out of the magistrates hands, and hung them at their own girdles. . . ."[96] Even when the Church is godly and the heresy real, spiritual pains constitute the extreme limits of its discipline. Violent courses can have none but an evil consequence. For if an accused man be an heretic in the hands of persecutors, "he disputes in feare, as the poor theefe: the mouse disputes with a terrible persecuting cat: who while she seems to play and gently tosse, yet the conclusion is a proud insulting and devouring crueltie." And, similarly, if the accused man be a faithful witness of truth, "disputes he not as a lambe in the Lyons paw, being sure in the end to be torne in pieces?"[97]

This is not the way of Christ, or of His followers. The Christian will remain humble, tolerant, and thankful in the light which God has bestowed upon him. He will patiently and charitably wait for the spread of God's truth amongst men whom he believes to be lost. He will recall that God's Church rests in divine hands and not in the hands of his own fallible wisdom. When men spurn and oppose the progress of truth he will do no more than pray "that out of them Gods elect may be called."[98] He will be far "from passing the sentence of death upon the least of the little ones of Jesus, (notwithstanding their spirituall weaknes, and sicknesses)."[99] He will wait upon the wisdom of the Lord and will shrink from the persecution of the errors of other men for fear that his own feet may be mired in heresy and his own eyes blinded by error.

Williams was far from condoning heresy and error. But he taught that mortal knowledge in these matters was extremely limited, that there was little the Christian can do to secure their reduction, and certainly nothing that the State can do about it. If God can tolerate idolatry and heresy, surely we can.[100] The Church should rear high walls to protect its internal purity and its own discipline, sealing itself agains the inroads of error. Its own internal discipline should be rigidly severe.[101] But those who are without the Church or who have been excluded from it are the tares that must be left for the final harvest.[102] We must leave them standing not only to prevent the plucking up of the good grain with the chaff but to prevent the destruction of the civil State through the wars and dissensions engendered by persecution.[103] Faith will rest most secure and the civil society will be grounded on its firmest foundations when we leave to God those things that are God's and content ourselves with the quest for a fuller and richer knowledge of that truth wherein we find peace and salvation.

A brooding scepticism permeates Williams's consideration of the probblem of heresy and error. He was deeply imbued with the sectarian ideal of a Church gathered up from the infinite marshes of sin and error by God's especial mercy and providence. This tiny knot of the godly enjoys the leadership and truth of God, dwelling aloof from the hosts of the lost who encompass it. Williams never stresses the typically Protestant faith in the implicit power of God's truth to conquer error. He rather counsels Christians to withdraw into churches formed of the regenerate, to preserve themselves from error by the walls of excommunication, and to leave the awful problem of the lost in God's hands. His reading of history taught him that certainty of truth had deluded men and had entrapped them in a disposition to impress that truth upon others. Truth, he suggested, should be subjectively, almost passively, held. We will gain all we need, fulfil our own destiny, if that truth which we possess accomplishes our salvation. Other men must find it in the same way by seeking the same end. Williams's pessimism, while it betokens the irreparable damage which relativism and sectarianism had done to the structural rigidity and the theological certainty of Calvinism, swept before it every impediment to the acceptance of the theory of toleration.

E. THE THEORY OF TOLERATION

Williams did not undertake a careful or systematic defence of toleration. His theory of religious liberty may be said to be implicit in all of his writings and to follow as a corollary from his masterly demolition of the doctrine of persecution. Williams distinguished clearly and deliberately between religious toleraton, which he regarded as inevitable if Church and State were to survive, and liberty of conscience, which he held to be desirable if both Church and State were to attain their ultimate fulfilment. He declared liberty of conscience to be a natural and fundamental right which has never been surrendered to the State and which, in fact, lies wholly beyond its proper jurisdiction.[104] His theory of religious liberty was rooted in the firm conviction that the sphere of Church and State must be entirely separated and that all elements of compulsion must be withdrawn from religious life and organization. "Even morality, as far as it is regulated by law, should be kept separate from the religious holiness demanded by the church."[105] Never in the seventeenth century was this separation of function, so essential in the development of religious liberty, more clearly or precisely envisaged. Finally, it should be indicated that in Williams's theory there were no reservations, no saving clauses of vague content, to vitiate the force of his arguments. Williams was prepared to face the wilderness of sectarian individualism which stems inevitably from religious liberty with equanimity and with serene confidence.

The Church, Williams argued, should perform its rites and extend its teachings under conditions of absolute liberty, eschewing, in its turn, the slightest coercion upon those who are without its communion. It must resolutely emancipate itself from the pernicious evils of enforced uniformity which it has inherited.[106] It will rely upon the magistrate for nothing more than the protection from violence which its members rightfully claim as members of the civil society. The true Church will avoid the political favour of the magistrate and will constantly recall that the structure of a National Church depending upon enforced uniformity is expressly contrary to God's Word.[107] No matter how seductive the prospects of a state religion may appear it will be avoided as a prison, for "who hath not found a pallace a prison, when forc't to keepe within it?" Even the true faith, directly ordained by God, "is a torment to that soule and conscience, that is forc't against its owne free love and choice, to embrace and observe it."[108] The fatal embrace of enforced conformity has caused the ruin of the Church and has implemented the slaughter of millions of souls that were precious to Christ.[109] The true Church will seek no other sanction than its own truth, defend itself by no other weapons than those with which Christ has armed it.

Religious toleration does not, however, leave the Church unprotected. The men and women who comprise it have experienced a spiritual regeneration which binds them to God by indissoluble ties. As an institution it is encircled by a spiritual wall which protects it from its mortal enemies without, while its spiritual preoccupation ensures the State of quiet civil conduct.[110] It refrains as part of its ethic from the forcible compulsion of men, thereby protecting the State from the ravaging ill of persecution and factional aggrandizement. The Church stills the rage of persecution by cleansing its thought and policy of "such unchristian practices, toward all that is man, capable of a religion and a conscience. . . ."[111] The fatal strife between Catholics and Protestants may well be assuaged when the implication and content of the doctrine of toleration are understood. For "it is but humanity, it is but Christianity to exercise meeknesse and moderation to all men."[112] Every man must be extended a complete liberty to try all things and to seek God in his own way. The Christian Church must be brought to realize that the slightest compulsion may well force men to accept that which they do not understand or that which they do not in conscience believe.[113] Compulsion, even the orthodox admit, cannot make Christians. Its effect is rather to destroy what religion men do have. Religious compulsion, however slight, is a "notorious and common pyrate, that takes and robbs, that fires and sinkes the (spirituall shipps and vessels) the consciences of all men, of all sorts, of all religions and perswasions whatsoever."[114] England must frame a liberty of conscience which not only rests upon political necessity but is rooted in the "equity and piety" which commend it as the only environment in which the gospel can be truly taught and freely received.

Religious liberty will yield a rich harvest of security to the State and transcendent spiritual blessings to the Church. The factions which persecution and clerical ambition have bred will be cured and Christianity may attain by tolerance the catholicity which bigotry has shattered. The great religious factions[115] not only have torn the seamless robe of Christ, but in their demands for exclusive hegemony over conscience have brought the State to the verge of ruin.[116] They have persecuted each other and have sought to win the approbation of the magistrate in order to secure the destruction of their rivals. They plead lustily "for mercie to mens consciences, when them selves are in the grates, and pits, and under hatches,"[117] only to exhibit their essential intolerance and fiendish bigotry once they have attained hope of mastery. When the State enforces religious liberty upon all men and all sects, these factional distempers will evaporate. Men will have no other defence, no other instrument of aggression, than the "two-edged sword of the spirit," with which the issue of truth and error will be finally resolved. From the shadows and mire of factional greed and cruelty a new and more glorious catholicity will be reared on the solid foundations of toleration. The Church will be revivified and unshackled when its spiritual nature is asserted and its spiritual weapons are refurbished.

Men must be brought to a fuller realization of the completely spiritual nature of religion, and the Church must conceive of itself spiritually before the priceless benefits of religious liberty may be won. The Church releases but reluctantly the sword of coercion which it dumbly grasps with the paralysed arm of persecution. It must relinquish the sword of force in full realization that Christ has provided it with adequate resources against heresy and error. "Those churches cannot be truly Christian . . . which either actually themselves, or by the civill power of kings and princes . . . doe persecute such as dissent from them or be opposite against them."[118] The Church possesses spiritual remedies with which it can maintain its own purity, and beyond that it cannot go.[119] The assistance of temporal power is not required in the warfare which it wages; its own spiritual weapons are omnicompetent.[120] The sword of coercion cannot touch the godly conscience, nor is it effective against the man who is dead in sin. A dead man cannot be killed.[121] The wolves of error which assail the Church are to be spiritually and mystically slain. Christ never intended that they should "be killed, their braines dasht out with stones, staves, halberts, guns."[122] Those men who violate the spiritual nature of Christ's message by the bloody arms of persecution make Him a temporal king by force, destroy His people, and delay the "sweet end of the comming of the Lord Jesus . . . to save mens soules . . . by his own blood."[123] The Church of Christ must seek in religious liberty penance for the wrongs which have been committed in the name of Christ and press towards the attainment of His Kingdom with the mighty gospel with which He has secured it.

Williams would admit no reservations to the toleration for which he pleaded so eloquently. Men must be left free to seek Christ in their own way, and the Church, he held, should not dare even to contrive a doctrinal system which might be imposed by suggestion or prescription upon conscience. He distrusted completely the efforts which his Calvinistic colleagues were undertaking at Westminster to define the fundamentals of faith. Such definitions are but a prelude to the coercive enforcement of a religious truth which a group of fallible men have elaborated to their personal satisfaction. He did propose, in vague terms to which no Christian of his period would have taken exception, certain teachings which appear to have universal validity.[124] But he hastened to point out that no definition of essential truth can have more than a subjective and relative meaning. Our knowledge of truth unfolds but slowly and is, at best, held feebly. God's chosen are scattered in all churches, in all ages, and in all nations. Any rigid definition of saving faith condemns not only men who are now in error and who will in the end be saved,[125] but likewise "the generation of the righteous, who have been generally for many generations ignorant of the Christian way of worship."[126] Doctrinal formulae, therefore, are both dangerous and unnecessary. Salvation is gained by individuals, not by Churches. The man who experiences regeneration gains from God a knowledge of truth sufficient for his own salvation, but he will not dare prescribe that truth to other men or to other ages. The daring and almost anarchistic sweep of Williams's argument is most clearly revealed in this amazing contribution to spiritual freedom. His theory really destroys the constitution not only of the organized Church but of the organized congregation. The Church is composed of men who have experienced regeneration and who worship God in thanksgiving and humility. But this relationship has little structural essence beyond association. The saint is bound only to God through the subjective experience of miraculous conversion. No authority can intrude into the awful intimacy of that relationship.

Williams had vindicated the benefits which accrue both to the State and to the Church when the principles of religious liberty are embraced. In his discussion of the relations of Church and State he had dwelt at length upon the stability, strength, and security which are gained by the State that divorces itself completely from the sectarian strife in which it engages at its own peril. Religious toleration, he reminded England, likewise promotes the economy of a nation. The history of Holland has demonstrated this as axiomatic, and in Holland Amsterdam, which has been the strongest citadel of religious toleration, has reaped the richest material rewards. There has descended upon Holland a "confluence of the persecuted" which drew "boats, drew trade, drew shipping, and that so mightily in so short a time, that shipping, trading, wealth, greatnesse, honour . . . have appeared to fall as out of heaven in a crown or garland upon the head of that poor fisher town."[127] Yet Holland has not gained the full benefits of religious liberty, since the Arminians and the Catholics still labour under restraints. England still enjoys the opportunity to "out-shoot and teach their neighbours" by extending unrestricted liberty of worship to men of all persuasions.[128] The civil and spiritual benefits which would flow from such a reformation have been historically vindicated. The economic gains which are the inevitable by-product of liberty of conscience should likewise not be ignored.

Every counsel of religion and policy, therefore, inclined Williams to advocate religious liberty as the model towards which the Christian world should aspire. He defended it with every argument which could be bent to his purpose and supported it with logical considerations which society could ill afford to ignore. He met the difficult problems which toleration presented to an age nurtured in the traditions of uniformity with candour, honesty, and a disarming sincerity. There are no evasions, no sectarian shifts in his thinking. And finally, Williams met the most difficult and decisive test of seventeenth century tolerance in his unequivocal demand that the benefits of toleration should be extended beyond the confines of the historically Protestant groups to men of all or of no religious persuasion.

All men who do not break the civil peace should be protected in absolute freedom of belief and worship whether they be Protestants, Catholics, Jews, Turks, or pagans.[129] The true Church will permit men to continue in unbelief or in false belief so long as they do not contravene the civil laws. There is no spiritual offence which can possibly justify the ruinous intervention of persecution in religious affairs. For false religion which lies without the Church can do the pious man no graver damage than poison which is not taken, nor will it harm the State save as its adherents happen to be bad subjects.[130] The Church has security in its internal discipline against the infection of heresy; the State guards itself against civil disturbances by the legitimate punishment of breaches of its laws. When the awful curse of persecution is lifted, the Church may at last proceed to repair the ravages that have laid it waste and to redeem men by "free conferrings, disputings and preachings of the Gospel of truth."[131]

There resides in all men of all faiths a fine devotion of conscience which betokens that faith which is the essence of religion. Thus Williams spoke with warm admiration of the noble death of Father Hartley whose faith as a Catholic could not be shaken by torture and death.[132] Those who would crush such resolved consciences would "turn up all roots, and lay all level and in blood" in their frenzied zeal to enthrone their own bigotry.[133] Satan deludes men into the awful error of canonizing their own opinions into infallible truths. The pious man is an humble and tolerant man. Thus Williams commended the temper of Jeremy Taylor, who in his *Liberty of Prophesying* had "excellently asserted the toleration of different religions, yea, in a respect, that of the papists themselves, which is a new way of soul freedom, and yet is the old way of Christ Jesus."[139] All men must have liberty to seek Christ in their own way, free from the dictation of the "holy and learned" who strive so eagerly to impose their wills.[135] All men must be left free before the judgment and mercy of God.

Williams is perhaps the strangest of a group of human spirits dislodged from traditional moorings by the hurricane of civil war and ecclesiastical disruption. The mind of one age always grapples dimly and feebly to engage the mind and spirit of a former age; when the attention is focused on a revolutionary and completely individualistic genius like Williams the task is almost insuperable. In the thought of Williams, considered both mad and incendiary by the orthodox in his own day, the modern mind discovers a kind of prescience, a kind of divination which taught him that the world was entering a new stage in which religious persecution must be abandoned as ineffective and as intolerably dangerous. Williams, in his voluminous denunciations of the iniquity of persecution, clung doggedly to a few principles upon which religious liberty has come to rest. He saw clearly that the civil State would be destroyed unless it withdrew from the sectarian bitterness and the clashing ambitions of rival orthodoxies which had for a century engulfed the Western world. He demonstrated to the satisfaction of reasonable men that persecution was in itself impious and destructive to the very essence of religious life. He posed a conception of religion, starkly mystical, intensely subjective, and wholly individualistic, before which religious liberty acquired the rich dignity of positive virtue. Roger Williams pleaded not for religious toleration but for religious liberty as the birthright of all men, whether pagan or Christian. His theology was ill-formed, chaotic, and subjective. But out of its very relativism, its proud assertion that men needed no more than the inward assurance of grace, flowed the strong necessity for freedom. There is in Williams's thought a complete honesty, an ultimate kind of logic which led him to accept without reservation the full implications of disorganization and ecclesiastical disintegration which the seventeenth century mind was discovering were implicit in religious liberty. He discarded the past without nostalgia to embrace the future in the assurance of a larger freedom and a nobler fulfilment of Christ's will.

NOTES

1. James Mackinnon, *History of Modern Liberty* (L., 1906-1908), III, p. 475.

2. Francesco Ruffini, *Religious Liberty* (London, 1912), p. 168.

3. Vernon Parrington, *Main Currents in American Thought* (New York: Harcourt, Brace, 1927), I, pp. 64-65.

4. Ernst Troeltsch, *Social Teaching of the Christian Churches* (New York: Macmillan, 1931), II, p. 934.

5. Parrington, p. 65.

6. Ruffini, p. 171.

7. H. B. Parkes, "John Cotton and Roger Williams Debate Toleration, 1644-1652," *New England Quarterly* IV, pp. iv, 750-51.

8. David Masson, *Life of John Milton* (London, 1871-1894), III, p. 113; James Ernst, *Roger Williams* (New York: Macmillan, 1932), p. 246.

9. Williams's place in contemporary English religious thought has been gravely distorted, in the judgment of this writer, by recent American biographers. His very great

contribution to the development of toleration cannot be denied, but a proper under-standing of English history and English thought in this period would make it impossible to regard him as the first apostle of religious toleration in England. Nor can he be said to have been the source of the devotion of the Independents and sectaries to religious liberty. In particular, we do violence to history when we credit to an author, whom we are considering in a biographical vacuum, the appearance of ideas similar to his in con-temporary or later works. The development of thought is a complex process in which every great thinker plays a part that must be carefully assessed in relation to the whole range of contemporary thought. The historian's quarrel with the biographer, of the new school, is that he wrests a complex figure from a complex setting, seeking to epitomize history in the far too simple terms of the individual.

10. Roger Williams, Mr. *Cottons letter lately printed, examined and answered*, (L., 1644) (ed. by R. A. Guild) "Narragansett Club Publ.", I, Providence, R. I., 1866), 42-43.

11. Michael Freund, *Die Idee der Toleranz* (Halle Saale, 1927), pp. 242-43.

12. Williams, Mr. *Cotton's letter*, pp. 44, 95.

13. John Cotton, *The bloudy tenent, washed, and made white in the blood of the Lambe*, etc. (L., 1647), pp. 3, 5-6.

14. Ibid., p. 20.

15. Ibid., p. 164-65.

16. Roger Williams, *The bloudy tenent of persecution for cause of conscience, discussed, in a conference between truth and peace*, etc. (L., 1644) (ed., by S. L. Caldwell) ("Narragansett Club Publ.", IV, Providence, R. I., 1867), Pref. (3).

17. Ibid., p. 121.

18. Roger Williams, *The bloody tenent yet more bloody*, etc. (L., 1652) (ed. by S. L. Caldwell) ("Narragansett Club Publ.", Providence, R. I., 1870), pp. 76-78, 161-68, 171, 187, 218-19, 243.

19. Williams, *The bloudy tenent*, p. 121.

20. Ibid., p. 214.

21. Ibid., p. 188.

22. Ibid., p. 217.

23. Williams, *The bloody tenent yet more bloody*, pp. 110-11, 300.

24. Williams, *The bloudy tenent*, pp. 308-09.

25. Ibid., p. 309.

26. Ibid., p. 311.

27. Ibid., p. 177-78.

28. Ibid., p. 350.

29. Ibid., p. 352.

30. Ibid., p. 367.

31. Ibid., pp. 367-68; Williams, *The bloody tenent yet more bloody*, p. 72.

32. Williams, *The bloudy tenent*, p. 184.

33. Ibid., pp. 184-85.

34. Ibid., pp. 368-69.

35. Ibid., pp. 372-73.

36. Williams, Mr. *Cottons letter*, p. 77.

37. Williams, *The bloudy tenent*, pp. 3-4.

38. Ibid., pp. 257-58.

39. Roger Williams, *Queries of highest consideration, proposed to Mr. Tho. Goodwin Mr. Phillip Nye Mr. Wil. Bridges Mr. Jer. Burroughs Mr. Sidr. Simpson. And to the commissioners*

from the Generall Assembly (so called) of the Church of Scotland; upon occasion of their late apologies for themselves and their churches, etc. (L., 1644) (ed. by R. Guild) ("Narragansett Club Publ.", II, Providence, R. I., 1867), pp. 25-26.

40. *Vide* Williams, *The bloudy tenent*, pp. 314-26, for the complete argument.

41. Ibid., pp. 344-45.

42. Ibid., p. 345. Williams was here specifically attacking the Directory.

43. Williams, *The bloody tenent yet more bloody*, p. 170; Williams, *The bloudy tenent*, p. 251.

44. Williams, *The bloudy tenent*, p. 4.

45. Williams, *The bloody tenent yet more bloody*, pp. 207, 238, 454; *Queries*, p. 35.

46. Williams, *The bloody tenent yet more bloody*, p. 71.

47. Ibid., p. 238.

48. Freund, p. 255.

49. Williams, *The bloudy tenent*, p. 142.

50. Williams, *The bloody tenent yet more bloody*, pp. 207-08, 365.

51. Ibid., p. 406.

52. Williams, *The bloudy tenent*, p. 221.

53. Ibid., pp. 224-25.

54. Ibid., p. 231.

55. Ibid., p. 237.

56. Ibid., p. 148.

57. Ibid., pp. 150, 160.

58. Ibid., p. 239.

59. Ibid., p. 378.

60. Ibid., pp. 399-400.

61. Mackinnon, pp. 475-76.

62. Williams, *The bloudy tenent*, Pref. (1.).

63. Ibid., pp. 7-9.

64. Williams, *Queries*, p. 35.

65. Williams, *The bloudy tenent*, p. 12.

66. Ibid., p. 13.

67. Ibid., p. 63.

68. Ibid., p. 58.

69. Williams to Endicott (1651), *The Letters of Roger Williams* ("Narragansett Club Publ.", VI, Providence, 1870), p. 216.

70. Williams, *The bloudy tenent*, p. 59; *The bloody tenent yet more bloody*, pp. 145, 147-49, 161.

71. Williams, *The bloudy tenent*, p. 60.

72. Ibid., p. 125.

73. Williams, *The bloody tenent yet more bloody*, 508-10.

74. Ibid., p. 515.

75. Williams, *The bloudy tenent*, p. 127.

76. Ibid., pp. 131-32, 135.

77. Ibid., p. 136.

78. Williams, *The bloody tenent yet more bloody*, pp. 70, 175, 179.

79. Ibid., pp. 328-39, 440.

80. Williams, *The bloudy tenent*, p. 137.

81. Williams, *The bloody tenent yet more bloody*, pp. 226, 474.

82. Williams, *The bloudy tenent*, p. 139.

83. Williams, *The bloody tenent yet more bloody*, pp. 208-09, 220-21.

84. Williams to Endicott (1651) Williams, *Letters*, pp. 216-17.

85. Williams, *The bloody tenent yet more bloody*, p. 493.

86. Ibid., p. 495.

87. Ibid., p. 496.

88. Ibid., p. 498.

89. Williams, *The bloudy tenent*, pp. 264-67.

90. Ibid., p. 270.

91. Ibid., pp. 74-75. He is here criticizing Cotton's remarks in this connection.

92. Ibid., pp. 76-80.

93. Ibid., pp. 80-81.

94. Ibid., p. 84.

95. Ibid., p. 91.

96. Ibid., p. 274.

97. Ibid., p. 277.

98. Ibid., p. 93.

99. Roger Williams, *Experiments of spiritual life & health, and their preservatives, etc.* (L., 1652), p. 4.

100. Williams, *The bloudy tenent*, p. 166.

101. In fact, Williams would apparently excommunicate persons who kneel during the Lord's Supper, who observe the Christmas rites, and who practice other "popish" superstitions. (Ibid., pp. 100-01.) But the punishment should be purely spiritual.

102. Ibid., pp. 110-16.

103. Ibid., pp. 169-170.

104. Parrington, pp. 71-72.

105. Preserved Smith, *A History of Modern Culture* (New York., 1930), I:491.

106. Williams, *The bloudy tenent*, Pref. (3-4).

107. Ibid., pp. 284-85.

108. Williams, *The bloody tenent yet more bloody*, p. 439.

109. Williams, *Queries*, p. 35.

110. Williams, *The bloudy tenent*, pp. 286-87.

111. Williams, *The bloody tenent yet more bloody*, p. 26.

112. Ibid., p. 28.

113. Williams, *The bloudy tenent*, p. 290.

114. Williams, *The bloody tenent yet more bloody*, p. 5.

115. Williams names four factions: the Catholics, the Anglicans, the Presbyterians, and the Independents. (Ibid., pp. 519-29). It is interesting to notice that his most damaging accusation against the Independents was based upon their intolerance in securing the ejection of Anglican and Presbyterian ministers. All men should be left free to preach Christ.

116. Ibid., p. 519.

117. Ibid., p. 522.

118. Williams, *The bloudy tenent*, p. 191.

119. Ibid., pp. 192, 193; Williams, *Queries*, p. 27.

120. Williams, *The bloudy tenent*, p. 200; Williams, *The bloody tenent yet more bloody*, pp. 246-47, 256-57, 260-61, 280, 292, 319, 353-54.

121. Williams, *The bloudy tenent*, p. 208.

122. Ibid., p. 145.

123. Ibid., p. 146; et cf. Williams, *Letters*, pp. 225-28.

124. Williams, *The bloody tenent*, p. 65; Williams, *The bloody tenent yet more bloody*, p. 21.

125. Williams, *The bloudy tenent*, p. 64.

126. Williams, *The bloody tenent yet more bloody*, p. 61.

127. Ibid., p. 9.

128. Ibid., p. 11.

129. Williams, *The bloudy tenent*, pp. 3-4, 142-43, 197, et passim; Williams, *The bloody tenent yet more bloody*, pp. 313-16; Williams, *Queries*, p. 27, et passim; Williams, *Mr. Cottons letter*, p. 77.

130. Williams, *The bloudy tenent*, p. 198.

131. Williams, *The bloody tenent yet more bloody*, p. 316.

132. Williams probably refers here to Fr. William Hartley, an Elizabethan priest. Hartley, a native of Nottinghamshire, was for some time a member of Saint John's College, Oxford. He was closely associated with Campion, and in 1584 was deported with him and other priests. Wood (*Athenae Oxonienses*) does not mention his subsequent return or death.

133. Williams to Endicott. Williams, *Letters*, p. 220.

134. Williams, *Letters*, p. 249. This letter, written while Williams was in England in 1652-1653, was addressed to Mrs. Sadleir, a daughter to Sir Edward Coke. Mrs. Sadlier's testy and orthodox reply was that she had read Taylor and had found the *Liberty of Prophesying* not to her stomach. "I say," she wrote, "it and you would make a good fire." (Williams, *Letters*, p. 252.)

135. Williams, *Letters*, p. 223, *et vide* "Letter to the Town of Providence" (1654-1655), ibid., p. 279.

Robert S. Alley

The Despotism of Toleration

The previous essays in this chapter have demonstrated the variety of attitudes expressed in the colonies on the subject of church and state. With the exception of Rhode Island, all of the original settlements accepted some form of religious establishment, along with restrictions on the free exercise of religious faith. These restrictions, to be sure, varied from the strict enforcements of Massachusetts Bay to the more lenient attitudes manifest in the middle colonies. But the principle of toleration prevailed as the underlying assumption of all efforts to deal with church-state issues. Research reveals no precipitate move toward religious freedom, but rather a moderating influence that called for greater inclusiveness respecting Protestants. The life of Samuel Davies, a Presbyterian pioneer who worked in Virginia from 1747 through 1759, offers an excellent example of this trend, one that maintained a clear bias on the part of the government against "religious excesses." In many ways Davies was a forerunner of the practices of the nineteenth century that created a de facto Protestant establishment.

Samuel Davies differentiated clearly between toleration and religious freedom, a difference drilled home unceasingly by Roger Williams. But unlike Williams, Davies believed that the state has the authority to tolerate religious diversity, and by logic, the right to restrict those religious expressions unacceptable to it. Davies went further—assuming that Virginia was a Protestant state, governed by Protestant presumptions. His quarrel with the authorities lay not in the area of freedom of conscience, but rather in the definition of tolerable religions. Thus, Davies wished simply to incorporate his dogmatic assumptions into government policy in place of the more restrictive ones practiced by a government that recognized a state church, the Church of England. Indeed, Davies did not object to that establishment, but wished merely to assert that the Parliament's 1689 Act of Toleration applied in Virginia, to the Presbyterians, in particular. On the other hand, he was convinced that the authorities should *not* tolerate Roman Catholics.

Davies believed in a Christian (read Protestant) state responsible for carrying out God's will. His religious convictions called upon him to assert the same things concerning Catholics that modern-day fundamentalists often claim about "secular humanists" and "main-line churches." Davies, therefore, is a paradigm for what is now described as "right-wing fundamentalism." Quite rightfully the leadership of this new wave of evangelicalism claims models in American history consistent with their practice. Davies's thought and actions may help to clarify the implications of this particular American tradition.

Davies's sojourn in Virginia was highlighted by two primary concerns. When the young Presbyterian representative of New Light theology moved to the colony in 1747, he was faced with an implacable church establishment, one that had successfully impeded the rise of Protestant dissent in Virginia for 140 years. A vigorous evangelist for his faith, Davies became the prime mover behind the application of legal toleration to dissenters in the colony. From his earliest sermons he abided by what he considered to be the rules of the 1689 Act of Toleration. He argued for and ultimately won (1759) his case that the act must apply in the colony since it was an act of Parliament.

Yet, Davies did not move to Virginia in order to make such a plea. His motivation was singular—to preach the Gospel as a New Light witness. His "call to preach" drove him to secure the right to do so in the colony. The Act of Toleration required dissenting ministers to obtain licenses from constituted authorities in order to preach at meetinghouses. Ever willing to submit to the requirements of the law, Davis applied for licenses. (Ultimately, he obtained eight.) He believed in an established church and found no fault with the Church of England in that role, as long as the law permitting dissent was observed.

The basis for this acceptance of religious establishment is found in the second characteristic of Davies's thought. For him enemies of the British nation were enemies of God. He identified Crown and Cross. Christ had died, he believed, for Protestant Britain. Thus, Davies found himself embroiled in political issues with the outbreak of the French and Indian War in 1755. In oratory anticipating twentieth-century evangelists, Davies warned that the French might win the conflict because God had determined to punish Britain for a lack of dedication to the faith. To be sure, the enemy in 1755 was not communism but Roman Catholicism; but, like his twentieth-century successors, Davies was confident that in the end Protestantism would triumph—in his case over godless Catholicism.

Britain was God's chosen nation. There was no fault with the system, only with people. Failing to view the world in relative terms, Davies spoke in absolutes, accepting war as inevitable until such time as the entire planet became Protestant. This world view had no place for the rights espoused by

Williams and soon to be expressed in calls for religious freedom. Davies believed that the state had the right to tolerate, or not tolerate, religious dissent. Further, he felt that God had ordained that Britain tolerate Protestantism, as manifest in the 1689 act, but that other forms of Christianity, Catholicism in particular, were condemned by God. Therefore, as God's chosen nation, Britain could not refuse toleration of Protestant dissent, but it must condemn error and heresy, that is to say, Catholicism.

Toleration became a means to an end for Davies. Religious freedom was not a right, but a privilege. Catholics, who were opposed to God, should not be tolerated. France was the political embodiment of Catholic error, and therefore must be opposed by citizens on moral grounds. Hence, Davies became the best recruiting officer in the colony.

Davies founded his thoughts on the subject of God's nation upon a familiar view of providence: ". . . . this world is a little territory of Jehovah's government; under the management of his providence: and particularly, that all the blessings of life are the gifts of his bounty; and all its calamities, the chastisements or judgments of his hand . . . . There is a set of little, conceited, smattering philosophers risen among us, who think they disprove all this, by alleging that earthquakes proceed from 'natural causes.'"[1]

Davies's clear conflict with the Deism of his age grew out of its rejection of primary causes. Davies, on the other hand, was convinced that the earthquake in Lisbon in 1755 was God's particular punishment of Portugese Catholics and their support of the anti-Christ, the Pope. God used natural events to punish and to throw "the world into ferment." He insisted, "These extraordinary ministers of his vengeance are generally these four: the FAMINE, SWORD, PESTILENCE, AND EARTHQUAKE."[2] Davies placed unusual natural events in the context of a gigantic struggle between good and evil, Christianity and paganism, Protestantism and Catholicism. Davies was concerned for the Christian State, a term he employed to describe Great Britain. It was a nation chosen by God and guarded by Him against harm. "It has pleased God to choose Great Britain out of the wide world, and to make her the object of his special care for many ages."[3] In contrast, Roger Williams refused to allow the term Christian to be applied to the state.

In sum, Davies believed in the British system and called upon people "to be loyal to the Hanover family in which liberty, the Protestant religion, and George III are inseparably united."[4] To the extent that he used the phrase, religious liberty meant to Davies only the granting of certain rights he felt were consistent with the system. While broader in his application of toleration than the Puritans of Massachusetts, Davies manifested a commitment to a theory of the Christian state that called upon the magistrate to act in the name of God.

The importance of Davies lies in his advocacy of a moderating principle that would support a broader Protestant hegemony. Already (prior to the Revolution) Virginia was experiencing an influx of Presbyterians in the west, and Davies's position was appealing to men like Patrick Henry. But the Davies formula was not applied by colonial authorities—even to Baptists, who, by the 1760s, were preaching a more radical brand of Protestantism. Even as it incorporated greater toleration into its policies, Virginia continued to persecute religious dissenters who insisted on complete religious freedom.

In the next decade, as Madison addressed the problems of establishment and religious persecution, he did not have to look across the Atlantic, or even to northern neighbor colonies. The conflict was homegrown. He had noted it in a series of letters to William Bradford shortly after returning home from Princeton at the conclusion of his education.* "If the Church of England had been the established and general Religion in all the Northern Colonies as it has been among us here and uninterrupted tranquility had prevailed throughout the Continent, It is clear to me that slavery and Subjection might and would have been gradually insinuated among us. Union of Religious Sentiments begets a surprizing confidence and Ecclesiastical Establishments tend to great ignorance and Corruption all of which facilitate the Execution of mischievous Projects."[5] After some comments on the merits of various courses of study, Madison returned to the theme of religious freedom with some of his most stinging prose, as he described the prevailing conditions in his home colony:

> I have indeed as good an Atmosphere at home as the Climate will allow: but have nothing to brag of as to the State and Liberty of my Country. Poverty and Luxury prevail among all sorts: Pride ignorance and Knavery among the Priesthood and Vice and Wickedness among the Laity. This is bad enough But It is not the worst I have to tell you. That diabolical Hell conceived principle of persecution rages among some and to their eternal Infamy the Clergy can furnish their Quota of Imps for such business. This vexes me the most of anything whatever. There are at this [time?] in the adjacent County not less than 5 or 6 well meaning men in close Goal [gaol] for publishing their religious Sentiments which in the main are very orthodox. I have neither patience to hear or think of any thing relative to this matter, for I have squabbled and scolded abused and ridiculed so long about it, [to so lit]tle purpose that I am without common patience. So I [leave you] to pity me and pray for Liberty of Conscience [to revive among us.][6]

Four months later, in another letter to Bradford, Madison informed his correspondent that there was some hope of redress for the persecuted religious minorities: "Our Assembly is to meet the first of May When It is expected something will be done in behalf of the Dissenters: Petitions I hear

---

*It is somewhat ironic that Davies left Virginia in 1759 to assume the presidency of the College of New Jersey in Princeton, and that Madison appears to have first experienced an understanding of religious freedom under the guidance of a successor to Davies, Scottish Presbyterian divine John Witherspoon.

are already forming among the Persecuted Baptists and I fancy it is in the thoughts of the Presbyterians also to intercede for greater liberty in matters of Religion."[7]

An 1810 history of Virginia Baptists by Robert Semple provides information regarding Baptist sentiments at the time. Quoting from minutes of a May 1774 Baptist meeting in Halifax County, Semple notes: "For three or four years, there had been severe persecutions against the Baptists, in many parts of Virginia. Letters were received at this association from preachers confined in prison, particularly from David Tinsley, then in Chesterfield jail."[8] The author repeats a resolution "entered into" at that time: "Agreed to set apart the second and third Saturday in June, as public fast days, in behalf of our poor blind persecutors, and for the releasement of our brethren."[9]

In April of that year Madison had written to Bradford: ". . . .the Clergy are a numerous and powerful body have great influence at home by reason of their connection with & dependence on the Bishops and Crown and will naturally employ all their art & Interest to depress their rising Adversaries; for such they must consider dissenters who rob them of the good will of the people and may in time endanger their livings and security."[10] On this same theme, Semple draws attention to an August 1775 meeting of Baptists:

> "It seems, that one great object of uniting the two districts at this time, was to strive for the abolition of the hierarchy, or church establishment, in Virginia. The discontents in America, arising from British oppression, were now drawing to a crisis; most of the colonies had determined to resist, and some were for independence. This was a very favourable season for the Baptists. Having been much ground under the British laws, or at least by the interpretation of them in Virginia; they were to a man, favourable to any revolution, by which they could obtain freedom of religion. They had known from experience, that mere toleration was not a sufficient check, having been imprisoned at a time, when that law was considered by many as being in force. It was therefore resolved at this session, to circulate petitions to the Virginia Convention or General Assembly, throughout the state, in order to obtain signatures. The prayer of these was, that the church establishment should be abolished, and religion left to stand upon its own merits: And, that all religious societies should be protected in the peaceable enjoyment of their own religious principles, and modes of worship.[11]

In July of 1775 Madison informed Bradford that he had requested an acquaintance at Princeton bring him two pamphlets, "An apology for the Church of England as by Law Established" by Josiah Tucker and "An Essay on Toleration with a particular view to the late Application of the Dissenting Ministers to Parliament" by Phil. Turneaux.[12] The following June Madison, a delegate to the Virginia Convention, was appointed to a committee to prepare a constitution and a declaration of rights. The dominant figure was George

Mason. Recalling those deliberations, Madison wrote in his "Autobiographical Notes" in 1832:

> Being young & in the midst of distinguished and experienced members of the Convention he [Madison] did not enter into its debates; tho' he occasionally suggested amendments; the most material of which was a change of the terms in which the freedom of Conscience was expressed in the proposed Declaration of Rights. This important and meritorious instrument was drawn by Geo. Mason, who had inadvertently adopted the word 'toleration' in the article on that subject. The change suggested and accepted, substituted a phraseology which—declared the freedom of conscience to be a *natural* and absolute right."

If Madison's memory is to be trusted, this appears to be the first occasion these two concepts (freedom of conscience and natural rights) were linked in his thought. And thus began James Madison's life-long struggle to secure and maintain freedom of religion for citizens of the commonwealth and the nation. Toleration, so decisively won by Davies in 1759, was put aside in favor of a concept that extended far beyond his theology and belief. In place of Mason's phrase Madison proposed the following: "all men are equally entitled to the full and free exercise of [religion] according to the dictates of Conscience." And he wished to add "therefore that no man or class of men ought, on account of religion to be invested with peculiar emoluments or privileges."

Madison realized he could not gain passage of the disestablishment provision at that time in Virginia, so he withdrew that portion in order to win the basic principle of religious freedom. As it finally appeared in the Declaration of Rights, the article read: "That religion, or the duty which we owe our Creator, and the manner of discharging it, can be directed only by reason and conviction, not by force and violence; and therefore, all men are equally entitled to the free exercise of religion, according to the dictates of conscience; and that it is the mutual duty of all to practice Christian forebearance, love, and charity towards each other." Historian George Bancroft described Madison's amendment to the Declaration as "the first achievement of the wisest civilian in Virginia."[13]

It would be another decade before establishment followed toleration into oblivion, but already those Presbyterians who owed their origins in Virginia to Samuel Davies were supportive of the Madison position. John Todd, Davies's successor, sent a memorial to the General Assembly in 1776, stating: "Therefore we ask no ecclesiastical establishments for ourselves; neither can we approve of them when granted to others."[14] And in 1777 Virginia Presbyterians affirmed: "Therefore, as it is contrary to our principles and interest; and, as we think, subversive of religious liberty, we do again most earnestly entreat that our Legislature would never extend any assessment for religious purposes to us, or to the congregations under our care."[15] The stage was set for the introduction of Thomas Jefferson's Act for Establishing

Religious Freedom in Virginia, offered to the General Assembly in 1779.

Until Samuel Davies insisted on the application of the 1689 Act of Toleration in Virginia, the establishment allowed no dissenters to worship freely. Davies understood the limits of that act, as well as its guarantees. After a decade of struggle, Davies successfully influenced colonial authorities to abide by that act of Parliament: In 1759 Governor Fauquier acted to satisfy Davies and the Presbyterians. At the time they neither asked nor sought anything beyond toleration. Moreover, the principle was clearly understood in the context of Davies's theology and it was employed against that background. The implication is unmistakable: Toleration meant acceptance of the concept of a Christian or Protestant state.

In arguing for the elimination of the word "toleration" from the Declaration of Rights, Madison intended to strike at the Davies definition of the term. Some years later Thomas Paine gave expression to the Madisonian position: "Toleration is not the opposite of intolerance, but it is the counterfeit of it. Both are despotisms. The one assumes to itself the right of withholding liberty of conscience, the other of granting it."

The evidence is persuasive that whenever persons advocate some form of Christian state or argue for the messianic role of the United States as God's chosen nation, there is a corollary, the introduction of toleration as a principle. And while the implementation may be benign in the beginning, the departure from the Madison principle of religious freedom as a natural right is replaced with the "despotism" of toleration.

A fitting footnote to the entire debate on the subject of toleration can be found in an address from French Jews to the French National Assembly on January 29, 1790: "America, to which politics will owe so many useful lessons, has rejected the word toleration from its code, as a term tending to compromise individual liberty and to sacrifice cartain classes of men to other classes. To tolerate is, in fact, to suffer that which you could, if you wish, prevent and prohibit."[16]

As will be evident in the next chapter, the Declaration of Rights signaled the beginning of the debate between those who advocated toleration, like Patrick Henry, and those who endorsed freedom of conscience, like Madison and Jefferson. Virginia proved to be, once again, the field on which the historic engagement took place.

NOTES

1. Samuel Davies, *Sermons on Important Subjects*, 4 vols. (London: W. Baynes, 1804-1810), III, pp. 263-64.

2. Davies, III, p. 261.

3. Davies, III, pp. 346, 370.

4. Davies, III, p. 93.

5. Letter from James Madison to William Bradford, January 24, 1774.

6. Ibid. Pennsylvania, under the influence of William Penn, had a much greater degree of freedom than did Virginia.

7. Letter from James Madison to William Bradford, April 1, 1774.

8. Robert Semple, A *History of the Rise and Progress of the Baptists in Virginia* (Richmond, 1810) p. 56.

9. Ibid.

10. Madison to Bradford, April 1, 1774.

11. Semple, p. 62.

12. Letter from James Madison to William Bradford, July 28, 1775.

13. George Bancroft, *The History of the United States*, 6 vols. (New York, 1883-1885), IV:416-17.

14. William H. Foote, *Sketches of Virginia: Historical and Biographical*, first series (Philadelpha: William S. Martien, 1850), p. 324.

15. Foote, p. 327

16. Edward F. Humphrey, *Nationalism and Religion in America, 1774-1789* (New York: Russell & Russell, 1965), p. 404. (First published in 1924.)

PART V

Madison and the Virginia Struggle

The essay by Marvin K. Singleton brings the light of modern historical inquiry to the period in Virginia life when Madison became fully involved in the practical struggle for religious freedom. It provides an important correction to the earlier effort of H. J. Eckenrode, *Separation of Church and State in Virginia*. However, in order to understand the context of the critical debates respecting freedom, assessment, and incorporation, a brief introduction dealing with the early history of church-state relations in Virginia has been included.

Robert S. Alley

The Church of England and Virginia Politics

The Church of England was the established religious organization from the founding of the colony in 1607. By a 1643 law the governor, or, in his absence, the lieutenant governor, was made head of the church in Virginia. Toward the end of the seventeenth century Governor Spotswood, in a letter to St. Anne's Parish, stated: "As the king is the sovreign of these plantations, so is he vested with the right of patronage of all ecclesiastical benefices, unless, when it appears that he has by other apt words granted the same away."[1]

In exercising this right, Spotswood came into conflict with James Blair, the first holder of the position of commissary. In that office Blair served as the deputy of the Bishop of London. There was no bishop in the colonies, so the direction of the church devolved upon the London bishop. Blair, in an effort to establish his own credentials vis-à-vis those of the governor, insisted that the determination of who should be minister for a given church lay not with the executive, but with the local vestry. Only after six months of inaction could the governor step in, according to Blair.[2] The commissary won his point and the vestries assumed a considerable authority. This victory placed the minister almost completely in the hands of a group of twelve men, "a local oligarchy of hard-fisted and often ignorant squires, who were interested in keeping expenses down. . . . Vestries were accustomed to ruling the ministers and the Assembly to ruling the church in general."[3] Acceptance of this condition is demonstrated by an act of the assembly in 1727 that fixed the salary of the clergy at 16,000 pounds of tobacco per year and required that the vestry provide a glebe of 200 acres for the minister.[4]

Later events show that Blair created conditions in which clergy were placed at the mercy of vestries, which were often composed of men who had little interest in the church or often espoused dissenting religious views. In 1748 the Reverend Mr. William Kay sued his vestry for nonpayment of

153

salary. The vestry was ordered by the court to pay, thus undermining the power these bodies had won earlier. The assembly sought to clarify the matter with an act "for the protection of the clergy" that granted the vestry nearly total control over the clergy. Governor Dinwiddie, in 1752, noted that the act took away patronage from the Crown. In writing to the Bishop of London, Dinwiddie commented: "Thus by the Laws of this Country the patronage of the Crown is utterly destroyed, and I am afraid any attempt to recover the right would be attended with bad consequences."[5]

Governor Dinwiddie believed that failure to restore jurisdiction to the Crown in these matters would result not only in general defection, but would also encourage dissenters who "begin greatly to increase."[6] The act was allowed to stand, however, in 1759 the Bishop of London wrote that no sooner were the vestries in possession of the patronage than they sought to be "absolute masters" of the clergy. He described assembly acts as making "a present to the vestry of the maintenance of the clergy, the jurisdiction of the Bishop, and the supremacy and rights of the Crown."[7] An example was a 1755 act of the assembly to allow the vestries to pay clergy in money instead of tobacco. The justification was a short supply of tobacco.

That action of the assembly was challenged by the Commissary, William Robinson, and in 1759 the Crown disallowed it and a similar act of 1758. Governor Fauquier called the king's disallowance a repeal of specific acts. The Reverend James Maury, contending that the Crown had disallowed not merely an act but the right of the vestry to alter salaries, brought suit against his vestry for damages. In 1763 a court, agreeing with Maury, ruled that he was entitled to recover damages from the vestry and his case was submitted to a local jury for determination of amount. It was at this juncture that Patrick Henry made his appearance in the famous "Parsons' Cause" and asserted that while the royal disallowance was legal, it was also tyrannical.[8] The jury was described by the commissary as "ignorant low-bred persons & seemed picked for the purpose, being chiefly composed of such as are known here under the denomination of 'new lights."[9]

Persuaded by Henry's arguments, the jury brought in a verdict of one penny damages. Historians have generally agreed that in his plea Henry spoke for the majority of the entire colony. It was not a class struggle, because by then the governor, the assembly, the vestries, and the people all sided against the clergy. The Bishop of London had recognized this earlier when he wrote in 1759 that undoubtedly "the Anglican clergy, in appealing to the power of the king against the colonial will, had awakened an embittered sentiment."[10]

The people of the colony were coming to resent outside interference in local affairs. The established clergy, at the mercy of the vestries, sought relief and the only source for it was outside Virginia. An appeal to London, no matter how justified, brought the ire of an aroused citizenry. Dissent, meanwhile, became identified with colonial interests and thus developed popular favor. The established church found itself in opposition to the entire governmental structure of Virginia. The church had appealed to England at precisely the wrong time. The clergy's position with respect to the mother country created even more difficulty as the Revolution approached. It was this peculiar complication, stemming in large part from the failure of the church to place a bishop in the colonies, that provided a particular opportunity for those who advocated greater freedom for religious dissent.

Madison had first responded to persecution of religious dissent in his letters to William Bradford in 1774. It was a persecution carried out in the name of the Anglican church. In spite of popular sentiment against the established clergy, along with the end to persecution, basic issues concerned with church/state relations lay dormant in the legislature until the spring of 1784. Then, as a member of the Virginia Assembly, Madison could do more than merely ask Bradford "to pity me and pray for Liberty of Conscience to revive among us."

In a letter to Thomas Jefferson on May 15, 1784 Edmund Randolph indicated that five questions would occupy the assembly for the spring session: "1. a general assessment; 2. restitution of British property; 3. payment of British debts; 4. the introduction of a stamp-act, under a less offensive name; 5. the making of Norfolk, the only port of entry and clearance."[11] He added: "The first has Henry for its patron in private; but whether he will hazard himself in public cannot be yet ascertained."

Henry, along with Richard Henry Lee, did become the chief advocates of assessment, "a proposition to make every man contribute something to the support of the Christian religion, as the only sure basis of public and private morality."[12] Lee remarked at the time: "Refiners may weave reason into as fine a web as they please, but the experience of all times shows religion to be the guardian of morals; and he must be a very inattentive observer in our country who does not see that avarice is accomplishing the destruction of religion for want of legal obligation to contribute something to its support."[13] This is the context for Marvin Singleton's historical account.

NOTES

1. William Meade, *Old Churches, Ministers and Families of Virginia* (Philadelphia: J. B. Lippincott, 1857), II, Appendix

2. William S. Perry, *Historical Collections Relating to the American Colonial Church* (Hartford: Church Press, 1870), I:226.

3. H. J. Eckenrode, *Separation of Church and State in Virginia* (Richmond, 1910), pp. 13, 20-21.

4. William W. Hening, *Statutes at Large* (Philadelphia, 1823), p. 204.

5. Perry, p. 400.

6. Ibid., p. 395.

7. Fulham Palace Paper, 14, 652. Bishop of London to the Lords of Trade, June 14, 1759.

8. Perry, p. 497.

9. Ibid., pp. 496-98.

10. Eckenrode, p. 26.

11. William C. Rives, *History of the Life and Times of James Madison* (New York, 1859-1868), I. p. 563.

12. Richard Henry Lee, *Memoir of the Life of Richard Henry Lee* (Philadelphia: H. C. Carey, I. Lea, 1825), I, p. 237. Cited by Eckenrode, p. 74.

13. Lee, II, p. 51. Quoted in Eckenrode, p. 75.

Marvin K. Singleton

Colonial Virginia as First Amendment Matrix: Henry, Madison, and Assessment Establishment

I

A balanced chronicle of the events surrounding Patrick Henry's effort during 1784 and 1785 to achieve tax support for Virginia teachers of the Christian religion is presently needed. There are, of course, brief references to the assessment controversy in biographical studies of the individual participants in it, and the assessment tiff and its fruits are mentioned by historians who stress the "internal revolution" aspect of the American Revolution.[1] These sources, together with H. J. Eckenrode's account in *Separation of the Church and State in Virginia*, long appeared adequate; after all, here seemed a charming little tug-of-war in young Virginia won fairly by the side better endowed with republican virtue. Jeffersonians especially cherished the episode, not only because Jefferson's Act Establishing Religious Freedom was eventually passed in lieu of Henry's measure, but also because of the wholesome way grass-roots opinion affected the legislative process. But at the same time Eckenrode's analysis grew stale, the Supreme Court, by extending to the states the First Amendment ban on "establishment of religion," during the 1940s directed renewed and heightened attention to this phase of Virginia's past. Even Supreme Court justices have commenced supporting church-state positions by advancing versions of the assessment affair as they rule upon First Amendment cases.

This article first appeared in A *Journal of Church and State* VIII: no. 3 (Autumn 1966). Used by permission.

The relevance of Virginia history to an understanding of the scope and spirit of the First Amendment ban on "establishment of religion" was recognized by the Supreme Court long before the ban was applied to the states through the Fourteenth Amendment. Chief Justice Waite, faced in 1878 with the problem of construing the word "religion" as used in the First Amendment, in *Reynolds* v. *United States* reasoned that, since the word is not defined in the Amendment and is not otherwise used in the Constitution, there was nowhere more appropriate to turn "than to the history of the times in the midst of which the provision was adopted." The Chief Justice thereupon traced the controversy over Henry's tax scheme and its alternative, Jefferson's Act for Establishing Religious Freedom, because the lessons of that contest were vivid to the Virginia delegation to the Constitutional Convention of 1787 at Philadelphia and entered into their understanding of the Bill of Rights. The approach of Chief Justice Waite has been followed by the Supreme Court in recent decades. Justice Black, writing for the majority in *Everson* v. *Board of Education* (1947), took notice of Virginia assessment history and conceded its contextual importance because the provisions of the First Amendment dealing with religion "had the same objective and were intended to provide the same protection" as Jefferson's Act. Justice Rutledge, however, in a strong dissent joined by Justices Frankfurter, Jackson, and Burton, insisted that the majority had insufficiently weighed Virginia events of the 1770s and 1780s. The dissent set forth in some detail the assessment fight in Virginia, and copies of the key documents of the affair were appended. Justice Rutledge's historical analysis, which is admitted to have borne fruit in at least one subsequent case,[2] has become the focal point of continuing debate among church-state disputants; and the debate itself reveals the need for a balanced narrative to which the judiciary, and other persons wishing to urge or deny historical parallels, may conveniently address themselves.

II

By 1776, the Anglican Church, designated in 1606 as the state church in Virginia in the first charter to the Virginia Company, was thoroughly on the defensive. The seat of authority for Anglicanism was England; and its prerogatives became for colonial patriots an unpopular reminder of English rule, in contrast to the Congregational establishments in New England, which had associated themselves with the patriot cause. That the Episcopal Church was sometimes considered a nucleus for loyalist sympathies would alone have inclined delegates to the Virginia Assembly to consider in 1776 its disestablishment.

But the causes of dissatisfaction reached back further in time. The Anglican Church had been privileged by the colonial administration in a variety of ways. There were franchise limitations based on religious grounds: in an act of 1769, recusants were denied a vote for legislative representatives, a denial which fed by the 1780s the under-representation in the Assembly of the western portions of Virginia, especially the Shenandoah Valley and Alleghanies areas. There were restrictions on dissenting ministers, who were not only unable to perform the marriage ceremony without paying a fee to the resident Episcopal minister, but whose very preaching was occasionally harassed by magistrate and gaoler.[3] Glebe lands were assigned for the support of the Anglican clergy, and tax monies were channeled to Episcopal vestry-men for assorted parish responsibilities. (True, there is evidence that vestry-men sometimes became dissenters without resigning their posts and pocketed vestry funds, but the General Assembly passed in 1759 an act intercepting this practice.) As the percentage of the population holding communion with the Episcopal Church dwindled, some sort of challenge had become inevitable.[4]

With these grievances in mind, the problems of the Revolutionary Convention and the General Assembly of 1776 are more easily comprehended. On May 15, 1776, the Revolutionary Convention, meeting in Williamsburg, named a committee to "prepare a Declaration of Rights, and such a plan of government as will be most likely to maintain peace and order in this colony; and secure substantial and equal liberty to the people." James Madison and George Mason were soon added to this committee. Madison, who had settled thoughts about the undesirability of establishment, sought an amendment to Mason's draft of the religion clause providing that "no man or class of men ought, on account of religion to be invested with peculiar emoluments or privileges." Madison, diffident about public speaking, asked Patrick Henry to sponsor his amendment; after all, Henry as a lawyer had pleaded effectively for dissenting persons, and his eloquence in the Two-Penny case was well known. Henry, however, did not uphold Madison's manifest intention to disestablish the Episcopal Church: and the Declaration of Rights, although it granted religious freedom as a right rather than as a privilege, left open the door for future assessment and tithing controversy.

When the Assembly met, on October 7, 1776, petitions from various sects asking disestablishment of the Episcopal Church were filed before it. The only notable resistance to disestablishment sentiment came, oddly enough, from the Methodists. The Society of Methodists, who considered themselves "in Communion with the Church of England," and who were formally to sever themselves from Virginia's Low-Church Anglicanism only by Christmas of 1784, memorialized the Assembly on October 28, 1776, asserting that "we are not Desenters" and praying that "as the Church of England ever hath been, so it may continue to be Established." But the Methodists failed to persuade. A "Committee on Religion" was appointed, with Thomas Jefferson as chairman, to consider the petitions and sift the issues raised by them. That these deliberations were fatal to the establishment is well known, but that the assessment question was expressly left open has not been sufficiently made clear. In the fifth section of the "Act for exempting the different societies of Dissenters from contributing to the support and maintenance of the church as by law established, and its ministers" is spelled out the postponement of the questions:

> And whereas a great variety of opinions hath arisen, touching the propriety of a general assessment, or whether every religious society should be left to voluntary contributions for the support and maintenance of the several denominations, and this difference of sentiments cannot be well accommodated, so that it is prudent to defer this matter to the discussion and final determination of a future assembly, when the opinions of the country in general may be better known: To the end, therefore, that so important a subject may in no sort be prejudged, *Be it enacted, by the authority aforesaid,* That nothing in this act contained shall be construed to affect or influence the said question of general assessment, or voluntary contribution, in any respect whatever.[5]

That this extraordinarily thorough statutory disclaimer has been overlooked has, as will be shown, borne severely on Henry's reputation; and its presence in the statute book suggests that the Episcopalians were not utterly without bargaining power, even in 1776. And, while between 1776 and 1779 the legislature repeatedly trimmed the privileges of the Episcopal Church (an act of January 1, 1777, ended enforcement of all tithe payments, and clergymen were banned by constitutional provision from acting as Assembly delegates), and several schemes for common assessment were defeated between 1776 and 1779, the issue remained very much alive. Not only had libertarians proven unable to secure passage for Jefferson's 1779 bill to establish religious freedom, but proponents of aid to religion remained able to point out that other young states were, as a matter of course, administering analogous laws, often with considerable rigor.[6] Moreover, that the Episcopal clergy were poorly enough off to warrant pity during and after the Revolution is conceded by all accounts: John Page wrote to Jefferson that

> Fontaine has been almost starved; Andrews has quitted his Gown, he says, to avoid starving. Nothing but a general Assessment can prevent the State from being divided between immorality, and Enthusiastic Bigottry. We have endeavored 8 years in vain to support the rational Sects by voluntary Contributions. I think I begin to see a Mischief arising out of the Dependence of the Teachers of the Christian Religion on their individual Followers, which may not only be destructive to Morality but to Government itself. . . . I have just read an outrageous piece against the Assessment, in which your Opinion is quoted and referred to . . . .[7]

Even the Presbyterians were not unaware that, "under the Smiles, & support of the Government," their church might "have more influence, and command a greater Respect" (as a 1784 Dinwiddie County petition phrased matters), and, deploring what they saw as a decline in morals during and after the Revolution, and representing religion as the necessary foundation of stable civil government, they so petitioned the Assembly.

Upon the subsidence of Revolution, and with piety becoming outspoken, Patrick Henry, well aware of his ascendancy in the House of Delegates, found it seasonable to press for common support; and, late in May, 1784, he broached his proposal with customary eloquence. Although his introductory speech in favor of his bill has not survived, some idea of its contents can be had from the jottings used by Madison to formulate a reply. Henry apparently cited precedents for compulsory taxation for religious purposes in other states, alleged the decay of nations which had eschewed such support, and sketched a black picture of Virginia's morality. Henry probably felt at ease with his subject: himself at least nominally religious (his religion is usually said to have been "sincere," though "after a Form of his own; for he was never attached to any Religious Society"),[8] he could appeal to the feelings of fellow believers. Perhaps equally to the point, he could count on a disproportionately Episcopal House of Delegates and strong friends in the Senate. In these quarters, Jefferson's notions of strict separation seemed "an untried experiment, and of very doubtful success"; and Jefferson himself, when first informed that Henry was a private patron of assessment and that he might publicly urge such a plan, was on his way to France to perform his duties as minister plenipotentiary. Jefferson, abroad during the entire assessment conflict, left behind no distinct political movement, and even his voluminous correspondence with his Virginia acquaintances conveys the impression that he was content to leave the problem in Madison's capable hands.

Henry's plan might have been threatened by Richard Henry Lee, who had fought with Henry for leadership in the Assembly and who remained influential there. But the assessment proposal found in Lee another supporter; and probably no force could have stayed passage of a measure favored by a Lee-Henry coalition had not Lee's absence on Congressional duty prevented such a coalition. Lee, writing to Madison, declared: "It is certainly comfortable to know that the legislature of our country is engaged in beneficial pursuits—for I conceive the Gen. assessment, and a wise digest of our military laws are very important concerns; the one to secure our peace, and the other our morals." Lee also claimed a "destruction of religion, for want of a legal obligation to contribute something to its support."[9] An ailing Edmund Pendleton delivered elegant but spindly speeches in favor of the measure. George Washington, sometimes said to have lent approval to the assessment levy idea, expressed his viewpoint to George Mason in terms very interestingly qualified:

Mount Vernon, October, 3, 1785
Dr. Sir: I have at this moment received yours of yesterday's date, enclosing a memorial and remonstrance against the Assessment Bill, which I will read with

attention. At *present* I am unable to do it, on account of company. The bill itself I do not recollect ever to have read: with *attention* I am certain I never did, but will compare them together.

Altho, no man's sentiments are more opposed to *any kind* of restraint upon religious principles than mine are; yet I must confess, that I am not amongst the number of those who are so much alarmed at the thoughts of making people pay towards the support of that which they profess, if of the denomination of Christians; or declare themselves Jews, Mahomitans or otherwise, and thereby obtain proper relief. As the matter now stands, I wish an assessment had never been agitated, and as it has gone so far, that the Bill could die an easy death; because I think it will be productive of more quiet to the State, than by enacting it into a Law; which, in my opinion, would be impolitic, admitting there is a decided majority for it, to the disquiet of a respectable minority. In the first case the matter will soon subside; in the latter, it will rankle and perhaps convulse, the State. The Dinner Bell rings, and I must conclude with an expression of my concern for your indisposition. Sincerely and affectionately, I am &c.[10]

John Marshall, a member of the House of Delegates during the first year of common support debate, voted in a manner which indicates agreement with Henry's designs. James Currie and Edmund Randolph likewise supported assessment.

The asssessment bill itself, although it was variously amended as the need for compromise arose, was at all times simpler than the former assessment plans submitted to the Assembly. The bill would require all taxpayers to "pay a moderate tax or contribution annually for the support of the Christian religion, or of some Christian church, denomination or communion of Christians, or for some form of Christian worship." A preamble sought to justify civil support of religion on grounds similar to those urged orally by Henry. A clause was eventually included permitting the secular taxpayer to designate his contribution for "the encouragement of seminaries of learning." The assessment would help make all Christian sects in Virginia "established" churches, even the Quakers and Menonists (Mennonites), who had little need and less desire for the assistance of the civil state in their simplistic devotions, and who viewed with skepticism a government which had, as late as 1776, considered a special tax on them because of their exemption from the militia.

Despite the over-representation in the House of Delegates of the tidewater counties, whose inhabitants were generally Episcopal in persuasion, and despite the notable personages willing to go along with Henry's measure, determined opposition soon arose. Henry had apparently over-estimated the potential support among the various sects to his plan. Madison recorded as follows the sectarian line-up: "The Episcopal people are generally for it (assessment) though I think the zeal of some of them has cooled. The laity of the other sects are generally unanimous on the other side. So are all the clergy, except the Presbyterians who seem as ready to get up an establishment which is to take them in as they were to pull down that which shut them out." Madison concluded: "I do not know a more shameful contrast than might be found between their memorials on the latter and former occasion." The initial Presbyterian support had stemmed, as Madison rightly observed, from clergymen drawn toward the idea of enhanced prestige and influence; but the laity felt otherwise, and the influential Hanover Presbytery was to perform an abrupt turnabout. The cessation of wobbling in Presbyterian ranks was partly induced by the securing of incorporation, late in 1784, by the Episcopal Church, the Episcopalians preventing similar status for the Presbyterian Church.[11] Nor were Presbyterians in the Assembly equivocal in their oppositon to Henry's plan. Such men as Zachariah Johnston, a Presbyterian from the Shenandoah Valley, balanced, to some degree, the Pendletons and Randolphs. Johnson, in an Assembly debate of the 1780s, declared that he would "leave his own church if it should become a State Church," and he gave credibility to his avowal by consistently opposing favors to ecclesiastical bodies.[12]

The Baptists, who had begun to proselytize in Virginia as early as 1714, and the "Separates" branch of whom had felt the brunt of the magistrates' interference with their evangelism, opposed with consistency the common support plan. Baptist petitions stated in plain terms their desire for separation of church and state, especially petitions from Madison's Orange County, a Baptist stronghold. The political drift of the "Great Awakening" found expression in these memorials by Baptists, whose preachers characteristically worked at some secular job during weekdays and thus did not need formal donative incomes. The Baptists were most numerous in the western counties, and they shared the Piedmont touchiness toward governmental regulation. Virginians living "west of the Blue Ridge" saw assessment as a 'half loaf.' As compared with Tuckahoe Virginia, they were new, poor, and radical. And indeed, the delegates to the Assembly were to vote on the assessment measure along sectional lines as well as sectarian ones.

The Assembly conflict deepened on November 11, 1784, when Madison and Henry delivered set speeches against each other's position. Beverley Randolph described the scene: "The Generals on the opposite sides, were Henry and Madison. The former advocated with his usual art, the establishment of the Christian Religion in exclusion of all other Denominations. By this," Randolph explained, "I mean that Turks, Jews & Infidels were to contribute, to the support of a Religion whose truth they did not acknowledge. Madison displayed great Learning & Ingenuity, with all the Powers of a close reasoner; but he was unsuccessful in the Event, having a majority . . . against him." Madison's arguments, many of them to reappear in his "Remonstrance," cogently drew upon history, and Madison could be an effective speaker to those who found themselves within earshot, but Henry's resolution passed on its first reading by a vote of 47 to 32. Madison and those who accepted his leadership on the question, including French Strother, Spencer Roane, and George Nicholas—men sometimes allied with Henry on other matters—had lost the first round. The vote showed a geographical pattern, with the western counties generally against, the middle countries divided, and the eastern and southeastern counties staunchly for, assessment. After the resolution had passed, the Speaker of the House of Delegates, John Tyler, named Henry as chairman of a committee to draw up a bill, and further strengthened Henry's position by selecting committee members favorable to assessment. On November 17, 1784, the bill for incorporation of the Episcopal Church was referred to another committee equally cordial to Henry, thus leaving his supporters in control of both crucial committees. Proponents of complete religious freedom took alarm: Jefferson uncharitably suggested in reply to Madison's plaints: "What we have to do I think is devoutly to pray for his death. . . . I am glad the Episcopalians have again shewn their teeth and fangs. The dissenters had almost forgotten them."[13]

Madison had a secular alternative to prayer: get Henry out of the legislature by having him elected governor. This uncontested election occurred on November 17, 1784, and Madison, whose satisfaction at this turn of events was augmented by his relief from Henry's interference with others of Madison's legislative interests, was one of three named to inform Henry of his elevation into a governorship which Henry had held before and was to hold again. Madison wrote to James Monroe: "Mr. Henry the father of the scheme is gone up to his seat for his family and will no more sit in the House of Delegates, a circumstance very inauspicious to his offspring." Madison's prophecy proved true: Henry, who was possibly less attached to his bill than had been supposed, had a full measure of indolence, a trait affecting his career in several ways. Whether he cared how much his absence might dishearten friends of assessment, or was too sanguine about the measure's chances, will never be known; but his leisurely ride homeward may have influenced America's development as much as Paul Revere's better publicized and speedier feat of equitation.

There remained, however, plenty of strife in the House of Delegates over the incorporation and common support bills: whenever the House was made a committee of the whole to debate these matters, the clerk prefaced developments by the phrase "after some time spent therein"—a phrase little used elsewhere in the *Journal*. The depth of the controversy is also shown in Madison's insistence that the vote counts be identifiable by voter, and other indicia of concern shortly appeared. On November 18, one day after Henry's promotion, a petition was filed from Rockingham County opposing assessment; and soon thereafter another such protest was received from Rockbridge: resistance to the "half-loaf" had begun. By December 4, 1784, Madison could declare the bill's fate "very uncertain," despite compromises in the wording of the bill made before the second reading and despite approval for a third reading on December 2.

The floor tactics used by Madison to delay action on the assessment can be in part surmised from events recorded in the *Journal*. Advocates of levy, such as Joseph Jones, an ardent supporter of common assessment, were promoted out of the House committee on religion with some frequency; and it is not unlikely that Madison and his lieutenants favored or engineered such happenings. On December 9, 1784, a committee was named to "inspect the enrolled bills," the members being mostly unfriendly to the support scheme.[14] Although these appointees were not numerous enough to do more than postpone action, they did effect a series of delays which held off the consideration of the third reading until the latter part of December. The incorporation bill, which received the greater part of the delegates' attention during mid-December, was passed on December 22, by a vote of 47 to 38, with Madison voting in the affirmative solely to remove one of the main Episcopal arguments for common support—namely, their fear of being unable to provide for a ministry.[15] Despite Madison's tactical concession, the margin of victory was rather small, and assessment proponents must have been shaken. After two days of debate, Henry's assessment measure was engrossed, on December 23, by a mere two-vote margin. When the plan came up for its third reading on December 24, it was moved to postpone the reading until November, 1785. The motion passed easily, and Madison's side had won a temporary victory, a victory they promptly consolidated by securing passage of a resolution designed to take the question before the people:

> *Resolved*, That the engrossed bill, "establishing a provision for teachers of the christian religion," together with the names of the ayes and noes, on the question to postponing the third reading of the said bill . . . be published in handbills, and twelve copies thereof delivered to each member of the General Assembly, to be distributed in their respective counties: and that the people be requested to signify their opinion respecting the adoption of such a bill, to the next session. . . .[16]

Except for this resolution, Madison himself would not otherwise have sought to stimulate anti-assessment sentiment, but the Nicholas brothers—George and Wilson Cary—and George Mason, encouraged Madison to compose some sort of paper against the levy, since the petitions which would certainly be circulated for the bill "ought to be met by a remonstrnace against it."[17]

There were plentiful signs that a memorial by Madison would not be apathetically received. By the end of April, Madison observed that the assessment bill had "produced some fermentation below the Mountains & a violent one beyond them. The contest at the next Session on this question will be a warm & precarious one"; and George Nicholas, writing about the same time, concurred, showing that the "fermentation" could indeed, as

Washington expressed it, "rankle and perhaps convulse, the State": "I have been through a considerable part of the country and I am well assured that it would be impossible to carry such laws into execution and that the attempt would bring about a revolution."[18] In this context, Madison wrote his famous "Memorial and Remonstrance on the Religious Rights of Man," urging separation of church and state. The "Remonstrance" was sent to the Nicholas brothers by the end of June, and they circulated it in longhand form until printed copies could be struck off.

The "Remonstrance" stated fifteen arguments against assessment. Whether or not the arguments were, as Gaillard Hunt has said, "the arguments of a Christian," it is clear that "the deep religious feeling of James Madison is stamped upon the Remonstrance."[19] Whereas Jefferson, in his Act Establishing Religious Freedom, after some rather peripheral reference to the Deity, had written of the issue from the viewpoint of the "natural rights of mankind," Madison's essay emphasized the threats to religion posed by civil interference. Portions of his rhetoric suggest that Caesar is being described from God's perspective: "If this freedom be abused, it is an offence against God, *not against man*: to God, therefore, *not to man*, must an account of it be rendered." Such an approach did not, of course, detract from the persuasive quality of the pamphlet.

Lurking among the more universal arguments against assessment is an objection entirely local to the Virginia of 1785: the tenth reason given by Madison is that the bill, if passed, would tend to add "a fresh motive for immigration" from Virginia. Many Virginians were anxious to avoid accelerating the exodus into new western lands; and a good deal of political activity, such as Madison's work with judicial reform, and such engineering programs as Washington's work on behalf of river navigation, was in part directed toward the mollification of restive Kentuck. And although Madison's warning avoided direct mention of the distaste most westerners would experience toward any new tax, since such an unspiritual consideration would have undercut the lofty tone of the "Remonstrance," economic factors eventually figured into the public's verdict. Bad weather damaged crops from the Spring of 1783 until the Spring of 1786; and, in addition, prices for agricultural commodities dropped sharply in 1785. That the tax rates were found oppressive and that a shortage of specie further made payment difficult is indicated by the frequent references in the pages of the *Journal* to the "scarcity of cash and severity of the late winter" (1783-84) and to litigation showing many western hamlets one year delinquent in tax payment. Sheriffs were occasionally permitted by statute to collect taxes in kind so as to evade the shortage-of-specie plea. Indeed, one quaintly-worded petition from Rockingham had objected in 1784 to the assessment as a tax:

. . . for the Confirmation of which Opinion we shall Cite no less authority than the Great Mr. Lock who says "that the whole jurisdiction of the

Majestrait reaches only to civil Concernments and that all civil power Right and Dominion is bounded . . ." which is so Pertinent that we need not Expatiate on it Onely say that if you can this year take five Dollars from me and give it to a Minister of any Denomination you may next year by the same Rule take Fifty or what not . . . .

Given such opinions in any quantity, and Madison's "Remonstrance" would have been unnecessary; and indeed, even before the "Remonstrance" had made a widespread impact, voters expressed themselves on the issue by returning to the Assembly many of its opponents in preference to its identifiable friends. Competition for seats in the Assembly was sharper than Virginians remembered it as ever having been. Such worthies as Edmund Pendleton were defeated on the issue, while Madison's star was adjudged to have ascended.

Well publicized religious conventions were called to determine sectarian policy toward assessment. On May 19, 1785, the Hanover Presbytery met, and several laymen took to task the clergymen responsible for the previous Fall's pro-assessment petition. A vote found the Hanover Presbytery unanimously against assessment, and such an expression of judgment was likely to be carefully weighed by all the Virginia Presbyterians: the Hanover Presbytery, thirty years old in 1785, was the acknowledged leader of all presbyteries to the South and West. A Presbyterian convention at Bethel on August 10, 1785, echoed the Hanover policy in terms suggestive of the influence of Madison's "Remonstrance" and of Jefferson's bill on religious freedom; and the Bethel memorial as filed expressly supported Jefferson's bill. The Baptists, who felt the "Remonstrance" to be an eloquent expression of their own position on church-state matters, condemned the assessment at general meetings at Powhatan on August 13, and at Orange on September 7, 1785. By the Fall of 1785, other sects were to protest the levy, including the Quakers and the Methodists (now distinct from the Episcopal Church); and dissatisfied members of the Episcopal laity made felt their opinions.

A fat sheaf of memorials opposed to the general levy greeted the Assembly when it convened in October, 1785. Although petitions signed by about 1,200 pro-assessment citizens were filed, over 10,000 signatures were affixed to anti-assessment petitions. Most of these latter petitions reflected some of Madison's reasons for the defeat of the bill. The levy would "tend to re-establishment of the church and persecution," asserted some of the simpler statements; while more ambitious petitions were dressed out with historical allegations, such as the claim that primitive Christianity had best flourished under civil oppression and had promptly stagnated when given state aid. Others of the anti-assessment petitions, however, were premised on starkly secular theories of public morality. One such petition from Montgomery declared, in stilted rhetoric, that religion was inessential to good morals: "Cannot it be denied that civil laws are not sufficient? We conceive it cannot, especially where the Observance of what is right and wrong . . . [is concerned]. Ideas of right and wrong, may be derived merely from positive law, without seeking a higher original." And into most of these petitions of a secular tendency were salted references to the civic virtues of the Greeks and Romans.[20]

At the outset of the 1785 Fall session of the Assembly, it became clear that Henry's bill would, as Washington had wished, "die an easy death." The bill was referred to a committee on religion, a committee then dominated by Madison. Zachariah Johnston was named chairman. The bill expired without being brought back onto the floor of the House. Madison then diligently shaped the enthusiasm generated by the past year's pamphleteering into support for religious freedom as embodied in Jefferson's bill for establishing religious freedom, which had remained orphaned by the sessions of 1779. Jefferson's bill, enacted January 19, 1786, of interest here only as a reciprocal to Henry's bill, is well treated elsewhere.[21] Its passage, however, settled the church-state question in Virginia, except for certain vestigal traces of establishment removed by 1802.[22]

III

Henry's labor on behalf of assessment brought upon him little admiration from historians: one Episcopal church historian saw "opportunism" in Henry's bid for common support, and Eckenrode has labelled the bill "reactionary." It is true that Henry's measure, laid alongside Jefferson's bill for establishing religious freedom, could have been judged in 1784 as anachronistic, if not reactionary. But Henry's submission of the bill was in itself not necessarily reactionary or opportunistic. Henry, though looking backward, was looking backward only eight years, and the intent of the 1776 legislature to keep open the question of assessment was clearly set forth in the statute of 1776 freeing dissenters from Episcopal taxes. His retrospective view of the issue, though mistaken and troublesome, was not an unnatural sort of mistake to fall into during the 1780s, when the values of the Revolution had not yet fully jelled into principles of good government. Indeed, in fairness to Henry, it should be noted that some dissenters had, during the late 1770s, petitioned simultaneously for Jefferson's bill and for a common assessment. It might also be recalled that Henry had represented Hanover for a good part of his political career, and at the time he strove for assessment, some of the Hanover Presbyterian clergy had petitioned for state aid. And to the extent that his bill was prompted by Episcopal vestrymen or ministers, action so inspired might be foolish or unthinking without being opportunistic. Moreover, what "opportunities" still eluded Henry in 1784? That his Virginia political fortunes were amply secured is attested by his 1784—and earlier—demonstrations of an ability to step into the governorship more or less at will; and Henry's national ambitions were probably nil. In short, despite a certain lack of fixed principle evidenced by the contrast between his Two-Penny position and his assessment views, and despite some unpleasantly pettifogging ratification politics by Henry,[23] there is no merit in identifying him as a villain in a controversy already most symmetrical.

Madison's role in the assessment fight has been diversely evaluated by posterity. Eckenrode has asserted that Henry's effort to implement assessment was defeated "by the spirit of the age rather than the skill of [its] opponents." This judgment is inaccurate. Madison and his colleagues proved themselves astute in their management of the threatened levy. Without the resources of a party behind him, without the machinery of caucus, and without charisma, Madison handled well both parliamentary matters and crystallization of public opinion. It is true that foes of common support had several factors working in their favor. New tax proposals are likely to be cried down during hard times, and there is much contemporaneous testimony of agricultural crisis brought on by drought, depredation, and low prices. Nevertheless, it would be easy to overrate the economic element in the adverse public reaction; and certainly tax problems were not solely endemic to Virginia during the Confederation period. More important was sectarian religious pride, with individual dissenters recollecting indignities and affronts from establishment days, and sectarian self-interest, which could not descry a need for formal apparatus to collect funds for their clergy and thus could hardly see assessment as other than a nuisance. A third factor, even more amorphous than the economic and religious factors, was the outspoken presence of a frankly secular element, an element to whom it would be very hard to justify any theory of assessment for ecclesiastical purposes.

Whether the assessment story warrants being considered a touchstone to the First Amendment, or even to Madison's intentions regarding the scope of the First Amendment, will be disputed for some years to come. As Leo Pfeffer has pointed out, the rationale behind Henry's assessment bill—the "'police' or 'welfare' power" of government[24]—is central to many litigated disagreements over the proper relation between church and state. Militant church groups now press for state and federal concessions to parochial schools, church-related businesses, and hospitals, all under the claim that impartial aid to several religions is not a wrongful establishment. Strict separationists, invoking the spirit of Jefferson and Madison, take umbrage at purported "give-aways" under urban-renewal or anti-poverty programs. Spokesmen for a flexible approach, such as Paul G. Kauper, assert that "the use of a metaphor, like the 'wall of separation,' does not afford much aid in the solution of concrete problems. Nor is it profitable to attempt to determine the solution to current problems by looking to James Madison for an answer."[25] In some quarters the disparagement of Justice Rutledge's Madisonian *Everson* dissent has been brusque: Edward Corwin, and, more recently, F. William O'Brien, S.J., have expressed such viewpoints. The tenor of Father O'Brien's criticism is suggested by the following criticism of the Virginia

Supreme Court for the *Almond v. Day* decision:

> One may speculate on how this state judge would apply these decisions [*Everson* and *McCollum*] to a case involving the use by an ex-G.I. of his government grants at Notre Dame, Howard, Southern Methodist, or some other religious school. The lesson to be learned is that it is no easy matter for the Court to correct a mistaken interpretation of the Constitution. Unless the justices are willing to submit to unconditional surrender, their subsequent compromises and distinctions will not prevent the unwholesome operation of bad law such as that of the *Everson* "no-aid" principle.[26]

As against the Kauper-Corwin-O'Brien approach is that of Justice Frankfurter, who wrote in his scholarly concurring opinion to *McCollum*: "We are all agreed that the First and the Fourteenth Amendments have a secular reach far more penetrating in the conduct of Government than merely to forbid an 'established church'. . . . We cannot illuminatingly apply the 'wall-of-separation' metaphor until we have considered the relevant history of religious education in America. . . ."[27] Fortunately the present Supreme Court shows a continued willingness to weigh First Amendment—and other—cases in the light of pertinent historical scholarship.[28]

NOTES

1. As in John R. Alden, "Reformation in the States," *The American Revolution 1775-1783* (New York: Harper, 1962), pp. 150-63. The most helpful of biographical studies are those of James Madison, especially Irving Brant, *James Madison: The Nationalist, 1780-1787* (Indianapolis: Bobbs-Merrill, 1948) and Irving Brant, "Madison: On the Separation of Church and State," *William and Mary Quarterly*, third series, VIII (1951), 3-24. (I am also indebted to Professor John R. Alden, of Duke University, and Professor Stanley Kutler, of the University of Wisconsin, for reading and commenting upon the historical portions of this essay.)

2. *Illinois ex rel. McCollum v. Board of Education*, 333 U.S. 203, 68 Sup. Ct. 461. 92 L.Ed. 649 (1948). In *McCollum*, Justice Frankfurter made thoughtful use of Justice Rutledge's *Everson* narrative, which had included copies of Henry's Bill Establishing a Provision for Teachers of the Christian Religion and Madison's *Memorial and Remonstrance Against Religious Assessments.*" Justice Reed in his dissent to *McCollum* (92 L.Ed. 672-682) discussed the First Amendment issue partly in terms of Virginia history other than the assessment phase.

3. Despite some suggestions otherwise (as in L. G. Tyler, *Tyler's Quarterly Historical and Genealogical Magazine* III [1922], 78), the records show legal actions against dissenters undertaken until the eve of the Revolution (for a discussion of one of these, see Robert Brock, *Archibald Cary of Ampthill* [Richmond: Garrett and Massie, 1937], p. 122). The tranquility of Madison's Orange County was exceptional (*The Papers of James Madison*, ed. William Hutchinson and William Rachal, 10 vols. [Chicago: University of Chicago Press, 1962-1977], I, p. 170).

4. Jefferson estimated that two-thirds of the people had become dissenters at the outbreak of the Revolution (*Notes on the State of Virginia*, ed. William Peden [Chapel Hill: University of North Carolina Press, 1955], p. 158).

5. *The Statutes at Large . . . the Laws of Virginia from 1619 to 1808*, ed. William W. Hening (Richmond: Bartow et al., 1810-1823). (Richmond: J. and G. Cochrane, (1821), p. 165.

6. P. E. Lauer, *Church and State in New England* (Baltimore: Johns Hopkins Press, 1892), pp. 89, 91-93. Rhode Island, however, because of rumors in 1716 of impending establishment, expressly forbade any but voluntary religious contributions. See C. F. James, *Documentary History of the Struggle for Religious Liberty in Virginia* (Lynchburg: J. P. Bell, 1900), for a specious attempt by W. G. Howell to derive from British precedent the assessment mandate.

7. Letter of August 23, 1785, printed in *The Papers of Thomas Jefferson*, VIII, pp. 428-431; and see E. C. Chorley, "The Planting of the Church in Virginia," *William and Mary Quarterly*, second series, X (1930), 211-13; Richard B. Davis, *Intellellectual Life in Jefferson's Virginia 1790-1830* (Chapel Hill: University of North Carolina Press, 1964), p. 128.

8. Quotation from "Judge Edmund Winston's Memoir of Patrick Henry," ed. Robert D. Meade, *Virginia Magazine of History and Biography* LIX (1961): 41; and see William Wirt, *Sketches of the Life and Character of Patrick Henry* (New York: Derby and Jackson, 1859), p. 418.

9. *The Letters of Richard Henry Lee*, ed. J. C. Ballagh, 2 vols. (New York: Macmillan, 1911-1914), II, p. 304.

10. R. L. Hilldrup, *The Life and Times of Edmund Pendleton* (Chapel Hill: University of North Carolina Press, 1939), p. 208; *The Writings of George Washington*, ed. John C. Fitzpatrick, 29 vols. (Washington: U. S. Government Printing Office, 1938), XXVIII, p. 285.

11. Madison to Jefferson, August 20, 1785, in *The Papers of Thomas Jefferson*, ed. Julian Boyd (Princeton: Princeton University Press, 1950), VIII, pp. 413-16, 415. The petition from the Hanover clergy is printed in James, *Documentary History*, p. 126.

12. John G. Paxton, "Zachariah Johnston," *Tyler's Quarterly Historical and Genealogical Magazine* V (1924), 185-92.

13. Quotations from Eckenrode, *Church and State in Virginia* (Richmond, 1910), p. 85; letter of December 8, 1784, *The Papers of Thomas Jefferson*, VII, pp. 557-60, 558 (italics omitted).

14. *Journal of the House of Delegates . . . 1781-1786* (Richmond: Dixon and Hunter, 1828), pp. 30, 64, and *passism*.

15. *Journal*, p. 79. Madison explained his vote to Jefferson in a letter of January 9, 1785, in *The Papers of Thomas Jefferson*, VII, pp. 588-98, 594-95.

16. *Journal*, p. 82.

17. Gaillard Hunt, "James Madison and Religious Liberty," *Annual Report of the American Historical Association for the Year 1901*, 2 vols. (Washington: U.S. Government Printing Office, 1902), I, p. 169; Kate M. Rowland, *Life of George Mason*, 2 vols. (New York: G. P. Putnam, 1892), II, p. 87.

18. Letters quoted in Eckenrode, p. 104; Brant, *James Madison: The Nationalist, 1780-1787*, p. 348.

19. Quotations from Hunt, I, p. 169; J. Frankfurter, *McCollum* 92 L.Ed. 661; and see Brant, "Madison . . .," *William and Mary Quarterly*, pp. 9-11.

20. Quotations from petition printed in *Virginia State Library: A Calendar of Legislative Petitions Arranged by Counties*, ed. H. J. Eckenrode (Richmond: D. Bottom, 1908), p. 7; Eckenrode, *Church and State in Virginia*, p. 110.

21. See especially *The Papers of Thomas Jefferson*, II, pp. 545-53; *Journal*, pp. 94-96, 148; Dumas Malone, *Jefferson and His Time*, Vol. I: *Jefferson the Virginian* (Boston: Little, Brown, 1948-1962), pp. 277-80.

22. The most important acts subsequent to Jefferson's Act for Religious Freedom were those of January 24, 1799, and January 12, 1802, *The Revised Code of the Laws of Virginia . . . .* (Richmond: Thomas Ritchie, 1819), I, pp. 78-81; and for the bitter dregs of disestablishment and a caveat, see *Terrett v. Taylor*, 9 Cranch (U.S.) 43, 3 L.Ed. 650 (1815).

23. Robert A. Rutland, *The Birth of the Bill of Rights 1776-1791* (Chapel Hill: University of North Carolina Press, 1955), pp. 166-67, 170, 192, 195; Brant, "Madison . . .," *William and Mary Quarterly*, pp. 12-17.

24. Leo Pfeffer, *Church, State, and Freedom* (Boston: Beacon Press, 1953), p. 98.

25. Paul G. Kauper, *Frontiers of Constitutional Liberty* (Ann Arbor: University of Michigan Law School, 1956), p. 143.

26. F. William O'Brien, S.J., *Justice Reed and the First Amendment: The Religion Clauses* (Washington: Georgetown University Press, 1958), p. 184.

27. 92 L.Ed. 659-669, 659-660.

28. For example, in *Garrison v. Louisiana*, 379 U.S. 64, 85 Sup.Ct. 209, 13 L.Ed. 125 (1964), Justices Black and Douglas make firm use of Irving Brant's "Seditious Libel: Myth and Reality," *New York University Law Review* XXXIX (1964): 1-19, in concurring with a decision holding that a criminal defamation statute of Louisiana was void for violating First Amendment safeguards. The concept of "establishment," like that of "bill of attainder" (see *United States v. Brown*, 381 U.S. 437, 85 Sup.Ct. 1707, 14 L.Ed.2d 484 [1965]), must ultimately be defined and applied in the light of historical wisdom: overemphasis on short-term anti-intellectual "tests" ought to be avoided in the First Amendment area.

PART VI

James Madison's Religion

The subject of Madison's religion has seldom been addressed by scholars, largely because he recorded so little of his religious sentiments. Yet his education at Princeton under the direction of President John Witherspoon, Presbyterian divine and signer of the Declaration of Independence, challenges the curious mind. And Madison whets the appetite of the researcher with just enough references to religious thinkers with whom he became acquainted during his college years. Further, the knowledge that Madison displayed concerning church history, particularly in the *Memorial*, suggests careful reading in that subject. In the essay that follows, Ralph Ketcham, who has written the most recent biography of Madison, explores the religion of Madison with a thoroughness that casts considerable light on a shadowy area in his thought.

Ralph L. Ketcham

James Madison and Religion
A New Hypothesis

Two factors, both largely circumstantial, have been principally responsible for the most common notions about the relationship of James Madison to religion. The first is that Madison was extremely reticent about expressing his ideas on matters of faith and personal conviction. In all his voluminous correspondence, public speeches, and miscellaneous papers, there are almost no references to his religious beliefs. Hence, the assumption has been widespread that Madison cared little about matters of religion. Secondly, Madison had always appeared deep in the shadow of Thomas Jefferson, and has thus acquired a comprehensive Jeffersonian coloration. In the field of religion it is therefore often assumed, in spite of almost no explicit evidence, that Madison shared Jefferson's varying degrees of deism and skepticism. But, as Adrienne Koch has pointed out in her *Jefferson and Madison: the Great Collaboration*, Madison had a brilliant mind of his own, and in no sense was he Jefferson's satellite or sycophant in matters of philosophy or conviction.

A serious effort to discover the reality of Madison's relationship to religion quickly runs afoul of his effective efforts to obscure this aspect of his life. But enough evidence is available to justify a new series of hypotheses about Madison's religion. Admittedly, the discoverable facts are not conclusive and the traditional assumptions cannot be proven erroneous, but a fresh approach is warranted in the light of new evidence, and is helpful in explaining some otherwise curious aspects of Madison's well-known public career.

In the midst of Madison's voluminous correspondence concerning the tariff debate, judicial review, nullification, and other matters which com-

This article first appeared in the *Journal of the Presbyterian Historical Society* 38: no. 2 (June 1960). Used by permission.

manded attention during his retirement, there appears an interesting letter responding to a request for Madison's opinion of a pamphlet claiming to prove, *a priori*, the existence of God. Following his customary denial of any particular insight or scholarship concerning the question asked, Madison proceeded to state that,

> . . . the belief in a God All Powerful, wise and good, is so essential to the moral order of the World and to the happiness of man, that arguments which enforce it cannot be drawn from too many sources. . . .
>
> But whatever effect may be produced on some minds by the more abstract train of ideas which you so strongly support, it will probably always be found that the course of reasoning from the effect to the cause, "from Nature to Nature's God," will be the more universal and more persuasive application.
>
> The finiteness of the human understanding betrays itself on all subjects, but more especially when it contemplates such as involve infinity. What may safely be said seems to be, that the infinity of time and space forces itself on our conception, a limitation of either being inconceivable; that the mind prefers at once the idea of a self-existing cause to that of an infinite series of cause and effect, which augments, instead of avoiding the difficulty; and that it finds more facility in assenting to the self-existence of an invisible cause possessing infinite power, wisdom and goodness, than to the self-existence of the universe, visibly destitute of these attributes, and which may be the effect of them. In this comparative facility of conception and belief, all philosophical reasoning on the subject must perhaps terminate.[1]

These few sentences, written in his seventy-fifth year, provide remarkable insight into Madison's religious and metaphysical speculations. Furthermore, implied in them is the essence of his view of the place of religion in society and the nature of religious experience. He was interested in theological and metaphysical speculations, yet was not devoted to any particular dogma. He accepted for the most part the eighteenth century assumption of harmony between the facts of nature and the rational ways of "Nature's God." He did not question the reality of psychic inclinations within man which led him to cleave to particular views of the nature and meaning of the universe. He attributed the ultimate rationale for religious aspirations to the finiteness of human understanding and the urge of men to know more-than-human insights. He understood the importance of religion to the psychological health of human beings and to the moral order of society. Finally, since the vital factor was inclination and personal conviction rather than dogmatic theology or ritual, the necessity for liberty of conscience and noninterference of public agencies in religious matters was clear. Madison's life from his first recorded activities to his death supported and illuminated these generalizations.

The Madisons, as was common among the Virginia gentry of the time, were adherents of the Anglican Church. Much that was congenial and enriching in Virginia plantation life was connected with the activities of this established church. As a vestryman, James Madison, Sr., participated in the practical affairs of the parish and took some mild part in the vigilance over public morality which also formed part of his duty.[2] One of the thorniest problems with which the elder Madison had to deal in his official position was that of enforcing Virginia statutes outlawing the activities of dissenting preachers. The decade of the 1760's was one of violent persecution of the dissenters, especially the Baptists who were very active in the Piedmont. They were stoned out of Culpepper County in 1765 and jailed in Spotsylvania County in 1768. The Madisons and their neighbors in Orange County had avoided direct persecution, but the controversy was there for the younger Madison, who was to be the future author of the First Amendment, to see.[3] The contradictory note is significant—the church life of his boyhood had been genuine and worthwhile, yet he had observed first hand the narrow-minded bigotry and cruelty of religious persecution. To assess the place of religion in the mind and life of James Madison, both sides must be understood. In a personal sense, what were his own answers to fundamental religious and philosophic questions, and in a public sense what were his views on the relationship between religious beliefs and institutions and society-at-large? Finally, since the personal answers foreshadowed his views on the latter question, it is logical to examine first Madison's own beliefs from which in some measure his more widely known arguments on the public matters follow.

Two sources stand out as preeminent in the intellectual background of Madison's religious views. First, the overall rationalism that saturated the theology of the eighteenth century and second, the rather rough-hewn Scottish "Common Sense" philosophy of the Rev. John Witherspoon, which was in one sense a reaction against rational theology and in another was a natural synthesis for the Enlightenment.

In the same letter in which Madison so succinctly expressed his religious opinions late in life, he referred to "the celebrated works of Dr. Clarke which I read 50 years ago," and, "The reasoning which could satisfy such a mind as that of Clarke."[4] The reference is to *The Being and Attributes of God* by the Rev. Samuel Clarke, published at London in 1704.[5] Clarke was an authority whom Witherspoon recommended to his students at Princeton as "one of the greatest champions of rational religion."[6] There can be little doubt that the kind of rational religion propounded in *The Being and Attributes of God* was fundamental to Madison's outlook.

In the generation following the publication of Sir Isaac Newton's *Principia Mathematica* in 1685, enlightened Anglican clergymen were quick to use the new natural philosophy in rational defense of their faith.[7] Among the foremost of these divines was "the celebrated Dr. Clarke" who published his Boyle Lectures of 1704 and 1705 under the imposing title *A Discourse Concerning the Being and Attributes of God, the Obligations of Natural Religion, and the Truth and Certainty of the Christian Revelation.* In a relatively brief space (119 pages), Dr. Clarke claimed to have proved as certainly as two times two is four, that there existed an eternal, infinite, and self-existing Being possessed of the attributes of omnipotence, perfect wisdom, and complete goodness. In so doing he explicitly denied the support of the Scriptures but rested his case solely on the kind of facts and reasonings which were sure to convince such atheists as Hobbes and Spinoza, whom Clarke used as his "whipping boys" throughout the discourse.[8]

The argument is a familiar one, and the method used is a curious combination of Aristotelian "black or white" procedure, and the principles of mathematical proof popularized by Newton and his fellow scientists. Clarke's whole proof of God rests on the assumption of the great chain of being which ultimately requires a first cause. Further assuming the necessity of cause-and-effect relationships in the universe, Clarke claimed to demonstrate the continuing power of the Eternal Being in the world.[9] Throughout the book added evidence of the need for a guiding hand is found in the great discoveries of the new science. The circulation of blood, the laws of mechanics, and the orderliness of the heavens are perpetually cited as proof of God's handiwork.[10] In short, "almost everything in the world demonstrates to us the great truth; and affords undeniable arguments to prove that the world and all things herein, are the effects of an intelligent and knowing cause."[11]

Once the existence of God has been established, the demonstration of his attributes proceeded with relative ease. In asserting God's all-powerfulness Clarke simply asked whether it is reasonable to suppose that a Being who created and controlled the Universe could in any way be thought limited in his power to do anything at all.[12] The proof of God's perfect wisdom was both *a priori* and *a posteriori*. "He who alone is self-existent and eternal, the sole cause and author of all things . . . must also know perfectly all consequences of those powers . . . and what in every respect is best and wisest to be done." Furthermore, "the proof of the Infinite wisdom of God, from the consideration of the exquisite perfection and consummate excellency of his works, is no less strong and undeniable."[13] In establishing God's moral perfection, Clarke took the familiar Enlightenment ground of defining evil intent as being "a direct choosing to act contrary to the known reason and nature of things," from which it is "manifest that the Supreme Cause and author of all things cannot but be infinitely removed."[14]

Two things about this argument are of special interest in understanding the mind of James Madison. First, Clarke gave expression to the obvious, if somewhat superficial, theological implications of the Newtonian world outlook. It was the kind of theology that largely carried the day in the first half of the eighteenth century,[15] and it is not surprising that in his youthful absorption of wisdom, Madison found great force in Clarke's argument. On the other hand, it is somewhat surprising to find Madison still referring to

Clarke's work as logically persuasive in 1825. In the light of this fact, it becomes apparent that Madison did not maintain his interest in theological controversy very long after his period of entrance into public life in 1776. He appears to have been uninfluenced either by Hume's devastating attack upon Clarke's brand of rationalism, or by Kant's reconstruction of the *a priori* argument concerning the moral order of the universe. In fact, Madison's reference to Clarke late in his life has a contradictory and almost nostalgic note about it, especially in the light of the statements he made in the final paragraph of his 1825 letter, and more particularly in view of the impact which Scottish philosophy made on him at Princeton and in the years immediately following his graduation.

When the infant College of New Jersey at Princeton was caught in the doctrinal struggle between the "New Light" and the "Old Light" Presbyterians in the years after the Great Awakening, it had the good fortune to look to the orthodox stronghold of Scotland for leadership untainted with clerical partisanship. In 1768, the Rev. John Witherspoon came to Princeton from Paisley.[16] As a student at the University of Edinburgh, he had been in the midst of the remarkable group of scholars known as the Scottish "Common Sense" School. Reacting against both the rationalism of Clarke and the Anglican Arminians, and the contradictory rational skepticism of Hume, the Scottish philosophers appealed to the "common sense" of mankind for "proof" that there was a God in Heaven and a moral order on earth.[17] On the floor of the Continental Congress, Witherspoon characteristically epitomized this philosophy when he said, "a person of integrity will pass as sound a judgment on subjects of this kind by consulting his own heart as by turning over books and systems."[18]

An examination of Witherspoon's writings[19] combined with his record at Princeton marks him as an incredible and perhaps somewhat overlooked figure in the growth of America. Under his leadership, Princeton was a hotbed of revolutionary patriotism, and produced one President, ten U.S. Senators, nine Governors, and nine members of the Constitutional Convention of 1787,[20] in addition to the usual steady stream of clergymen and business leaders. Witherspoon was always first and foremost a minister of God. His inclination, however, was to neglect theological disputation and emphasize sermons and lectures on the Law of Love and the necessity of good works in this world. Such sermon topics as "The Nature and Extent of Disciple Religion" (text, "Let your light so shine before men that they may see your good works. . . .") and "The Trial of Religious Truth by Its Moral Influence (text "Therefore, by their fruits shall ye know them") were typical of him.[21]

In his classroom lectures to undergraduates, Witherspoon was unusually open-minded for a clergyman of his day. His method in moral philosophy, which included such subjects as political theory, economics, and international law, was to summarize for his students the views of various authors, criticize them, and then suggest his own view of these topics. In ethics, Butler, Shaftesbury, Wollaston, Leibnitz, Hutcheson, and even the "infidel" Hume were presented and criticized.[22] Throughout, Witherspoon never lost sight of his basic point of departure, that of a Christian minister leading his flock toward the true light. The significant thing is that he felt the way to do this was to hold up to challenge by all opponents the tenets he supported. The notes taken by Witherspoon's students do not bear out the charge that he severely limited freedom of inquiry at Princeton.[23]

It is easy to over-emphasize the conjectures about the influence of books or men on the thinking of individuals, but in the cases of the influence of Clarke and Witherspoon on Madison there is more evidence than might be expected at first glance. In addition to the letter of 1825, already cited,[24] explicitly emphasizing Clarke, there is the combination of Witherspoon's use of Clarke in his pre-Revolutionary lectures and the presence of Clarke's books on a list of theological works prepared by Madison in 1824 for use at the University of Virginia.[25] The personal relationship between Witherspoon and Madison was unusually strong. Madison stayed at Princeton six months beyond his graduation, partly to pursue further reading under Witherspoon's direction. They were close and cooperating colleagues in the Confederation Congresses of 1781 and 1782. Upon the completion of Madison's work at the Constitutional Convention, Princeton conferred upon him a Doctor of Laws degree accompanied by warm words from Witherspoon: "as it has been my peculiar happiness to know, perhaps more than any of them [the trustees], your usefulness in an important station, on that and some other accounts, there was none to whom it [the honorary degree] gave more satisfaction than to [me]."[26] Finally, during Madison's very busy days in the first Federal Congress, he reported to Jefferson his disappointment at not finding Witherspoon at Princeton, where he had gone especially to see "the old Doctor."[27] That Clarke and Witherspoon were far more than casual influences upon Madison would seem to be beyond doubt.

Certainly there is much of the ideas of these two men in the thought and writings of Madison. His expressions of adherence to the rational religious ideas of Clarke are countless. In the Virginia address of 1799 he argued that a free press "dispelled the clouds which long encompassed religion" and disclosed its "genuine lustre." In closing this same "Address," Madison appealed to "the Almighty Disposer of Events" for assistance in reaching "the summit of happiness and glory, to which we are destined by nature and nature's God."[28] As Secretary of State, Madison dismissed one of Talleyrand's frequent allusions to bribery saying his suggestion "arraigned the justice of Heaven, and the order of nature."[29] His Presidential addresses and decrees contain the usual references to "Divine Providence," "Creator," and "Order of Nature" which are in the rational tradition of Clarke. This is not to say that Madison consciously had reference to Clarke in these statements— such expressions were commonplace in his time, and were in the ordinary vocabulary of most educated men. The point is that Madison had at the base of his religious thinking the rationalism of eighteenth century Anglican theology.

In a provocative review of Brant's second volume of *The Life of Madison*, T. V. Smith stated that Madison achieved a "spiritual amplitude unsurpassed on this continent." Furthermore, Professor Smith saw a "toughness of fiber" in Madison's outlook which he ascribed to the hard-headed Scottish Presbyterian ideas of John Witherspoon.[30] This suggests that Madison's outlook on religious matters was more complex than the almost naive confidence and simplicity of Anglican rationalism. He took seriously Presbyterian skepticism about the goodness and rationality of human beings. He understood that religion rested on more than sheer reason; that, in Witherspoon's words, "The being and infinite perfection and excellence of God may be deduced from reason, contemplation, sentiment and tradition."[31] Indeed, the very basis of religion and morality was a kind of combination of inclination and conscience which would guide men if but given the chance, although it was admitted that men often failed to hear or heed this guidance. The fact that this outlook was seriously at odds with the complacent rationality of Clarke did not seem to bother Madison. He appears to have been able here, as elsewhere, to sacrifice a narrow consistency to concepts which were practical and sensible to him.[32]

Madison's religious views become clearer in two further experiences which occupied his attention before he was completely absorbed in his public career. Both in his graduate study at Princeton under Witherspoon, and in the years 1772-1775 when he was at Montpelier suffering from epileptoid hysteria, Madison undertook serious study of the Scriptures and theology. There is positive evidence that he never intended to make the ministry his life work, nor was religious study the only topic that engaged his attention in these years. He simply was interested in basic theological questions, a concern which was heightened by his illness and fear of an early death. He wrote his friend William Bradford in 1772 that "a watchful eye must be kept on ourselves, lest while we are building ideal monuments of renown and bliss here, we neglect to have our names enrolled in the annals of Heaven . . . my sensations for many months past have intimated to me not to expect a long or healthy life." Following this Madison advised Bradford to "season" his studies "with a little divinity now and then."[33] During these same years Madison conducted family prayers which, once again, suggests no more than that he partook of the usual activities of religious people of the time. An interesting pocket-sized booklet entitled *The Necessary Duty of Family Prayer, With Prayers for Their Use*, published in 1768, survives in the collection of Madison's pamphlets at the University of Virginia.[34]

Evidence relating to the substance of Madison's religious studies during this period is scanty. Four large pages of closely written notes in Madison's hand on The Gospel of St. John, The Acts of the Apostles, and the Proverbs of Solomon have been dated 1772 by Irving Brant.[35] These notes contain Scriptural passages, the key ideas in them, and occasionally, digressions such as comparisons with Mohammedan practices, etc. The emphasis is on ethics, guides to action, and recognition of the humble virtues of Christianity, although there are some citations dealing with problems of sin and the after life. The notes on the whole indicate serious and systematic study, but are hardly thorough or extensive enough to suggest professional use of them.

That theology and church history were studied during this period is substantiated by Jefferson's request to Madison to compile a list of theological books for the University of Virginia, since he knew that Madison had undertaken extensive study at one time of that subject. There is no other time in Madison's career when he either had the time or faintly suggested that he was making such a study, although his continued interest in religious study is indicated by a request to a friend in London in 1821 for a book entitled *The Apocryphal New Testament Translated from the Original Tongues*.[36] Thorough lists of books on the first five centuries of Christian History indicate systematic study of that period. A request from Jefferson for speed in compiling the list caused Madison to simply list the well-known theological works of the remaining centuries. Again the impression is that of the serious and systematic layman of wide curiosity, rather than that of the professional student of divinity.[37]

More indicative than these activities of the state of Madison's religious and philosophic thinking during the 1770's is a correspondence which passed between Madison and his college friend, Dr. Samuel Stanhope Smith, in 1778 when Madison was a member of the Virginia Governor's Council. Although Madison's letters have been lost, the subject of the intercourse and much of his position in the discussion is clear. Smith introduced the exchange cordially:

> Perhaps I may prove a relaxation to you in the midst of other business to attend to a few metaphysical ones. I would not have troubled you on such subjects, if I had not known your taste for them, and your quick discernment of every error or mistake, and even of every hint that may lead to the *discovery of any truth*.

Obviously, Madison had a reputation as a keen debater of theological questions, and Smith was confident of the interest the young Virginia Councillor would have in his speculations.

The subject of "liberty and necessity" was then taken up with learning and vigor. Kames, Hume, and Locke were mentioned in an off-hand manner indicating assumption on Smith's part that Madison was familiar with their arguments. Smith stated he would "embrace the idea of liberty and will endeavor to explain it consistently with our experience. Nothing can be more fallacious than to begin with an abstract theory of divine prescience, a subject so far superior to human intellect, and from there to reason to the action of human creatures." Furthermore, Smith asked whether there was "any cause for the existence of a Deity, that one may not also assign to the existence of the Universe alone. I do not doubt his being. But I doubt whether it can be proved by speculative reasoning. Is it not a kind of indelible sentiment of the heart? . . ." The practical, non-rationalistic outlook of Smith is apparent. This kind of "Common Sense" outlook formed the philosophic language in which Madison and Smith conducted their speculations.

Turning directly to the question of liberty and necessity, Smith started with the proposition that we

> have an evident consciousness of liberty and freedom of movement. This is an effect which flows from the combination of a variety of senses, propensities, instincts and their balance in our constitutions. They mutually connect each other's impulse and however each alone might draw with irresistable force; yet altogether they produce a state of mind loose and free to move . . . . They are calculated to *rouse* and *animate* the mind and *set it in motion* but not necessarily *determine* its movement toward any precise point.

In short, Smith was proposing that argument for freedom of the will rested ultimately on the obvious consciousness of freedom which human beings feel, and further argued that the source of freedom in the mind was based on the existence of many conflicting tendencies, no one of which was strong enough to rule. The similarity between the microcosmic view and the "extended republic" theory of the tenth *Federalist* is strikingly apparent. Smith continued with a detailed analysis of how he thought the mind and will operated to implement this freedom, in a way which suggested that he, like Madison, had absorbed much of the thinking of Locke's *Essay Concerning Human Understanding*.[38]

In the next letter, Smith significantly acknowledged Madison's reply: "I have read over your *theoretical* objections against the doctrine of moral liberty, but *practically* you seem to be one of its disciples. I remember the manner in which you have formerly expressed yourself upon that intricate subject." Smith made it perfectly clear that Madison had countered his argument with the logic of Jonathan Edwards: "You will say that if the sentiments of duty are more pleasing than others they will have their necessary effect, otherwise they will make but a vain opposition against their fatal antagonists."[39] In other words, Madison's position was that of seeing the logical force of the rejectors of freedom of the will, but yet he retreated when asked to accept the legitimate, practical implications of that logic. Madison was as convinced as Smith was that, in fact, men *did* exercise freedom of choice, even though his logic could not prove it. This is remarkably similar to the position he took in his 1825 letter—rather than being absolutely convinced logically of God's existence, Madison simply asserted that the mind "finds facility in assenting to the self-existence of an invisible cause." Here is the end result of Madison's theological study and religious concern. The good "common sense" insight upon which Witherspoon had encouraged him to rely proved more convincing to him than the quasi-mathematical "proof" of the rationalist Clarke. Yet, he never abandoned what light reason could give to him. He had the "spiritual amplitude" and "toughness of fiber" to accept the finiteness of his human understanding. The experience of mankind dictated that both freedom and religious insight were real, yet the contradiction which reason forced upon him made Madison modest and tolerant rather than self-confident and fanatic in matters of conscience.

Recognition of this subtle position helps resolve some apparent paradoxes in Madison's career. He never became a member of the Episcopal Church,[40] yet attended its services and treated the clergy of Orange County with kind respect. He relished Voltaire's devastating jibes at religion, yet frequently in his career he had the cordial support of various religious groups. It seems probable that Madison had a deep personal attachment to some general aspects of Christian belief and morality. The importance of this personal faith both to Madison's relationship to religious groups throughout his public career, and in his crucial formulation of the American doctrine of the free conscience, form the remaining and more familiar parts of the story of James Madison and religion.

One of the most striking features of Madison's life was the warm feelings of mutual respect which generally existed between him and a wide variety of religious groups. There were exceptions, of course. Madison showed his suspicion of some of the less sophisticated sects in a comment to Bradford in 1774 which Hunt omitted from his edition of Madison's writings.

> I agree with you that the world needs to be peopled, but I should be sorry if it should be peopled with bastards as my old friend Dod [a clergyman friend from Princeton] seems to incline. Who could have thought the old monk had been so lecherous? I hope his religion, like that of some enthusiasts, was not of such a nature as to fan the amorous fire.[41]

In 1814, Madison demonstrated his occasional Enlightenment antagonism toward clericalism in a bitter comment on New England's resistance to the War of 1812: "The greater part of the people in that quarter have been brought by their leaders, aided by their priests, under a delusion scarcely exceeded by that recorded in the period of witchcraft. . . ."[42] Hostility to "enthusiasts" and New England theocracy hardly amounts to hostility toward religion.

The record of cordial relationships is impressive. Madison consistently opposed anti-Catholic prejudices. During a Congressional debate over naturalization in 1795, a Massachusetts Representative ridiculed certain tenets of the Catholic religion, to which Madison replied that he "did not approve the ridicule attempted to be thrown out on Roman Catholics. In their religion there was nothing inconsistent with the purest Republicanism. . . . Americans had no right to ridicule Catholics. They had, many of them, proved good citizens during the Revolution."[43] He was similarly cordial to Jews in America and wrote occasionally to members of that religion expressing his respect for their fortitude and patriotic attachment to the United States. In 1818 an eminent American Jew wrote Madison that his co-religionists owed many of the blessings they enjoyed in America to Madison and his colleagues.[44] When the Bill of Rights was before Congress, Madison wrote to Washington that "one of the principal leaders of the Baptists lately sent me word that the amendment had entirely satisfied the disaffected of his Sect. . . ."[45] Finally, among the phamphlets Madison left to the University of Virginia, there are sermons sent to Madison by preachers or their friends, tracts dealing with various phases of theological controversy, and even some writings of the English Methodist leader John Wesley.[46] Madison's tolerant, sympathetic, and interested attitude toward religious questions and institutions was recurrent and consistent.

An interesting story pieced together by Lyman Butterfield illuminates most graphically the mutually fruitful relationship that often existed between Madison and the powerful religious sects that sprouted all over America during the years of his public career. It is the story of Elder John Leland, a Baptist evangelist who preached in the Virginia Piedmont from 1776 to 1791, after which he continued his activities in New England for another forty years, never wavering from his staunch support of the Jeffersonian Party, to which he had been converted in Orange County under Madison's influence.[47]

Like most Virginia dissenters, Leland was a vigorous supporter of separation of church and state. During the fight over religious assessments in 1784 and 1785, Leland violently opposed to the assessment, was a lobbyist in Richmond where he no doubt worked with Madison, who during this period wrote the *Memorial and Remonstrance* opposing any connection between church and state. Leland's devotion to the principle of separation was so intense that his first reaction to the Federal Constitution of 1787 was to favor rejection because it neglected the vital question of religious freedom. As the foremost leader of one of the largest sects in Virginia at the time,[48] his influence was highly significant. A letter from Joseph Spencer, a Baptist friend in Orange County, to Madison just before Madison left for home to campaign for election to the Virginia Convention of 1788, urged him to stop and see Leland to dissuade him from his opposition to the Constitution. The meeting took place between February 20-28, 1788. Madison convinced Leland that the Constitution was not hostile to religious freedom, and Leland re-enforced Madison's willingness to support an amendment explicitly guaranteeing that freedom. Madison, with Leland's full support, won election to both the 1788 Convention and to the First Federal Congress.

The tie between Leland and Madison grew. Leland corresponded with

Washington attesting to Madison's political sagacity, and engaged in political activity on Madison's behalf. After his removal to New England, Leland continued his vigorous Jeffersonian "politicking." The town of Cheshire, Massachusetts, where Leland preached from 1800-1808, voted for Republican governors by an average plurality of 200-2 during that period![49] This solid alliance between Leland and Madison was highly significant. Madison received important support in his fight for religious liberty. In the other direction, Leland "effectively transmitted certain fundamental tenets of Jeffersonian political thought to an inarticulate and growing mass of voters."[50]

The substance of Madison's doctrine of the free conscience is justly famous and has been carefully developed by many eminent authorities.[51] It was brilliantly and most completely enunciated by Madison in his *Memorial and Remonstrance against Religious Assessments* in 1785. In objecting to a bill to pay teachers of religion out of public funds, Madison stated that

> we hold it for a fundamental and undeniable truth, that religion, or the duty we owe to our Creator and the manner of discharging it, can be directed only by reason and conviction, not by force or violence (Virginia Declaration of Rights, 1776). The religion then of every man must be left to the conviction and conscience of every man; and it is the right of every man to exercise it as these may dictate. This right is in its nature an unalienable right. It is unalienable, because the opinions of men depending only on the evidence contemplated by their own minds, cannot follow the dictates of other men. . . . We maintain, therefore, that in matters of religion, no man's right is abridged by the institution of Civil Society, and that religion is wholly exempt from its cognizance.[52]

Madison then proceeded to marshal other arguments in support of liberty of conscience.

2. Since Civil Society itself had no right to meddle in religious beliefs and practices, certainly the legislature which is its creature, has no such right.

3. "Who does not see that the same authority which can establish Christianity, in exclusion of all other religions, may establish with the same ease any particular sect of Christians, in exclusion of all other sects?"

4. "Equal title to the free exercise of Religion" implies the right to believe in no religion at all, as well as the right to believe and worship as one chooses.

5. Civil Magistrates can neither be competent judges of religious truth, nor should they bolster civil policy with official religious sanction.

6. The Christian religion does not need civil support. Its truth and power are prior to human society and do not require laws in their behalf.

7. History records that "ecclesiastical establishment" serves to corrupt and stultify true religion, not promote its purity and efficacy.

8. History further testifies that civil governments do not need religion for their support; on the contrary, religious establishments had often served as oppressors of the peoples' liberty.

9. The assessment marks a first step in the direction of persecution and bigotry departing from the generous policy of offering asylum for the oppressed, and leads to "the Inquisition from which it differs only in degree."

10. Good citizens will be driven from the state if required to pay a religious tax.

11. Religious strife and violence will be encouraged by laws which meddle with religion.

12. "The policy of the bill is adverse to the diffusion of the light of Christianity." It sets up walls of separation between Christianity and regions of darkness, thus preventing dissemination of the light of the former.

13. An attempt to enforce a religious assessment, obnoxious to many citizens, will weaken the support for the rest of the laws of society.

14. There is no clear evidence that a majority of the people support the assessment. In fact, the burden of the evidence points in the opposite direction.

15. Finally the right of freedom of conscience "is held by the same tenure with all our other rights. . . . Either we must say that the will of the legislature is the only measure of their authority; and that in the plenitude of this authority, they may sweep away all our fundamental rights; or, that they are bound to leave this particular right untouched and sacred. . . ."[53]

The arguments presented in the *Memorial and Remonstrance* were an important part of the battle to enact Jefferson's famous statute establishing religious freedom in Virginia, a fight which Madison led and master-minded throughout. The Episcopalians, strong in the tidewater countries, and the Presbyterians, traditionally dominant in the Piedmont and Shenandoah Valley, had temporarily joined forces in 1784 to secure passage of a bill to pay teachers of religion out of public funds. Such eminent men as Patrick Henry, Richard Henry Lee, John Marshall, and Philip Barbour favored the bill. Madison, backed by the Nicholases, Archibald Stuart, Spencer Roane, and others, fought the bill with the arguments Madison summarized in the *Memorial and Remonstrance*. By making articulate the public opinion which opposed the religious assessment and by shrewdly sowing dissention between the Episcopalians and Presbyterians, Madison managed to defeat the bill and secure the passage of Jefferson's statute in its place.[54] Writing to Jefferson, Madison, in a rare mood of exaltation, stated that: "I flatter myself [that] this country [has] extinguished forever the ambitious hope of making laws for the human mind."[55]

There is no principle in all of Madison's wide range of private opinions and long public career to which he held with greater vigor and tenacity than this one of religious liberty. The strength of this consistency was heightened significantly by the substitution of the concept of freedom of conscience for the Lockean idea of toleration. The difference was dramatically stated by Thomas Paine: "Toleration is not the opposite of intolerance, but it is the counterfeit of it. Both are despotisms. The one assumes to itself the right of withholding liberty of conscience, the other of granting it. The one is the pope armed with fire and faggot, the other is the pope selling or granting indulgences."[56]

Madison's devotion to religious liberty stemmed in part from his repulsion at the persecution of dissenters in pre-Revolutionary Virginia. He wrote Bradford,

> that diabolical, hell-conceived principle of persecution rages. . . . This vexes me the worst of anything whatever. There are at this time in the adjacent country not less than five or six well-meaning men in close jail for publishing their religious sentiments, which in the main are very orthodox. I have neither patience to hear, talk or think of anything relative to this matter; for I have squabbled and scolded, abused and ridiculed, so long about it to little purpose, that I am without common patience. So I must beg you to pity me, and pray for liberty of conscience for all.[57]

The unusual vehemence of this plea makes it fitting that Madison's first public act of major importance should have been the substitution of the idea of freedom of conscience for that of "fullest toleration." In drawing up the Virginia Declaration of Rights in June 1776, Madison was instrumental in changing the draft proposed by George Mason to include the doctrine making complete religious liberty one of the inalienable rights of man.[58] In addition to being the main legislative manager in securing the passage of Jefferson's Virginia Statute Establishing Freedom of Religion, Madison, always using to good advantage the powerful arguments of the *Memorial and Remonstrance,* guided the adoption of the first amendment to the Federal Constitution.[59]

After the establishment of the Federal Constitution, Madison was unwavering in his support of complete separation of church and state. He opposed having chaplains for the Congress paid out of public funds, asking "could a Catholic clergyman ever hope to be appointed Chaplain? To say that his principles are obnoxious or that his sect is small, is to lift the veil at once and exhibit in its native deformity the doctrine that religious truth is to be tested by numbers, or that the major sects have a right to govern the minor."[60] On the same principle, he opposed government support of chaplains for the armed forces. In both cases he favored voluntary contributions for support of such clergymen as the members of the group desired. He opposed presidential proclamation of religious holidays, or if proclamation was necessary, it should be "absolutely indiscriminate, and merely recommendatory, or, rather, mere designation of a day on which all who thought proper might unite in consecrating it to religious purposes, according to their own faith and forms."[61] While President he vetoed bills to incorporate the Protestant Episcopal Church in the District of Columbia and to reserve public lands for a Baptist Church in Mississippi, both on the grounds that they violated the clause of the first amendment which declared that "Congress shall make no law respecting a religious establishment."[62]

This is one place in Madison's thought where he appears to have been absolutely doctrinaire in his stand. Religious liberty ought to be defined

> as distinctly as words can admit, and the limits to this authority [religious laws] established with as much solemnity as the forms of legislation express. . . . Every provisions for them [laws] short of this principle, will be found to leave crevices at least through which bigotry may introduce persecution; a monster feeding and thriving on its own venom, gradually swells to a size and strength overwhelming all laws human and divine.[63]

The vigor of Madison's advocacy of separation of church and state has sometimes led to the implication that he was hostile to religion, and felt its effect in society a pernicious one. A careful look at the record would seem to refute this implication. Madison made it clear again and again, as he did in the *Memorial and Remonstrance*, that the separation was as necessary for the vitality and salutary influence of religion as it was for the tranquility of society. It is no doubt true that Madison saw the primary defense of religious freedom in its status as one of the inalienable rights of man, but it is also true, and of considerable importance, that he saw that same principle as a great bulwark to the strength of religious sentiments.

In his lectures on Moral Philosophy, John Witherspoon was a consistent advocate of religious freedom, often citing in its support the dangers oppression presented to sound religion. "We ought to guard against persecution on religious account . . . because such as hold absurd tenets are seldom dangerous. Perhaps they are never dangerous, but when they are oppressed."[64] Although his remark about "absurd tenets" indicated that "the old Doctor" was something less than fully tolerant of views other than his own, it is to his credit that he had great confidence in his ability to uphold the correctness of his own convictions in the open market. That Madison shared this confidence seems clear from his words and deeds throughout his life.

In the debates over the Statute of Religious Freedom in 1786, Madison secured the defeat of any reference to Christianity because he did not want "to profane it by making it a topic of legislative discussion, and particularly by making His religion the means of abridging the natural and equal rights of all men, in defiance of His own declaration that His Kingdom was not of this world."[65] During the years of retirement at Montpelier, Madison received with his usual cordiality scores of letters and sermons from clergymen who always treated the ex-President with the utmost respect. Madison's reply to a New York City clergyman upon receipt of a sermon, illustrates this mutual sympathy:

> It is a pleasing and persuasive example of pious zeal, united with pure benevolence and of a cordial attachment to a particular creed, untinctured with sectarian illiberality. It illustrates the excellence of a system which, by a due

distinction, to which the genius and courage of *Luther* led the way, between what is due to Caesar and what is due God, best promotes the discharge of *both* obligations. . . . A mutual independence is found most friendly to practical religion, to social harmony, and to political prosperity.[66]

The Board of Visitors of the University of Virginia, of which Madison was a member, resolved that "Should the religious sects of this state, or any of them, establish within or adjacent to, the precincts of the University, schools for instruciton in the religion of their sect, the students of the University will be free, and expected to attend worship at the establishment of their respective sects. . . . "[67]

What he considered to be the blessings of the separation of church and state in Virginia was a source of great satisfaction to Madison as he viewed the history of his native state. In answer to a request for information on this account, Madison wrote,

That there had been an increase of religious instruction since the Revolution can admit of no question. . . . The old churches built under the establishment at public expense have in many instances gone to ruin, or are in a very delapidated state, owing chiefly to a desertion of the flocks to other worships . . . among the other sects, meeting houses have multiplied and continue to multiply; tho' in general they are of the plainest and cheapest sort. But neither the number nor style of the religious edifices is a true measure of the state of religion. Religious instruction is now diffused throughout the community by preachers of every sect. . . . On a general comparison of the present and former times, the balance is certainly and vastly on the side of the present, as to the number of religious teachers, the zeal which activates them, the purity of their lives, and the attendance of the people on their instructions. It was the Universal opinion of the century preceding the last, that Civil Government could not stand without the prop of a Religious establishment and that the Christian religion itself, would perish if not supported by a legal provision for its clergy. The experience of Virginia conspicuously corroborates the disproof of both opinions. the Civil Government, tho' bereft of everything like an associated hierarchy, possesses the requisite stability. . . . Whilst the number, the industry and the morality of the Priesthood, and the devotion of the people have been manifestly increased by the total separation of church and state.[68]

Certainly Madison's greatest contribution to the development of civil liberties in the United States had its roots in both his devotion to the freedom of the human mind and in his concern for the vitality of religious sentiment in the community at large.

In addition to feeling that religious liberty served many purposes, Madison also applied his inevitable principle of dispersal of power to his view of the place of religion in society. He wrote Bradford in 1774.

If the Church of England had been established . . . in all the northern colonies as it has been among us here, and uninterrupted tranquillity had prevailed throughout the continent, it is clear to me that slavery and subjection might and would have gradually insinuated among us. Union of religious sentiments begets a surprising confidence, and ecclesiastical establishments tend to great ignorance and corruption; all of which facilitate the execution of mischievous projects.[69]

In his fight against assessments, Madison reported to Jefferson that the jealousy of the Presbyterians and Episcopalians was helpful. "I am far from being sorry for it, as a coalition between them could alone endanger our religious rights. . . ."[70] In the Virginia Convention of 1788, Madison, urging adoption of the Federal Constitution, asked,

Is a Bill of Rights a security for religion? If there were a majority of one sect, a bill of rights would be a poor protection for liberty. . . . Freedom arises from a multiplicity of sects, which pervades America, and which is the best and only security for religious liberty in any society. For where there is such a variety of sects, there cannot be a majority of any one sect to oppress and persecute the rest. . . . It is better that [religious] security should be depended upon from a general legislature, than from one particular state. A particular state might concur in one religious project. But the United States abound in such a variety of sects, that there is a strong security against religious persecution, . . . that no sect will ever be able to outnumber and oppress the rest.[71]

Just as in politics and economic affairs, Madison was tough-minded enough to want to base his cherished principles upon facts and circumstances, and was not willing to rest them on noble sentiments or pious declarations.

The source of Madison's ideas about religious liberty and the place of religion in society are not directly traceable. His outburst to Bradford about his objection to persecution in Virginia suggests that his own observation of a contrary practice was important. The devotion of the God-dominated Witherspoon to the cause of freedom of conscience must also have been a powerful influence upon the young Virginian. Indeed, the fact that Madison went to another state and religious environment for his college education no doubt impressed upon him the need for open-mindedness on questions of faith and ritual. The Lockean tradition of religious toleration was basic, although Madison went far beyond Locke in following the logic of making private opinion immune from magisterial control. His study of the histories of England and Holland re-enforced his view that religious liberty fostered both public tranquillity and spiritual health.[72] Rives reported that "Mr. Madison was accustomed to quote with great approbation" Voltaire's remark that "If one religion only were allowed in England, the government would possibly become arbitrary; if there were but two, the people would cut each others throats; but, as there are such a multitude, they all live happy and in peace."[73] Obviously the Enlightenment reaction against ecclesiastical corruption and religious superstition was part of Madison's intellectual heritage. Certainly there was a diverse and fortunate accumulation of factors in the background of the man who, more than any other person, formulated and put into practice the unique American doctrine of the free conscience.

In generalizing about the nature and importance of Madison's views on religious matters, two factors stand out beyond what is well known about the ideas of the fourth president. First, Madison's own religious and metaphysical beliefs were more profound and complex than has usually been recognized. Second, there was an intimate and fruitful relationship between Madison's religious views and sympathies, and the signal contributions he made to the philosophy of religious liberty in a free society.

That Madison was a child of the Enlightenment and aware of the ideas of perfectibility and melioration which were part of that age, has been a commonplace observation. That his thinking deeply and consciously went beyond this has not always been so obvious. In a letter Madison wrote to a friend in 1821, he stated that "afflictions of every kind are the onerous conditions charged on the tenure of life; and it is a silencing if not a satisfactory vindication of the ways of Heaven to man that there are but few who do not prefer an acquiescence in them to a surrender of the tenure itself."[74] It would be difficult to find a neater and more compassionate balance between hopeful optimism on the one hand and pessimistic despair on the other. Madison was thoroughly indoctrinated with a sense of awareness of an orderly, benevolent universe. Yet, his tough assessment of the frailty of man's nature, the finiteness of human understanding, and the occasional inclination of the world to be simply "out of joint," would have warmed the heart of Presbyterian John Witherspoon. The contradiction of these positions is as apparent today as it was to the controversialists of the eighteenth century. That James Madison possessed the kind of deep understanding and humble faith which could resolve or at least absolve that predicament is a conclusion to which the record of his life and thought gives strong support. This reticence and lack of flippancy on Madison's part is perhaps the clearest indication of his difference from Jefferson on the question of religion. Jefferson's skepticism and eager willingness to depart from orthodoxy are in considerable contrast to Madison's consistent reserve. Madison took notes on the meaning of the Scriptures, while Jefferson compiled his own condensation of the New Testament. The difference in method and pretension is significant and meaningful.

In the light of this insight, it becomes unwarrantable to portray Madison as a Voltairian skeptic who championed religious liberty with tongue-in-cheek, presuming that the expulsion of religion from the care of the state would lead to its decline or at least immunization. The very opposite inference is more tenable. Madison saw that in the final analysis he could not demonstrate with assurance the logical rectitude of his religious views, any more than he could accept the claims of theologians of other persuasions that they had absolutely proved the validity of their doctrines. Madison insisted, rather, that religious sentiments were based on dispositions and inclinations of the human mind and spirit. To apply state power in support of these kinds of experiences was obviously absurd.

Accepting this logic, and retaining his sense of the reality of religious insight, Madison became a consistent and sympathetic supporter of the right of religious and non-religious groups and individuals to seek their own lights and pursue their own kinds of salvation. Like de Tocqueville, he saw very clearly the mutually beneficial results of separation of church and state. The contribution which this sort of magnanimous solution made to the civil peace and religious vitality of the United States was and is very great indeed.

NOTES

1. Madison to Frederick Beasley, November 20, 1825, Gaillard Hunt, ed., *The Writings of James Madison*, 9 vols. (New York, 1904), IX, pp. 230-31.

2. William C. Rives, *History of the Life and Times of James Madison*, 3 vols. (New York, 1859-1868), I, p. 49.

3. Irving Brant, *The Life of James Madison*, 4 vols. (Indianapolis, 1941-1954), I, pp. 51-53, 69-72.

4. Hunt, IX, p. 230.

5. Samuel Clarke, *Being and Attributes of God* (London, 1735), 10th Edition.

6. Notes of John E. Calhoun, "Lectures in Moral Philosophy," taken in 1774, p. 3. Similar references are in the Hunter Notes, 1772, but the references to Clarke were deleted from Witherspoon's published works (1815), which in most places are identical to the recorded notes of his students. Apparently Witherspoon lost his liking for Clarke in his later years, but it should not be overlooked that Witherspoon did think highly of Clarke's work during the years Madison was at Princeton (1769-1772), and recommended him to his students at that time. The Notes are deposited in the Archives of the Firestone Library, Princeton University.

7. Ernest C. Mossner, *Bishop Butler and the Age of Reason* (New York, 1936), provides excellent insight into the use of Newton by theologians of the eighteenth century.

8. Clarke, p. 7.

9. Ibid., p. 12.

10. Ibid., pp. 102-105.

11. Ibid., p. 48.

12. Ibid., 69.

13. Ibid., pp. 100, 102.

14. Ibid., p. 113.

15. Mossner shows how both the orthodox defenders of Christianity and the deistical opponents argued within the Newtonian framework, *passim*, pp. 13-105.

16. Thomas J. Wertenbaker, *Princeton, 1746-1896* (Princeton, 1946), pp. 55-56.

17. Herbert W. Schneider, *The History of American Philosophy* (New York, 1946), pp. 246-250.

18. Brant, I, p. 78, in a speech Witherspoon made in the Continental Congress in 1778 in regard to dealing with the prisoners captured at Saratoga.

19. The best available edition of Witherspoon's writings is *The Works of John Witherspoon, D. D.*, 9 vols. (Edinburgh, 1815), although as noted, *supra*, fn. 6, there are significant differences between this edition and his lectures to Princeton students in pre-Revolutionary days.

20. Wertenbaker, pp. 115-16.

21. Witherspoon, Sermon 14, pp. 323-51 and Sermon 16, pp. 302-40.

22. *Lectures in Moral Philosophy*, delivered at Nassau Hall by John Witherspoon. A True Copy by John E. Calhoun, Princeton, N.J., 1774, pp. 25-78. Notes taken by Andrew Hunter in 1772 seem to be identical to the Calhoun notes.

23. Even Irving Brant accepts this charge, I, p. 119, although Brant did not know of the existence of the student notes at Princeton when he wrote his first volume. Personal letter from Irving Brant, June 18, 1953.

24. *Supra*, p. 2.

25. Hunt, IX, pp. 203-207. Clarke appears on this list in the midst of a dozen authors whose fame has far outlasted Clarke's—Butler, Wollaston, Priestley, and Paley, for example.

26. Rives, II, p. 518.

27. Madison to Jefferson, New York, May 1, 1791, Hunt, VI, p. 46.

28. "Address of the General Assembly to the People of the Commonwealth of Virginia," January 1799, Ibid., VI, pp. 336, 340.

29. Madison to John Armstrong, Department of State, June 6, 1805, Ibid., VII, p. 183.

30. T. V. Smith, "Saints, Secular and Sacerdotal—James Madison and Mahatma Gandhi," *Ethics* 59: (October, 1948): 42, 45.

31. John Witherspoon, "Lectures on Moral Philosophy," in *The Development of American Philosophy*, eds. Walter G. Muelder and Laurence Sears (Boston, 1940), p. 109.

32. There are many other examples of apparent inconsistencies and changes of mind in Madison's thought and action which are well-known—his vacillations on the constitutionality of the National Bank, Judicial Review, and state's rights to mention some important instances. Although detailed explanation cannot be given here, it can be shown that Madison overlooked these inconsistencies to accomplish larger and wiser ends such as defining a practical concept of freedom for the United States within the limitations of time and circumstances.

33. Hunt, I, p. 10. Brant, I, pp. 109-34, brilliantly solves some of the mysteries surrounding these years of Madison's life, especially the diagnosis of the nature and seriousness of his illness.

34. Isaiah Woodward, *The Necessary Duty of Family Prayer, With Prayers for Their Use*, (n.p. 1768). This book, dedicated to Anglican Archbishop Tillotson, is a collection of Scriptural readings and anecdotes for daily use. Its date would suggest it might have been used at Montpelier during the years of Madison's year-round residence there from 1772-1775. At any rate, it was preserved by Madison and placed by him in the collection of materials he left to the University of Virginia.

36. Madison Papers, Library of Congress, vol. 91, miscellaneous papers.

36. Madison to Richard Rush, April 21, 1821, Hunt IX, p. 55.

37. Ibid., IX, pp. 202-07; *Letters and Other Writings of James Madison*, 4 vols., Published by Order of Congress (New York, 1865), IV, pp. 447-48, 450-51.

38. Locke, of course, was a dominant influence among the intellectuals of the English-speaking world during the eighteenth century, and it is no surprise to find Madison and Smith debating within a Lockean framework.

39. All quotations are from two letters, one undated, and the other dated September 15, 1778, Hampden-Sidney College, from Dr. Samuel Stanhope Smith to Madison during the period when Madison was a member of the Virginia Council of State. Smith had been a classmate of Madison's at Princeton, succeeded to the leadership of the college upon Witherpoon's death, and was a long-time friend of Madison's. Deposited in the Madison Papers, L. C., vol. I. The correspondence was weighty, running to 20 large papers of fine writing for two letters.

40. Brant, I, pp. 113, 118.

41. Madison to William Bradford, Orange County, April 1, 1774, cited in Brant, I, p. 115.

42. Madison to Wilson Cary Nichols, Washington, November 26, 1814, Hunt, VIII, p. 319.

43. January 1, 1975, Annals, 3rd Congress, 1035. Cited in Ibid., VI, p. 231.

44. Letters of Madison to Mordecai Noah, May 15, 1818, and to Jacob de la Motta, August, 1820, and Noah's letter to Madison, May 6, 1818. Ibid., VIII, p. 412; IX, p. 29.

45. Madison to Washington, November 20, 1789, Ibid., VI, p. 429.

46. The University of Virginia has over 400 pamphlets left by Madison. Around 10 percent of this total deal with religious and theological matters. Madison portfolios, Manuscript Division, Alderman Library, University of Virginia.

47. Lyman H. Butterfield, "Elder John Leland, Jeffersonian Itinerant," *Proceedings of the American Antiquarian Society* 62 (October 1952): 155-242. Rives neglected Leland completely, and Brant makes only passing reference to "a Baptist preacher" Madison was urged to see on his way to Orange County in the Spring of 1788. Brant, III, p. 188. Butterfield's account is thoroughly convincing and contributes significantly to an understanding of Madison's relationships with religious groups. This paragraph and the following two are based upon Butterfield's article.

48. The Baptists underwent a great religious revival in Virginia between 1785-1791 and by 1790 there were 204 churches and 20,443 Baptists in Virginia. Annual Register of the Baptist Denomination in North America, 1792. Ibid., pp. 180-81, 196.

49. Ibid., p. 216.

50. Ibid., p. 242.

51. See Stuart Gerry Brown, "Plural Values and the Neutral State: The American Doctrine of the Free Conscience," *Syracuse Law Review* (Fall, 1953): 28-41. Also Brant, I, pp. 128-31, 241-50; II, pp. 343, 356, relates Madison's part in the development of doctrine.

52. Hunt, II, pp. 184-85.

53. Ibid., II, pp. 185-91.

54. Brant, II, pp. 343-55.

55. Madison to Jefferson, Richmond, January 22, 1786, Hunt, II, p. 216.

56. Thomas Paine, *Rights of Man* (1791), p. 74.

57. Hunt, I, p. 21.

58. Brant, I, pp. 241-50.

59. Brown, pp. 30-36.

60. Elizabeth Fleet, ed., "Madison's Detached Memoranda," *William and Mary Quarterly*, third series, III (October, 1946), p. 558. The passage is a piece entitled

"Monopolies, Perpetuities, Corporation Ecclesiastical Endowments," undated.

61. Madison to Edward Livingston, July 10, 1822, Congress Ed., *Writings*, III, p. 275.

62. Veto messages, February 21 and February 28, 1811, Hunt, VIII, pp. 132-33.

63. Fleet, pp. 554-55.

64. Witherspoon, "Lectures on Moral Philosophy," Calhoun Notes, 1774.

65. Fleet, p. 566.

66. Madison to Rev. F. L. Schaeffer, December 3, 1821, Congress Ed., *Writings*, III, p. 242.

67. "Record of the Board of Visitors of the University of Virginia," October 1, 1822, 169. Deposited in the Manuscript Division of the Alderman Library of the University of Virginia.

68. Madison to Robert Walsh, March 2, 1819, Hunt, VIII, pp. 430-32.

69. Madison to William Bradford, January 24, 1774, Ibid., I, p. 19.

70. Madison to Jefferson, August 20, 1785, Ibid., II, pp. 163-64.

71. Speech in Virginia Convention, June 12, 1788, Ibid., II, p. 176.

72. Madison to Edward Livingstone, March 2, 1819, Ibid., IX, p. 102.

73. Rives, II, pp. 220-21. The observation is in Voltaire's article on "Tolerance" in *Dictionaire Philosophique* which Jefferson had sent Madison from Paris. Pointed out by Douglass Adair, "Intellectual Origins of Jeffersonian Democracy," unpublished doctoral dissertation, Yale Unversity, 1944, p. 244.

74. Madison to John G. Jackson, December 27, 1821, Hunt, IX, p. 77.

PART VII

The Courage to Doubt
in a Secular Republic

No two scholars at work today understand the Madison tradition more clearly than Robert Rutland and Daniel Boorstin. Together these essays define the heritage to which this volume is dedicated.

Robert A. Rutland

James Madison's Dream: A Secular Republic

Any clear-headed historian who reaches his ninetieth year in reasonably good health is going to be asked a lot of silly questions, as Dumas Malone found to be the case in 1982. But like all wise men, Malone was able to turn the tables when he rephrased a mindless query about American history into a sensible one. The question as it finally came out: "What is the most fortunate aspect of American history?" The biographer of Thomas Jefferson scarcely hesitated. "The fact that we became a nation and immediately separated church and state—it has saved us from all the misery that has beset mankind with inquisitions, internecine and civil wars, and other assorted ills," Malone said. "Jefferson's part in this is what he wanted remembered, and it is certainly a great contribution to mankind." Reminded that Madison helped Jefferson push the 1786 Statute on Religious Freedom through the Virginia legislature, Malone added: "Yes, of course Madison felt the same way—nearly all the Founding Fathers did." (In his homespun way, Professor Malone was making the same point that the English historian J. B. Bury struck in his *History of Freedom and Thought*, where he says the idea "that coercion of opinion is a mistake . . . is the most important [conclusion] ever reached by men" [p. 6, 1957 edition]. The broad implications of complete separation of church and state are weakened by the claims one hears that the Constitution is a logical offshoot of the Judeo-Christian ethic, or such a proclamation as the one recently passed by Congress and signed by President Reagan declaring 1983 to be the "Year of the Bible.")

Such a testimonial from an eminent scholar reminds us that the shared wisdom of the Revolutionary generation not only spread the blessings of

From *Free Inquiry* 3: no. 2 (Spring 1983). Copyright © 1983 by *Free Inquiry*. Reprinted by permission.

liberty after 1776 but also spared the American people much of the tragedy that has marked mankind's story since Cain and Abel fell out. In James Madison's case, the perceptions he gained as a Princeton graduate were nurtured by experience in Orange County, Virginia, and strengthened when he contrasted the healthy intellectual climate in places where there was no established church with the mind-blight he witnessed in his native community.

After Madison took his cram course in classics at Princeton so that he could earn the baccalaureate degree in barely more than two years, he worried about his future and eventually returned to Montpelier to contemplate his career plans. In the drafty halls of his father's plantation home Madison heard the news from his neighborhood and wrote his college friend (in the winter of 1773-74) of his hope to travel northward in the spring. "I want again to breathe your free Air. . . . I have indeed as good an Atmosphere at home as the Climate will allow: but have nothing to brag of as to the State and Liberty of my Country," Madison confided. Poverty and luxury prevailed side by side, "among all sorts: Pride ignorance and Knavery among the Priesthood and Vice and Wickedness among the Laity."

> This is bad enough But It is not the worst I have to tell you. That diabolical Hell conceived principle of persecution rages among some and to their eternal Infamy the Clergy can furnish their Quota of Imps for such business. This vexes me the most of any thing whatever. There are at this [time] in the adjacent County not less than 5 or 6 well meaning men in close Gaol for publishing their religious Sentiments which in the main are very orthodox.

Confessing that he had "neither patience to hear talk or think of any thing relative to this matter, for I have squabbled and scolded abused and ridiculed so long about it, [to so lit]tle purpose that I am without common patience," Madison suggested that the only resource left was "to pray for Liberty of Conscience [to revive among us.]"[1]

Many men who have seen twenty-two winters make statements that they later amend or repudiate, but James Madison was acting and talking as consistently on the matter of religious freedom at eighty-two as he had been at twenty-two. Lip service was never his game. His discussions with James Madison, Sr., vestryman of St. Thomas Parish in Orange County, are unrecorded, but we can assume that between his Princeton experience and his fireside discussions there took shape in Madison's mind a lifelong aversion to religious bigotry that antedated his association with that other great libertarian, Thomas Jefferson.

Revolutions have a way of changing things swiftly; hence the men involved in the proceedings of 1775 and 1776 gloried in alluding to their experiences later as "a revolt." Thus, when Madison complained in 1774 of the misery inflicted by one set of Christians upon another, he was standing on the brink of events that transformed the entire political and social structure of the thirteen colonies in less time than it now takes to send a First Amendment case from appeal to the Supreme Court. Things happened fast, including the election of Madison himself to the Virginia Convention of 1776. There in Williamsburg, while George Mason and the older leaders whipped their frothy ideas into the heavy batter of republicanism, Madison made his first move. Ready to cut all ties with England, the convention moved to declare independence and write a constitution and bill of rights for the free state of Virginia. Mason personally handled most of the business (he hated committee work), but when it came to his article on religion the Truro Parish vestryman only saw the need to guarantee "that all Men shou'd enjoy the fullest Toleration in the Exercise of Religion, according to the Dictates of Conscience, unpunished and unrestrained by the Magistrate, unless, under Colour of Religion, any Man disturb the Peace, the Happiness, or Safety of Society, or of individuals." [2] But for Madison, there the landmark Article 16 of the Virginia Declaration of Rights would have stood through the final reading. When Madison thought about it, however, he saw a shorter, broader, and hence a better way of expressing Mason's idea. So he moved to amend the phrase simply to read: "all men are equally entitled to the free exercise of religion, according to the dictates of conscience."[3] The wording stuck, and in time the world read it and marveled that such common sense could come from the wilderness state of Virginia.

Before Madison would pursue his thoughts on the national stage, there were still battles to be won in his home territory. Jefferson wrote his statute on religious freedom in 1779 but was not able to bring it before the Virginia General Assembly as he had planned. With this bill cached in his desk, Jefferson went to France and carried on the diplomacy necessary to keep the young republic from being swallowed up by old enemies and new friends.

Meanwhile, by 1784 Madison found duties enough to keep himself busy in the Virginia House of Delegates. One of the hottest issues concerned the status of the old Anglican church. Out of sentiment and natural conservatism, many of the Virginia public men decried what was happening and wanted to use the commonwealth's political structure to save the feeble leftovers of the established church. Church-going in Virginia had long been on the decline as communicants found more reasons for attending Sunday horse races or cockfights than for being in pews. In 1784 a foreign traveler in Richmond noted that the village had only "one small church, but [it was] spacious enough for all the pious souls of the place and the region. If the Virginians themselves did not freely and openly admit that zeal for religion, and religion generally, is now very faint among them, the fact might easily have been divined from other circumstances."[4] In the face of such realities there were still many members of the General Assembly disposed to aid the Protestant Episcopal church, and they seemed determined to carry a so-called General Assessment bill (designed to collect and distribute tax money to all Christian churches in the name of "public morality") despite widespread but inarticulate opposition from many constituents. Passage of the bill, said to be Patrick Henry's "pet," seemed likely.

In this confused situation Presbyterians occupied an ambiguous position. Convinced that a religious subsidy would pass, the Hanover Presbytery first declared that "religion as a spiritual System is not to be considered an object of human Legislation" and in the next breath made a bid to share in the proceeds of "a general assessment for teachers of Christianity."[5]

Such a compromise was anathema to Madison, who had no intention of retreating from the high ground he occupied when helping fashion Article 16 of the Virginia Declaration of Rights. He had seen conservative forces in the General Assembly come within an eyelash of passing the legislation—officially known as the "Bill establishing a provision for the teachers of the Christian religion" at the October 1784 session—with some sly maneuvering needed by its opponents to postpone final action on the bill and publicize its provisions in the interim. George Nicholas in neighboring Albemarle County had entreated Madison to bestir himself so that apathy would not allow the bill to become law.[6] Surely Madison discussed the matter with his neighbors, including the obstreperous Elder John Leland, a Baptist minister who loathed all forms of church-state alliances. A host of Episcopalians as well as dissenters were eager to cut all church-state ties. However, a focal point for the opposition was needed, and the usual way to protest pending legislation in the 1780s was by a petition.

Partly from pressure, then, and partly from personal conviction, Madison took pen in hand and wrote a cogently reasoned, anonymous attack on the General Assessment bill. By the end of June it was ready for distribution, most likely through Nicholas and other young men in the Piedmont whom Madison could trust to keep his secret—Archibald Stuart, John Breckinridge, and the tidelands patriarch at Gunston Hall who was eager to knock the tax-subsidy props from beneath the church he attended and loved, George Mason. The Library of Congress copy of the protest is in Madison's handwriting. No doubt he sent a copy to Mason, who was eager to see it in print. From an Alexandria press Mason broadcast copies of the *Memorial and Remonstrance* to friends and neighbors. Mason sent with it a covering letter that honored Madison's request for anonymity. The petition, Mason explained, "was confided to me by a particular Freind [sic], whose name I am not at Liberty to mention."[7] So active was Mason in supporting Madison's remonstrance that there was speculation that he was its real author.[8]

Madison's motive in seeking a cloud of anonymity over his attack on the General Assessment bill is uncertain. He told Jefferson copies had been dispatched "thro' the *medium of confidential persons*."[9] Hamilton Eckenrode speculated that most Virginians were inclined to support the bill, until the protest movement began to swell.[10] The phalanx committed to its passage was imposing. A fortuitous circumstance was the fact that Patrick Henry was still governor and thus unable to use his oratory in the House of Delegates to overwhelm the opposition. Carter Henry Harrison, Charles Mynn Thruston, Wilson Miles Cary, John Page, and lesser lights also were convinced that religion needed bolstering. Richard Henry Lee and Edmund Pendleton were not legislators, but in Richmond their support of the General Assessment bill was certainly no secret.[11]

In these circumstances Madison may have thought it prudent to eschew the role of rabble-rouser. There was much to be done at the October 1785 session of the legislature, and Madison was too good a politician to go out of his way to alienate those men whose votes or support he would need if the reforms of the court system and the whole legal code were to pass a House of Delegates fairly balanced in terms of conservative and progressive members. So it may have been prudence and expediency that caused Madison to mantle his authorship of "one of the truly epoch-making documents in the history of American Church-State separation."[12]

A comparison between the fifteen-paragraph *Memorial and Remonstrance* and John Locke's "Letter on Toleration" (1685) leads to the speculation that Madison had occasion to use Locke's treatise in preparing his own. Assertions of intellectual dependence are often based on slender textual coincidences, but there are a number of similarities between the views of Madison and Locke toward religious ties between church and state. For example, Madison speaks of the "metes and bounds" between the temporal and spiritual establishments while Locke marked "the true bounds between the church and the commonwealth." Madison denies to "the Civil Magistrate" any power over religion because "Religious truth" and "the means of salvation" are beyond the concerns of the state. With Locke, the whole jurisdiction of the magistrate is concerned only with "civil goods" such as life, liberty, and property and ought not "in any way to be extended to the salvation of souls." Indeed, Locke held that "the magistrate ought not to forbid the holding or teaching of any speculative opinions in any church, because they have no bearing on the civil rights of his subjects."[13]

If this comparison of Locke and Madison seems strained, there is one indisputable similarity between the "Letter on Toleration" and the *Memorial and Remonstrance*. Neither Locke nor Madison wanted his authorship revealed. A modern scholar has noted that "Locke's timid anxiety to conceal his identity was excessive"; Madison sent his petition to a close circle of friends who were enjoined to secrecy.[14] "My choice is that my name may not be associated with it," Madison wrote his friend Edmund Randolph.[15]

Whether Madison gleaned his "wall of separation" arguments from a growing number of volumes in his personal library or drew upon experience and practical politics as his guides, the result is beyond doubt. Because of his labors the campaign against the General Assessment bill had all the aspects of a well-organized endeavor. What is not generally known is that Madison was not only seeking anonymity but was so circumspect that another opponent of the General Assessment bill actually had a more active following. While at least thirteen of Madison's petitions were circulated (and in time bore 1,552 signatures), another (also anonymous) petition writer found that his attack on the "Teachers of Christian Religion" measure gained more widespread support. Twenty-nine petitions, signed by 4,899 Virginians, came from the pen of this unknown opponent of a church-state tie. This petition was based on an argument that carries beyond Madison's—the General Assessment bill was not only contrary to the Virginia Declaration of Rights and to the enlightened republicanism pronounced there, but the proposed act was in conflict with "the Spirit of the Gospel." Whoever wrote this petition, which was easily the most popular of the several circulating protests, was clearly an active Christian (and probably a Baptist) who believed the General Assessment bill would do nothing to check "that Deism with its banefull Influence [which] is spreading itself over the state."[16]

Obviously, more Virginians were made aware of this zealous protest than Madison's calmer one, and it is also notable that in Westmoreland County at least eleven women signed the remonstrance based on "the Spirit of the Gospel." Thus, while Madison's role in shaping opposition to the bill is noteworthy, his protest was signed by a minority of all the protesting Virginians who were recorded as opponents of the General Assessment bill (since 10,929 signed some kind of anti-assessment petition). Almost eighty petitions opposed to the General Assessment bill flowed into the legislative hopper after October 27, 1785. Some were printed, and some came in longhand, but less than one-fifth of them were based entirely on Madison's work. Only eleven counties mustered enough support for the bill to send favorable petitions to Richmond. Faced with such odds, the conservatives retreated. The bill that seemed so certain of passage in November 1784 was, one year later, allowed to die in a pigeonhole.

With the passage of time, history tended to forget the other protests of 1785-1786 and focused upon Madison's. Madison himself was no longer shy about his role, and in his seventy-fifth year he remembered that chiefly because of the *Memorial and Remonstrance* the churchmen in the General Assembly were "entirely frustrated, and under the influence of the public sentiment thus manifested the celebrated Bill 'Establishing Religious freedom' [was] enacted into a permanent Barrier agst. future attempts on the Rights of Conscience as declared in the great charter affixed to the Constitution of the State."[17] Strengthened by the victory over churchmen in 1785, Madison resurrected Jefferson's 1779 bill to cut all religious ties asunder at the 1786 legislative session. With Patrick Henry now governor and out of the way, it passed handily.

Madison did not pause to rest. His dominant role in drafting the Constitution and forcing the First Amendment upon a reluctant Congress in 1789 is well known. In the light of history, it would have been an irony had any other man performed the task—certainly no one in the House of Representatives or Senate could match his record as a fighter for religious freedom.

Some thirty years later Madison was still as concerned about the need for separation of church and state as he had been in 1774. Around 1832 he wrote a retrospective memorandum on the scenes of public life he had witnessed and also set down a few of his fears. Among the latter was a feeling that "the danger of silent accumulations & encroachments by Ecclesiastical Bodies have not sufficiently engaged attention in the U.S."

At the time, several New England states still had ties with religious bodies, and with some pride Madison pointed out that "there is one State at least, Virginia, where religious liberty is placed on its true foundation and is defined in its full latitude." Madison hailed the "general principle . . . in her declaration of rights, . . . unfolded and defined, in its precise extent, in the act of the Legislature, usually named the Religious Bill." "This act is a true standard of Religious liberty . . . as long as it is respected & no longer, these will be safe," Madison warned.

Warming to the issue, Madison called on the errant states to build an impenetrable wall separating the church and state and thus "make the example of your Country as pure & compleat, in what relates to the freedom of the mind and its allegiance to its maker, as in what belongs to the legitimate objects of political and civil institutions." Before dropping the subject, Madison alluded to offshoots of a church-state relationship that worried him. "Besides the danger of a direct mixture of Religion & civil Government, there is an evil which ought to be guarded agst in the indefinite accumulation of property from the capacity of holding it in perpetuity by ecclesiastical corporations." The power accumulating to such groups, Madison wrote, "never fails to be a source of abuses." He compared the latent dangers in church property-holding with those "in the minute tax of 3 pence on tea" of yesteryear.

With Madison the line between church and state had to be drawn with absolute firmness. "The establishment of the chaplainship to Congs is a palpable violation of equal rights as well as of Constitutional principles." And what about presidential proclamations involving religious feast days and fasts? Even though they come as "recommendations only, they imply a religious agency" and are therefore suspect. On balance, Madison reasoned, even these proclamations are not a good idea, and he appears to have regretted those issued during his presidency. "They seem to imply and certainly nourish the erroneous idea of a *national* religion," he explained. "During the administration of Mr. Jefferson no religious proclamation was issued."[18] Looking back, Madison wished he had followed the same rule.

NOTES

1. Madison to William Bradford, Jan. 24, 1774, *The Papers of James Madison*, eds. William T. Hutchinson et al., 14 vols. to date (Chicago and Charlottesville, Va., 1962-),

I, p. 106. Words in brackets from copybook version.

2. Robert A. Rutland, ed., *The Papers of George Mason*, 3 vols. (Chapel Hill, N.C.: University of North Carolina Press, 1970), 1, p. 278.

3. Ibid., 1, pp. 289-91. The final wording seems to have represented a further compromise, as Madison's first thought was to add a prohibition on "peculiar emoluments" based on religious ties.

4. Johann D. Schoepf, *Travels in the Confederation* [1783-1784], translated and edited by Alfred J. Morrison, 2 vols. (Philadelphia, 1911), vol. 2.

5. Virginia Historical Society: Records of the Proceedings of Hanover Presbytery from the Year 1755 to the Year 1786 (typed copy by George S. Wallace, 1930), pp. 327-27.

6. Nicholas to Madison, Apr. 22, 1785, in Hutchinson, 8, pp. 264-65.

7. Mason to Washington, Oct. 2, 1785, in Rutland, 2, p. 830.

8. Kate Mason Rowland, *The Life of George Mason, 1725-1792*, 2 vols. (New York, 1892), 2, p. 87.

9. Madison to Jefferson, Aug. 20, 1785, in Hutchinson, 8, p. 345 (italicized words in code).

10. Hamilton J. Eckenrode, *Separation of Church and State in Virginia* (Richmond, 1910), p. 95.

11. David John Mays, ed., *The Letters and Papers of Edmund Pendleton, 1734-1802*, 2 vols. (Charlottesville, Va.: University Press of Virginia, 1967), 2, p. 474.

12. Anson Phelps Stokes, *Church and State in the United States*, 3 vols. (New York, 1950), 1, p. 391.

13. John Locke, *Epistolia de Tolerantia: A Letter on Toleration*, ed. by Raymond Klibansky and J. W. Gough (Oxford, 1968), pp. 65, 67, 121.

14. Locke, p. 45; Rutland, 2, pp. 830, 832.

15. Madison to Randolph, July 26, 1785, in Hutchinson, 8, p. 328.

16. Virginia State Library: Westmoreland County petition.

17. Madison to George Mason [of Green Spring], July 14, 1826 (Virginia Historical Society).

18. Elizabeth Fleet, ed., "Madison's 'Detached Memoranda,'" *William and Mary Quarterly*, 3rd ser., 3 (1946): 554-62.

Daniel J. Boorstin

The Founding Fathers and the Courage to Doubt

In late winter of February 1790, when Benjamin Franklin at the age of eighty-four was gravely and painfully ill and suspected that he did not have much longer to live, he received a letter from his old friend Reverend Ezra Stiles, then president of Yale, asking him for the specifics of his religion. It was a serious matter for Stiles. He had spent some years experimenting with electricity at Franklin's suggestion, and then spent many years reflecting on whether he really believed in the Christian doctrine when he accepted ordination.

Franklin's reply was laced with Franklin wit. He said, "I believe in one God, Creator of the universe. That He governs it by His providence. That He ought to be worshiped. That the most acceptable service we render Him is doing good to His other children." But Stiles had also asked him what he thought of the divinity of Jesus. To which Franklin replied, "I think the systems of morals and his religion as he left them to us, the best the world ever saw or is likely to see; but I have, with most of the present Dissenters in England, some doubts as to his divinity; though it is a question that I do not dogmatize upon, having never studied it, and think it needless to busy myself with it now, when I expect soon an opportunity of knowing the truth with less trouble."

With his usual political concern, Franklin added the request that Stiles should not make his letter public because, Franklin said, "I've ever let others enjoy their religious sentiments, without reflecting on them for those that appeared to me unsupportable and even absurd. All sects here, and we have a great variety, have experienced my good will in assisting them with subscrip-

From *Free Inquiry* 3: no. 3 (Summer 1983). Copyright © 1983 by Free Inquiry. Reprinted by permission.

tions for building their new places of worship; and, as I never opposed any of their doctrines, I hope to go out of the world in peace with them all."

I think this parable represents the beliefs of at least many of the Founding Fathers and the spirit that formed their making of the Constitution. I would like, from the vantage point of Franklin's skepticism, to try to offer a larger historical perspective, to take the discussion of religion in politics out of the halls of legislatures and try to put it into macroscosm of world history.

The United States was the first modern nation founded on purpose in the bright light of history. The mere existence of the nation was itself a kind of Declaration of Independence from the folk gods and religious and semireligious myths that had always and everywhere surrounded governments and their rulers. Kings and queens were customarily crowned and hallowed by priests, bishops, cardinals, and popes. And they had good reason to want the odor of sanctity. Queen Elizabeth I, for example, made trouble for the author who wrote too freely describing the dethroning of her predecessor Richard II. Prudent divine-right sovereigns saw their protection lay in controlling the prying research of inquiring historians. They preferred simply to legitimize themselves by descent from the Trojans or from the gods.

Some would say that religious liberty is probably the most distinctive and certainly one of the greatest contributions of the American experience to all human progress. Religious liberty in the United States is the product of not only the courageous personal humility of the Founding Fathers, as well as a by-product of some happy facts of American history. These are no less important because they appear obvious, but we're inclined to ignore them.

First, since the founding of the nation—by an act of revolution and by the framing of a Constitution—was accomplished in a relatively brief time, living men and women could see that it was a product of their struggles, discussion, and handiwork, not the fiat of some sanctified, myth-enshrouded past.

Second, the nation was created from areas with diverse sects. Oddly enough, the fact that the colonies already had their several and various established churches contributed to this necessity. A federal nation was plainly not founded on an orthodox religious base. In Europe, the Protestant Reformation came as a disruptive force into the relatively monolithic world of the medieval church. In England, for example, Protestant orthodoxy was indelibly identified with national identity. In the American colonies, religious variety preceded political unity and had to be accommodated within it.

Third, the diffusion of American colonial settlements with no one capital, the great distance of colonial urban centers from one another, and the oceanic separation from London or Rome, all made religious independence a fact of geography as well as of theology. So much of the population was at the edges and out beyond the range of the churches. One of the consequences of this was a different line of historical development of the relation between church and state, one which is so grand and so unqiue that we are perhaps inclined to ignore it. Over there, the development was generally from religious orthodoxy enforced by the state, to toleration—and only later to religious liberty. Historically speaking, of course, religious toleration is to be sharply contrasted to religious liberty. Toleration implies the existence of an established church, and toleration is always a revocable concession rather than a defensible right. In the United States, for the first time in modern Western history, the nation leaped from the provincial religious preference of its regions into religious liberty for the whole nation. The Founding Fathers despised the condescension that was implied in the very concept of toleration. That was a stage necessary for Old World nations, but not for our New World nation.

Religious persecution, that is to say, the punishment, torture, execution, or civil disability of individuals for their refusal to embrace a particular religious doctrine, is a modern Western and especially a Christian invention. It was virtually unknown in Greek and Roman antiquity. Socrates was condemned to death for essentially a political crime. In Rome, where religion seems to have been more in the nature of a patriotic ritual than an affirmation of doctrinal orthodoxy, the execution of Christians in the first three centuries was less because of governmental opposition to their theology than for their refusal to participate in the imperial rites. It is well known, of course, that as the Roman empire expanded the Romans simply incorporated the local deities into the Roman pantheon.

Judaism, monotheistic and theocratic, did offer more basis for intolerance. While the Jews detested and opposed idolatry, their religion remained in many respects national or perhaps even tribal. Of the Eastern regions, Buddhism was notoriously free from intolerance. The only example of Buddhism appearing to become the basis for persecution—in seventeenth-century Japan—turns out to have been for political and not for theological purposes and was stirred by the fear of Christian missionaries. Hinduism, with its wealth of pantheistic lore, was not a persecuting religion and did not encounter problems of religious warfare and genocide until it encountered Islam, which was of course a successor to Christianity.

Christianity then, along with its beliefs, sought also the spirit of intolerance and persecution. The Protestant Reformation did not help much against these particular evils. It brought a new version of religious (now Protestant) persecution, and it was a long time before the Reformation brought political liberalism and religious liberty. Some of the most bitter religious wars in Western history—the Thirty Years War, for example, between 1616 and 1648, which we are told killed one-tenth of the population of Germany, mainly for religious doctrinal reasons—were taking place at the very time that the New England Puritans were settling in the New World in quest of their own religious liberty, and incidentally, their freedom to persecute in their own way.

But after the American Revolution, Washington, Jefferson, and others could see what the New England Puritans could not see, that their government was not described and foremodeled in the Bible but was the prudential product of human struggle, compromise, and the pursuit of decency.

From the force of circumstances, as well as from long and deep reflection, our Founding Fathers brought forth this nation in the wholesome atmosphere of the courage to doubt. Federalism in politics meant pluralism in religion, which incidentally meant a faith in the wisdom of mankind but a doubt of the wisdom of orthodox man. Their spirituality, their God, was a God of common human quest and not the God of anybody's dogma.

There is no more eloquent apostle of the courage to doubt than Jefferson. Belief in the happy diversity of mankind and human thought was for him probably his first religious axiom after belief in God. "Rebellion to tyrants is obedience to God," was the motto that Jefferson chose for his seal in 1776. Jefferson's God was a God not of orthodoxy, but of diversity. "As the creator has made no two faces alike," Jefferson said, "so no two minds, and probably no two creeds," and he substantiated this view with the latest psychology and medicine of his day. He believed that the study of the variety of creation was itself an act of worship. In 1811, when Jefferson was about to resume friendly relations with his old friend John Adams, from whom he had been separated by bitter differences of opinion, he asked, "Why should we be dissocialized by mere differences of opinion in politics, in religion, in philosophy, or anything else? His opinions are as honestly formed as my own. Our different views of the same subject are the result of a difference in our organization and experience." So it's not surprising that Jefferson refused to accept the dogma of any religious sect. He made his own humanist anthology of the teachings of Jesus and we reap a rich harvest of his differences with John Adams from his treasure trove of correspondence in his last years.

An eloquent and reverent expression of the implications of this courage to doubt—a belief in religious liberty and the creator's delight in the multiformity of men's minds—was offered by Thomas Paine, who was a prophet and publicist of the American Revolution and never a favorite of dogmatic theologians.

This is what Paine wrote in the *Rights of Man* in 1792: "If we suppose a large family of children who . . . made it their custom to present to their parents some token of their affection and gratitude, each of them would make a different offering, and most probably in a different manner. Some would pay their congratulations in themes of verse and prose, by some little devices as their genius dictated, or according to what they thought would please, and, perhaps the least of all, not being able to do any of those things, would ramble into the garden or the field and gather what it thought the prettiest flower it could find, though, perhaps it might be but a simple weed. The parent would be more gratified by such a variety. . . . But of all unwelcome things, nothing could more afflict the parent than to know that the whole of them had afterward gotten together by the ears, boys and girls, fighting, scratching, reviling, and abusing each other about which was the best or the worst present."

In this way, Paine, as Jefferson did on so many occasions, affirmed his belief in some divine ordination of diversity and man's duty to preserve the opportunity to express that diversity.

The courage to doubt, on which American pluralism, federalism, and religious liberty are founded, is a special brand of courage, a more selfless brand of courage, than the courage of orthodoxy. A brand that has been far rarer and more precious in the history of the West than the courage of the crusaders or the true believer who has so little respect for his fellow man and for his thoughts and feelings that he makes himself the court of last resort on the most difficult matters on which wise men have disagreed for millennia.

PART VIII

Madison and the First Amendment

It would be convenient for the chronicler of Madison's contributions to freedom of religion if it were demonstrable that he alone wrote the First Amendment to the Constitution. However, modern historians are satisfied that the final draft of that amendment, and in particular the language concerning religion, was the work of several men along with Madison. Yet, there is little doubt that the sentiments expressed in the final wording conformed to Madison's basic principles. It is proper to conclude, therefore, that the Supreme Court has been correct in interpreting the First Amendment almost exclusively in terms of Madisonian ideas espoused in the *Memorial and Remonstrance*. As the excerpts from the Everson case make clear, Justices Black and Rutledge were equally committed to Madison as the touchstone for rulings on the religion clause.

However, Donald Drakeman raises significant questions about a too easy assumption of Madisonian authorship, which may tend to cloud the main issue. Drakeman believes Madison "should instruct the inquiry into the meaning of the First Amendment." But he reminds the reader that current decisions ought better to be made in light of Madison's dedication to freedom of conscience, rather than in terms of any particular historical action by him. Again, it is important to recall the risks of undergirding principles with too much historical "evidence." Further, those who find the Black thesis convincing need to consider seriously the evidence as interpreted by Drakeman.

The focus of modern inquiry should be upon the ideas espoused, not on the specific historical events. Were the principles of religious freedom bound to particular events in the past, those events would of necessity become masters over current practice. And if history were in turn to become dogma, what reckoning would occur if later inquiry demonstrated flaws in a particular description of events? Senator Ervin is an excellent example of a person who came to support the Madisonian principles because he saw in them the best means of preserving a free democratic society. His commitment to the principle of religious liberty and to separation of church and state was born in the crucible of twentieth-century political reality, even as Madison was affected by current conditions, leading him to seek to extinguish "forever the ambitious hope of making laws for the human mind."

Sam J. Ervin, Jr.

Colonial History and the First Amendment: A Senator's View

Religion is man's belief in and reverence for a superhuman power recognized as the creator and governor of the universe. Believers call this power God.

I am a Presbyterian whose Scotch-Irish, English, and French Huguenot ancestors came to America before the Revolution. All of them were Protestants. Most of them dissented from the established churches in the lands of their origin.

Religious faith, which is tolerant of other beliefs, is, in my opinion, the most wholesome and uplifting power on earth. Religious faith is not a shelter to which men and women can flee to escape the storms of life. It is, indeed, an inner spiritual strength that enables them to face those storms with courage and serenity.

The Constitution makes two references to religion. One appears in Article 6, Section 3, of the original Constitution, and the other is found in the first words of the First Amendment and the Bill of Rights.

Article 6, Section 3, provides that all legislative, executive, and judicial officers "of the United States and the several States shall be bound by oath or affirmation to support this Constitution, but no religious test shall ever be required as a qualification to any office or public trust under the United States."

The First Amendment provides in pertinent part that "Congress shall make no law respecting an establishement of religion, or prohibiting the free exercise thereof."

If we are to understand the meanings of these provisions, we must understand the historic events that prompted the Founding Fathers to embody them in the Constitution.

From *Free Inquiry* 3: no. 3 (Summer 1983). Copyright © 1983 by *Free Inquiry*. Reprinted by permission.

RELIGIOUS INTOLERANCE

The ugliest chapters in history are those that recount the religious intolerance of the civil and ecclesiastical rulers of the Old World and their puppets during the generations preceding the framing and ratifying of the First Amendment.

These chapters of history reveal the casting of Christians to the lions in the Colosseum at Rome; the bloody Crusades of the Christians against the Saracens for the possession of the shrines hallowed by the footsteps of the Prince of Peace; the use by the papacy of the dungeon and the rack to coerce conformity and of the fiery faggot to exterminate heresy; the unspeakable cruelties of the Spanish Inquisition; the slaughter of the Waldenses in Alpine Italy; the jailing and hanging by Protestant kings of English Catholics for abiding with the faith of their fathers; the jailing and hanging by a Catholic queen of English Protestants for reading English Scriptures and praying Protestant prayers; the hunting down and slaying of the Covenanters upon the crags and moors of Scotland for worshiping God according to the dictates of their own consciences; the decimating of the people of the German states in the Thirty Years War between Catholics and Protestants; the massacre of the Huguenots in France; the pogroms and persecutions of the Jews in many lands; the banishing of Baptists and other dissenters by Puritan Massachusetts; the persecution and imprisonment of Quakers by England for refusing to pay tithes to the established church and to take the oaths of supremacy and allegiance; the banishing, branding, imprisoning, and whipping of Quakers, and the hanging of the alleged witches at Salem by Puritan Massachusetts; and the hundreds of other atrocities perpetrated in the name of religion.

It is not surprising that Blaise Pascal, the French mathematician and philosopher, was moved more than three hundred years ago to proclaim this tragic truth: "Men never do evil so completely and cheerfully as when they do it from religious conviction."

One of my life's most rewarding experiences was that of serving for a time on the North Carolina Supreme Court with the late Chief Justice Walter P. Stacy, one of America's wisest jurists of all time. He possessed an uncanny capacity to phrase truth in unforgettable words.

When he wrote his opinion in *State v. Beal*, 199 N.C. 278, 302 (1930), Chief Justice Stacy made these comments on the nature and history of religious intolerance:

> There are those who feel more deeply over religious matters than they do about secular things. It would be almost unbelievable, if history did not record the tragic fact, that men have gone to war and cut each other's throats because they could not agree as to what was to become of them after their throats were cut. Many sins have been committed in the name of religion. Alas! the spirit of

proscription is never kind. It is the unhappy quality of religious disputes that they are always bitter. For some reason, too deep to fathom, men contend more furiously over the road to heaven, which they cannot see, than over their visible walks on earth.

Religious intolerance was fostered in Great Britain and virtually all the nations of Europe by unholy alliances between governments and particular churches recognized and established by law as the sole custodians of religious truth.

The objective of the unholy alliance in each nation was to persuade or coerce the people to accept and practice the political and religious orthodoxy sanctioned by the state and the establshed church. As pragmatists, state and church sought to accomplish this objective by imprisoning the minds and spirits of the people within intellectual and spiritual jails.

The British Parliament made the Church of England the established church in Great Britain. It created the crime of seditious libel to punish those who spoke ill of the government or its officers, and the crime of blasphemous libel to punish those who spoke ill of the established church. Besides, the British Parliament enacted laws compelling the people to pay tithes or taxes for the support of the established church, and to attend its worship services, denying those who dissented from its doctrines the capacity to hold civil office in government, and forbidding ministers of dissenting congregations to administer the sacraments to their members.

As a consequence of these attempts to regulate relations between men and religion, dissenters from the established church were compelled to make contributions of money for the propagation of religious opinions they disbelieved, required to listen to the exposition of religious doctrines they rejected, and denied the right to hold civil offices in government. Besides, they sometime had their marriages annulled and their children adjudged illegitimate for daring to speak their marital vows before ministers of their own faith rather than clergymen of the established church.

ESTABLISHED CHURCHES IN THE COLONIES

While they were joined by many Germans and French Huguenots and smaller numbers of Dutch, Swedes, and Swiss, natives of the British Isles constituted by far the greater part of those who migrated from the Old World to the thirteen British colonies in America.

A substantial proportion of the colonists were dissenters from the churches established by law in the lands of their origins.

Like the colonists who conformed to the established churches, these dissenters came to America to better their economic lots. But they were also motivated by the hope that they would find in the New World the political and religious freedom denied them by the civil and ecclesiastical rulers of the Old.

When they reached America, however, they discovered to their disappointment that in many of the colonies predominant groups had set up established churches here and that they were compelled in such colonies to pay taxes for the support of established churches whose doctrines they disbelieved. Moreover, most of the churches had established religious qualifications in their oaths for public office holders. As a result, these tests were designed to exclude dissenters, Catholics, Jews, deists, or unbelievers.

There is more than a modicum of historical truth in this statement of Artemas Ward, a humorist of a bygone generation:

> The Puritans nobly fled from a land of despotism to a land of freedom, where they could not only enjoy their own religion, but could prevent everybody else from enjoying his.

The colonies of Virginia, North Carolina, South Carolina, Georgia, and Maryland had established churches, and the Anglican Church was the favorite under their laws.

In the colonies of Massachusetts, Connecticut, and New Hampshire, the Congregational church was the established church.

In the colony of New York, the Dutch Reformed and Anglican churches were, in turn, established by law.

The people in these nine colonies were compelled by law to pay taxes for the support of these established churches, and in some cases to attend their services.

The dissenters were outraged by these requirements. They believed it tyrannical for government to attempt to regulate by law the relationship between an individual and his God. Moreover, as they pondered verses 15 to 22 of Chapter 22 of Matthew, "Render, therefore, unto Caesar the things that are Caesar's, and unto God the things that are God's," they concluded that in addition to being tyrannical, the attempt to regulate religion by law was also sinful.

SEPARATION OF CHURCH AND STATE IN THE STATES

The dissenters accepted as absolute truth this declaration, which had its origin in the North Carolina Constitution of 1776:

> All persons have a natural and inalienable right to worship Almighty God according to the dictates of their own consciences, and no human authority shall, in any case whatever, control or interfere with the rights of conscience.

As a consequence, they demanded the separation of church and state in

America.

During the Revolution and the years immediately following it, the dissenters found staunch allies in their fight for separation of church and state among non-churchmembers and those adherents of established churches who believed that it was abhorrent to reason as well as for earthly government to regulate the relationship between human beings and religion.

The separation of church and state presented no problems in Rhode Island, where Baptists led by Roger WIlliams had settled under a royal charter granting complete religious freedom to all, or in Delaware, New Jersey, and Pennsylvania, where establishment never acquired a foothold.

When their revolt against Great Britain converted the thirteen colonies into self-governing states, Rhode Island retained separation under its original charter, and Delaware, New Jersey, and Pennsylvania did so under constitutions adopted in 1776. North Carolina, New York, Georgia, and Virginia granted the right of freedom of worship to all and disestablished religion within their borders before the drafting of the First Amendment, and South Carolina did likewise before the amendment was ratified.

Hence, the only states maintaining any financial and legal relationship to religion at the time the First Amendment became a part of the Constitution were Connecticut, Maryland, Massachusetts, and New Hampshire. These four states were able to do this after the adoption of the First Amendment because the amendment applied originally to the federal government and not to the states.

But in those four states there was no single established church at that time. As a concession to those demanding complete separation of church and state, they had substituted for single established churches multiple establishments and were providing for an impartial use of taxes for the support of all churches they deemed respectable.

The last of these four states to terminate such relationship to religion was Massachusetts, which did so in 1833. . . .

THE FIRST AMENDMENT

After the Constitution of the United States was drafted and submitted to the states for ratification or rejection, many Americans were dissatisfied with it because it did not contain any bill of rights, or any provision relating to religious freedom other than Article 6 prescribing that no religious test should be required as a qualification for any office or public trust in the United States.

When New York, New Hampshire, and Virginia ratified the Constitution, they adopted resolutions that insisted that the Constitution should be amended by incorporating in it guaranties of religious freedom and freedom from taxation for the support of religion.

North Carolina and Rhode Island both postponed ratifying the Constitution and their conventions resolved they would not ratify it unless it was amended to provide for the disestablishment of religion.

As a result of the actions of these five states and the demands of multitudes of Americans in the other original states, the Constitution was amended in these respects by the First Amendment, which, as part of the Bill of Rights, was adopted by the requisite number of states by December 15, 1791.

The Constitution was so amended as a result of efforts of James Madison, who was elected a representative from Virginia to the First Congress, which met after its ratification.

As soon as this Congress convened, Madison began his great fight to have the First Amendment added to the Constitution. Some of his colleagues did not want the amendment to deny to government the power to support religion, and others insisted that the religious clauses of the amendment should merely prohibit a *single* established church.

But Madison contended at all times that the First Amendment should embody in it provisions that Congress should pass no law respecting an establishment of religion or prohibiting its free exercise.

He triumphed after much effort. On September 23, 1789, Madison made a report to the House of Representatives concerning the action of the conference committee of the Senate and House, which had been appointed to reconcile varying views as to the language of the First Amendment. This committee agreed with Madison and recommended the words that are now incorporated in the First Amendment. Hence James Madison, whom historians call the Father of the Constitution, really phrased the establishment and free-exercise clauses of the First Amendment.

As has been observed, the First Amendment was originally an inhibition on the federal government and not on the states.

In July 1868, the Fourteenth Amendment was added to the Constitution. Section 1 of this Amendment provides that no states shall deprive any person of liberty without due process of law.

The Supreme Court clearly adjudged for the first time in *Cantwell* v. *Connecticut*, 310 U.S. 296, which was decided in 1940, that the fundamental concept of liberty embodied in the Fourteenth Amendment embraced the liberties guaranteed by the First Amendment relating to religion, and that in consequence the First and Fourteenth amendments in combination forbid the states as well as the federal government to make any law or take action respecting the establishment of religion or prohibiting its free exercise, and thus secure to all people in the United States religious freedom. This ruling has been subsequently reaffirmed by the Supreme Court in many cases.

The First and Fourteenth amendments do this by erecting a wall of separation between government and religion at all levels and in all areas of the United States. By prohibiting any official relationship between government and religion, they forbid government to undertake to control or support religion and deny any religious group or groups the power to control public policy or the public purse.

The constitutional separation of government and religion is best for government and best for religion. It enables each of them to seek to achieve its rightful aims without interference from the other. Besides, it is wise. History reveals that political freedom cannot exist in any nation where religion controls government and that religious freedom cannot survive in any nation where government controls religion.

Moreover, constitutional separation of government and religion is indispensable to the domestic tranquility of the United States, "whose people came from the four corners of the earth and brought with them a diversity of religious opinion." As the Supreme Court revealed in *Abington School District v. Schempp* and *Murray v. Curlitt*, 374 U.S. 203, 214 (1963): "Today authorities list 83 separate religious bodies, each with a membership exceeding 50,000, existing among our people, as well as innumerable smaller groups." These organizations compete for the religious allegiance of the people.

By securing the absolute equality before the law of all religious sects and requiring government to be neutral in respect to them, the constitutional separation of government and religion makes the love of religious freedom and the other things that unite our people stronger than their diversities and enables Americans of varying religious faiths to live with each other in peace.

As made applicable to the states by the Fourteenth Amendment, the religious clauses of the First Amendment accomplish their wholesome objectives in their entirety in these ways:

1. They prohibit the federal government and the states from establishing any religious test as a qualificaiton for any public office at any level of government.[1]

2. "The establishment of religion clause of the First Amendment means at least this: Neither a state nor the federal government can set up a church. Neither can pass laws which aid one religion, aid all religions, or prefer one religion over another. Neither can force nor influence a person to go to or remain away from church against his will or force him to profess a belief or disbelief in any religion. No person can be punished for entertaining or professing religious beliefs or disbeliefs, for church attendance or non-attendance. No tax in any amount, large or small, can be levied to support any religious activities or institutions, whatever they may be called, or whatever form they may adopt to teach or practice religion. Neither a state nor the federal government can, openly or secretly, participate in the affairs of any religious organizations or groups or vice versa. In the words of Jefferson, the clause against establishment of religion by law was intended to erect a wall of separation between church and state."

3. The free-exercise clause of the First Amendment secures to every person the absolute right to accept as true the religious beliefs that appeal to his conscience and to reject all others, to practice the religious beliefs he

accepts in any mode of worship not injurious to himself or others, to seek by peaceful persuasion to convert others to his religious beliefs and practices, and to be exempt from taxation for the support of religious activities or teachings. A person is denied religious freedom if he is taxed to support any religious faith, including his own.[2]

OPPOSITION TO THE FIRST AMENDMENT

Numerous Americans of the utmost sincerity are not in intellectual and spiritual rapport with the First Amendment's separation of government and religion. Whether they are hostile to the principle of separation itself or do not understand what it entails, I do not know and will not surmise.

One group demands that the public schools of the states teach religion to the children attending them; and the other group demands that government provide public funds to aid and support private schools maintained by various churches to teach their religious doctrines to the children attending them. In so doing, the second group demands that the taxes of Caesar be used to finance the things of God.

While one is concerned with the public schools and the other with private religious schools, both groups base their demands on the assumption that governmental fidelity to the First Amendment frustrates the religious education of children.

This assumption is without foundation. While it forbids government to teach religion, the First Amendment leaves individuals, homes, and non-governmental institutions, such as Sunday schools, churches, and private schools, free to do so. Indeed, it encourages them to do so by securing religious freedom to all.

Churches should look to their members and their friends only for the financing of their undertakings, and no church should engage in any undertaking, no matter how laudable it may be, that its members and friends are unable or unwilling to finance.

NOTES

1. *Torcaso v. Maryland,* 367 U.S. 488 (1961).
2. *Cantwell v. Connecticut,* 310 U.S. 296 (1940); *Jones v. Opelika,* 316 U.S. 584 (1942); *West Virginia Board of Education v. Barnette,* 319 U.S. 624 (1943); *Follett v. City of McCormick,* 321 U.S. 573 (1944); *Kovacs v. Cooper,* 336 U.S. 77 (1949); *Sherbert v. Verner,* 374 U.S. 398 (1963); *Flast v. Cohen,* 392 U.S. 83 (1968).

The *Everson* Case

Everson v. *Board of Education*
330 U.S. I (1947)

MR. JUSTICE BLACK DELIVERED
THE OPINION OF THE COURT

A New Jersey statute authorizes its local school districts to make rules and contracts for the transportation of children to and from schools. The appellee, a township board of education, acting pursuant to this statute authorized reimbursement to parents of money expended by them for the bus transportation of their children on regular buses operated by the public transportation system. Part of this money was for the payment of transportation of some children in the community to Catholic parochial schools. These church schools give their students, in addition to secular education, regular religious instruction conforming to the religious tenets and modes of worship of the Catholic Faith. The superintendent of these schools is a Catholic priest.

The appellant, in his capacity as a district taxpayer, filed suit in a State court challenging the right of the Board to reimburse parents of parochial school students. He contended that the statute and the resolution passed pursuant to it violated both the State and the Federal Constitutions. That court held that the legislature was without power to authorize such payment under the State constitution. The New Jersey Court of Errors and Appeals reversed, holding that neither the statute nor the resolution passed pursuant to it was in conflict with the State constitution or the provisions of the Federal Constitution in issue. . . .

The only contention here is that the State statute and the resolution, in so far as they authorize reimbursement to parents of children attending parochial schools, violate the Federal Constitution in these two respects, which to some extent, overlap. First. They authorize the State to take by taxation the private property of some and bestow it upon others, to be used for their own private purposes. This, it is alleged, violates the due process clause of the Fourteenth Amendment. Second. The statute and the resolution forced inhabitants to pay taxes to help support and maintain schools which are dedicated to, and which regularly teach, the Catholic Faith. This is alleged to be a use of State power to support church schools contrary to the prohibiton of the First Amendment which the Fourteenth Amendment made applicable to the states. . . .

Second. The New Jersey statute is challenged as a "law respecting an establishment of religion." The First Amendment, as made applicable to the states by the Fourteenth, commands that a state "shall make no law respecting an establishment of religion, or prohibiting the free exercise thereof." These words of the First Amendment reflected in the minds of early Americans a vivid mental picture of conditions and practices which they fervently wished to stamp out in order to preserve liberty for themselves and for their pos- terity. Doubtless their goal has not been entirely reached; but so far has the Nation moved toward it that the expression "law respecting an establishment of religion," probaby does not so vividly remind present-day Americans of the evils, fears, and political problems that caused that expression to be written into our Bill of Rights. Whether this New Jersey law is one respecting the "establishment of religion" requires an understanding of the meaning of that language, particularly with respect to the imposition of taxes. Once again, therefore, it is not inappropriate briefly to review the background and environment of the period in which that constitutional language was fash- ioned and adopted.

A large proportion of the early settlers of this country came here from Europe to escape the bondage of laws which compelled them to support and attend government favored churches. The centuries immediately before and contemporaneous with the colonization of America had been filled with turmoil, civil strife, and persecution, generated in large part by established sects determined to maintain their absolute political and religious supremacy. With the power of government supporting them, at various times and places, Catholics had persecuted Protestants, Protestants had persecuted Catholics, Protestant sects had persecuted other Protestant sects, Catholics of one shade of belief had persecuted Catholics of another shade of belief, and all of these had from time to time persecuted Jews. In efforts to force loyalty to whatever religious group happened to be on top and in league with the government of a particular time and place, men and women had been fined, cast in jail, cruelly tortured, and killed. Among the offenses for which these punishments had been inflicted were such things as speaking disrespectfully of the views of ministers of government-established churches, non-attendance at those churches, expression of non-belief in their doctrines, and failure to pay taxes and tithes to support them.

These practices of the old world were transplanted to and began to thrive in the soil of the new America. The very charters granted by the

English crown to the individuals and companies designated to make the laws which would control the destinies of the colonials authorized these individuals and companies to erect religious establishments which all, whether believers or non-believers, would be required to support and attend. An exercise of this authority was accompanied by a repetition of many of the old-world practices and persecutions. Catholics found themselves hounded and proscribed because of their faith; Quakers who followed their conscience went to jail; Baptists were peculiarly obnoxious to certain dominant Protestant sects; men and women of varied faiths who happened to be in a minority in a particular locality were persecuted because they steadfastly persisted in worshipping God only as their own consciences dictated. And all of these dissenters were compelled to pay tithes and taxes to support government-sponsored churches whose ministers preached inflammatory sermons designed to strengthen and consolidate the established faith by generating a burning hatred against dissenters.

These practices became so commonplace as to shock the freedom-loving colonials into a feeling of abhorrence. The imposition of taxes to pay ministers' salaries and to build and maintain churches and church property aroused their indignation. It was these feelings which found expression in the First Amendment. No one locality and no one group throughout the Colonies can rightly be given entire credit for having aroused the sentiment that culminated in adoption of the Rights' provisions embracing religious liberty. But Virginia, where the established church had achieved a dominant influence in political affairs and where many excesses attracted wide public attention, provided a great stimulus and able leadership for the movement. The people there, as elsewhere, reached the conviction that individual religious liberty could be achieved best under a government which was stripped of all power to tax, to support, or otherwise to assist any or all religions, or to interfere with the beliefs of any religious individual or group.

The movement toward this end reached its dramatic climax in Virginia's tax levy for the support of the established church. Thomas Jefferson and James Madison led the fight against this tax. Madison wrote his great *Memorial and Remonstrance* against the law. In it, he eloquently argued that a true religion did not need the support of law; that no person, either believer or non-believer, should be taxed to support a religious institution of any kind; that the best interest of a society required that the minds of men always be wholly free; and that cruel persecutions were the inevitable result of government-established religions. Madison's *Remonstrance* received strong support throughout Virginia, and the Assembly postponed consideration of the proposed tax measure until its next session. When the proposal came up for consideration at that session, it not only died in committee, but the Assembly enacted the famous "Virginia Bill for Religious Liberty" originally written by Thomas Jefferson. The preamble of that Bill stated among other things that

Almighty God hath created the mind free; that all attempts to influence it by temporal punishment, or burthens, or by civil incapacitations, tend only to beget habits of hypocrisy and meanness, and are a departure from the plan of the Holy author of our religion who being Lord both of body and mind, yet chose not to propogate it by coercions on either . . .; that to compel a man to furnish contributions of money for the propagation of opinions which he disbelieves, is sinful and tyrannical; that even the forcing him to support this or that teacher of his own religious persuasion, is depriving him of the comfortable liberty of giving his contributions to the particular pastor, whose morals he would make his pattern. . . .

And the statute itself enacted

That no man shall be compelled to frequent or support any religious worship, place, or ministry whatsoever, nor shall be enforced, restrained, molested, or burthened, in his body or goods, nor shall otherwise suffer on account of his religious opinions or belief. . . .

This Court has previously recognized that the provisions of the First Amendment, in the drafting and adoption of which Madison and Jefferson played such leading roles, had the same objective and were intended to provide the same protection against governmental intrusion on religious liberty as the Virginia statute. Prior to the adoption of the Fourteenth Amendment, the First Amendment did not apply as a restraint against the states. Most of them did soon provide similar constitutional protections for religious liberty. But some states persisted for about half a century in imposing restraints upon the free exercise of religion and in discriminating against particular religious groups. In recent years, so far as the provision against the establishment of a religion is concerned, the question has most frequently arisen in connection with proposed state aid to church schools and efforts to carry on religious teachings in the public schools in accordance with the tenets of a particular sect. Some churches have either sought or accepted state financial support for their schools. Here again the efforts to obtain state aid or acceptance of it have not been limited to any one particular faith. The state courts, in the main, have remained faithful to the language of their own constitutional provisions designated to protect religious freedom and to separate religions and governments. Their decisions, however, show the difficulty in drawing the line between tax legislation which provides funds for the welfare of the general public and that which is designed to support institutions which teach religion.

The meaning and scope of the First Amendment, preventing establishment of religion or prohibiting the free exercise thereof, in the light of its history and the evils it was designed forever to suppress, have been several times elaborated by the decisions of this Court prior to the application of the First Amendment to the states by the Fourteenth. The broad meaning given the Amendment by these earlier cases has been accepted by this Court in its decisions concerning an individual's religious freedom rendered since the Fourteenth Amendment was interpreted to make the prohibitions of the First applicable to state action abridging religious freedom. There is every reason to give the same application and broad interpretation to the "establishment of religion" clause. The interrelation of these complementary clauses was well summarized in a statement of the Court of Appeals of South Carolina, quoted with approval by this Court, in Watson v. Jones, "The structure of our government has, for the preservation of civil liberty, rescued the temporal institutions from religious interference. On the other hand, it has secured religious liberty from the invasions of the civil authority."

The "establishment of religion" clause of the First Amendment means at least this: Neither a state nor the Federal Government can set up a church. Neither can pass laws which aid one religion, aid all religions, or prefer one religion over another. Neither can force nor influence a person to go to or to remain away from church against his will or force him to profess a belief or disbelief in any religion. No person can be punished for entertaining or professing religious beliefs or disbeliefs, for church attendance or non-attendance. No tax in any amount, large or small, can be levied to support any religious activities or institutions, whatever they may be called, or whatever form they may adopt to teach or practice religion. Neither a state nor the Federal Government can, openly or secretly, participate in the affairs of any religious organizations or groups and vice versa. In the words of Jefferson, the clause against establishment of religion by law was intended to erect "a wall of separation between Church and State."

We must consider the New Jersey statute in accordance with the foregoing limitations imposed by the First Amendment. But we must not strike that state statute down if it is within the state's constitutional power even though it approaches the verge of that power. New Jersey cannot consistently with the "establishment of religion" clause of the First Amendment contribute tax-raised funds to the support of an institution which teaches the tenets and faith of any church. On the other hand, other language of the amendment commands that New Jersey cannot exclude individual Catholics, Lutherans, Mohammedans, Baptists, Jews, Methodists, Non-believers, Presbyterians, or the members of any other faith, because of their faith, or lack of it, from receiving the benefits of public welfare legislation. While we do not mean to intimate that a state could not provide transportation only to children attending public schools, we must be careful, in protecting the citizens of New Jersey against state-established churches, to be sure that we do not inadvertently prohibit New Jersey from extending its general State law benefits to all its citizens without regard to their religious belief.

Measured by these standards, we cannot say that the First Amendment prohibits New Jersey from spending tax-raised funds to pay the bus fares of parochial school pupils as a part of a general program under which it pays the fares of pupils attending public and other schools. It is undoubtedly true that children are helped to get to church schools. There is even a possibility that some of the children might not be sent to the church schools if the parents were compelled to pay their children's bus fares out of their own pockets when transportation to a public school would have been paid for by the State. The same possibility exists where the state requires a local transit company to provide reduced fares to school children including those attending parochial schools, or where a municipally owned transportation system undertakes to carry all school children free of charge. Moreover, state-paid policemen, detailed to protect children going to and from church schools from the very real hazards of traffic, would serve much the same purpose and accomplish much the same result as state provisions intended to guarantee free transportation of a kind which the state deems to be best for the school children's welfare. And parents might refuse to risk their children to the serious danger of traffic accidents going to and from parochial schools, the approaches to which were not protected by policemen. Similarly, parents might be reluctant to permit their children to attend schools which the state had cut off from such general government services as ordinary police and fire protection, connections for sewage disposal, public highways and sidewalks. Of course, cutting off church schools from these services, so separate and so indisputably marked off from the religious function, would make it far more difficult for the schools to operate. But such is obviously not the purpose of the First Amendment. That Amendment requires the state to be a neutral in its relations with groups of religious believers and non-believers; it does not require the state to be their adversary. State power is no more to be used so as to handicap religions, than it is to favor them.

This Court has said that parents may, in the discharge of their duty under state compulsory education laws, send their children to a religious rather than a public school if the school meets the secular educational requirements which the state has power to impose. It appears that these parochial schools meet New Jersey's requirements. The State contributes no money to the schools. It does not support them. Its legislation, as applied, does no more than provide a general program to help parents get their children, regardless of their religion, safely and expeditiously to and from accredited schools.

The First Amendment has erected a wall between church and state. That wall must be kept high and impregnable. We could not approve the slightest breach. New Jersey has not breached it here.

Affirmed.

MR. JUSTICE RUTLEDGE, WITH WHOM MR. JUSTICE FRANK-
FURTER, MR. JUSTICE JACKSON AND MR. JUSTICE BURTON
AGREE, DISSENTING.

* * *

I

Not simply an established church, but any law respecting an establishment
of religion is forbidden. The Amendment was broadly but not loosely
phrased. It is the compact and exact summation of its author's views formed
during his long struggle for religious freedom. In Madison's own words char-
acterizing Jefferson's Bill for Establishing Religious Freedom, the guaranty he
put in our national charter, like the bill he piloted through the Virginia Assembly, was "a Model of technical precision, and perspicuous brevity." Madison could not have confused "church" and "an establishment of religion."

The Amendment's purpose was not to strike merely at the official establishment of a single sect, creed or religion, outlawing only a formal relaxation
such as had prevailed in England and some of the colonies. Necessarily it was
to uproot all such relationships. But the object was broader than separating
church and state in the narrow sense. It was to create a complete and permanent separation of the spheres of religious activity and civil authority by
comprehensively forbidding every form of public aid or support for religion.
In proof the Amendment's wording and history unite this Court's consistent
utterances whenever attention has been fixed directly upon the question.

"Religion" appears only once in the Amendment. But the word governs
two prohibitions and governs them alike. It does not have two meanings, one
narrow to forbid "an establishment" and another, much broader, for securing "the free exercise thereof." "Thereof" brings down "religion" with its
entire and exact content, no more and no less, from the first into the second
guaranty, so that Congress and now the states are as broadly restricted
concerning the one as they are regarding the other.

No one would claim today that the Amendment is constricted, in "prohibiting the free exercise" of religion, to securing the free exercise of some
formal or creedal observance of one sect or of many. It secures all forms of
religious expression, creedal, sectarian or nonsectarian wherever and however taking place, except conduct which trenches upon the like freedoms of
others or clearly and presently endangers the community's good order and
security. For the protective purposes of this phase of the basic freedom street
preaching, oral or by distribution of literature, has been given "the same high
estate under the First Amendment as . . . worship in the churches and
preaching from the pulpits." And on this basis parents have been held
entitled to send their children to private, religious schools. Accordingly,
daily religious education commingled with secular is "religion" within the

guaranty's compehensive scope. So are religious training and teaching in whatever form. The word connotes the broadest content, determined not by the form or formality of the teaching, or where it occurs, but by its essential nature regardless of those details.

"Religion" has the same broad significance in the twin prohibition concerning "an establishment." The Amendment was not duplicitous. "Religion" and "establishment" were not used in any formal or technical sense. The prohibition broadly forbids state support, financial or other, of religion in any guise, form or degree. It outlaws all use of public funds for religious purposes. . . .

Donald L. Drakeman

Religion and the Republic: James Madison and the First Amendment

Since the Supreme Court's decision in *Reynolds* v. *United States*[1] in 1878, James Madison's views on the proper relationship of church and state have been a subject of discussion in many cases involving the religion clauses of the First Amendment.[2] With Thomas Jefferson, Madison has been viewed by many scholars and judges as the spokesman for the founding fathers on the subject of religious liberty.[3] One commonly held perception of Madison's influence on the First Amendment was summarized by Justice Wiley Rutledge of the United States Supreme Court as follows: "All the great instruments of the Virginia struggle for religious liberty [in which Madison played an important role] . . . became the warp and woof of our constitutional tradition, not simply by the course of history, but *by the common unifying force of Madison's life, thought and sponsorship*. He epitomized the whole of that tradition in the Amendment's compact, but nonetheless comprehensive phrasing."[4]

These statements raise two important issues in constitutional interpretation.[5] First, is it correct to say that Madison provided a "common unifying force" in the evolution of religious liberty in Virginia and in the adoption of the religion clauses of the First Amendment? As discussed below, Madison originally opposed the inclusion of a bill of rights in the Constitution and probably did not draft the language adopted as the First Amendment.[6] Moreover, Madison's view of the scope of the First Amendment's religion clauses was rejected by Congress. Is it fair to read Madison's acts and writings into the Constitution?

Even if we conclude that Madison's "life, thought, and sponsorship" is a

Portions of this essay are reprinted from *A Journal of Church and State* 25, no. 3 (Autumn 1983): 427–45. Used by permission.

valid context in which to interpret the First Amendment, the second issue is what Madison thought the First Amendment meant. While Madison's brilliant "Memorial and Remonstrance Against Religious Assessments"[7] has been often quoted by the Court, his declarations of national days of prayer and fasting as well as his condemnation of congressional and military chaplains have generally been ignored.[8] Perhaps a complete reading of Madison can provide a picture not only of the rationale behind the separation of church and state, but also of its inherent tensions.

MADISON'S VIEWS ON THE NEED FOR A BILL OF RIGHTS

The original Constitution did not provide for the protection of individual rights, and Madison, a delegate to the Constitutional Convention, did not participate in the brief debate over the inclusion of a bill of rights. Madison's lack of concern over the absence of a bill of rights was rooted in his concept of federalism. Because the Constitution did not grant to the federal government any power over religion, all matters of religion would be reserved to the exclusive authority of the states. To include a provision relating to religion would be to invite a limitation on individual rights. Noting that "a religious establishment wd. have taken place in [Virginia], if the legislative majority had found as they expected, a majority of people in favor of the measure [to provide a tax to support teachers of Christianity] . . .," Madison concluded that "the invasion of private rights is *chiefly* to be apprehended, not from acts of Government contrary to the sense of its constituents, but from acts in which the Government is the mere instrument of the major number of the constituents."[9]

Thus, Madison feared the use of the government by a majority to oppress the minority. He thought that if the federal government were given any power over religion it could be used in a way that inhibited the freedom of conscience. In response to popular demand, however, he agreed to support a bill of rights that would include a guaranty of religious freedom.[10]

WHO WROTE THE FIRST AMENDMENT?

Irving Brant, author of a multi-volume biography of Madison,[11] believes that Madison clearly influenced, and probably drafted, the final version of the religion clauses. Brant's views have been summarized as follows:

> He says that the First Amendment was written by Madison; that he produced this positive and all-inclusive [statement]: "'Congress shall make no law respecting the establishment of religion or prohibiting the free exercise thereof,'" and that this amendment "was Madison's further answer in behalf of all the American people, to every attempt, no matter how small or innocent it might seem to be, to establish religion by financial or other means."[12]

The opposite view has been expressed as follows:

> Madison's insistence was that the full and equal rights of conscience be not infringed by state or federal interference. This requirement was omitted. Madison called for a protection of one's civil rights regardless of his religious view; this concept was not reflected in the committee amendment. Madison called for a prohibition against establishment. The accepted amendment restricts Congress alone, from laws *respecting an* establishment.[13]

This author takes issue with Brant, saying, "Madison was not the author of the first amendment, nor does the amendment reflect his attitude toward the role of government in religion."[14] Accordingly, Madison's "pre-constitution period writings are not reflective of the meaning of the first amendment and cannot be used as interpretative of the amendment's meaning."[15]

Unfortunately, this issue cannot be completely resolved. The records of the House proceedings are scanty, and there appear to be no minutes of the meetings of the conference committee that produced the final version of the First Amendment.[16] We can, therefore, only speculate about the amendment's author and purpose.

Madison proposed two amendments to the Constitution relating to religion. The first read as follows: "The civil rights of none shall be abridged on account of religious belief or worship, nor shall any national religion be established, nor shall the full and equal rights of conscience be in any manner, or in any pretext, infringed."[17] The second stated, "No State shall violate the equal rights of conscience. . . ."[18]

A select committee of the House of Representatives, of which Madison was a member, considered the amendments relating to religion, and reported to Congress the following proposals that were clearly based on Madison's original drafts: "[N]o Religion shall be established by law, nor shall the equal rights of conscience be infringed." The second stated, "No state shall infringe the equal rights of conscience. . . ."[19]

After discussion and referral to the arrangement committee,[20] the House of Representatives passed the following amendment, which was proposed by Representative Fisher Ames of Massachusetts: "Congress shall make no law establishing religion, or to prevent the free exercise thereof, or to infringe the rights of conscience." This version was based on a proposal of Samuel Livermore of New Hampshire. According to the House reporter: "Mr. LIVERMORE was not satisfied with [Madison's] amendment. . . . He thought it would be better to read in this manner, that Congress shall make no laws touching religion, or infringing the rights of conscience."[21] This was the first suggestion that the Constitutional language should prohibit laws "touching" (i.e., "respecting" as it was ultimately adopted) religion or the establishment thereof.

The House also passed an amendment reading, "No State shall infringe . . . the rights of conscience. . . ."[22]

234 Of Religious Liberty

The Senate approved an amendment that resembled the House version of the first religion amendment, but omitted the last phrase. The Senate version read, "Congress shall make no law establishing articles of faith or a mode of worship, or prohibiting the free exercise of religion. . . ."[23] This revision of the House version caused the appointment of a conference committee, of which Madison was a member, which produced the form of the amendment that was enacted: "Congress shall make no law respecting an establishment of religion, or prohibiting the free exercise thereof."[24] The second religion amendment approved by the House, which would have applied to the states, was not approved by the Senate.[25]

Did Madison draft the language of the religion clauses that were adopted? Probably not. Madison's proposals were not chosen. Rather, the House adopted the Ames version, which closely resembled Livermore's proposal. Thus, Ames' and Livermore's language, not Madison's, provided the verbal nucleus for the First Amendment's separation of church and state.

As the head of the House's delegation to the conference committee,[26] Madison undoubtedly influenced the final choice of language, although the paucity of records prohibits us from discovering the extent of Madison's influence. In light of Madison's interest in such issues, however, it is reasonable to assume that Madison was an important member of the conference committee. It is unlikely that the committee would have agreed upon an amendment that was not acceptable to Madison without Madison voicing strong opposition in Congress.

Even if Madison did not draft the language adopted as the religion clauses of the First Amendment, did it sufficiently reflect his beliefs to allow us to consider his thought as its inspiration? According to Madison, the "most valuable" proposal was the one that prohibited the states from violating the rights of conscience.[27] That proposal, of course, was not accepted. Does the First Amendment otherwise embody Madison's views? As two centuries of church-state litigation has shown, it is very difficult to determine what the First Amendment means. Although some have argued that the final version of the First Amendment "demonstrates a religious opinion clearly distinguishable from the Madison proposals,"[28] it is not clear that the Amendment was a repudiation of Madison's views.

Although it is possible to debate interminably over the linguistic difference between Madison's original proposal and the final version of the religion clauses of the First Amendment, the historical record is too incomplete to provide certain answers. Based on the available evidence, however, three reasonable conclusions can be made. First, Madison's desire to prohibit the states from infringing upon the equal rights of conscience was clearly rejected. Second, the language of the First Amendment was not drafted by Madison. Third, although Madison was not the Amendment's draftsman, his interest in the relationship of church and state, as well as his service on the conference committee, suggests that the final version of the

Amendment was not contrary to Madison's position. Had it been contrary to his views, Madison certainly would have taken up his experienced pen to bring pressure on the legislative body as he had in his "Memorial and Remonstrance Against Religious Assessments."[29]

To return to the original question, is it fair to read Madison's acts and writings (particularly those relating to the struggle for religious liberty in Virginia) into the religion clauses of the First Amendment? The answer is no to the extent that Madison's thought may be viewed as representative of the views of the Congress that enacted the Amendment. Rather, Madison stood at the forward edge of Congress, pushing it clearly to require a greater degree of separation of church and state (at both federal and state levels) than many members desired.

Although it is clear that not all of the founding fathers viewed the First Amendment as the embodiment of James Madison's views, there are good reasons to look to Madison for guidance in interpreting the First Amendment. Madison was deeply involved in church-state issues on federal and state levels at the time the First Amendment was enacted. He was also an influential member of the Congress that approved the Amendment. Thus, while Madison's views should not be treated as dispositive interpretations of the First Amendment, they should be accorded substantial weight as those of a profound thinker and statesman who influenced (to an indeterminate extent) the adoption of the First Amendment.

MADISON'S VIEWS ON THE SEPARATION OF CHURCH AND STATE

Recently, controversy has arisen over the nature of Madison's views on the separation of church and state. For example, Robert L. Cord, in a systematic attack on the Supreme Court's reading of Madison and other Founding Fathers entitled *Separation of Church and State: Historical Fact and Current Fiction*,[30] argues that Madison did not intend that there be as strict a separation between church and state as the Supreme Court has decreed. Cord accuses the Supreme Court of relying too heavily on the historical analysis of Leo Pfeffer and other "strict separationist" scholars and advocates.[31] Basing this argument on his interpretation of the words and deeds of the Founding Fathers, Cord asserts that his book shows "conclusively that the Pfeffer interpretation of the Establishment Clause of the First Amendment is incorrect."[32] Cord's conclusion is that nondiscriminatory aid to religion by government is consistent with the First Amendment.[33]

Although discussion of Cord's thesis is beyond the scope of this article, his interpretation of Madison is certainly relevant. There are, as he notes, examples of actions by Madison that run counter to the "strict separationist" position. Madison's "Memorial and Remonstrance," however, is an eloquent call for a strict separation between church and state. How these disparate positions can be reconciled may suggest that both Cord and the "strict separationists" have erred on the side of simplicity. In an effort to articulate a grand theory of Constitutional interpretation, they have overlooked the cultural complexities of the issues.

Madison did not leave volumes of material on his views of the relationship between church and state. As a practical politician he had little time to compose scholarly dissertations on the subject. Rather, he spoke to the issues when they arose, generally with a particular political end in mind. As a result, the views of Madison on church and state issues are always set in the context of conflict, with Madison taking the role of advocate rather than dispassionate scholar.

To obtain the best picture of Madison's views, his writings and activities in the area of church and state should be reviewed. Then, having seen the evidence that Pfeffer, Cord, and others have used to support their theories, we can try to understand Madison's position in light of the culture that enveloped the new nation.

MEMORIAL AND REMONSTRANCE

The *Memorial and Remonstrance* is the centerpiece of Madison's works on the separation of church and state. Leo Pfeffer has extolled it as "one of the great documents in the history of human liberty. . . ."[34] Justice Rutledge called it "at once the most concise and the most accurate statement of the views of the First Amendment's author concerning what is an 'establishment of Religion.'"[35]

The *Memorial and Remonstrance* was drafted by Madison in 1784 in response to a proposal of the Virginia legislature (of which Madison was a member) to levy a tax to support "Teachers of the Christian Religion." The bill was proposed by Patrick Henry and had the support of many leading Virginians, including George Washington, John Marshall, and Richard Henry Lee.[36] In early debates on the bill, Madison fought a potentially losing battle, finally succeeding in having the vote on the bill postponed for several months by agreeing to support a bill incorporating the Protestant Episcopal Church.[37]

The Memorial and Remonstrance was circulated as a petition, and did not bear Madison's name as author. The precise amount of its influence is debatable, but Madison's work was certainly an important component of the effort to defeat the bill.[38] Ultimately, not only was the bill voted down, but the surge of antiestablishment thought caused the enactment of Jefferson's "Act for Establishing Religious Freedom," which had lain dormant since 1779.[39]

Madison began the *Memorial* by saying that it is a "fundamental and undeniable truth, 'that Religion . . . can be directed only by reason and conviction, not by force or violence.'" Religion, which Madison described as "the duty which we owe to our Creator," is precedent to "the claims of Civil Society." Thus, "in matters of Religion, no man's right is abridged by the institution of civil society and . . . Religion is, wholly exempt from its cognizance." This precedence of religion extends even to unorthodox religions and, arguably, to the irreligious. Madison noted: "Whilst we assert for ourselves a freedom to embrace . . . the Religion which we believe to be of divine origin, we cannot deny an equal freedom to those whose minds have not yet yielded to the evidence which has convinced us."[40]

Having established that each person has an individual duty to his creator, Madison asserted that this duty will not necessarily be protected in a democracy because "the majority may trespass on the rights of the minority."[41] Madison warned: "The same authority which can force a citizen to contribute three pence only of his property for the support of any one establishment may force him to conform to any other establishment in all cases whatsoever[.]"[42] Thus, Madison argued, religious groups should fear the power of establishment because it would grant the right to the government to infringe on individual liberties and would give the majority the power to select any religion in vogue.

Likewise, the people should not allow government to align itself with religious groups for the benefit of the government. Madison referred to the historical evils wrought by established churches that, in some cases, "have been seen to erect a spiritual tyranny on the ruins of Civil authority; in many instances they have been seen upholding the thrones of political tyranny; in no instance have they been seen the guardians of the liberties of the people."[43] For Madison, a proper government does not need the support of an established church.

Two key themes can be distilled from the *Memorial and Remonstrance*. First, all individuals are free, by the nature of religion itself, to choose a religion; and it is a violation of this basic human liberty for the law to require them to support any religious institution. Thus, Madison's commitment to religious freedom for all individuals provides the basis for his arguments against religious establishments. Second, as institutions, church and state must maintain totally separate spheres of influence, with neither supporting the other.

OTHER WRITINGS SUPPORTING STRICT SEPARATION

Madison often reiterated his belief in the separation of church and state so that neither institution could influence the other. Admitting the difficulty of building an impenetrable wall, Madison noted in a letter written late in his life:

238 James Madison On Religious Liberty

[I]t may not be easy, in every possible case, to trace the line of separation between the rights of religion and the Civil authority with such distinctness as to avoid collisions and doubts on unessential points. The tendency to usurpation on one side or the other, or to a corrupting coalition or alliance between them, will be best guarded agst. by an entire abstinence of the Gov't from interference in any way whatsoever, beyond the necessity of preserving public order, and protecting each sect agst. trespasses on its legal rights by others.[44]

In his "Detached Memoranda" (which are generally dated fairly late in Madison's life, after his retirement)[45] Madison evidenced fear that the perpetual duration of the charters of religious corporations would enable them to accumulate exhorbitant wealth, thus giving them control over the people and the government. In one of the "Detached Memoranda," Madison stated that all corporations, including ecclesiastical corporations, should be prohibited from the "indefinite accumulation of property [and] the capacity of holding it in perpetuity . . . ."[46] These statements showed an evolution of Madison's thinking, since in 1788 Madison had noted that "[religious] freedom arises from that multiplicity of sects, which pervades America, and which is the best and only security for religious liberty in any society . . . . [I]t is a strong security against religious persecution, and is sufficient to authorize a conclusion that no one sect will ever be able to out-number or depress the rest."[47] In both cases, however, Madison's goal was to keep church and state from influencing each other.

In the "Detached Memoranda," Madison also said that the appointment of chaplains to the House of Representatives and the Senate was improper because the practice violated both the Constitution and the "pure principle of religious freedom."[48] The ability of the majority in Congress to elect a chaplain of a particular faith or denomination would "shut the door of worship against the members whose creeds & consciences forbid a participation in that of the majority. . . ."[49]

Madison also registered his objection to military chaplains, saying: "Better also to disarm in the same way, the precedent of Chaplainships for the army and navy, than erect them into a political authority in matters of religion."[50]

In the "Detached Memoranda," Madison also decried religious proclamations by the president. Referring to days of prayer, fasting, or thanksgiving proclaimed by each of the presidents (including Madison) other than Jefferson, Madison raised five arguments in opposition:

1. That governments ought not to interpose in relation to those subject to their authority but in cases where they can do it with effect . . . .
2. The members of the government as such can in no sense be regarded as possessing an advisory trust from their Constituents in their religious capacities. . . .

3. They seem to imply and certainly nourish the erroneous idea of a *national* religion . . . .

4. The tendency of the practice [is] to narrow the recommendation to the standard of the predominant sect . . . .

5. [T]he liability of the practice to a subserviency to political views; to the scandal of religion, as well as the increase of petty animosities.[51]

ACTIONS SUPPORTING STRICT SEPARATION

Madison's first public venture in the realm of church and state came when he was a young member of the committee of the House of Burgesses of Virginia that was charged with the responsibility of drafting a declaration of rights. The committee's draft, prepared by the eminent George Mason, provided for "the fullest Toleration in the Exercise of Religion,"[52] thus assuring some degree of religious freedom within the context of an established church. Madison was dissatisfied with the committee's proposal, and he introduced an amendment that would have disestablished the Anglican Church. Madison's amendment met with great opposition, and he was forced to replace it with one that emphasized religious liberty but did not outlaw religious establishments.[53]

As president, Madison twice vetoed legislation that he believed violated the establishment clauses of the First Amendment. In one case, Congress had passed "An Act incorporating the Protestant Episcopal Church in the town of Alexandria, in the District of Columbia." Madison vetoed the act because the church's internal governance would become subject to government regulation or support.[54] A week later, Madison vetoed another church-related bill. The bill, "An act for relief of . . . the Baptist Church at Salem Meeting House, in the Mississippi Territory," provided for a piece of government-owned property to be set aside for a Baptist church. Madison noted that the bill "comprises a principle and precedent for the appropriation of funds of the United States for the use and support of religious societies, contrary to the article of the Constitution . . . . "[55]

ACTIONS OPPOSING STRICT SEPARATION

In contrast to Madison's opposition to legislative and military chaplains was his membership on the congressional committee that recommended the appointment of the first congressional chaplain.[56] There is no record that Madison publicly resisted the chaplaincy system until the "Detached Memoranda" were composed (and even the "Detached Memoranda" were probably not widely circulated).

In the "Detached Memoranda," Madison admitted that he had declared national days of prayer and fasting as president. His rationale for doing so is vague, however. Madison noted that "it was understood" that he was "disinclined" to issue such proclamations and that some individuals "supposed

. . . that [such proclamations] might originate with more propriety with the Legislative Body . . . ."[57] Accordingly, a resolution calling for the proclamation of a national day of prayer and fasting was passed by Congress early in the War of 1812.

According to Madison's "Detached Memoranda," in complying with the Congressional request, Madison sought to establish a day on which people could, if they desired, pray together rather than a day on which the people should (or must) pray.[58] Madison's four proclamations, however, had more explicitly religious content than the "Detached Memoranda" may suggest. For example, the proclamation of 9 July 1812 included the following:

> I . . . . recommend [a day] be set apart for the devout purposes of rendering the sovereign of the Universe . . . the public homage due to His holy attributes . . . and especially offering fervent supplications that in the present reason of calamity and war He would take the American people under His peculiar cause and protection; that he would guide their public councils, animate their patriotism, and bestow his blessing on their arms; that He would inspire all nations with a love of justice and of accord and with a reverence for the unerring precept of *our holy religion* to do others as they would require that others should do to them . . . .[59]

In only one of the proclamations of public days of prayer and fasting did Madison speak directly to the issue of the conjunction of religion and government. Although Madison did not raise any questions as to the advisability or constitutionality of the proclamations, he emphasized that they were designed to be recommendations rather than mandates. He declared: "If the public homage of a people can ever be worthy of the favorable regard of the Holy and Omniscient Being to whom it is addressed, it must be that in which those who join in it are guided only by their free choice, by the impulse of their hearts and the dictates of their consciences . . . ."[60]

Madison's presidential proclamations were not his first encounters with the use of days of prayer and fasting. In the early days of the Revolution, a twenty-three-year-old Madison had little sympathy for local preachers who refused to observe a day of fasting proclaimed by the Virginia House of Burgesses:

> A Scotch Parson in an adjoining County refused to observe the fast or preach on that day. When called on he pleaded Conscience . . . . The Committee it seems have their consciences too: they have ordered his Church doors to be shut and his salary to be stopped . . . . If the Convention should connive at their proceedings, I question, should his insolence not abate if he does not get ducked in his new Canonicals and act under the lawful authority of gen. Gage if he pleases.[61]

A few years later, James Madison introduced into the Virginia legislature a "Bill for Appointing Days of Public Fasting and Thanksgiving" drafted by Thomas Jefferson. Under that bill, the General Assembly (or in its absence, the governor or chief magistrate) was empowered to declare a day of prayer or fasting and thanksgiving on which every "minister of the gospel shall . . . perform divine service and preach a sermon, or discourse, suited to the occasion . . . on pain of forfeiting fifty pounds for every failure, not having a reasonable excuse."[62]

PUBLIC RELIGION

Madison's willingness to use religious proclamations may have been rooted in his intense patriotism and his desire to see the new Republic succeed. As a savvy, experienced politician, Madison was undoubtedly aware of the political power of the religious beliefs of the people.[63] This power may have manipulated Madison as much as he manipulated it. The religious force that lay at the heart of the proclamations was the virtually ubiquitous perception of the divine destiny of the new American nation—a common consciousness that scholars have labeled "public religion" or "civil religion."

Public religion is a concept developed by social scientists and historians to explain the cross-fertilization of religion and the secular elements of culture. The literature on public religion is too vast to be summarized here. It should be sufficient, however, to describe the prevailing concepts as recently synthesized by John F. Wilson, a historian of American religion.[64]

Wilson states that the "influence and significance of Christianity [was] a cultural reality in the new nation . . . ."[65] The Protestant Christian myth and theology shared by so many of the citizens of the new Republic provided a cultural framework in which the events of the world were viewed.[66] Thus, even while Madison and others were severing the formal ties between church and state, the cultural ties were growing stronger.

The crux of eighteenth-century public religion in America was that the new nation had a special role in world history. Its citizens viewed the nation as having a "national covenant" with God.[67] As a result, "the national experience [is placed] in a universal framework. . . . America is placed at center stage in the concluding act of world history."[68]

Public religion becomes particularly important in times of major national conflict when the viability of the national covenant is questioned. In such times the nation's leader must reaffirm the national covenant to unite the nation. Wilson notes: "[T]here is a pronounced periodicy in the religious references made by [Presidents while in office]. These seem to have been closely correlated with perceived threats to the society. Religious language about the public realm is occasioned by national crisis."[69]

Although Madison's motives for declaring days of prayer and fasting will never be known, it is likely that they were intended (at least in part) to unite the divided country during the War of 1812 by focusing attention on the national covenant that superseded regional and political factionalism.

Similar reasons may have been behind Madison's willingness to support the legislative chaplaincy system. From the Puritan settlers through George Washington, homage had been paid to the divine mission of the new world. Even Benjamin Franklin (not known as a devout churchman) proposed that the Constitutional Convention commence with a prayer.[70] Although Madison found substantial support for his efforts to separate state from church, he may not have been terribly troubled over not separating the legislature from God's daily blessing. The symbolism of a representative of God ordaining each session of Congress, combined with the fact that the vast majority of Congressmen were undoubtedly Christians, may have overwhelmed any objection by Madison on philosophical grounds.

RELIGION VERSUS RELIGIOUS INSTITUTIONS

Madison was fearful of the potential for abuse by churches that had the backing of governmental power. His early efforts to sever church from state in Virginia set a lifelong principle from which he never deviated: There must be strict separation between the government and religious institutions. As president, Madison struck out again at potential establishments involving governmental support of religious institutions. He vetoed the incorporation of a church and also vetoed a bill setting aside land for a church in a new territory. Thus, Madison registered opposition when he saw the state attempt to aid religious institutions.

The line between government and religious belief, however, is far less clear. The widely-held view of the national covenant precluded a strict separation of religion and the state. For many Americans, the role of the state was defined in explicitly religious terms. Thus, the state could not be segregated completely from religious belief and symbolism. The nature of the public religion demanded Madison's presidential proclamations of days of prayer and fasting. The proclamations (and, similarly, the legislative and military chaplains) must be viewed not as the intermeddling of church and state but as the result of a cultural fusion of religion and the new nation.

To return to Professor Cord's thesis: Did Madison believe that nondiscriminatory aid to religion was constitutional? The answer is—sometimes. Aid to churches and other religious organizations was improper in Madison's view. Although Madison was probably never faced with a completely nondiscriminatory situation, such as a bill to support teachers of all religions, his broad language in the *Memorial and Remonstrance* and elsewhere shows his opposition to the conjunction of the institutions of church and state. For Madison, the goal is "mutual independence." He wrote: "The experience of the United States is a happy disproof of the error. . . that without a legal incorporation of religious and civil policy, neither could be supported. A mutual independence is found most friendly to practical Religion, to social harmony, and to political prosperity. . . .[71]

As to nondiscriminatory "aids" to religious belief—such as the declaration of days of prayer and fasting—Madison found them permissible but he was uncomfortable with them. As president he declared them, thus suggesting that he did not believe them to be unconstitutional. At least later in life, however, he found them philosophically undesirable. Similarly, legislative chaplains, which were designed to invoke God's blessing on the nation's leaders, did not lend the support of government to specific religious institutions. So, Madison raised no constitutional objections when he was in Congress, despite his later qualms. Religious myth and symbolism was part of the American culture during Madison's life. No matter how much he could separate church from state he could not separate religion from the Republic.

CONCLUSION

How should this analysis of Madison affect the interpretation of the religion clauses of the First Amendment? First, no individual's views on church and state, including Madison's, were written into the Constitution. The First Amendment to the Constitution was the product of considerable negotiation and political compromise. The vagueness of the final version was probably its greatest political strength. Madison's views, however, should instruct the inquiry into the meaning of the First Amendment.

Second, in Madison's day, religion and government in America were culturally linked. In assessing the value of Madison's thought in the consideration of contemporary questions, the ways in which "public religion" may have evolved should be considered. To do so would be well beyond the scope of this article; but it should be noted that there are many who see a continuing link between religious thought and the nation's destiny.[72]

Third, if Madison's guidance on Constitutional issues is sought, we should understand that his chief fear was the infringement of the freedom of conscience. His efforts to limit the power of religious institutions and to separate them from government stem from his fervent desire to prohibit church or state from limiting religious freedom.

Finally, we should remember that issues of church and state are often extremely complex. Even Madison admitted the difficulty of tracing "the line of separation between the rights of religion and the Civil authority" in a time essentially free of income taxes, public schools, and the other complications of twentieth-century American life. Every contemporary Constitutional issue simply cannot be put in an eighteenth-century pigeon hole.

NOTES

1. 98 U.S. 145 (1878). In *Reynolds,* the Court said, "[A]t the first session of the first Congress the amendment now under consideration [the First Amendment] was proposed with others by Mr. Madison." 98 U.S. at 164.

2. The First Amendment religion clauses are as follows: "Congress shall make no law respecting an establishment of religion, or prohibiting the free exercise thereof." U.S., *Constitution,* Amend. I. Madison's views of church and state have been discussed in at least forty federal cases and fifty-five state cases, including virtually every major Supreme Court case.

3. This article's focus on James Madison is not intended to minimize the influence of Thomas Jefferson and others on the development of scholarship and judicial decisions on the First Amendment.

4. *Everson* v. *Board of Education,* 330 U.S. 1, 39 (1946) (emphasis added). In *Everson,* the majority opinion also discussed Madison. The opinion, by Justice Black, read, "This Court has previously recognized that the provisions of the First Amendment in the drafting and adoption of which Madison and Jefferson played such leading roles, had the same objective and were intended to provide the same protection against governmental intrusion or religious liberty as the Virginia [Bill of Religious Liberty]." 330 U.S. at 13.

5. By using Justice Rutledge's statements, I do not mean to suggest that Rutledge necessarily speaks for the Supreme Court (or other courts). His views have, however, been adopted by a number of judges and scholars. They are illustrative of an extreme (but not necessarily uncommon) interpretation of the legislative history of the First Amendment.

6. See pp. 236–39 of this essay.

7. William T. Hutchinson et al., eds., *The Papers of James Madison,* 13 vols. (Chicago: University of Chicago Press, 1962-69), 8, 2 pp. 98-304. There are two major compilations of Madison's works. The more recent compilation, published by the University of Chicago Press, only included Madison's writings through 1791 at this writing. It will be used for all of Madison's works until that time. The earlier compilation, edited by Gaillard Hunt, was completed during the period 1900-1910; Gaillard Hunt, ed., *The Writings of James Madison,* 9 vols. (New York, 1904). This will be used for references to Madison's works after 1791.

8. See pp. 243–45 of this essay.

9. Hutchinson 11, p. 298 (emphasis in the original, i.e., by Madison). Madison is referring to the bill presented to the General Assembly of Virignia that provided for a general assessment to support "teachers of the Christian religion."

10. Ibid., 11, p. 297. Madison had to make this promise to obtain Virginia's ratification of the Constitution; see Irving Brant, "Madison: On the Separation of Church and State," *William and Mary Quarterly,* third series, 8 (January 1951): 12.

11. Brant's four volume series chronicles Madison's entire life. The last volume was published in 1961. Irving Brant, *The Life of James Madison,* 4 vols. (Indianapolis: Bobbs-Merrill, 1941-54).

12. Anson Phelps Stokes, *Church and State in the United States,* 3 vols. (New York: Harper & Brothers, 1950) 1, p. 548. Brant's view is followed to some extent in Richard E. Morgan, *The Supreme Court and Religion* (New York: Macmillan Publishing Co., 1972), p. 24. ("Thus while it is impossible to refer to any 'intent' of the Framers of the First

Amendment, the evidence establishes at least a presumption in favor of the hard-line Madisonian position.")

13. Clifton Kruse, "The Historical Meaning and Judicial Construction of the Establishment of Religion Clause of the First Amendment," *Washburn Law Journal* 2 (Winter 1962):73 (emphasis in the original).

14. Ibid., p. 65.

15. Ibid.

16. Stokes, 1, p. 548.

17. Hutchinson, 12, p. 201.

18. Ibid., p. 202.

19. Ibid., p. 757.

20. *Annals of the Congress of the United States. The Debates and Proceedings in the Congress of the United States*, Vol. 1, compiled from Authentic Materials by Joseph Gales, Sr. (Washington: Gales and Seaton, 1834), p. 796 (hereafter cited as *Annals of Congress*).

21. *Annals of Congress*, p. 759. Note that both Ames and Livermore represented states having established churches. It has been suggested that Livermore's purpose in using the word "touching" was to prohibit federal interference with state establishments; see, for example, Joseph M. Snee, "Religious Disestablishment and the Fourteenth Amendment," *Washington University Law Quarterly* 1954 (December 1954): 371-407. I tend to agree. In any event, Anson Phelps Stokes notes that Livermore has "received almost no public credit for his services in suggesting the essential part of the phraseology of our religious freedom guarantee . . . ." Stokes, 1, p. 543.

22. Ibid., p. 748.

23. Stokes, 1, p. 548.

24. *Annals of Congress*, p. 948.

25. See Kruse, pp. 71-72.

26. *Annals of Congress*, p. 547.

27. It is possible that Madison's enthusiasm was primarily rhetorical. There seemed to be little doubt that some form of restriction against involvement in religious matters would be applied to the federal government. A restriction applicable to the states, however, could have the effect of disestablishing churches in several states and would have made major changes in the relationship of church and state in virtually all of the states. Thus, Madison had little to lose, and possibly much to gain, by drawing attention to the restriction on the states.

28. Kruse, p. 73. Perhaps the most careful analysis of the debates on the religion clauses is found in Michael J. Malbin, *Religion and Politics: The Intentions of the Authors of the First Amendment* (Washington, D.C.: American Enterprise Institute, 1978), in which the author attempts to explain the positions of the various political factions warring over the First Amendment. Malbin concludes that nondiscriminatory aid to religion was not forbidden in the framers' minds by the First Amendment. In general, however, Malbin seems to believe, unlike this author, that one can discern a clear legislative intent behind the religion clauses of the First Amendment.

29. See Ralph Ketcham, *James Madison: A Biography* (New York: Macmillan Company, 1971), p. 162 et. seq.

30. Robert L. Cord, *Separation of Church and State: Historical Fact and Current Fiction* (New York: Lambeth Press, 1982).

31. See, for example, Leo Pfeffer, *Church, State, and Freedom*, rev. ed. (Boston: Beacon Press, 1967).

32. Cord, p. 81.

33. Ibid., p. xiv. Not long ago, a federal judge used Cord's thesis to provide a basis for ignoring a long line of Supreme Court cases on the Establishment Clause of the First Amendment. In upholding the constitutionality of prayers led by teachers in the public schools, the judge noted that "the Court agrees with the studied conclusions of Cord that it should be clear that the traditional interpretation of Madison and Jefferson [advocating a strict separation between church and state] is historically faulty if not virtually unfounded . . . . " (*Jaffree* v. *Board of School Commissioners*, Civ. No. 82-079211, mem. op. at 28 [S.D. Ala. 1983]). This decision was immediately stayed by Supreme Court Justice Powell and later reversed by the federal court of appeals. This case shows, however, the influence that historical scholarship may have on current First Amendment issues.

34. Pfeffer, p. 11. Pfeffer notes that the "Memorial and Remonstrance" until revived by Justice Rutledge in the *Everson* case, was known to only a few historical students." Ibid.

35. *Everson* v. *Board of Education*, 330 U.S. at 37.

36. Gaillard Hunt, "James Madison and Religious Liberty," *Annual Report of the American Historical Association for the Year 1901* (1902): 168.

37. Pfeffer, p. 111. Pfeffer explains that the incorporation was believed to be necessary to order the affairs of the Protestant Episcopal Church following its split from the Anglican Church as a result of the Revolution. The incorporation bill stated that the Episcopal clergy held little to the church property and dealt with other similar issues. Hutchinson, 8, p. 196.

38. The editors of the most recent collection of Madison's writings note that "While at least thirteen of JM's petitions were circulated (and in time bore 1,552 signatures), another (and still anonymous) petition writer found that his attack on the 'teachers of Christian Religion' measure gained more widespread support. Twenty-nine petitions, signed by 4,899 Virginians, came from the pen of this unknown opponent of a church-state tie." Hutchinson, 8, p. 297 (ed. note).

39. Pfeffer, p. 113. Hutchinson, 8, pp. 195, 401 (ed. notes).

40. Ibid., 8, p. 299.

41. Ibid., 8, p. 300.

42. Ibid.

43. Ibid.

44. Letter to Rev. Adams (1832), Hunt, 9, p. 487.

45. See Elizabeth Fleet, ed., "Madison's 'Detached Memoranda,'" *William and Mary Quarterly* 3 (October 1946): 532-68. Fleet concludes that Madison drafted the "Detached Memoranda" after his retirement from the presidency in 1817 (p. 535).

46. Fleet, p. 556.

47. Hutchinson, 11, pp. 130-31.

48. Fleet, p. 558.

49. Ibid.

50. Ibid., p. 559.

51. Ibid., pp. 560-61.

52. Hutchinson, 1, p. 173.

53. Madison's amendment read: "That Religion or the duty we owe to our Creator, and the manner of discharging it, being under the direction of reason and conviction only, not to violence or compulsion all men are equally entitled to the full and free exercise of it according to the dictates of conscience; and therefore that no man or class of men ought, on account of religion to be invested with peculiar emoluments or privileges; nor

subjected to any penalties or disabilities . . . ." Hutchinson, 1, p. 174.

54. Saul K. Padover, *The Complete Madison* (New York: Harper and Brothers 1953), p. 307.

55. Ibid., p. 308.

56. See Cord, p. 23.

57. Fleet, p. 562.

58. Brant, *The Life of James Madison*, 6, p. 28.

59. James D. Richardson, *Messages and Papers of the Presidents, 1789-1897*, 10 vols. (Washington, D.C.: Bureau of National Literature and Art, 1901) 1, p. 513 (emphasis added).

60. Ibid., p. 533.

61. Hutchinson, 1, p. 161.

62. Julian P. Boyd, ed., *The Papers of Thomas Jefferson*, 17 vols. (Princeton: Princeton University Press, 1950) 2, p. 556.

63. The historian Perry Miller notes that the Federalists denounced Madison's proclamation as a trick designed to inspire public (and perhaps divine) support for the unpopular War of 1812; Perry Miller, *The Life of the Mind in America* (New York: Harcourt, Brace and World, Inc., 1965), pp 38-39.

64. John F. Wilson, *Public Religion in American Culture* (Philadelphia: Temple University Press, 1979). Wilson describes his book as a "clarification and delineation of the controlling concept [of public religion]" (p. viii).

65. Ibid., p. 10.

66. As Wilson notes, this "cultural hegemony of republican Protestantism" did not end until at least the beginning of the twentieth century, and possibly later. Ibid., p. 14 et. seq. This does not signify the end of the public religion. Rather, the nature of the "national convenant" constantly changes to reflect social changes and new issues. Ibid., p. 40.

67. Ibid., p. 28.

68. Ibid., p. 29.

69. Ibid., p. 56.

70. "Debates in the Federal Convention of 1787 as Reported by James Madison." *Documents Illustrative of the Formation of the Union of the American States* (Washington, D.C.: Government Printing Office, 1927), pp. 295-96.

71. Padover, p. 310.

72. See, e.g., individuals ranging from Jerry Falwell and the Moral Majority to scholars such as Robert Bellah; see, for example, Robert N. Bellah, *The Broken Covenant: American Civil Religion in Time of Trial* (New York: The Seabury Press, 1975).

PART IX

Nineteenth-Century Reactions

In order to make sense out of events in the twentieth century respecting religious freedom, it is absolutely essential that one understand the ways in which religion became a part of the cultural fabric of the nineteenth century. The de facto Protestant establishment that emerged by the middle of the century provides some clear reminders of the risks involved in such arrangements. Left essentially free from interference by the Supreme Court, Protestant leadership created numerous links with state governments and public institutions. Madison might well have viewed these developments as proof of the case he had made all his life concerning church-state relations.

Robert S. Alley

The Protestant Establishment

The survey of historical events surrounding James Madison would suggest to the reader that the America of the nineteenth century was devoted to the principles of religious freedom. Indeed, it was public pressure that convinced Madison he should support a Bill of Rights in 1789. The star in that collection was, for Madison, freedom of conscience. Yet within a very few years the public pronouncements of Protestant clergy made it clear that a kind of "voluntary establishment" was emerging: "As they watched the erosion of the establishments in Connecticut and Massachusetts, the New England clergy could not believe that morals could survive the severing of church from state. Yet when the divorce came there appeared a conception of the relation of religion to society that accepted the American commitment to freedom and the voluntary principle in church-state relations without making sacrifice of the precious conception that religion was the essential ingredient of the public weal."[1]

By the end of the first quarter of the nineteenth century the leadership of many Protestant denominations were speaking unreservedly about the new nation as a "Christian" republic. John Wilson in his essay identifies this as the fourth period in church-state relations in the nation, a time when "evangelical forces in the United States" sought "to recover in an informal way what had been their legal position before disestablishment" (p. 106). Historian Paul Nagel observed that this sentiment suddenly "took over the tone of the great American sermon and the Fourth of July oration."

The causes of this affirmation are, I believe, quite numerous, but at least two contributing forces have significance. First, the churches experienced phenomenal growth after 1800. The irony of this outcome was that both Roger Williams and Madison had predicted it. Madison returned to that theme often: ". . . the lapse of time now more than 50 years since the legal

251

support of Religion was withdrawn sufficiently prove that it does not need the support of Government and it will scarcely be contended that Government has suffered by the exemption of Religion from its cognizance, or its pecuniary aid."

Both men had time after time insisted that the churches would be stronger if they were free and voluntary. That was precisely the case. The problem was that once this healthy specimen considered its condition, it drew the perverse conclusion that now was the time to gain that control denied by the Bill of Rights. Part of the difficulty was that many clergymen had never accepted the second part of the Madison formula: that the government had not "suffered" from the divorce.

The mission fever that captured most denominations by 1820 resulted in the rapid development of complex organizational structures and educational institutions. These, in turn, provided the religious leadership with an unanticipated power base from which to press, with missionary zeal, for laws based on moral and religious principles:

> One question they left for later generations to answer, of course, was the extent to which a free people, persuaded by religious influences that sumptuary laws were vital to the national interest, might end by enforcing practices deemed by dissenters prejudicial to their own rights and freedom. The tendency of later constitutional development to regard such sumptuary law as tending toward an establishment of religion, would have been incomprehensible to the early republican theocrats. Legislation inevitably had a moral content, and legislatures were responsible for the health of the whole society. Sumptuary law, therefore, was not a matter of church and state at all.[2]

The second factor of importance is described well by Nagel:

> I think one reason for this [the national emphasis upon a 'Christian America'] is that around the time of the death of Adams and Jefferson, ten years before Madison's death, there is dramatic shift in the sense of comfort, as opposed to uneasiness, over the Republic. Ten years after the War of 1812 the new democratic movement wanted to seem to be positive to brotherhood. They wanted to present something positive as opposed to what they thought was the negativism of the Republicans. Politics had a lot to do with it.

The first inclination of the student of the colonial period might be to wonder how Madison might have reacted to such a primary shift in attitude. But Madison lived through more than one-third of the nineteenth century and there is no need for such speculation. For Madison was aware of what was happening. In 1833, the very year that Massachusetts became the final state to abolish religious establishment, the venerable Virginian received a pamphlet from one Jasper Adams [The Relations of Christianity to Civil Government in the United States] with a request for Madison's views. In the publication Adams set forth an attack upon the notion "that Christianity had no connection with our civil constitutions of government." Rather, he argued, "the people of the United States have retained the Christian religion as the foundation of their civil, legal, and political institutions." He believed that the nation did indeed have a national religion. Remarking upon Adams's argument, Adrienne Koch wrote: ". . . he lamented that the view was gaining ground that religion and government had no connection with each other and found this view 'in the highest degree pernicious in its tendency' to all our institutions, pervasively corrupting the morals of the American people."[3]

Adams appears to have sent his pamphlet to numerous political luminaries of the time. In contrast to Madison's strong dissent were the comments of Justices John Marshall and Joseph Story. Marshall observed, "The American population is entirely Christian, and with us, Christianity and religion are identified." Story was more strident, writing, "I have read it with uncommon satisfaction. I think its tone and spirit excellent. My own private judgment has long been (and every day's experience more and more confirms me in it) that government can not long exist without an alliance with religion to some extent; and that Christianity is indispensable to the true interests and solid foundations of free government."

Madison responded, in spite of rheumatism "which makes my hand and fingers as averse to the pen as they are awkward in the use of it." He turned directly to Adams's argument that there should be an established Christian state, noting that in Europe "few of the most enlightened judges . . . will maintain that the system has been favorable either to Religion or to Government." He then noted, "It remained for North America to bring the great and interesting subject to a fair, and finally to a decisive test." In responding to the charge that religion left to itself would "run into extravagances injurious both to religion and to social order," Madison was to the point in suggesting that Adams was reflecting "excessive excitement." He went on to affirm that "Reason will gradually regain its ascendancy." His firmest point he made his conclusion: "The tendency to a usurpation on one side or the other, or to a corrupting coalition or alliance between them, will be best guarded against by an entire abstinence of the Government from interference in any way whatever, beyond the necessity of preserving public order, and protecting each sect against trespass on its legal rights by others."

Koch, remarking upon this response, observed, "he tried to establish a *secular* moral order as the American political system, and thought it might be good, perhaps even the best order ever devised." Thus Madison was consistent on the principle to the end of his life, a point well noted by Koch: "On the whole, it seems fair to say that Madison came as close to making an absolute of religious liberty as he ever did of any value in the bouquet traditionally available to men. . . ."[4]

For Madison, it would have been a more felicitous turn of history if the nation had been responding to the words of Zelotes Fuller as reprinted in this section. His analysis harks back to the founding fathers as likewise do the words of David Moulton and Mordicai Myers in their 1832 report regarding the appointment of chaplains in New York State. The latter reminded the state legislators that "there is an *evil spirit* abroad, seeking to infuse its baleful influence among the people, to obtain a dominant power in the civil government, through which to manage all the political concerns of the nation, and thus to establish ecclesiastical dominion on the ruins of our free republican institutions, and the civil and religious liberties of our country."5 And they concluded: "But it is not true that christianity as such is the law of the land. The constitution is the 'supreme' law of the land; by virtue of which the 'mosque,' the 'synagogue,' the 'christian church,' and all other churches and religions are placed on equal grounds."6

Fuller was equally direct in his 1830 address: "Never I beseech of you, encourage a certain 'Christian party in politics,' which under moral and religious pretenses, is officiously and continually interfering with the religious opinions of others, and endeavouring to effect by law and other means, equally exceptionable, a systematic course of measures, evidently calculated, to lead to a union of Church and State." And it was the circumstances that made these pleas necessary which brought about a virtual Protestant establishment by mid-century. "In the early nineteenth century, Protestant denominations hoped to achieve by voluntary means what establishment had not been able to do—to bring about what Horace Bushnell called 'a complete christian commonweath.' They were convinced that the Christian state they envisaged would be so liberal and tolerant that persons of good will could hardly oppose it, for to them it combined freedom and truth."7

Indeed, by the middle of the century Bushnell provided an excellent description of a Protestant mood sweeping the country: "The wilderness shall bud and blossom as the rose before us; and we will not cease; till a christian nation throws up its temples of worship on every hill and plain; till knowledge, virtue and religion, blending their dignity and their heathful power, have filled our great country with a manly and happy race of people, and the bands of a complete christian commonwealth are seen to span the continent."8

To be sure, there was no official church, no established order, but the hegemony claimed by Protestants seemed almost complete. "Despite the absence of a legally established faith, foreign travelers and thoughtful Americans believed that evangelical Protestantism had made itself the religion of the land and that its clergymen were the arbiters of public morals."9

Timothy Smith goes on to affirm that by "1860 the clergy had recovered whatever influence over public affairs they had lost in the generations of Thomas Jefferson and Andrew Jackson, and enjoyed it without let or hindrance from legal sanctions."10 Thus, Smith contends, "Protestants were now willing to entrust the state with the task of educating children, confident that education would be 'religious' still."11

Faced with resistance this kind of attitude could turn violently intolerant.[12] Phrases such as the following flowed freely from responsible Protestant leaders Ezra Stiles Ely (1828); Charles G. Finney (1837); Gardiner Spring (1820):

> We are a Christian nation: we have a right to demand that all our rulers in their conduct shall conform to Christian morality; and if they do not, it is the duty and privilege of Christian freemen to make a new and a better election.[13]

> And multitudes will never yield, until the friends of God and man can form a public sentiment so strong as to crush the character of every man who will not give it up.[14]

> Liberty, without godliness, is but another name for anarchy or despotism.[15]

By 1860 the mood of the country was largely fashioned along the lines described. The Madison legacy might well have appeared dead to those lingering supporters of religious freedom as they viewed the political and social landscapes. Winthrop Hudson, in his classic *The Great Tradition of the American Churches*, observed: "The ideals, the convictions, the language, the customs, the institutions of society were so shot through with Christian presuppositions that the culture itself nurtured and nourished the Christian faith."[16]

Well, perhaps. Yet there is the gnawing thought that those who assess that period in our history have on occasion failed to examine the premise. Was Roger Williams correct when he insisted that just such a coalition undermines the essentials of the Christian faith? Madison was to pose the same query numerous times in his career.

Certainly it is fair to describe the mid-nineteenth century as a time of "voluntary" establishment. Fear of Roman Catholics, fanned by immigration from Europe, inflamed latent prejudices and caused a retrenchment against forces distinctly different from the mainstream. Attaching themselves to the tradition of theocracy tempered by toleration, the nation's institutions reflected a Protestant bias. In so doing the institutions of government departed from the principles of the First Amendment. It is essential to make this clear. It was not a matter of the times changing in such way as to demand new applications of an old principle. Rather the principle espoused by Madison and Williams was simply abandoned.

At least two factors combined to cause the collapse of this incipient theocratic alternative. The immigration effectively recreated the conditions that prevailed prior to the revolution, i.e., a variety of religious expressions sufficiently at variance to necessitate a new accommodation. The result was a slow erosion of the more flagrant violations such as the Protestant domination of New York public schools. At the same time, the decline in anti-

Catholicism was evident even in the defeat of Al Smith in 1928. Further, a war had thrust America onto a world stage. Finally, there is merit in Handy's argument that: "During the period of religious and economic depression, then, the 'Protestant era' in America was brought to a close; Protestantism emerged no longer as the 'national religion.' The test of depression was a severe one; it laid bare certain weaknesses in American Protestantism. But the repudiation of the virtual identification of Protestantism with American culture by an able and growing group of religious leaders freed many Protestants to recover in a fresh way their own heritages and their original sources of inspiration."[17]

Beyond all these reasons, in some ways more immediately significant was the collapse of the Protestant theological center. Biblical criticism, rampant by the close of the nineteenth century, brought about an awareness that no single definition of Protestant Christianity was broad enough to encompass a majority. In short, the presumed meaning of a Christian nation was lost in a swell of discontinuity among religious factions. If the first fracture to reach national attention was that between Fundamentalism and the remainder of Protestants in the Scopes trial, no less important were the fissures caused by various degrees of acceptance of the critical method respecting the Bible. Thus, the Enlightenment that had in the eighteenth century so molded the founding thinkers, now effected a marked disjunction respecting the Bible.

The denouement came in the 1960s with the "Death of God" movement and the experience of loss of theological direction. If Christians ever knew what they meant by describing the nation by their religious label, after World War II the consensus was gone.

During the period when this loss of focus was occurring another approach to the Puritan heritage of the "city on the hill" emerged with Woodrow Wilson. Historian Louis Hartz, in 1968, discussed what he termed a potential "nationalist Americanism": "The matter of the nationalist response goes back, in fact, to the moment of the migration itself. For when the English Puritan comes to America, he is no longer completely 'English,' which means that he has to find a new national identity. And where is that identity to come from if not from Puritanism itself, the ideal part which he has extracted from the English whole and which alone he possesses. Hence the part becomes, as it were, a new whole and Puritanism itself blossoms into 'Americanism.'"[18]

Hartz believed that with Wilson there was born a new American "messianism" in which the President sought to impose our institutions, "seeking to evangelize the results of a peculiar experience."[19] Certainly Wilson gave support to the thesis with remarks such as this one regarding the prosecution of the war. "In a righteous cause they have won immortal glory and have nobly served their nation in serving mankind. God has indeed been gracious."[20]

What becomes evident here is that the culture has appropriated the Christian tradition, nationalized it, and sanitized it. This civic piety becomes nonsectarian and serves our coins and the CIA.[21] While it often lies dormant, this new American "faith" fuels nationalistic messianism in times of stress. And the problem appears to be that religious leaders have often failed to recognize the cultural transfer. Many clergy speak to America in theological terms, assuming that their peculiar version of God must perforce be the God of Christian America since there is only one God and he has revealed himself in a particular fashion. In this situation mischief abounds.

It is this precise problem that confronted the Supreme Court by the sixties when citizens began to clamor for nonsectarian prayer in schools, as well as Bible-reading. There was a dualism at work such that even Billy Graham found himself claiming two gods. But the "true believer" cannot long abide generalized, nonsectarian, prayers. Thus, certain church groups sought to impose their own definitions upon this acculturated religion.

Because the notion of God is so diffused in current debates, concerned citizens have difficulty in identifying a proper definition of the divine. In this situation "In God We Trust" is often equated with dogmatic, trinitarian Christianity. The United States is awash with deities and with churches anxiously seeking to amalgamate them and define them in terms of ancient dogma. In this confusion the principle of religious freedom is more and more often viewed with suspicion. Its opponents in the 1980s seek to make that same equation espoused by Patrick Henry and the supporters of the Assessment Bill.

An excellent example of this confusion focuses upon the *Engel* v. *Vitale* Supreme Court decision of 1962. Justice Hugo Black delivered the opinion of the Court in which he unmistakably affirmed the right of persons to practice voluntary prayer in schools. He wrote that the colonists came to America on many occasions. ". . . filled with the hope that they could find a place in which they could pray when they pleased to the God of their faith in the language they chose."

In spite of this position of the Court, the fact that it outlawed prescribed prayer in New York public schools allowed those who preferred toleration to freedom to argue that the Court "had kicked God out of the schools." In the public mind then there was created a confusion between free exercise and establishment.

That confusion has prevailed for two decades during which Americans were told that any effort to enforce the establishment clause led necessarily to a violation of free exercise. Conversely, any effort to insist that prescribed prayer was a violation of the free exercise of the minority was met with the contention that catering to minority sentiment was tantamount to establishing secularism as a religion in the classrooms. These convolutions test the Madisonian principle, as they test the American citizen. Madison would, I believe, respond as he did to Jasper Adams in 1833. And he would stand not upon a technicality of the First Amendment, but rather upon the natural rights of man and liberty of conscience. Indeed, the First Amendment is most significant to our democracy at those special times when the majority seeks to assert an ideology. It is then that Jefferson's warning at the close of his Bill for Religious Freedom is most appropriate to be read: "the rights hereby asserted are of the natural rights of mankind, and that if any act shall be hereafter passed to repeal the present, or to narrow its operation such act will be an infringement of natural rights.[22]

Persons committed to Madison's vision of a free conscience in a secular democracy are obligated to demonstrate that the alternative to a sterile religious dogma seeking to establish a national faith is *not* the equally depressing hopelessness of a totally relativistic world. Henry Steele Commager insists that Madison and his contemporaries were dedicated to a nation of morality and virtue, justice and happiness. The Madison challenge, anchored in natural rights, is to "establish more firmly the liberties, the prosperity, and the happiness of the Commonwealth." If we cannot respond positively then Madison's mantel falls unattended.

NOTES

1. Elwyn Smith. "The Voluntary Establishment of Religion," in *The Religion of the Republic,* ed. Elwyn Smith (Philadelphia: Fortress, 1971), p. 155.

2. Ibid.

3. Adrienne Koch, *Madison's "Advice to My Country,"* (Princeton: Princeton University Press, 1966), p. 37.

4. Ibid., p. 48.

5. David Moulton and Mordecai Myers, *Report of the Select Committee of the New York State Assembly on the Several Memorials Against Appointing Chaplains to the Legislature.* Reprinted in Joseph Blau, ed., *Cornerstones of Religious Freedom in America* (Boston: Beacon, 1950), pp. 152-53.

6. Blau, p. 154.

7. Robert T. Handy, "The Magna Charta of Religious Freedom in America," *Union Seminary Quarterly Review* 38 (1984): 312.

8. Horace Busnell, *Barbarism the First Danger: A Discourse for Home Missions* (New York, 1947), p. 32.

9. Timothy L. Smith, *Revivalism and Social Reform* (New York: Harper, 1957), p. 11.

10. Ibid., p. 38.

11. Timothy Smith, "Protestant Schooling and American Nationality, 1800-1850," *Journal of American History* LIII (1966-1967): 687.

12. See also Ray Billington, *The Protestant Crusade, 1800-1860* (Chicago: Quadrangle Books, 1964), for an analysis of anti-Catholic feeling.

13. Ezra Stiles Ely, as quoted in Robert T. Handy, *A Christian America* (New York: Oxford, 1984), p. 50.

14. Charles G. Finney, ibid.

15. Gardiner Spring, ibid.

16. Winthrop Hudson, *The Great Tradition of the American Churches* (New York: Harper, 1953), p. 108.

17. Robert T. Handy, "The American Religious Depression," in *Religion in American History*, eds. John Mulder and John Wilson (Englewood Cliffs, N.J.: Prentice Hall, 1978), p. 442.

18. Louis Hartz, "The Nature of Revolution," *Hearings Before the Committee on Foreign Relations*, United States Congress, Second Session, February 26, 1968, p. 118.

19. Ibid., p. 133.

20. Woodrow Wilson, *Selected Literary and Political Papers and Addresses of Woodrow Wilson* (New York: Grosset & Dunlap, 1927), II, p. 277.

21. On the CIA building in Virginia is the inscription "You shall know the truth and the truth shall make you free."

22. "Act for Establishing Religious Freedom," written by Thomas Jefferson and made law by the Virginia legislature in 1786.

Zelotes Fuller

The Tree of Liberty:
An Address in Celebration of the
Birth of Washington

Wisely and justly has it been asserted, that *all mankind are born free and with equal rights:* that the rights of conscience, of private judgment, and the freedom of opinion and of speech, are natural and unalienable—that they are, by the principles inherent in their very natures, born *free* and *equal,* by a certain code which existed before all civil governments—that these blessings, are, as a *legacy,* guaranteed by Almighty God, to every individual.

These invaluable privileges and blessings, Washington and his distinguished associates, restored to the people of America, after nearly eight years of bloody and unequal warfare; and secured the free exercise and enjoyment of the same, by the noble constitution, under which it is our country's boast, glory and happiness, still to exist.

This was an event which electrified every American bosom, and sent a powerful impulse of the love of liberty among the different nations of the world; and by it, was set an example, worthy of good men, and of the imitation of every nation under Heaven. By it monarchs were made to gather paleness on their tottering thrones, and holy inquisitors to contemplate the future, with direful apprehensions. It was, we trust, the dawning of an epoch, in the ultimatum of which, the lawless thrones of all tyrants shall crumble to dust, and those iron sceptres, which for ages have been wielded over the consciences and persons of degraded millions, shall fall harmless from the palsied hand of tyranny, to be grasped no more forever—and when civil and religious liberty shall unite to bless, to make thrice happy, the whole world of mankind!

From Zelotes Fuller, *The Tree of Liberty: An Address in Celebration of the Birth of Washington* (Philadelphia, 1830).

Something more than half a century, gone by, a numerous widespread and happy nation was given to the world. Great has been our prosperity. Under the mild, liberal and wise government of our choice, we have flourished as a nation, beyond all others. Witness our fruitful fields—our flocks and herds upon a thousand hills—our commerce floating in every breeze of heaven—our homes and store houses filled with plenty—our colleges and seminaries of learning, and our temples and altars of religion. We have covered the seas with our ships; yea, we have rivalled Britain in her commerce, in mechanical ingenuity, and in every species of internal improvement. We are protected by just and equal laws, are blest with ample means of support for ourselves and families, the means of charity for our poor and aged, and the means of instruction for our children. Many learned institutions have grown up among us, that are in their nature powerful, but rigorous—free, but not licentious—and equal, with but removing those distinctions, necessary to the order and subordination of society.

By the generous system of laws we have adopted, all religions are tolerated and protected. We enjoy the exalted privilege of worshipping Almighty God agreeably to the dictates of our own consciences, and there is no one to molest or to make us afraid. We can sit down under our own vine and fig tree, and enjoy the life that was made for man. Surely this is a boon worthy the holy religion of Jesus, yea, worthy an infinitely merciful God—worthy of Him, who has created all men free and the lawful proprietors of equal rights.

Ours is the only government under heaven, where liberty can, in truth, be said to dwell—and the numberless advantages of such a government, for moral, religious and intellectual improvement, may be learnt from the prosperous state of our country since the time she assumed her just and proper station among the nations of the earth. Contrast the situation of America, with those nations where tyranny reigns in all its cruelty, degrading millions of wretched subjects almost to a level with the overladen brute, which cringes beneath the cruel lash, of his more brutish and unfeeling master; and the superiority of our government over all others, will, *must* be apparent.

Here in our beautiful America, are enjoyed all the sweets of freedom and equality, of individual rights and halcyon peace. Here just and liberal sentiments, civil and religious, are tolerated, and flourish in rich luxuriance and perennial beauty. Not so with other nations. Look to Switzerland and Poland, to Holland and Venice, to Russia, and instead of freedom and equality, civil and religious liberty, with all their attendant blessings, you will behold the ravages of tyranny and the dessolations of oppression—instead of liberty and its happy fruits, will be seen degrading vassalage, with all its concommitant evils and bitter consequences. You may indeed look to the empires of Europe, Asia, or Africa, and turn from them with disgust, to our own beloved and highly favoured America—the asylum of the persecuted and oppressed, the land of peace and plenty, yea, the paradise of the world.

What more could wisdom ask or desire for us, in a national capacity, than what we now enjoy? What addition or alteration could be made, as it respects either our civil or religious liberties, that would be of any material advantage? No government, we humbly conceive, could possibly be more favourable to a general diffusion of knowledge, of correct and virtuous principles—more favourable to the cultivation and enriching of the human mind with all that is useful and good, with all that refines and embellishes the mind—more favourable to the promotion of moral and religious improvement, than the government under which we exist.

Wisely did the framers of the constitution of our government, after defining with unexampled accuracy the rights of the citizens, and limiting the authority of Congress, expressly prohibit the latter from interfering with the religious opinions of the people. There has been no change as yet in this particular, and we most sincerely pray, that there never may be. Every species of creeds, and varieties of faith, receive equal toleration and protection. The freedom of inquiry and the right of private judgment, the freedom of the press and of public speech, are still our rich inheritance—they are privileges which the laws of our common country guarantee to every citizen. This is as it should be. These privileges are just and unalienable, they originate in perfect equity, they are the birthright of every individual, and should not be infringed by any one; nor will they be, willingly or designedly, by any *real* friend to the peace and happiness of human kind.

No government under heaven, affords such encouragement, as that of America, to genius and enterprise, or promises such rich rewards to talent and industry. Here, if a man rise to eminence, he rises by merit, and not by birth, nor yet by mammon. This is as it ought to be—this is perfect justice. By the liberal government of our country, ample provision is made, for the encouragement of the honest and ingenious artist, and due support is given to every laudable undertaking. Here, talent is not frowned into silence or trampled in the dust, for the want of gold to support its dignity, nor for the want of noble parentage; but commands the respectful attentions, of all the truly wise and candid, however obscure the corner from whence it emanates, and receives that encouragement and support from a generous government, to which it is justly and lawfully entitled.

Here, every man labours for himself, and not to pamper the pride of royalty, not to support kingly pomp, luxury and dissipation! Here, no ghostly priest stalks forth, and by virtue of her prerogative, seizes upon a tenth, of the hard earnings of the industrious poor, leaving them in a state of want and wretchedness; but they may apply their little all, to the conveniences of themselves and families. He who toils and labours, in the field or in the shop, or in whatever employment he may engage, has the high satisfaction to reflect, that it is wholly for the comfort and happiness of himself or family, if he so please, and that he is not bound by law, to contribute to the support of an artful, tyrannical and corrupted priesthood. . . .

. . . We fear not, that the rights and privileges, guaranteed to us by our most excellent constitution, will be infringed by those abroad, but they may be by a certain class at home, if no precaution be taken to prevent it.

Brethren and friends of America! Something more than half a century ago, Washington and his distinguished companions, nobly asserted, and more nobly defended, the rights and privileges we have been considering. The names of these men, and their unwearied exertions in the cause of freedom, are worthy of our highest admiration, and deserve to pass down the current of time to other generations, that they may live for ever in the grateful recollections of all the most virtuous of the human race. May we and our children rise up and call them blest—rise up and rally round the institutions they have given us, and prove ourselves worthy to be called their sons. May we preserve these rights and privileges, and hand them unimpaired, down to the generation that shall come after us, as a priceless inheritance, yea, the richest earthly boon to man.

If that was a righteous cause in which the fathers of our liberty bled, and who can doubt it, then does not justice demand, that we who now live and enjoy the glorious fruits of their toil and patriotic exertions, should be ready and willing to support and defend with our property and if need there should be, with our lives, the rich inheritance they have left us!

If such be the feelings of our fellow countrymen, if such be the full purpose of their souls, if such their steadfast resolution;—if the principles and feelings, which led the heroes of '76, to declare themselves independent of the British crown, continue to cheer and warm the hearts of each succeeding generation of the happy sons of America, which may God send, then will it be safe to predict that, long shall she remain in the sanctuary of liberty, and the dwelling place of millions of happy freemen. Then will it be safe to say of America that—

The *union* of her states in rapture shall run
Till nature shall freeze at the death of the sun!

Fifty-three years have we been in possession of national independence and political freedom. Our fathers willed themselves free and independent, and behold, liberty followed the sun in his path! *To continue free, we have but to will it!* And will you not do it. O people of America—ye who know the sweets of liberty? To support the liberties of your country, as did our fathers, so have ye pledged your lives, your fortunes, and your sacred honor. And are ye not ready to make good the pledge? Ye who are the friends of American freedom, and of humankind, have but one answer to give, and that answer is yea! Ye will duly honor the cause, that is committed to your keeping. Ye will never prove false to the liberties of your country—nor violate the pledge of your fathers—the pledge of yourselves as Americans.

Remember that the civil and religious liberty which ye enjoy, and which ye hold to be the birth-right of every man, was purchased with toil, and blood, and suffering. Dear was the price which it cost—precious the lives that were sacrificed. Never, O never suffer yourselves to be robbed of such an invaluable heritage, nor quietly submit to any infringement of the rights and privileges which it confers.

I have said, we fear not that the civil and religious rights and privileges, which our excellent constitution guarantees, will be infringed by those abroad, but they may be by a certain class at home, if no precaution be taken to prevent it. Yea, we deem it a truth, too evident to admit of doubt, and too generally conceded to require proof on the present occasion, that it is the intention of a certain religious sect in our country, to bring about, if possible, a union of church and state. To effect this purpose, a deep and artful scheme has been laid, and which may ultimately be consummated, unless it is speedily and vigorously opposed. Yea, the declaration has gone forth, that in ten years, or certainly in twenty, the political power of our country, will be in the hands of those who shall have been educated to believe in, and probably *pledged* to support, a certain creed. Merciful God! forbid the fulfilment of the prophecy! Forbid it all ye, who have at heart, the prosperity and happiness of our nation!

People of this free and happy land! we ask, will you give your consent to the political dominancy of any one religious sect, and the establishment of their religious creed by law? Will you in any way encourage certain popular religious measures, got up by a certain popular religious sect, in our humble opinion, for a very *unpopular* object, but which in the view of many, is very popular to approve? Be assured, whatever may be the *ostensive* objects of these measures, if they should be generally adopted, they will tend to infuse the spirit of religious intolerance and persecution into the political institutions of our country, and in the end, completely to annihilate the political and religious liberty of the people. Are you willing that a connection should be formed between politics and religion, or that the equal rights of conscience, should in any degree be mutilated? Are ye prepared to bow your necks to an intolerant and persecuting system of religion; for instance, like that of England? Are ye prepared to submit to such an unrighteous system of tithes, taxations and exactions, for the support of a *national religion*, as the great mass of her people are compelled to submit to? Are ye prepared to debase yourselves, like so many beasts of burden, before a dissipated nobility and an intolerant corrupted priesthood? It cannot be. I feel certain, that I am addressing those of my countrymen, who are too enlightened and intelligent, too patriotic and independent in their principles, whose feelings are too lofty and whose souls are too noble, who love liberty too well and prize it too highly, ever to submit to such degradation and wretchedness. No! sooner may we perish—sooner let yonder fields be strewed with our bones—sooner shall the tented battle ground, be stained with our blood, as with the blood of our fathers! for what is life without liberty to him, whose bosom glows with the patriotic fire of '76, and who scorns to be a slave? Ye who imbibe the principles and feelings of Washington and his associates, in the days that tried men's souls; ye who are genuine republicans at heart, cannot we think, long debate, which of the two choose, slavery or death.

Be it your care, then, to repel every encroachment upon your sacred rights and privileges—to see that the equal rights of conscience—the freedom of religious opinion—the provisions and the spirit of the constitutions of the political government of our country, are never trampled in the dust, by bigotry, fanaticism, or superstition. Let not the base spirit, of civil and religious intolerance, that bane of our free institutions and misfortune of our country, ever receive from you the least encouragement. Forbid that clerical ambition should ever obtain a leading influence in the political councils of the nation. Keep down that spirit, where it ought to be kept, *in silence and darkness*, that would overthrow the liberty of our country, and establish on its ruins an ecclesiastical hierarchy. Crush the demon of tyranny in the very embryo of his existence. Certain it is, that you *now* have power to do this, and it is no less certain, that it is your imperious *duty* to do it.

Never I beseech of you, encourage a certain *"Christian party in politics,"* which under moral and religious pretences, is officiously and continually interfering with the religious opinions of others, and endeavouring to effect by law and other means, equally exceptionable, a systematic course of measures, evidently calculated, to lead to a union of Church and State. If a union of church and state should be effected, which may God avert, then will the doctrines of the prevailing sect, become the creed of the country, to be enforced by fines, imprisonment, and doubtless death! Then will superstition and bigotry frown into silence, everything which bears the appearance of liberality; the hand of genius will be palsied, and a check to all further improvements in our country, will be the inevitable consequence. If we now permit the glorious light of liberty to be extinguished, it may never more shine to cheer a benighted world with the splendour of its rays. Was it, may we ask, for a *few* years only, of freedom and independence, that our fathers raised the standard of rebellion? Was it for no more than this, they braved an empire's power, endured the toil, hardships and suffering, of an unequal and bloody warfare—that they closed their unarmed ports against the navies of Britain, and bid defiance to the authorities of ancient days and the threats of parliaments and thrones? It is for you to say, O people of America. The destinies of your country, are in your own hands. They are committed to your own keeping. It is for you to say, which ye will have, liberty or slavery, knowledge or ignorance, happiness or misery. I have said, *to continue free you have but to will it.*

If we do not choose the wiser and the better part—if by our negligence or want of zeal, we suffer the liberties of our country to be subverted—if we permit a corrupted priesthood to gain ascendency in the civil government, then shall the like direful fate of other countries, where this has been, and is still the case, be the fate of ours. The abuses which have been practised, the hellish cruelties which have been perpetrated, and the immense amount of suffering which has been inflicted, under governments where the clergy have borne rule, cannot easily be described. Youth and beauty, age and virtue, genius and rank, were equally unable to relax the iron grasp of clerical tyranny. Even now there are regions where the infuriated demon of persecution unfurles her bloodstained banner, and demands that unnumbered victims should bleed at the foot of her unrighteous throne! The past history of the Christian Church, should be a solemn warning to us, never to permit an alliance to be formed, between the priesthood and the civil magistracy—between *Church and State powers.*

To perpetuate our excellent government, and to defend it from the attacks of its enemies, is a duty we owe to ourselves, to our children, and to succeeding generations. It is what we owe to those, who fleeing from persecution, from slavery and wretchedness, in the land of their nativity, have here sought refuge, as the only country under heaven, where freedom and equality, peace and plenty, can be said to dwell—as the only genuine Republic, on the face of the whole earth. To perpetuate our excellent government, is a duty we owe to the whole world. It was long since predicted, that the fate of other Republics, ere this, would have been the fate of ours. "Oh, people of America! weighty is your responsibility! The destinies of mankind hang upon *your* breath. The fate of all the nations of the earth is entrusted to *your* keeping. On you devolves the task of vindicating our human nature, from the slanders heaped on it by superstitious ignorance, and the libels imagined by designing ambition. With you rests the duty, for with you is the power, to disprove the blasphemies of temporal tyrants, and spiritual craftsmen. On you the whole family of human kind turns the eye of expectation. From the Hellespont to the icy sea—from the Don to the Atlantic, suffering Europe hopes in your liberty, and waits for the influence of the virtue she dreams must be yours. On the shores of the ravaged Tagus, the ruined Tiber, the barbarous Tanais and Danube, the palace crowned Thames and Luxurious Seine, where wealth displays its splendour, and poverty its wretchedness—there, in each varied realm and distant region, does the oft defeated patriot, and oft disappointed believer in the latent excellence and final enfranchisement of trampled humanity, breathe his sighs, and wing his hopes to the far off land, which annually celebrates, not only its own, but the world's festival, and renews, in the name of human kind, the declaration of human independence.

Say, will you disappoint these high expectations? Will ye prove false to the cause ye have espoused? Will ye belie the sacred pledge ye have made? It *cannot* be, that ye will.

Proud, happy, thrice happy America! the home of the oppressed—the asylum of the emigrant—where the citizens of every clime, and the child of every creed, roams free and untrammelled as the wild winds of heaven—

baptized at the font of liberty in fire and blood—cold must be the heart that thrills not at the mention of thy name! Search creation around my countrymen, and where do you find a land that presents such a glorious scene for contemplation! Look at our institutions—our seminaries—our agricultural and commercial interests—and above all, and more than all, look at the gigantic strides we are making in all that ennobles mankind! When the old world with its pride, pomp, and circumstance, shall be covered with the mantle of oblivion—when thrones shall have crumbled, and dynasties shall have been forgotten—then will our happy America, we trust, stand amid regal ruin, and national desolation, towering sublime like the last mountain in the deluge; majestic, immutable, and magnificent, in the midst of blight, ruin, and decay—the last remnant of earth's beauty—the last resting place of liberty and the light of heaven!

PART X

The Twenieth Century: Establishment and Free Exercise

The aftermath of the Civil War brought new amendments to the Constitution. The result was an extension of the First Amendment to include the states. The Supreme Court did not immediately turn its attention to the subject of church and state, but by 1879 in *Reynolds* v. *United States* the question of "free exercise" became a part of the Court's agenda. Other decisions such as *Pierce* v. *Society of Sisters* (1925) indicate a growing involvement by the Court in religion questions. In 1940 in *Minersville School District* v. *Gobitis* the Court began the consideration of a collection of cases that have made the church-state issue a central one for the Supreme Court down to the present. Both parts of the First Amendment, establishment and free exercise, have received close attention by the Court, and the two essays included here offer a careful analysis of the cases that proved most significant.

John W. Baker

Belief and Action:
Limitations on Free Exercise of Religion

Despite the fact that the First Amendment specifically states that "Congress shall make no law . . . ." there were many knowledgeable people who were surprised when the Supreme Court, in *Barron v. Baltimore* (1833), held that the restrictions on government actions found in the Bill of Rights were not applicable to the actions of the several states. While the facts and pleadings in *Barron* dealt only with the constitutional requirement that private property shall not be taken for public use without just compensation, the effect of the decision was to declare that all of the Bill of Rights, including the free exercise of religion clause, protected the people only from the infringements of the national government.[1]

In 1868 the Fourteenth Amendment was added to the Constitution, and in its relevant parts it states: "All persons born or naturalized in the United States, and subject to the jurisdiction thereof, are citizens of the United States and of the State wherein they reside. No State shall make or enforce any law which shall abridge the privileges or immunities of citizens of the United States; nor shall any State deprive any person of life, liberty, or property, without due process of law . . . ."

The Amendment does not make specific reference to religion or to most of the other rights protected by the Bill of Rights. There has been a good deal of disagreement between legal scholars on whether there was any intention that the Fourteenth Amendment be related to the Bill of Rights. There

This is an edited version of an address delivered by the author to the Conference on Church, State, and Politics, sponsored by The Roscoe Pound–American Trial Lawyers Foundation, 1981. Copyright © 1985 by The Baptist Joint Committee on Public Affairs. This version is used by permission. The death of John Baker in December 1984 saddened his friends and deprived the nation of a staunch advocate of religious liberty.

is no question that some of the Amendment's spokesmen saw a relationship. Thaddeus Stevens, who introduced the proposed amendment in the House of Representatives, stated:

> The first section prohibits the States from abridging the privileges and immunities of citizens of the United States, or unlawfully depriving them of life, liberty, or property, or of denying to any person within their jurisdiction the "equal" protection of the laws.
>
> I can hardly believe that any person can be found who will not admit that every one of these provisions is just. They are all asserted, in some form or other, in our Declaration or organic law. But the Constitution limits only the actions of Congress, and is not a limitation on the States. This amendment supplies that defect, and allows Congress to correct the unjust legislation of the States, so far that the law which operates upon one man shall operate *equally* upon all.[2]

A prominent analyst of the Fourteenth Amendment's historical origins declared that one of the major objects the Congress had in submitting the proposed amendment to the states for ratification was the nationalization of the Bill of Rights.[3]

Such conclusions have been strongly challenged by other constitutional scholars who assert that existing evidence does not support the idea that Congress and the states, in adding the Fourteenth Amendment, intended to make the Bill of Rights applicable to the states.[4] Chief Justice Earl Warren suggested that the history of the Fourteenth Amendment is "at best . . . inconclusive";[5] and Justice Brennan concluded that the "record left by the framers of the Fourteenth Amendment . . . is . . . too vague and imprecise," and that the Amendment remains "capable of being interpreted by future generations in accordance with the vision and needs of those generations."[6]

The spirit of Justice Brennan's statement had an earlier expression by the Court in *Cantwell v. Connecticut* (1940), which held that the "liberty" in the Fourteenth Amendment made the religion clauses of the First Amendment applicable to the states. Scholars may argue about the intent of the framers and the ratifying states, but the Court has held that the religion clauses have been nationalized.

FREE EXERCISE OF RELIGION: JUSTIFICATION AND MEANING

Justifications of the Free Exercise Clause

As has been pointed out, one of the motivating drives of those who colonized this nation was an intense desire to protect and practice their own religious beliefs. Such a drive made an indelible mark on the mores of our society. An overwhelming majority of Americans appears to have adopted the ideas of our forebears that a person who is guided by religious beliefs is not a great menace to our society and that he or she should be protected from government infringement of those beliefs and actions.

J. M. Clark has suggested[7] that there are at least three justifications for religious freedom:

1. Religious liberty can be justified because it is inseparable from freedom of speech—a justification for one is a justification for the other. The Court has even considered the two together in several cases. A free society can exist only where there is free speech—and, therefore, where there is religious freedom.

2. Religion represents ideas and idealism which serve as a valuable element in the entire society—even though the society may reject the conclusions of the idealist. For example, many Americans who are not conscientious objectors themselves agree with the idea that a person has the right to choose, for religious reasons, to be a conscientious objector to war. A justification of religious liberty on this basis, however, does not give the courts substantial guidance in deciding religious liberty cases.

3. The most important justification for religious liberty relates to fairness to the individual. As Clark says: "The violation of a man's religion or conscience often works an exceptional harm to him which, unless justified by the most stringent social needs, constitutes a moral wrong in and of itself. . . . The moral condemnation implicit in the threat of criminal sanctions is likely to be very painful to one motivated by belief. Furthermore, the cost to a principled individual of failing to do his moral duty is generally severe, in terms of supernatural sanction or the loss of moral self-respect."[8]

These may not be considered as a complete justification of religious liberty to a religious person but they, and particularly the last one, serve as bases for interpretation "by future generations in accordance with the vision and needs of those generations."

"Religion" in the Law

If the free exercise of religion is a "good" worthy of constitutional protection, some brief attempt should be made to define "religion" in terms which aid in discussing the free exercise of that religion.

A leading English legal dictionary does not even attempt to define "religion."[9] *Black's Law Dictionary* defines it as "Man's relation to Divinity, to reverence, worship, obedience, and submission to mandates and precepts to supernatural or superior beings. In its broadest sense includes all forms of belief in the existence of superior beings exercising power over human beings by volition, imposing rules of conduct, with future rewards and punishments." The standard legal definition of the term "religion" is the one given by the Supreme Court: "The term 'religion' has reference to one's views of his relations to his Creator, and to the obligations they impose of reverence for his being and character, and of obedience to his will."[10] However well such a definition may have fitted the concept of religion current in 1890 when it was written, it does not come to grips with the problem of non-theistic religions—a problem which will be discussed below.

Theologian Paul Tillich developed the idea that "religion" should be defined as a person's "ultimate concern." It seems that Judge Augustus N. Hand supported that idea when he said: "Religious belief is a belief finding expression in a conscience which categorically requires the believer to disregard elementary self-interest and to accept martyrdom in preference to transgressing its tenets."[11]

Such an "ultimate concern" definition is appealing in that it focuses on function rather than content. It does not, thereby, place unnecessary preconceptions on the content of free exercise of religion: "it is adequately limited because it excludes beliefs capable of compromise; and it is consistent with the preferred status given to religious freedom under the first amendment because of the importance which the law should attach to the ultimate concerns of individuals."[12] There are difficulties from the legal point of view in such a definition. As a definition depending entirely on the psychology of the individual, it becomes entirely too subjective for analysis and puts courts in the difficult position of attempting to determine the sincerity of beliefs. Such a definition also tends to equate the nature of belief with the intensity with which that belief is held and invites inquisitorial methods in direct opposition to constitutional guarantees.

Other scholars have developed different definitions of the term "religion"—all of them with problems of their own. But this is not a theological study. It can rather quickly be concluded that the term "religion" is not subject to a precise, all-inclusive definition. However, there is every indication that the founders *intended* that the word be interpreted broadly by the courts. "The free exercise of religion protected by the First Amendment extends far beyond the freedom of worship; it includes the right to believe, to practice, to preach, and to teach. Moreover, it includes the right of no religion, . . . [and] it protects disbelief as well."[13]

FREE EXERCISE OF RELIGION: THE SCOPE OF THE PROTECTION

The Supreme Court has stated that the free exercise clause of the First Amendment "embraces two concepts—freedom to believe and freedom to act. The first is absolute, but, in the nature of things, the second cannot be."[14] It is clear that the problem that confronts a court in hearing a free exercise of religion case is drawing an intelligent and logical distinction between permissible actions based on religious beliefs and impermissible ones.

The Supreme Court has given some guidance. When a court evaluates an assertion that free exercise of religion has been infringed, it will apply the tests developed by the Supreme Court in the establishment cases—i.e., it will look first for a secular primary purpose and effect, and excessive entanglement of government with religion will be considered. If the state's actions pass these tests, the court will apply other tests for determining when state action unconstitutionally burdens, denies, or limits freedom of action based on religious beliefs. These tests were developed over many years and were distilled by the Supreme Court in *Wisconsin* v. *Yoder* (1972). In *Yoder* can be found a three-part test: (1) the court must determine whether or not a legitimate religious belief is held and whether the activity affected by state action is pervasively religious; (2) the court must inquire as to whether the state action places a burden or inhibition on free exercise rights; (3) assuming an affirmative response to these two, the court must decide if the burden is justified by a compelling state interest which cannot be served by less restrictive means.

The first of the tests presents some potential problems for a court, but these are largely evidentiary problems. Even though there may be a general uniformity of belief within a sect, a member may hold beliefs which differ from those of his fellows without lessening the validity or viability of those beliefs. Ultimately, the trier of fact must make a judgment on whether a legitimate religious belief is held and whether the activity is pervasively religious. However, "religious beliefs need not be acceptable, logical, consistent, or comprehensible" to others in order to merit First Amendment protection.[15]

The second test rests on an objective basis. Does the state action burden or inhibit the free exercise of religion? A *de minimis* burden may be accommodated to the test, but state action which denies "a benefit because of conduct mandated by religious belief, thereby putting substantial pressure on an adherent to modify his behavior and to violate his beliefs" burdens religion. "While the compulsion may be indirect, the infringement upon free exercise is nonetheless substantial."[16] "The Free Exercise Clause . . . withdraws from legislative power, state and federal, the exertion of any restraint on the free exercise of religion. Its purpose is to secure religious liberty in the individual by prohibiting any invasions thereof by civil authority. Hence it is necessary in a free exercise case for one to show the coercive effect of the enactment as it operates against him in the practice of his religion."[17]

The third test qualifies somewhat the absolute statement above. Even if there is a burden on religion as a result of state action, the state may justify placing that burden if it can demonstrate a paramount or compelling interest which cannot be served by less restrictive means. Thus, the Court, in its first free exercise case, permitted the government to make illegal the plural marriages sanctioned by the Church of Jesus Christ of Latter-day Saints on the grounds that it had a compelling interest in protecting morals.[18] Similarly, the state interest in protecting the health and safety of its citizens was deemed sufficient to permit the banning of the so-called "snakehandling" cults.[19] The burden of proof of both the compelling state interest and the fact that less restrictive means of serving that interest are not available rests on the state when it infringes on free exercise of religion.

As clear as the free exercise tests may seem, litigation abounds hinging on the question of the legitimate burdens which the state may place on the free exercise of religion. The metes and bounds of the protection remain unclear. However, there have been some clear determinations of the scope of the protection in specific cases.

FREE EXERCISE OF RELIGION: CURRENT PROBLEMS

Despite what seems to be a progressive expansion of the protections of the free exercise clause for both theistic and nontheistic religions, there are many unsettled questions about the degree to which the state can limit, regulate, or control churches and their religious mission. The churches prefer to call any state attempts to so limit, regulate, or control "government intrusion into religion." This is a loaded phrase, but it is indicative of the emotion which the churches bring into existing and potential litigation under the free exercise clause.

At the heart of the church-state conflicts and tensions lies a problem of definition. The state, which must deal with the church in a multitude of ways, would like a clear definition of the word "church." Religious organizations resist having the state make that definition for two basic reasons. First, the Constitution clearly gives to the state only secular powers and specifically denies to it any authority over religious matters. Thus, as they see it, the churches alone have legal competence to define what is church and what is not church. Second, the broad spectrum of ecclesiology, belief, and practice within American religious organizations makes it impossible to arrive at a single definition which will fit all of them. To try to force all of them into a preferred mold would be unconstitutional under the establishment clause alone in addition to inhibiting the free exercise of religion to an unconstitutional degree. Any legislation or administrative regulation which attempts to establish an exclusive definition of "church" will be resisted in the legislatures and in the courts by all segments of organized religion.

Flowing from its determination that the state may not define "church" is the religious community's unshakable belief that the church and only the church must define for itself the nature and content of its religious mission. It is a truism that a definition establishes parameters which are limits. If the state defines the religious mission of a church, it is limiting that mission. Only when the state can demonstrate a compelling interest which cannot be served by less restrictive means may it limit or regulate specific actions which constitute the religious mission of the church, but it cannot under any circumstances develop a definition which sets the metes and bounds of the religious mission of any or all churches.

CONCLUSIONS

Churches are not above the law, but neither is government above the law. They are both bound by the Constitution and laws "made in pursuance thereof." The churches recognize the difference between religious belief and action on that belief. They would not argue against state control of actions that present a "clear and present danger" to society; but beyond that they insist that the state must clearly demonstrate a compelling interest which cannot be served by less restrictive means before it embarks on efforts to regulate actions based on religious beliefs. The burden of demonstrating that compelling interest lies squarely on the state. The church must not be expected to make the case that the state does not have a compelling interest.

The special status that the First Amendment gives to religion has its disadvantages as well as its advantages. Because an organizaton is religious, it is forbidden by the establishment clause from receiving public funds. But because an organization is religious, it is protected by the free exercise clause from state demands for reporting or disclosure.

Those organizations or individuals who break the law must expect to pay the penalty set by the law if their offense is determined not to be justified. Religious organizations and their members are no exception. With the exception of claims under the Constitution, they should neither demand nor expect special treatment under the law.

James Madison, the father of the Constitution and of the Bill of Rights, wrote in the famed *Memorial and Remonstrance*: "[I]t is proper to take alarm at the first experiment on our liberties." The churches seem more determined than ever to react strongly to any attempts to limit unjustifiably the free exercise of religion.

NOTES

1. Massachusetts was the last state to give up an established church as a result of an 1833 amendment to its constitution. See J. C. Meyer, *Church and State in Massachusetts* (Cleveland: 1930), pp. 201-20.

2. Quoted in the appendix to Justice Black's dissent in *Adamson v. California*, 332 U.S. 46, 104 (1947).

3. H. E. Flack, *The Adoption of the Fourteenth Amendment* (Baltimore: 1908), p. 94.

4. C. Fairman, "Does the Fourteenth Amendment Incorporate the Bill of Rights?" II *Stanford Law Review* 5 (1949). See also Graham, "The Antislavery Backgrounds of the Fourteenth Amendment," II *Wisconsin Law Review* 610, 659 (1950).

5. *Brown* v. *Board of Education*, 347 U.S. 483, 489 (1954).

6. *Oregon* v. *Mitchell*, 400 U.S. 112, 278 (1970).

7. J. M. Clark, "Guidelines for the Free Exercise Clause," 83 *Harvard Law Review* 327, 336, 337 (1969).

8. Clark, *supra*, 337.

9. J. Burke, *Osborn's Concise Law Dictionary*, 6th ed. (London: 1976).

10. *Davis* v. *Beason*, 133 U.S. 333, 342 (1890).

11. *United States* v. *Kauten*, 133 F. 2d 703, 708 (CA 2 1943).

12. S. L. Worthing, "'Religion' and 'Religious Institutions' under The First Amendment," 7 *Pepperdine Law Review* 313 (1980).

13. L. Pfeffer, *Church, State, and Freedom*, rev. ed. (Boston: 1967) pp. 609, 610.

14. *Cantwell* v. *Connecticut* 310 U.S., 303, 304. (1940).

15. *Thomas* v. *Review Board of the Indiana Employment Security Division*, U.S. 101 S. Ct. 1425, 1431 (1981).

16. *Id.* 1432.

17. *Abington* v. *Schempp*, 374 U.S. 203, 222, 223 (1963).

18. *Reynolds* v. *United States*, 98 U.S. 145 (1879). See also *The Late Corporation of the Church of Jesus Christ of Latter-day Saints* v. *United States*, 136 U.S. 1 (1890), *Davis*, *supra*, 133 U.S.

19. In *Pierce* v. *Society of Sisters*, 268 U.S. 510 (1925), Catholics won the point that parents have the right to send their children to parochial schools. The pleadings in this pre-*Cantwell* case did not stress the religious issue but gave emphasis to property and business rights. Most subsequent parochial school litigation has centered around the establishment clause.

A. E. Dick Howard

The Supreme Court and the Establishment of Religion

Thomas Jefferson brought the "wall of separation" into the permanent lexicon of American relations between church and state when, in 1802, he wrote a letter (oft quoted) to the Danbury Baptist Association on his understanding of the meaning of the First Amendment's religion clauses: "Believing with you that religion lies solely between man and his God, that he owes account to none other for his faith or his worship, that the legislative powers of government reach action only, and not opinions, I contemplate with solemn reverence that act of the whole American people which declared that their legislature should 'make no law respecting an establishment of religion, or prohibiting the free exercise thereof,' thus building a wall of separation between church and state."

Jefferson's "wall of separation" is no exception to the tendency of walls to dominate debate. Much ink has been spilled by lawyers and judges, by historians and theologians, over the wall of separation—on whether the concept fairly expresses the purposes of the First Amendment, whether the wall is in fact as absolute and impervious as the language suggests and how the separation of church and state is to evolve in light of new demands vying with old traditions.

The establishment clause collected gloss only slowly. The Supreme Court's first look at the establishment clause did not come until 1899, when the justices sustained a federal appropriation for a public ward to be administered as part of a hospital run by Catholic nuns.[1]

The seminal case in the modern Court is *Everson* v. *Board of Education* (1947). Though much First Amendment law has been written in the subsequent three decades, Justice Hugo Black's majority opinion remains the starting point for any consideration of the current Court's approach to religious liberty. A man self-taught in the Greek and Roman classics and in British and American history, Black was fond of advising his law clerks to read Tacitus or *Fox's Book of Martyrs*. Black took a preeminently Whig view of history, and *Everson* is an example.[2]

The specific holding in *Everson* was that New Jersey had not violated the establishment clause by authorizing local boards of education to reimburse parents for the cost of having their children ride the public buses to school, including to a parochial school. The opinion is of wider interest, however, for its effort to provide a roadmap for the reading of the First Amendment.

After reviewing the history of religious persecution, Black went straight to Madison and Jefferson for inspiration. Pointing to Madison's "great Memorial and Remonstrance" and Jefferson's Bill for Establishing Religious Freedom, Black declared that "the provisions of the First Amendment, in the drafting and adoption of which Madison and Jefferson played such leading roles, had the same objective and were intended to provide the same protection against governmental intrusion on religious liberty as the Virginia statute." Then Black laid down surely the most famous dictum in any Supreme Court opinion on the meaning of the establishment clause:

> The "establishment of religion" clause of the First Amendment means at least this: Neither a state nor the Federal Government can set up a church. Neither can pass laws which aid one religion, aid all religions, or prefer one religion over another. Neither can force nor influence a person to go to or to remain away from church against his will or force him to profess a belief or disbelief in any religion. No person can be punished for entertaining or professing religious beliefs or disbeliefs, for church attendance or non-attendance. No tax in any amount, large or small, can be levied to support any religious activities or institutions, whatever they may be called, or whatever form they may adopt to teach or practice religion. Neither a state nor the Federal Government can, openly or secretly, participate in the affairs of any religious organizations or groups and *vice versa*. In the words of Jefferson, the clause against establishment of religion by law was intended to erect "a wall of separation between church and State."

Notwithstanding his use of the "wall of separation" metaphor, Black was able to sustain the New Jersey law—which he admitted approached the "verge" of the state's constitutional power—by viewing it as general public welfare legislation, a statute to help children get safely to school, public or private. The First Amendment, Black thought, "requires the state to be neutral in its relation with groups of religious believers and non-believers; it does not require the state to be their adversary."

Everson has been an important and influential opinion. To begin with, it settled (on this the justices apparently were unanimous) that the establishment clause applies to the states. This was not a foregone conclusion. In the same year of Everson, Justice Black, dissenting in Adamson v. California, had argued that the Fourteenth Amendment applies to the states all the provisions of the Bill of Rights—a proposition that Justice Frankfurter and other critics on and off the bench derided.[3] Moreover, as to establishment, some wondered how the Court could apply to the states a provision which, they argued, was put in the Constitution primarily to keep Congress from interfering with state establishments existing at the time the First Amendment was proposed.[4]

Everson's influence went beyond interpretation of the Federal Constitution. State constitutions have often been interpreted by state courts even more restrictively of state aid to private schools than the First Amendment.[5] Everson's "child benefit" theory offered a way to soften some of those state provisions, and the doctrine thus found its way into the decisions of some state courts.

Everson spawned much academic comment, much of it critical. Paul Freund has called the dichotomy between pupil benefit and benefit to the school "a chimerical constitutional criterion."[6] Erwin Griswold has ridiculed Black as an "absolutist,"[7] and as to Black's use of history Paul G. Kauper concluded, "Nothing in the historical research to date lends authority to Justice Black's broad interpretation."[8]

Everson was only the opening shot in the war over the reach of the establishment clause. Subsequent years have seen repeated occasions for the Supreme Court to assess the applications of separationism. The "wall of separation," as Justice Jackson once remarked, has been as serpentine as the walls at Mr. Jefferson's University of Virginia. In 1948 the Court struck down an Illinois "released time" program under which religious instructors were permitted to come into public classrooms, but four years later the justices upheld a New York program which released students during school hours to receive religious instruction off the school grounds.[9]

The Court came down against prayers and Bible-reading in the public schools. The Court thought it unnecessary to ask whether unwilling children were coerced into taking part in these exercises; a finding on coercion (relevant to a free exercise claim) is not a prerequisite to showing that the establishment clause has been violated. But the "wall" was found not to have been breached when states enacted Sunday-closing laws notwithstanding the laws' religious origins; it was enough that they now served a secular purpose.[11] Nor was there a breach (Board of Education v. Allen) when New York lent textbooks to students in parochial schools, even though textbooks are far more central to the educational process than was schoolbus transportation in Everson[12]

The Court's cases between Everson and the end of the Warren era (1969) saw, in addition to significant holdings, important evolution in establishment doctrine. Black had painted with a broad brush in *Everson*. Later cases showed how difficult it was to apply Black's dictum that government could do nothing to "aid" religion. Similarly, "neutrality" has proved a coat of many colors. As for the "wall of separation," Justice Stewart, dissenting in the first of the school prayer cases (1962), complained of the "uncritical invocation of metaphors like the 'wall of separation,' a phrase nowhere to be found in the Constitution."[13]

Some justices could not conceal the difficulties of construing the establishment clause. Justice Douglas joined in approving the New Jersey bus transportation plan and, in 1952, wrote the majority opinion permitting "released time" programs off school premises. Said Douglas, "We are a religious people whose institutions presuppose a Supreme Being."[14] Yet Douglas subsequently became one of the Court's strictest separationists. Concurring in the 1962 prayer decision, Douglas confessed that he had changed his mind about *Everson*—a holding which, he said, "seems in retrospect to be out of line with the First Amendment."[15] And in 1968 Douglas dissented from the New York textbook decision.

As they groped for ways to apply the establishment clause, the justices devised additional tests. The major innovation between *Everson* and the advent of the Burger Court was the test stated by Justice Clark in the 1963 Bible-reading and Lord's Prayer cases, *Abington School District* v. *Schempp* and *Murray* v. *Curlett*. Clark said that two questions had to be asked about a challenged law: what is the enactment's purpose, and what is its primary effect? In order to be valid, "there must be a secular legislative purpose and a primary effect that neither advances nor inhibits religion." The purpose and effect tests quickly become boiler plate in establishment clause options, both during the Warren years and since.

I. THE TENSION BETWEEN
FREE EXERCISE AND ESTABLISHMENT

Securing free exercise of religion and prohibiting an establishment of religion are two ways of attaining a common object—religious liberty. Freedom to worship as one chose and freedom from exactions to support a religious establishment were implicit in Madison's proposal for a religious freedom section in Virginia's first Bill of Rights. Neither Jefferson nor Madison thought the fight for religious liberty complete in Virginia until both rights were secure. It was natural, therefore, that the First Amendment should contain both a free exercise and an establishment clause.

We now see that, though the two clauses may complement each other, they sometimes conflict. Concurring in the Court's 1963 ruling against prayers and Bible reading in public schools, Justice Brennan noted this conflict. There are some practices, he thought, which, though questionable under the establishment clause, might be permissible in the interest of free exercise. Brennan's examples included provision of chaplains and places of worship for prisoners and soldiers cut off from civilian opportunities for public communal worship.[16]

In several cases the Burger Court has had to worry about how to reconcile potential tensions between free exercise and establishment. The possibility of conflict seemed not to trouble the Court in *Yoder*. There Chief Justice Burger granted the establishment implications of allowing a religious group an exemption from general laws. But he concluded that enforcing the compulsory attendance laws on the Amish would have such a telling impact on their religious practices that the Court should come down on the side of free exercise.

Other cases have proved more troublesome to the justices. Programs of aid to parochial schools have provoked the sharpest quarrels among the justices. In *Nyquist* Justice Powell read the Court's precedents as requiring that, in order to resolve the tension that "inevitably exists" between free exercise and establishment, the state must maintain "an attitude of 'neutrality,' neither 'advancing' nor 'inhibiting' religion."[17] For Powell and the majority, that approach meant striking down New York's efforts to relieve the financial pinch felt by parents whose children were in private schools. The dissenters, on the other hand, saw free exercise interests imperiled by the Court's ruling. Justice White argued that, in light of the free exercise clause, a state "should put no unnecessary obstacles in the way of religious training for the young." Likewise, Chief Justice Burger thought that "where the state law is genuinely directed at enhancing the freedom of individuals to exercise a recognized right . . . then the Establishment Clause no longer has a prohibitive effect."

II. "BENEVOLENT NEUTRALITY"—THE ACCOMMODATION OF RELIGION

Of all the themes in the religion cases perhaps none had greater appeal than "neutrality." Justice Black appealed to that standard in *Everson* when he said that the First Amendment "requires the state to be a neutral in its relations with groups of religious believers and non-believers." Yet, like the "wall of separation" metaphor, "neutrality" has proved an elusive standard, difficult of application to concrete facts. Black thought government was being neutral when it reimbursed parochial school parents for the cost of bus transportation. Yet when Justice Douglas, in *Zorach*, invoked the neutrality principle in upholding New York City's released time program, Black dissented.

A wag once commented that there are as many kinds of natural law as there are pies at the Leipzig Fair.[18] The same could be said for "neutrality" under the Constitution's religion clauses. Professor Kurland states his neutrality principle in terms of equality of treatment: "The freedom and separation clauses should be read as stating a single precept: that government cannot utilize religion as a standard for action or inaction because these clauses, read together as they should be, prohibit classification in terms of religion either to confer a benefit or to impose a burden."[19]

Kurland's notion of neutrality leads him to endorse government aid to parochial schools. Paul Freund also points to neutrality as a central premise of the religion clause. Yet Freund's idea of neutrality brings him to oppose parochaid.[20]

In an age of limited government—before government began to play a role in ordering such a vast range of social and economic activities—it mattered less precisely what one meant by "neutrality." Strict separationists, such as Jefferson and Madison, would have argued that the neutrality ordained by the First Amendment required the government give no aid of any kind to religion. Two hundred years later, in an age of positive government, equating neutrality with a strict "no-aid" position invites a more spirited argument. Donald Giannella has maintained that the founding fathers expected religion to play a part in the established social order but also assumed that the state would play a minimal role in forming that order. In our own time, his argument runs, the question of how to treat religious groups and interests "has become a fundamentally different one" from that confronting the founders. Political equality for religious groups requires that they be able to participate in and have access to the benefits of government programs on the same terms as other groups.[21] Were the Supreme Court to adopt Giannella's reasoning, a "no-aid" theory—of the kind Justice Black had in mind—would have to give way to "neutrality" of the sort conceived by Professor Kurland. The implications of such a shift would be the most marked in education cases, notably those involving aid at the elementary and secondary level of private education.[22]

On the Court, Chief Justice Burger himself has been an especially active spokesman for neutrality—or, as he puts it, "benevolent neutrality." His first religion opinion, Walz v. Tax Commission, turns on this principle. Rejecting what he called "absolute" readings of the First Amendment, Burger seems to have joined the ranks of those, on the Court and off, who have criticized the "absolutist" Justice Black and, specifically, Black's opinion in Everson. Cautioning against relying on "too sweeping utterances" in earlier cases, Burger in Walz argued for "play in the joints productive of a benevolent neutrality which will permit religious exercise to exist without sponsorship and without interference."

In the context of tax exemptions, Burger had little difficulty in lining up his brethren in support of "benevolent neutrality" (only Douglas dissented in Walz). But subsequent cases have shown Burger (along with White and Rehnquist) to be emphatically more of an accommodationist than the majority of his colleagues. Granted, Burger wrote for the majority in Lemon v. Kurtzman, invalidating the Pennsylvania and Rhode Island aid programs. But rather than resting his holding on the programs having an impermissible effect of aiding religion, he relied on the excessive entanglement likely to result from the states' need to police the programs to prevent aid to parochial schools' religious functions.

Burger's commitment to accommodating religion became clear in *Nyquist*. Burger, dissenting in part, saw tuition grant and tax relief programs as "general welfare" statutes—sustainable, as in *Everson*, on the theory that it was individual parents, not the parochial schools, who should be viewed as the beneficiaries of the aid. Burger adopted the argument traditionally put forth by Catholic proponents of parochaid—a principle of equal treatment for Catholic parents who must pay tuition costs for their own children while also paying taxes to support public schools.

> It is beyond dispute that the parents of public school children in New York and Pennsylvania presently receive the "benefit" of having their children educated totally at state expense; the statutes enacted in those States and at issue here merely attempt to equalize that "benefit" by giving to parents of private school children, in the form of dollars or tax deductions, what the parents of public school children receive in kind. It is no more than simple equity to grant partial relief to parents who support the public schools they do not use.

Indeed, it is hard to escape the conclusion that, apart from the bare question of the constitutionality of help for the patron of private schools, Burger agrees with the policy underlying aid programs. That agreement is reflected in the closing paragraph of Burger's *Nyquist* dissent, where he invoked the "debt owed by the public generally to the parochial school systems" and praised the "wholesome diversity" those schools make possible.

Justices White and Rehnquist have also taken the accommodationist point of view. Indeed, White was in that camp in the parochaid cases even before Burger; White dissented in part in *Lemon* v. *Kurtzman*. Invoking the principle of benevolent neutrality, Rehnquist is disturbed that the Court should "throw its weight on the side of those who believe that our society as a whole should be a purely secular one."[23] Rehnquist's opinion in *Mueller* v. *Allen*, upholding Minnesota's system of tax deductions for tuition and other educational expenses of parents, represents at least a limited victory for the proponents of benevolent neutrality. Both in finding a secular purpose in the Minnesota statute and in refusing to hold that the statute had a primary effect of advancing religion Rehnquist made much of the public interest in a pluralistic system of education and the essential fairness of recognizing the burden lifted from taxpayers' shoulders by patrons of private schools.

III. THE POROUS WALL: MARSH V. CHAMBERS

Relaxing the Court's three-part establishment test is but one avenue for accommodating state recognition of religion. Another road is to bypass that test altogether. This is what the Court did in another 1983 case, *Marsh v. Chambers*. There Chief Justice Burger rejected an establishment clause challenge to Nebraska's long-standing practice of paying a chaplain to open legislative sessions.

The Court of Appeals for the Eighth Circuit had applied in *Marsh* the traditional three-part test and had concluded that Nebraska's practice violated all three prongs of that test. In looking to history, however, Burger sidestepped the three-part test altogether. Burger found Nebraska's practice to be "deeply imbedded in the history and tradition of this country." That history included the action of the First Congress—the same session that voted to submit the First Amendment to the states for ratification—in appointing a chaplain to open sessions with a prayer.

Marsh's enquiry into history and tradition carves out an exception to the Court's usual approach to establishment clause cases. Justice Brennan, in dissent, thought the exemption a "narrow" one, posing little threat (he said hopefully) "to the overall fate" of the establishment clause. Brennan went through the motions of applying the conventional three-part test, but he devoted many more pages and much more effort to resting his arguments on the "underlying function" of the establishment clause.

Marsh reflects an air of a pragmatic concern about other cases that might be brought before the Court. The majority's invocation of history may signal a concern over their being pestered with suits challenging the use of "In God We Trust" on coins or the opening of sessions of court with the cry "God save the United States and this Honorable Court." In an age in which Americans are quick to take a remarkable range of issues to court, religious and otherwise, the Court has some reason to wonder what religious practice will surface in the next round of cases.

Indeed, the ink was hardly dry on *Mueller* and *Marsh* before the Court, early in the next term, heard arguments in a challenge to Pawtucket, Rhode Island's display of a crèche at the Christmas season. In *Lynch v. Donnelly*, the justices split 5 to 4 in upholding the display. Chief Justice Burger, who wrote the court's opinion, observed that the crèche (owned by the city and erected in a privately owned park) was displayed alongside more secular seasonal figures, such as Santa Claus and his reindeer. Burger concluded that the crèche, rather than carrying an explicitly sectarian message, served to engender "a friendly community spirit of good will in keeping with the season."

The chief justice's opinion in *Lynch* carries something of the flavor of both *Marsh* and *Mueller*. Burger did apply the three-part establishment test, but he wasted few words in finding all three aspects of the test satisfied in *Lynch*. At the same time, however, he characterized the Court as having shown an "unwillingness to be confined to any single test or criterion in this sensitive area." He devoted a fair proportion of the *Lynch* opinion to history, an approach that recalls his opinion in *Marsh*.

The chief justice may have had a broad agenda in mind in *Lynch*. The passages devoted to history are not confined to the practice of displaying crèches. Instead, Burger developed a more general thesis of "an unbroken history of official acknowledgement by all three branches of government of the role of religion in American life from at least 1789." In so doing, he supplied examples of the proclamation of Christmas and Thanksgiving as official holidays, of references to God on coins and in the pledge of allegiance, and of public galleries' display of religious art. Throughout, Burger's opinion is characterized by a distaste for "absolutist" readings of the establishment clause and by an effort to accommodate the nation's religious traditions.

Justice Brennan wrote for the four dissenters in *Lynch*. Dissenting opinions have a way of wavering between hope and fear, and Brennan's opinion is no exception. On the hopeful side, he saw *Lynch* as reaching "an essentially narrow result" turning largely upon the particular way in which Pawtucket displayed the crèche. He saw as an open question, for example, the constitutionality of the display of a crèche by itself or the erection of other religious symbols such as crosses.

On the fearful side, however, Brennan showed obvious concern that the Court's tendency to accommodation presaged a weakening of the traditional limits implicit in establishment clause jurisprudence. He was concerned that the Court's "less than vigorous application" of the three-part test suggested that the majority were not really committed to that standard. Moreover, he was troubled by the Court's "broader and more troubling theme"— the scope and range of practices that government might "acknowledge." Brennan saw the danger that, in so doing, government would be implying approval of or favoritism toward one set of religious beliefs.

In *Lynch*, as in *Marsh*, the majority had signaled their unwillingness to uproot practices that, while carrying strong religious symbolism, have become widely absorbed into the civic consciousness of Americans. The struggle, of course, goes on. In the term of Court following that in which *Lynch* was decided, the Court set several church-state cases for argument. One case involved an Alabama law permitting public school teachers to start the school day with a moment of silence "for meditation and silent prayer"; the second, a Michigan school district's "shared time" program, in which public school teachers were sent into parochial schools to teach remedial and enrichment classes; the third, a Connecticut law giving employees in the private sector a right not to work on a day the employee designated as the sabbath. In all three cases, appellate courts had struck down the statutes as amounting to an establishment of religion. In all three cases, the Reagan administration filed amicus briefs defending the statutes. The Court's decisions in the *Mueller*, *Marsh*, and *Lynch* cases raised expectations that, in the 1984 term, the justices would reach accommodationist results in the cases from Alabama, Connecticut and Michigan (to which the Court added a case from New York involving a challenge to the use of federal funds to send teachers into parochial schools). Those expectations were confounded when, in June and July of 1985, the Court handed down decisions invalidating, in each of the four cases, the practice being challenged. Two of the cases turned on narrow grounds; the Alabama decision does not appear to rule out carefully drafted moment-of-silence laws, nor does the Connecticut decision seem to forbid statutes requiring reasonable accommodation of an employee's religious practices. The two parochaid cases, from Michigan and New York, are drawn in broader terms and reaffirm the separationist lines drawn by the Court in the seventies.[24]

IV. PRAGMATISM AND DOCTRINE
IN THE SUPREME COURT

Justices of the Supreme Court often seek to anchor their opinions in history. In the Court's first interpretation of the free exercise clause, *Reynolds* v. *United States*, Chief Justice Waite looked to the writings of Jefferson for an "authoritative" understanding of the First Amendment. In *Everson* Justice Black looked to the fight led by Madison and Jefferson in disestablishment in Virginia as having had the "same objective" as the First Amendment.

Historians are not slow to criticize the Court's use of history. Mark DeWolfe Howe voiced his disenchantment with the justices' effort to play historian: "The judge as statesman, purporting to be the servant of the judge as historian, often asks us to believe that the choices he makes—the rules of law that he establishes for the nation—are the dictates of a past which his abundant and uncommitted scholarship has discovered." Howe thought that "illusion born of oversimplification" has brought the Court to favor the Jeffersonian version of the "wall of separation"—a political principle grounded in rationalism—over Roger Williams's version—a theological concern to preserve the "garden of the church" in the "wilderness of the world." Modern liberals, according to Howe, have not sufficiently recognized the complexities of motive which fashioned the policy of separation. Howe was concerned that the Court's "current inclination to extract a few homespun absolutes from the complexities of a pluralistic tradition" would stand in the way of accommodating the religious strands in American life.[25]

The years since *Everson* have brought so much gloss on the First Amendment that the Court has fallen into the habit—natural to judges as to lawyers—of putting gloss on gloss. Thus it becomes more important to reconcile an opinion with *Allen* or *Lemon* than to go back to first principles. Moreover, the tradition of a "living Constitution"—a continuing process of reinterpretation—affects religion decisions as much as any other. Finally, the justices—again like lawyers—often seem more comfortable with immediate, real life problems than with theory and abstract principle. Thus they get the feel of the issue before them—aid to parochial schools, or whatever—and try their hand at what seems like a workable approach to the problem. As a result we see the Court evolving pragmatic decisions in which aid to primary and secondary schools is one thing, and aid to colleges another.

Justice Holmes once remarked that a "page of experience is worth a volume of history." Holmes had a way of writing pithy, readable opinions that sometimes made things seem simpler than they actually were. With the advent of the Burger Court, constitutional adjudication seems to have taken on a more ad hoc, episodic quality—in constitutional cases generally, not just in religion cases.[26] But since so much of the case law on establishment, especially aid to education, comes from the Burger era, the present Court's pragmatic instincts have particular importance in understanding judicial glosses on the First Amendment's religion clauses. The justices are by no means oblivious to the origins of the First Amendment. The contours of the religion cases, however, often owe as much to pragmatic institutions as to doctrine grounded in historical judgments.

NOTES

1. *Bradfield v. Roberts*, 175 U.S. 291 (1899).

2. A. E. Dick Howard, "Mr. Justice Black: The Negro Protest Movement and the Rule of Law,." 53 *Virginia Law Review* 1030, 1068-69 (1967).

3. *Adamson v. California*, 332 U.S. 46, 59 (Frankfurter, J., concurring), 68 (Black, J., dissenting) (1947); see Charles Fairman, "Does the Fourteenth Amendment Incorporate the Bill of Rights?: The Original Understanding," 2 *Stanford Law Review* 5 (1949).

4. *Abington School District v. Schempp*, 374 U.S. 203, 309-10 (1963) (Stewart, J., dissenting).

5. A. E. Dick Howard, *State Aid to Private Higher Education* (Charlottesville, Va.: Michie-Bobbs, 1977), p. 27; Howard, "State Courts and Constitutional Rights in the Day of the Burger Court," 652 *Virginia Law Review* 873, 907-12 (1976).

6. Paul A. Freund, "Public Aid to Parochial Schools," 82 *Harvard Law Review* 1680 (1969).

7. Erwin Griswold, "Absolute Is in the Dark," 8 *Utah Law Review* 167 (1963).

8. Paul G. Kauper, "*Everson v. Board of Education*: A Product of Judicial Will," 15 *Arizona Law Review* 307, 317 (1973).

9. *McCollum v. Board of Education*, 333 U.S. 203 (1948); *Zorach v. Clauson*, 343 U.S. 306 (1952).

10. *Engel v. Vitale*, 370 U.S. 421 (1962) (Regents' prayer); *Abington School District v. Schempp*, 374 U.S. 203 (1963) (Bible-readings, Lord's Prayer).

11. *McGowan v. Maryland*, 366 U.S. 420 (1961).

12. *Board of Education v. Allen*, 392 U.S. 236 (1968).

13. *Engel v. Vitale*, 370 U.S. 421, 445-46 (Stewart, J., dissenting).

14. *Zorach v. Clauson*, 343 U.S. 306, 313 (1952).

15. *Engel v. Vitale*, 370 U.S. 421, 443 (Douglas, J., concurring).

16. *Abington School District* v. *Schempp*, 374 U.S. 203, 296 (1963) (Brennan, J., concurring).

17. 413 U.S. at 788.

18. Arnold Brecht, an international lawyer.

19. Philip B. Kurland, *Religion and the Law* (Chicago: University of Chicago Press, 1962), p. 112.

20. Freund, "Public Aid to Parochial Schools," 82 *Harvard Law Review* 1680, 1686 (1969).

21. Donald A. Gianella, "Religious Liberty, Nonestablishment, and Doctrinal Development. Part II: The Nonestablishment Principle," 81 *Harvard Law Review Rev.* 513, 514-15 (1968).

22. Michael J. Malbin argues that, under the "original meaning" of the establishment clause, federal aid to private schools would have been allowed, perhaps even aid limited to religious schools, depending upon there being a secular purpose and upon how one defined "religion." Malbin, *Religion and Politics: The Intentions of the Authors of the First Amendment* (Washington, D.C.: American Enterprise Institute, 1978), preface. *See also* Walter Berns, *The First Amendment and the Future of American Democracy* (New York: Basic Books 1976), pp. 1-32.

23. 421 U.S. at 395 (Rehnquist, J., concurring and dissenting).

24. See *Wallace* v. *Jaffree*, 105 S. Ct. 2479 (1985); *Estate of Thornton* v. *Caldor, Inc.*, 105 S. Ct. 2914 (1985); *School Dist. of the City of Grand Rapids* v. *Ball*, 105 S. Ct. 3216 (1985); *Aguilar* v. *Felton*, 105 S. Ct. 3232 (1985).

25. Mark De Wolfe Howe, *The Garden and the Wilderness: Religion and Government in American Constitutional History* (Chicago: University of Chicago Press 1965), pp. 4-10, 174.

26. See A. E. Dick Howard, "The Burger Court: A Judicial Nonet Plays the Enigma Variations," 43 *Law and Contemporary Problems* 7 (1980).

PART XI

The Legacy of Madison

With all the evidence amassed in this volume concerning Mr. Madison's views and actions regarding religious liberty, one would naturally expect to discover a considerable legacy in the present. The opening essay by Senator Weicker reflects the power of Madison's thought to affect politicians of principle today. The brief comments that constitute the central part of this chapter bear witness to Madison's extraordinary influence. The concluding article completes the picture that Professor Howard began in the first chapter.

Lowell P. Weicker, Jr.

The Bible or the Constitution?

My perspective on religion in America is not that of a historian or a theologian, and I have been accused by at least one New Right politician of flunking constitutional law. That is not true by the way, but neither do I pretend to know it as well as Sam Ervin or Leo Pfeffer. No, my perspective is that of a Member of Congress sworn in all I say and do to uphold the Constitution of the United States, as written by the founders, amended by Congress and the states, and interpreted by the Supreme Court. And if upholding that Constitution means opposing the president and the tide of public opinion on any of a number of church-state issues before the Congress, then so be it. The choice is not mine to do differently.

During the Ninety-seventh Congress, a coalition was built around the issues of religious liberty and the separation of powers. By standing together, we were able to stop Senator Jesse Helms from seeing his school-prayer bill enacted into law. Unfortunately, Senator Helms is from the "try, try again" school of politics, and in March he presented his calling card to the Ninety-eighth Congress in the form of another bill to promote school prayer.*The president is again pushing his alternative: a constitutional amendment to do the same. Tuition tax credits ad vouchers for private and parochial schools are again on the agenda, with the administration optimistically factoring them into future deficits.

Abortion, another issue with serious church-state ramifications, is likely to come up again in an appropriations rider, if not in a full-fledged bill or

From *Free Inquiry* 3: no. 3 (Summer 1983). Copyright © 1983 by *Free Inquiry*. Reprinted by permission.
*Senator Helms's latest effort on this subject was overwhelmingly defeated by the Senate in the summer of 1985. —Ed.

constitutional amendment.

So while we can celebrate the fact that the First Amendment emerged from the Ninety-seventh Congress relatively unscathed, we must be prepared to link arms again in the Ninety-eighth.

In my home state, our license plates proudly proclaim Connecticut to be "The Constitution State," a motto dating back to 1650, when we were the first state to adopt a bill of rights. And it was Mark Twain's "Connecticut Yankee in King Arthur's Court" who decried established religion because it invariably "means death to human liberty and paralysis to human thought."

Unfortunately, Connecticut's record in this regard is not without blemish. Until its disestablishment in 1818, nearly two hundred years after the Pilgrims came to America in search of religious liberty, Congregationalism was Connecticut's official creed. This no doubt made life difficult for the Baptists in Danbury, to whom in 1802 Thomas Jefferson wrote a now-famous letter: "Believing with you that religion is a matter which lies solely between man and his God," wrote Jefferson, "I contemplate with solemn reverence that act of the whole American people which declared that their legislature should 'make no law respecting an establishment of religion or prohibiting the free exercise thereof' *thus building a wall of separation between Church and State.*" (Emphasis added.)

That wall, embodied in the First Amendment, is perhaps America's most important contribution to political progress on this planet. For as Theodore White put it, "Never in civilization, since the earliest ziggurats and temples went up in the mud-walled villages of prehistoric Mesopotamia, had there been any state that left each individual to find his way to God without the guidance of the state."

By building this wall between church and state, we stop either from putting barriers between people and their own beliefs. From the first, this was a wall under constant barrage from both sides. It has been battered by courts and Congresses, local governments and boards of education, preachers and presidents. James Madison noticed this tendency when as a small boy he happened by a window of the local jail and heard one of the prisoners, who turned out to be a persecuted Baptist minister, preaching the Gospel to a crowd outside.

As a young man just out of Princeton, Madison used livid language in a letter to a friend to express his horror that such practices continued in Virginia. "That diabolical, hell-conceived principle of persecution rages among some," wrote Madison, "and to their eternal infamy, the clergy can furnish their quota of imps for such business."

Just a few years later, he would muster his great skills of persuasion and his reading of John Locke and other writers of the Enlightenment to author "A Memorial and Remonstrance Against Religious Assessments." When I rediscovered that document during the Senate floor debate on school prayer last year, I couldn't resist reading it in its entirety to my colleagues. What genius it contains.

When Madison was engaged in debate in the Virginia legislature with the equally eloquent Patrick Henry, Henry is reported to have named city after ancient city that had fallen after religion decayed. He further asserted that the lack of a tax for support of the church in Virginia was the reason for what he called an alarming decline of morals in that state. Henry appeared to have won the day, but Madison one-upped him in the history department. In every one of those ancient civilizations, said Madison, the church had in fact become an established church, and that was the chief cause of its decay.

History books are full of such examples, but so are the daily papers of 1983. In India, we read about Hindus killing Muslims. We read about Shiite Muslims battling Sunnite Muslims in Iran and elsewhere in the Middle East. We read about Protestants and Catholics terrorizing each other in Belfast, Northern Ireland. Where does it all end? The answer is that it doesn't until that wall between church and state is solidly in place and held together with the mortar of cooperation and good will.

And it does no good for the folks on one side of the wall to keep their side in good repair if the others let it fall into ruin. That is why every generation of clergy, lay people, and politicians alike must prop up the wall. Today, we do that by fighting radical rewrites of the First Amendment that are masquerading as good, old-fashioned morality.

The most religious among us should actually take the lead against such proposals, because they are the ones with the most to lose if religious liberty becomes a freedom of the past. Indeed, on the national level, many church leaders have come out against school prayer because at best it would be "a least common denominator prayer addressed to whom it may concern." But the message hasn't yet filtered down to the congregations and parishes. It hasn't reached the people who make up the school-prayer majorities in the Harris polls. People need to be reminded that not so many years ago, right here in America, Baptists were being thrown in jail for preaching the Bible as they knew it. They need to be reminded that Catholics, until the election of John F. Kennedy in 1960, were considered by many to be unfit to hold high public office. They need to be reminded that Mormons and Jews were mocked and shunned and excluded from clubs and communities. People need to be reminded, because it could happen again.

I should think that my Catholic friends would be especially wary of mixing government with religion. American history is rife with examples of discrimination against them. In the mid-nineteenth century, a struggle ensued in the New York City school system over the daily reading of the King James Version of the Bible and the use of other texts disparaging of the Catholic church. This Protestant bias in the public schools was a primary reason that the archdiocese decided to set up a system of parochial schools.

School-prayer supporters vow that the prayer they have in mind should be both nondenominational and voluntary. But to a child who is six, or even twelve, no prayer recited in school will be truly voluntary. Peer pressure is often at its strongest then—when everyone else bows their head, you bow your head; and when everyone else mutters a prayer, so do you, whether or not you believe it, whether or not it goes against everything you have been taught at home and at church.

I myself attended a private school where not only prayer but worship was mandatory, and believe me it was Protestant in form. As a WASP with an Archbishop of Canterbury among my ancestors, I had all the right credentials to feel at ease; but even I felt uneasy, because the form of worship was Presbyterian. My Jewish and Catholic friends were forced to participate or go stand in the park. And we looked on them as something different, just as they must have looked on themselves. Now this school, mind you, was private. No one was there because they had to be. They chose to be, or their parents chose it for them. Public school students have no such choice. Their attendance is compulsory.

Many clergy are sincerely concerned about the fall in church attendance and the dwindling number of applicants to seminaries, and well they might be. But making prayer and other forms of religious expression a government program won't help matters. Government itself is suffering many of the same symptoms. Fewer and fewer people are bothering to vote. Many young people look down on politics as a profession. Political parties, like many churches, have become complacent, too comfortable with their monopolies to get out there and compete. People look at our two-party system and find the ideas and the candidates they have to offer stale and uninspiring. There's the problem with politics and with the church.

Yet, rather than go about fixing up their respective failings, church and state are proposing to join forces. As chairman of the Small Business Committee, I must say that I have never seen a merger between two weak companies succeed, and that is what is being attempted here. In this country, government and religion must stand on their own. If they cannot, then the fault lies not in the Constitution but in those institutions themselves.

We should take to heart Madison's prescription for a free yet moral secular society. According to biographer Irving Brant, Madison's remedy lay in fair laws, proper administration of them, the education of youth, and better adult example. We hear a lot of talk about law and order, but almost always it is in terms of crime on the streets. We underestimate the demoralizing example set by some of the most privileged and best educated in the country who break the law on a daily basis. Whether we are talking about Abscam or Watergate or whatever, we see a privileged group acting as though they were above the law, acting as though because their crime is more sophisticated it bears no similarity to sticking a knife in someone's back. Yet these same individuals may at the same time be some of the most vocal proponents of school prayer. Better adult example, that is what is needed today, not school prayer, or a ban on abortion based on some people's religious beliefs, or even a law proclaming 1983 the "Year of the Bible."

In a recent radio address, the president urged Americans to "face 1983 with the Bible." I don't believe it is up to a congressman or a senator or even the president to espouse or encourage any one religion, or even religion in general. It is not our job to do the convincing, to take up on Monday where the minister left off on Sunday or the rabbi on Saturday. What I *can* and do encourage, espouse, promote, and plead for is greater understanding of the principles on which our nation was built. So I say to my fellow citizens: Face 1983 with the Constitution. And I say the same to my colleagues in the Congress. For we serve our constituents best when we do our best by that document.

I was recently reelected to my third term. Two years ago, when I began the first of the filibusters against bills seeking to strip the federal courts of jurisdiction over busing, abortion, and school prayer, the common wisdom was that messing with any one of these issues was tantamount to writing your political obituary. But I am living proof that that just isn't so. In fact, these issues may well have provided my margin of victory. Not that the majority of Connecticut voters necessarily agreed with me on school prayer, or abortion, or busing. Many disagreed, and vehemently so. But what they did endorse was the notion that the Constitution represents the best of what America is about. They may not refer to it as a matter of course in their daily lives. But they know it is a tough document that sets some high standards for us all, and they want their senator to stand up and fight for those standards.

People are like this in Connecticut and all over this country. They may say they favor the president's constitutional amendment for school prayer, but when the issues are laid out for them in plain language that is simple and straightforward, they think twice. They begin to consider the consequences. They begin to understand what Madison meant when he urged the American people "to take alarm at the first experiment on our liberties." They begin to realize that by allowing a simple prayer in school today, we invite an inquisition tomorrow. "One is the first step," said Madison, "the other the last one in the career of intolerance."

But before this deeper kind of understanding can take place, somebody has to take the time and the trouble to put the issues in perspective. Somebody has to be the first to stand up and say: "Wait a minute. This may sound like a good idea but it's not." It is hard. It won't win you friends, at least not right away. Sometimes even your loved ones won't understand. But it has to be done.

I'd like to ask you to imagine with me the scene in "A Man for all Seasons," after the hero, Sir Thomas More, a devout Catholic and leading citizen, has refused to bless the annulment of the king's first marriage. King Henry, hoping to get even, has sent a spy to More's household. Recognizing him for what he is, More's daughter cries: "He's a spy. Arrest him. Father, that man is bad."

More answers: "There's no law against that." But his son-in-law inter-jects: "There is. God's law." More replies: "Then God can arrest him."

Meanwhile, More's daughter is getting more and more exasperated as it becomes clear that the spy will be allowed to escape. "While you talk, he's gone," she complains.

"And go he should if he was the Devil himself," says More, "until he broke the law."

Sarcastically, his son-in-law inquires: "So now you'd give the Devil benefit of law?"

"What would you do?" More asks him. "Cut down a great road through the law to get after the Devil?"

And his son-in-law replies: "Yes, I'd cut down every law in England to do that."

That was when More had him. "Oh?" he said, "and when the last law was down, and the Devil turned around on you, where would you hide, the laws all being flat? This country's planted thick with laws—man's laws, not God's—and if you cut them down do you really think you could stand upright in the winds that would blow then?"

The wall of separation between church and state is just this sort of law. With it, we are sheltered from the winds of intolerance. Without it our nation could hardly stand as it does today, a haven where people of all religions can live together in peace.

In conclusion, what we are all fighting for is the freedom to interpret life and the world around us as we choose. Our purpose is not to promote Catholicism or Judaism or Buddhism; or the faith of Islam. For, indeed, it may be that none of these is the true faith. Perhaps there is one but it has yet to be proclaimed. And when the day does come to pass when it is to be proclaimed, then in America, if nowhere else on this planet, it will be taught and it will be heard. We hold that door open to the future by fighting for religious freedom today.

Michael Novak

The Wisdom of Madison

Should I ever be forced to a desert island and allowed to take only three books, James Madison's *The Federalist* would be one of them. It is one of the great books about the building of democracy, in all its practical glory, that the world has ever seen. Yet it is sadly neglected. One sees at the United Nations how few have grasped its elementary lessons, how few have ever even encountered them.

This first became apparent to me when, at a meeting in Europe in November 1981, several leaders of Solidarity quoted Madison and argued that they could never succeed in creating democracy in Poland until, as in *Federalist No. 10*, some commercial and industrial enterprises independent of state control could be established. Without an independent commercial and industrial base, they said, state tyranny is imposed simply by taking away the jobs of dissidents. In a nation of one employer, a dismissed architect loses the prospect of ever practicing his craft.

Religious leaders from Africa, Asia, and elsewhere seek a form of political economy that will be free of oppression while enhancing their traditions. Yet only in contemplation of how to create a free society, which liberates religion as it liberates human beings, will one discover the secret of keeping vigorous the traditions that people freely cherish—religious, cultural, and aesthetic. No one more clearly than Madison saw his way through the problems of religious traditions in a pluralist environment—and in a practical way. In the future, both in the inevitable rebellions against Marxism and in the persistent inquiry into ways in which to build free societies while retaining religious and cultural pluralism, Madison will be the best teacher.

From *Free Inquiry* 3: no. 3 (Summer 1983). Copyright © 1983 by *Free Inquiry*. Reprinted by permission.

More than any other American and more than any other figure in the intellectual world, he is the master of practicality in political economy.

A Trinitarian to the bitter end, I would like to make three points. First, it seems so plain that what our founders did exceeds even our current understanding of it. They had learned from the bitter experience of the religious wars that they had to treat well the matter of religion. They had to do so in a practical way that would work. Indeed, that emphasis on practicality is what saved them. They discovered a way of allowing human beings of the most varied sorts of motivations, interpretations of the world, and sense of their own place within the world to cooperate in building institutions and in carrying out a multitude of diverse activities in harmony. It didn't matter so much to them *why* each individual acted well, from whatever faith or philosophy. It mattered how each acquitted his public responsibilities and how cooperatively. Theirs was an extraordinary discovery: that human beings can be one in practice yet various in their image of what they are doing on this planet. Almost everybody else in the world believes "If you're not with me, you're against me." The art of practical compromise and daily cooperation is one of the world's rare social treasures.

Second, do we not have a classic American posture, a common experience, that Madison foretold? When we gather together, each group imagines itself a small, embattled faction threatened by hostile hordes—in this case, by Moral Majoritarians. If we went to a meeting of the Moral Majority, they would have exactly the same image of us, and they would be scared to death of the rising tide of secular humanists. Madison wrote very well on factions and their necessary role, each watching the other like a hawk, with none dominating.

Third, I have noticed that here and elsewhere the moralizing and religious certitude of right-wing forces elicits much greater fear than does that of left-wing forces. We ought to remember that today, if you go to a university, practically the only groups that will forbid you from speaking are on the Left. It's very important that we understand where the dangers of repression come from.

Adam Smith commented on two new experiments of his time, one in South America and the other in North America. He predicted that the South American experiment (which had already been tried for more than a thousand years in the Holy Roman Empire) would end exactly as the liberation theologians are telling us it has ended, in poverty and oppression. Jefferson predicted the same, and Madison too.

The North American experiment, he thought, would end in unparalleled prosperity and unprecedented liberty. He made the prediction not on the basis of natural resources, which in South America seemed superior then and seem even more so today, and not on the basis of the quality of the people, there more aristocratic and here poorer, including criminals and dissidents. The difference he detected lay in the new idea on which America was being established, its new *ordo*, the *novus ordo seclorum*—as it says on the seal of the United States, the "new order of the ages." What was new about this order that excited Smith and of which Madison was to be a chief articulator?

First, it didn't trust political leaders to make decisions of conscience, religion, information, or ideas. It separated the state from the church, the press, and the universities. It freed a whole set of moral and cultural institutions concerned with conscience, information, and ideas, and made them independent of political control. That was a great step forward, but not unprecedented; Geneva and some other European cities had already made substantial experiments in this regard.

Second, neither did the new order trust political leaders to make all of the economic decisions. To an unprecedented degree, it separated the economy from the state. This was the more novel and decisive separation, grounding the first in economic practicality. Madison argued that commerce and industry are indispensable to democracy because they multiply diverse interests and focus attention on practical, negotiable interests, rather than on absolutist passions on which compromise is impossible.

I strongly agree that we should not call the United States a Judeo-Christian republic. On the other hand, neither should we call it a secular state. Secular is an equivocal word. A secular state may be neutral or it may be a state whose worldview is quite different from Judaism or Christianity, with a positive morality to which some might not subscribe. A truly neutral state would honor all those ways of ordering the classical human patterns of doubt and search, as Daniel Boorstin puts it, which are as crucial to the dark night of the soul of the Jewish or Christian believer as to the atheist. We share a common night.

The fundamental insight of the founders might be regarded as plain, ordinary secular wisdom based on the scrupulous study of historical experiments. The founders ransacked dusty libraries to discover what went wrong in Constantinople, what went wrong in Venice, and what went wrong in London in order to invent workable remedies. But this same insight may also be said to be derived from a classical Jewish-Christian conviction, the doctrine of sin. In any case, as I understand the wisdom of the Founding Fathers, they said that you can't trust the state, not in the moral-cultural order and not in the economic order. Each of the three systems—political, economic, moral-cultural—was intended to check the other two. That wisdom was later to be embossed on many American coins in the phrase, "In God We Trust." Its operational meaning is, "Nobody else."

You can't trust any human being all the time. On the other hand, most people are decent, responsible, and generous most of the time. The first premise makes democracy necessary, the second makes democracy possible. Likewise for capitalism and pluralism.

This notion of sin is not Islamic, Hindu, or from any of the other world religions. It arises out of the Jewish-Christian experience, and in any case from common observation. It is as open to persons who are not Jewish or Christian as to those who are.

If this way of looking at our tradition is correct, the operational meaning of a phrase like "In God We Trust" is: Don't trust anyone with too much power, on the one hand, and, on the other hand, open the spiritual way for ordinary Americans of any and every background. In a word, keep the shrine of transcendence empty. People with different conceptions of God will fill that place as each sees fit. And others, in place of the symbol God, will fill it with something like the courage to doubt, an insistence on free inquiry, or a capacity to question any institution and any arrangement whatever. A constitution by which the state does not insist upon filling that shrine, but keeps it empty so as to injure the consciences of none, is an operationally sound fulfillment of "In God We Trust." It allows transcendence according to each human conscience.

There was a story going around Poland last summer about two ways to solve the Polish crisis, a miraculous way and a realistic way. The realistic way would be if Our Lady of Czestahowa should suddenly appear, with Jesus at her right hand and with all the angels and saints, and solve the Polish crisis. The miraculous way would be for all the Polish people to cooperate. This is the way much of the world still works—repressing dissent, homogenizing differences, enforcing false unities.

The great discovery of this country, not well understood in the contemporary world, is that Madison and his colleagues worked out a way by which we could cooperate with one another to solve crises while leaving space, not only to each individual (because the task is not solely private), but also to social, public, and institutional associations of individuals—open spaces in which might arise radically different answers to such questions as "Who am I or who are we—under these stars and on this spinning planet—to be remembered when we are dead?"

Dumas Malone

The Madison-Jefferson Friendship

The friendship between Jefferson and Madison was one of the greatest in history. But it hasn't attracted nearly as much attention as, for example, Jefferson's friendship with John Adams. One reason for that is of course that there was, in the case of Adams and Jefferson, a reconciliation and that gave it a certain dramatic quality. But the other factor is that they were separated to a greater extent than were Jefferson and Madison. This geographical fact led to a considerable difference in the nature and volume of the correspondence.

It was a wonderful friendship, nevertheless. They always saw eye to eye. And I am of the opinion, though I never found proof, that Madison was at his best in Jefferson's company. From the scant evidence we possess we know that they played chess together, but mostly they just talked. And their conversations were so frequent and extensive that it becomes difficult to determine where one man's thinking begins and the other's ends. In studying Madison as secretary of state under Jefferson it was impossible to make the slightest distinction concerning their thoughts on public matters.

They were loyal friends. Madison did some things as President that Jefferson wouldn't have done, yet Jefferson never criticized his friend. For example, Madison signed the bill creating the Second Bank of the United States and Jefferson had argued against the constitutionality of the first bank. Because Madison had done it, Jefferson kept entirely quiet about it.

Granted their near mirror-image condition respecting their public lives, there were times when the evidence suggests that Madison did temper Jefferson on critical issues. For example, Jefferson espoused the doctrine that the earth belongs to the living generation. Madison saw limitations in this idea because he believed one must be concerned with continuity in human affairs. As you know, Jefferson carried his idea so far that he thought the

Constitution should be revised every twenty years. Madison saw the danger of this position and calmed Jefferson down, essentially putting on the brakes in that connection.

Madison *was* a better constitutionalist than Jefferson; he was the more judicious of the two. Jefferson had the more daring mind: he tried things out on Madison and Madison would provide the caution.

On those rare occasions when one does detect public difference, Madison consistently exhibited that caution. For instance, Jefferson, while agreeing that the Supreme Court should be the final judge regarding individual rights, found problems with the Court's role in deciding disputes over parts of the Constitution. Jefferson believed these matters should be resolved by conventions. Madison saw this as completely impractical, opting for the federal judiciary as arbiter. But even here, these were differences of emphasis.

Madison was the more judicious and balanced of the two. Yet, in the end, Jefferson was not likely to be extreme in conduct. I mean, when it got right down to it he'd be realistic. Madison, of course, knew that and when Jefferson said something extreme, Madison didn't think he was going to act in an extreme fashion, because he seldom did.

I regard the work of Madison and Jefferson on the subject of religious freedom as extremely important. When you consider the religious conflicts around the world, which have been and remain the bitterest of all conficts, we have been awfully lucky. We have had some religious conflicts, some religious persecution in America, but relatively little, on the whole, as compared to Europe. It's a wonderful thing that we adopted the principle of religious freedom at the very beginning. The two men may not have been entirely consistent about other forms of freedom, although they were powerful advocates of them, but on religious freedom they were absolutely consistent.

As Madison and Jefferson looked back over history they thought the clergy and the nobles and the kings had tried to prevent the growth of learning and there is a good deal of truth in that. Jefferson thought the clergy was an obstacle to the freedom of the mind. And for him freedom of religion and intellectual freedom were the same thing.

Jefferson and Madison thought there was safety in numbers in connection with religious groups. There was much more toleration where there were a lot of different groups rather than one, which bears out Madison's famous remarks in the *Federalist* papers.

The atmosphere of the time, the spirit of the age, when Jefferson and Madison grew up, and when the Bill for Religious Freedom was passed, was much more liberal than it was when Jefferson died. In the days when Jefferson was a student and Fauquier was Governor of Virginia, it was stylish to be liberal. Fauquier was an extremely liberal and generous man. However, there was an intellectual reaction following the French Revolution and I am sure it was more to one's disadvantage to be unorthodox in the last decade of

Jefferson's life than it was in the revolutionary period.

There was a de facto Christianity by the middle of the eighteenth century, predominantly Protestant it was true. Jefferson and Madison would have found problems with this incursion of religion. They would have been rigid on this question and would have approved of the Supreme Court rulings on the subject of prayer in schools.

Madison's legacy is connected to the Constitution and the Bill of Rights. I don't think we would have had the Constitution, nor the Bill of Rights, without Madison. Further, Madison deserves the title of the father of the Republican party (ancestor of the present Democratic party) more than Jefferson. He started it. Yet Madison lacked Jefferson's gift with the language and he was not quotable, perhaps making his extraordinary legacy less clear to the public.

Sam J. Ervin, Jr.

Madison and the Schools

As Professor Howard suggests in his conclusion to this section, that few have pursued education "more assiduously than did Madison," Senator Ervin's examination of American schools reminds the reader of Madison's legacy in this critical dimension of democracy.—Ed.

THE PUBLIC SCHOOLS

For generations before the school-prayer cases, the public schools of various states conducted religious exercises each school day conforming to the religious beliefs that prevailed in the communities where the schools were located. The school-prayer cases are *Engel v. Vitale, School District of Abington Township v. Schempp,* and *Murray v. Curlett.*

The *Engel* case, 370 U.S. 421 (1962), involved the constitutionality of a New York regulation requiring the following prayer to be said aloud by each class in a public school in the presence of a teacher at the beginning of each school day: "Almightly God, we acknowledge our dependence upon Thee, and we beg Thy blessings upon us, our parents, our teachers, and our country."

The *Abington School District* and *Murray* cases, which were consolidated for decision, involved the constitutionality of a Pennsylvania statute that required that "at least ten verses from the Holy Bible shall be read, without comment, at the opening of each public school on each school day," and a rule of the School Commissioners of Baltimore, Maryland, that required the

From *Free Inquiry* 3: no. 3 (Summer 1983). Copyright © 1983 by *Free Inquiry*. Reprintd by permission.

holding of opening exercises in the schools of the city consisting primarily of "reading, without comment, of a chapter in the Holy Bible and/or the use of the Lord's Prayer."

It was provided in each instance that any child would be excused from participating in the prescribed religious exercises on the request of his parent or guardian.

By a vote of 6 to 1 in the *Engel* case and 8 to 1 in the *Abington School District* and *Murray* cases, the Supreme Court ruled that by using their public school systems to require these religious exercises, New York, Pennsylvania, and Maryland violated the establishment clause of the First Amendment, and that the regulation, statute, and rule requiring them were therefore unconstitutional.

The Court dismissed as immaterial the circumstance that any child was excused on request from participating in the exercises on the ground that governmental coercion is not an essential ingredient of governmental establishment of religion.

The rationale of the rulings was thus summarized in the opinion in the *Abington School District* and *Murray* cases: "They are religious exercises required by the state in violation of the command of the First Amendment that the government maintain strict neutrality, neither aiding nor opposing religion."

These rulings shocked sincere people throughout the nation. It is not surprising that this was so. The custom of holding religious exercises in public schools had been followed in many states for generations, and the school authorities in these states had acted on the assumption that it was proper for these schools to teach the religious beliefs that prevailed in the communities in which they operated.

Many sincere persons charge that the school-prayer cases show the Supreme Court to be hostile to religion. This charge is untrue and unjust. In these cases the Supreme Court was faithful to its judicial duty. It enforced the First Amendment, which commands government to maintain strict neutrality respecting religion, neither aiding nor opposing it.

In these and other cases, the Supreme Court recognizes the supreme value of religious faith in the lives of individuals and through them in the life of the nation.

The First Amendment forbids the states to teach religion to the children attending their public schools. Without impairing this principle to any degree, the Supreme Court makes this observation in its opinion in the *Abington School District* and *Murray* cases:

> It might well be said that one's education is not complete without a study of comparative religion or the history of religion and its relationship to the advancement of civilization. It certainly may be said that the Bible is worthy of study for its literary and historic qualities. Nothing we have said here indicates

308 James Madison On Religious Liberty

that such study of the Bible or of religion, when presented objectively as part of a secular program of education, may not be effected consistently with the First Amendment. [374 U.S. 203, 225]

It is to be noted, moreover, that the school-prayer cases do not question the soundness of the prior ruling in *Zorach* v. *Clauson*, 343 U.S. 306 (1962), where the Supreme Court held that the New York system of released time for religious instruction did not violate the First Amendment. Under this system, the state authorities in charge of public schools released from their customary studies an hour a week children who, acting without any pressure from them, desired to receive religious instruction in churches or church schools outside public school property.

Those who demand that public schools be made instruments to teach religion to the children attending them suggest varying ways to achieve their objective.

Since the school-prayer cases adjudged the religious exercises involved in them to be repugnant to the First Amendment because they were required by state authorities, they propose initially that state authorities sanction voluntary religious exercises in public schools. Despite their good faith, this proposal is fatally defective. In the nature of things, religious exercises sanctioned by public authorities are not, in reality, voluntary.

They propose secondarily that Congress deprive federal courts of jurisdiction to hear and determine cases in which states are alleged to have taught religion to the children attending their public schools in violation of the First Amendment. If it should take such action, Congress would nullify the First Amendment in substantial part by abolishing judicial enforcement of one of the amendment's commands.

They propose finally that Congress and the states amend the Constitution to authorize the states to teach religion to children attending their public schools. If consummated, this forthright proposal would repeal the First Amendment in substantial part insofar as it applies to the public schools.

As a general rule, those who demand that the public schools of the states be made instruments to teach religion are motivated by their desire to have the children attending them taught the religious beliefs of their particular sect of Christianity.

The word *religion* as used in the Constitution is not restricted in its meaning to any particular sect of Christianity, or to the Christian religion in general. It embodies Buddhism, Judaism, Muhammandanism, Shintoism, and all other religions; and the Constitution confers on all persons of all religious persuasions an equality of constitutional right. If those who demand that the public schools be made instruments to teach religion would pause and ponder these things, the ardor of their demand might abate.

PRIVATE SCHOOLS THAT TEACH RELIGION

The Supreme Court held in *Pierce v. Society of Sisters*, 268 U.S. 510 (1925), that a state statute requiring all children to attend the public schools was unconstitutional because the guaranty of liberty of the due process clause of the Fourteenth Amendment gave Catholic parents a constitutional right to send their children to a Catholic school to receive both secular and religious instruction from it.

Although multitudes of Catholics revere and understand the First Amendment in its entirety and oppose taxation of any Americans to support the teaching of any religion, Catholics comprise the majority of those who insist that government give financial aid to private schools that teach religion.

The Catholic church establishes and operates its parochial schools to teach the children of Catholic parents its religious doctrines and observances. Since the First Amendment forbids the public schools to teach any religion, Catholic parents who desire their children to be taught the Catholic faith send their children to parochial rather than public schools. As taxpayers, these Catholic parents pay taxes to help the state to maintain the public schools; and as parents, they bear the added expense of the instruction of their children in parochial schools.

Many of these parents and others demand that government should provide public funds either directly or indirectly to aid and support the parochial schools. They base their demand on the propositions that it is unjust to compel Catholic parents to pay taxes for the support of public schools and bear the additional expense occasioned by sending their children to the parochial schools, and that the Catholic church saves the government enormous outlays of money because Catholic children go to parochial rather than public schools.

Without questioning the validity of the unadorned facts underlying these assertions, these observations are of crucial import:

1. The Catholic parents voluntarily impose the additional financial burden on themselves by sending their children to the parochial schools to obtain instruction in the Catholic faith, instruction that the First Amendment forbids the public schools to give them.

2. The Catholic church operates the parochial schools to ensure that it rather than government will control the education of Catholic children.

Justices Jackson and Rutledge present irrefutable reasons in their dissenting opinions in the *Everson* case why government must refuse to give financial aid and support, either directly or indirectly, to parochial and other private schools that teach religion if the religious freedom the First Amendment establishes is to endure in the United States. Justice Jackson added the warning that government may regulate the private schools it subsidizes.

As Justice Jackson stated in his dissent in the *Everson* case, 330 U.S. 1, 22-28, the First Amendment occupies first place in the Bill of Rights because its objective occupies first place in the minds of the Founding Fathers. He made the objective of the Bill of Rights clear in the opinion he wrote for the Court in *West Virginia Board of Education* v. *Barnette*, 319 U.S. 624, 638 (1943):

> The very purpose of a Bill of Rights was to withdraw certain subjects from the vicissitudes of political controversy, to place them beyond the reach of the majorities and officials and to establish them as legal principles to be applied by the courts . . . One's right to freedom of worship . . . and other fundamental rights may not be submitted to vote; they depend on the outcome of no elections.

The Oklahoma court proclaimed truth when it said in *Cline* v. *State*, 9 Okla. Crim. 40, 130 P. 510:

> The crowning glory of American freedom is absolute religious liberty, every American has the unquestioned and untrammeled right to worship God according to the dictates of his own conscience, without let or hindrance from any person or any source.

It is just as sinful and tyrannical now as it was in the day of Jefferson and Madison for government to tell people what they must think about religion, or to compel them to pay taxes for the propagation of religious opinions they disbelieve.

May America cherish the First Amendment and thus keep religious freedom inviolate for its people as long as time shall last.

Robison B. James

Beware of Sheep in Goats' Clothing

As I reflect on the Madison legacy and how I encountered it in the Virginia House two centuries after Madison served there, I can see that I confronted "Mr. Madison on the church-state issue" in two rather different ways.

On perhaps a dozen occasions the church-state question arose quite explicitly as a matter of principle, or of "high principle" as I might put it, during those 1976-1983 years. Jefferson more than Madison, but both of them together, were a kind of living presence at such times. I was not alone in feeling this, and the deference we paid these two men was far more than ceremonial. Virginia's legislature is one of those least prone to fudge the line of separation between church and state, in my judgment. Nevertheless, I am sure that such a question as "voluntary" public school prayer would show Virginia's legislators to be significantly less absolutist on church-state separation than Madison would probably be, if he could rejoin us at this late date.

The second way in which I encountered the Madison legacy was a matter not of explicit principle but of presumption and routine practice. For me it is intellectually the most interesting way in which Madison lives on. It may also be the more important of the two, since the presumption and the practice I have in mind can quickly rise to the level of principle, if they are challenged by religious zealots.

After I'd been in the House about a year, I read Madison's *Federalist* 10 and 51. That bit of homework allowed me to put a name on what I had been observing and analyzing. (I teach ethics.) I then saw clearly that it was *the spirit of James Madison*, more than anything else, which presided over the business of the House. True, we talked about Jefferson more. But if the voice was the voice of Jefferson, the hands were the hands of Madison. And I mean the hands which usually got things done—the same hands that would have your wallet, figuratively speaking, if you were not wary.

311

It was unquestionably true, as Madison said, that our "principal task" as legislators was "the regulation of these various and interfering interests"—by which Madison meant the clashing *economic* interests. And just as undeniably it could be said that our mandate "involves the spirit of party and faction in the necessary and ordinary operations of government . . ." (*Federalist* 10). Yet we hoped and believed that none of these special interests would tyrannize or subvert the common good, because it would be met and contained by an interest of a conflicting sort. In other words, we were following a "policy of supplying, by opposite and rival interests, the defect of better motives . . ." (*Federalist* 51).

And what has all this to do with Madison's views on church and state? An answer is to be found in an incident which took place on January 17, 1978. The occasion was a legislative breakfast sponsored by the Virginia Council of Churches. The newly inaugurated governor was speaking to an audience comprised principally of clergy and Virginia legislators. The situation gave me a passing twinge of that mild "identity crisis" I occasionally experienced during my early years in the General Assembly. Was I a sheep or a goat? Even though I had been ordained, I was a university professor by vocation, not a church official of some sort. So I settled back, feeling secure as one of the goats.

Then the governor came to that part of his brief speech that had "Madison" written all over it. "Those of us in government," he said, "may not always be in complete agreement with the positions that members of the clergy take in the secular world, because our approach is somewhat different." Turning to the clergy, he continued, "By and large you concern yourselves with making people better, and thereby making things better. Our approach is to try to make things better, taking people pretty much the way they are."

A few days later I got hold of the governor's speech writer. Had he been steeping himself in the Madisonian legacy in some bookish way? "Not at all," he replied. "That part of the speech sprang full blown out of my head."

At first I was disappointed. But then it struck me that the incident gave more credit to Madison the way it happened than if it had happened as I imagined. Madison was so built into the way we normally went about our business that no one needed to look him up in a book. We didn't cite his name. We lived his views.

Or, rather, we should live his views. For in saying that the Virginia legislature normally operates in an unconsciously Madisonian way, I am paying it a compliment. With whatever faults it has, and no doubt there are plenty, it tends to get this issue right: you should beware of sheep in goats' clothing, because when sheer religious passion becomes the spring of governmental initiatives, legislation will so outstrip or outrage the aspirations of the people that there'll be hell to pay. Put otherwise, sheep in goats' clothing can easily turn into wolves.

Paul C. Nagel

Madison the Intellectual

I have always admired Madison as an intellect. I first got acquainted with him
when I taught American Constitutional history. I marvelled at his role in the
Constitutional Convention and his quiet work afterwards. I suppose that
James Madison is perhaps the best example we have (including that of
Woodrow Wilson) of the natural-born professor who got misdirected into
politics. It would have been marvelous, I think, to have had him teaching
history or philosophy, maybe theology in the larger sense of the word. His
was a wonderful mind and what a model for any public spirited person today
in his example to us of the importance of thoughtful, closely reasoned approaches to contemporary issues. He recognized them, understood them. He
just had difficulty translating what he knew when it was his move politically.

Madison's career increasingly marks him as very possibly one of the
three or four seminal minds in American political thought and perhaps our
most discerning critic and advocate of republicanism. In an age when the
nature of a republic is so battered and in such jeopardy, the times we live in
only add to the keenness of his understanding and to the cogency of his
alarm, his concern.

Respecting Madison's presidency, he had to reap as he and Jefferson had
sown in the two Jefferson administrations. It was he who had to try to hold
the Republic together. I suspect, like many intellectuals, it was very difficult
for him to break from the intellectualization of problems and to have settle
for less. His presidency was a great tragedy. It was a legacy, a cross he had to
bear while Jefferson was up in Albemarle wishing him well, glad to get out of
town.

I have difficulty getting beyond Madison as a wonderful thinker about

Interview with the editor, January 28, 1985.

government with such a keen appreciation for human nature. I found him less susceptible to the naiveté and the cheerfulness, the optimism of the eighteenth-century Enlightenment. He was far more aware of the delicacies in human nature as men and women emerged into modernity. I wish that the generation of historiography begun with George Bancroft could have had that in mind before they began to trumpet the certainty of the triumph of the American system. This Eden that Providence had held in reserve for the chosen people is part of the American outlook, and unfortunately the outlook of American historians who think today that if it weren't for certain conspiracies we'd be ushering in the golden age of the learned plowman.

No better example for that human frailty for both Madison and Jefferson was the recollection of those horrible religious wars which were not all that far back. The Jeffersonian and Madisonian system, which was one of stepping back from centralism, has to be remembered as much as anything else as one drawing back from human nature with a healthy skepticism.

My guess is that the concern which did more to make John Adams feel an overriding camaraderie with Madison and Jefferson was his complete agreement with them that church and religion had to be kept absolutely apart from and free from political entanglement. He had the strongest views in that regard and those views moved in and out of his exchanges with Jefferson both before their rupture in friendship and afterwards. Adams's and Jefferson's religious views were very similar. And while he and Madison did not write each other on the subject, it gave Adams a sense of kinship with Madison.

I think this is an important point that it would be well to remember today. As intense as the political acrimony was in the age of Adams and Madison, there were some principles which immediately brought the true statesmen together. Now, this was not the empty-headed, muddled kind of thinking used in addressing principles that I am afraid we have resorted to today to get people on the same platform, e.g., mother and the flag. There *were* some pressing questions in the minds of Federalists and anti-Federalists, or Republicans, at the time, which arose from their general acceptance of the fact that the republic was a fragile business, a very delicate experiment. Adams, along with Madison, saw that if republicanism in the new world, this experiment all the rest of civilization was watching, got bound up in religious disputation, that would be the quickest way to destroy it. I think he and Madison believed it would be a greater danger than if the country got into an ill-timed war. It was passion, unreasoning exchanges in the body politic, that they wanted to avoid.

Robert Holsworth

Madison and the Rights of Society

There is a great sobriety in the American constitutional structure. It is not taking any bets on people, that they are going to be able to act without having passions and interests really shape and direct those actions. Madison and his colleagues were hedging their bets against people, the general population. In addition, they wished to limit the power of any particular member of the government. I think, in many ways, we have been served very well by that extremely sober outlook. This is noticeably true when one examines our political style. As a nation, we have not normally fallen into the trap that has plagued other countries where following charismatic leaders has thoroughly undermined the pursuit of democracy.

There are certain problems that arise with that point of view. For instance, I don't think the Madisonian position particularly encourages popular participation in government. Thus, while we find that the sober attitude concerning human nature has helped us to avoid some of the real problems that have afflicted modern society, at the same time we do have levels of apathy and ignorance about politics. It is something that is almost inexcusable in a modern democratic, technological society. The Constitution is a "script" that was written for the nation, that on occasion may become restrictive.

Madison did have concern that people who were getting involved in state politics were not always the most responsible members of the community at the time. People had taken the democratic ideas a little too far, denying office on the ground of intellect, as they demanded the average person, the representative type. The principal constitutional idea was to discover how you could have the most worthy people to run the government. It was felt that filtering peoples' ideas through representatives would aid this effort. Madison had a great belief that the worthiest people, politicians, would be elected at the national level, so it is not surprising that he did not want

315

316 James Madison On Religious Liberty

critical issues to be decided at the state level.

Today, we don't elect people in a Madisonian way. Jacksonian democracy has given much more popular control over elections. It is quite a distance from the founders, who certainly did not envision having presidential elections decided on the basis of extended campaigns for popular support. Indeed, the nation was well into the nineteenth century before presidential candidates ran personal campaigns. Our campaigns today would have certainly distressed the founders. It is doubtful that Jefferson, a reluctant public speaker, would thrive under such conditions or that a Washington would even bother to run.

In some ways, we have the worst of both worlds. The Madisonian structure for insuring the election of worthy people has crumbled, while the idea that the public arena can be used to pursue private advantage has been elaborately developed and refined. There are some commentators today who see the proliferation of PACs and the aggressiveness of business in the political arena as a sign that the Madisonian system is functioning well. I think not. I tend to believe that a better future is dependent on combining popular participation with an explicit commitment to the public good.

Robert A. Rutland

Madison and Free Exercise

The text for this sermon comes from the first verse of John Adams, Chapter 1: "Soon after the Reformation, a few People came over into this New World for conscience's sake. Perhaps this, apparently, trivial incident may transfer the great seat of empire in America. It looks likely to me." John Adams wrote that in 1755.

A few years before, in 1749, Benjamin Franklin (who as we know was full of common sense) said "History will . . . afford frequent opportunities of showing the Necessity of a Publick Religion, from its Usefulness to the Public; the Advantage of a Religious Character among private persons; the Mischevious [sic] of Superstition, and the Excellency of the Christian Religion above all other antient or modern."

At the Philadelphia outpost of the British empire in 1749, I'm sure Franklin was in tune with his times. Thirty-eight years later he was again in touch with his times when as a delegate to the Constitutional Convention he watched and worked with efforts to prevent the establishment of a national religion.

A great deal happened between the middle of the eighteenth century and its last two decades. Just as a great revolution had taken place in the minds of Americans, so had the pendulum of leadership swung from the older men to the younger men with fresh, new ideas. One of the youngest was James Madison; certainly one of the freshest minds belonged to him.

By remembering how Madison came to regard government vis-à-vis religion, perhaps we can send a few signals to our fellow Americans who need a refresher course in constitutional history.

From *Free Inquiry* 3: no. 3 (Summer 1983). Copyright © 1983 by *Free Inquiry*. Reprinted by permission.

The writing, ratification, and implementation of the Constitution in 1787 and 1789 was a clear warning to the eighteenth-century philosophers that American society was at once experimental and at the same time rooted in the orderly past. While most men had lived under monarchies for centuries, where they used the crown to eliminate risk and stabilize the social order, the American experience from 1776 onward was to proceed in a contrary direction.

No doubt the collective wisdom of the preceding two thousand years benefited the Founding Fathers when they saw the philosophical underpinning for their revolution and its aftermath. But the American War for Independence proved many things. One was that a small country can defeat a large country under certain circumstances. It also proved that a monarchy is not the only way to run a state for civilized people and that a government based on republicanism rather than authoritarianism can flourish over a broad geographic area and maintain its sovereignty and security while permitting its citizens to enjoy the blessings of personal freedom. These were enormous accomplishments.

What was the key element in the whole riddle of good government that Americans tried to solve as the glorious century ended? Was it the founding of a nation on the premise that people can be trusted? Was it the deeper understanding that somehow divine Providence was, as George Bancroft said, to oversee America's future? Happy America, to which Providence gave the tranquility necessary for her growth as well as the trials that were to discipline her for action.

Or was the founding of the United States the culminating historical event after a long series of constitutional developments beginning roughly with Mosaic law, picking up a little from the Sermon on the Mount, and then fusing them all in a secular document? We can only guess that the movement, because it was a great experiment, started at the moment the Revolution began. I'm reminded of Catherine Albanese's *Sons of the Fathers: The Civil Religion of the American Revolution*, which suggests that the Revolution "was in itself a religious experience" for those involved.

After doing considerable research on the First Amendment, I believe that its purpose, in terms of the Founding Fathers, was not to protect *personal* liberties. The point, as they conceived it, was to maintain republican movement through the widest public discussion of what the republic was all about. You might argue that point, but it is a fact that the Supreme Court repeatedly said that the states and not the federal government are involved in religion.

In 1833, Madison got a letter and a pamphlet from the Reverend Jasper Adams, who called for the reestablishment of church and state. He asked for Madison's comments and whether he had changed his mind. He went into the historical background and said that Holland was really the first country where they began to talk about toleration. The prevailing opinion in Europe, England not excepted, was that religion could not be preserved without the support of government and that government could not succeed without established religion, that there must at least be an alliance of some sort between them.

Madison couldn't see this at all. He said: "The tendency of usurpation on one side or to a corrupting coalition or alliance between them will be best guarded against by an entire abstinence of the government from interference in any way whatsoever, beyond the necessity of preserving public order and protecting each segment from trespasses on its legal rights."

He also mentioned the fact that every president had had trouble with proclamations involving religion except one. That one was Jefferson, who did not issue any; and Madison, looking back, wished he had done the same.

I don't see that anything has changed insofar as how Madison would feel if he came back today. He had an absolute feeling about religious freedom; it was not relative. Every time we've chipped away at it—and we certainly have chipped away at it—we have diluted and weakened the original concept, which was to have no religious tie in any way whatsoever.

A. E. Dick Howard

Madison and the Republic

What is the Madisonian legacy? In posing that question, one might recall Jefferson's instructions for his tomb at Monticello. He wanted three accomplishments recorded: the writing of the Declaration of Independence, the founding of the University of Virginia, and his authorship of the Virginia Statute for Religious Freedom. There is no mention of his holding of high offices, such as that of president or secretary of state.

Likewise, the legacy of James Madison does not lie in his public offices, not even the presidency. His bequest to later generations inheres in Madison's having been the architect of the Constitution and the central figure in the shaping of the grand themes of American constitutionalism.

I turn, therefore, to contemporary issues. The question I would pose is this: Were Madison here, what would he think of our stewardship of America's constitutional system? In mulling that question, and because of the central role the Supreme Court has come to play in interpreting the Constitution, I propose to concentrate on the intersection of several essential Madisonian themes with modern Supreme Court decisions.

FEDERALISM

A proper concern for the federal structure calls for the balancing and protection of *both* the national and state spheres of competence. Madison's career reflects a concern about both sides of the federal balance—national dignity and states' competence. Depending upon the issues of the moment, Madison would direct his attention to that side needed to bring the system into balance. Thus Madison's "nationalism" is evident in his proposals for the federal

Constitution, spurred by his perception of the weaknesses of the Articles of Confederation. But Madison was equally concerned to curb excessive federal power—a concern given voice in his authorship of the Virginia Resolves in 1799.

In modern terms, the application of these Madisonian concerns ought to be, first, the Supreme Court's willingness to police Congress' use of the powers delegated to it under Article I of the Constitution, and, second, the Supreme Court's acting as an arbiter of federalism—a function as the "balance-wheel" of the federal system.

As to the first prescription, Chief Justice John Marshall, in his opinion in *McCulloch v. Maryland* (1819), said that it was the Court's duty to see through a "pretext" by Congress—legislation by Congress which, purporting to rest on powers properly drawn from Article I, in fact is not within Congress' competence. Since the so called "constitutional revolution" of 1937, however, the Supreme Court has largely abandoned the policing of limits on Congress' Article I powers. Through the use of a "rationality" test—it is enough that there be some rational relation (it may be a post hoc rationalization) between the statute's object and an Article I power—the Court has taken the path of judicial abdication.

The Court's unwillingness to play any significant role in defining the limits of Article I powers can be understood only as a reaction to the excesses of the pre-1937 period, when judges too often were willing to second-guess legislative judgments about the country's social and economic needs. In the modern Court, however, reaction has become overreaction, leaving Congress in effect to be (in this sphere) the judge of its own powers—hardly in accord with Madisonian precepts about checks and balances.

As to the second assumption—the Supreme Court as the arbiter of federalism—the Court does indeed play that role in protecting federal interests against state encroachments. Examples abound in decisions involving state actions found to be excessive burdens on commerce and in decisions holding that state laws have been preempted because of the operation of federal statutes or regulations. The Court is far more reluctant, however, to play its part in protecting legitimate state interests against federal intrusion. Indeed, in *Garcia v. San Antonio Metropolitan Transit Authority* (1985), the Court concluded that if the states "as states" want protection with the constitutional system, they must look to Congress, not to the courts—a position that ignores both principle and history.

Scholars such as Herbert Wechsler and, more recently, Jesse Choper have argued that "political safeguards" suffice to protect that states' interests and that, accordingly, the Court ought to play no part on the states' behalf. This thesis, however, overlooks the decline of those "political safeguards." Institutional safeguards at one time included the states' election of senators and states' control over franchise and apportionment—the former abolished by constitutional amendment, and the latter sharply limited by judicial opinions and by federal statutes. Political safeguards have also become attenuated. State political parties have declined, and political action committees (PACs) have grown in influence. In general, the growth of the Federal Government has led to an "iron triangle"—bureaucrats, interested legislators (often committee or subcommittee chairmen), and lobbyists. Faced with such evolutions in institutions and politics, it is hard to suppose that Madison would approve of the states—an indispensable ingredient in the federal balance—being accorded so little protection by a court which, by and large, does its job in attending to national interests.

FACTION

Madison voiced a special concern, as he put it in *Federalist* No. 10, about the need "to break and control the violence of faction." Measures "are too often decided, not according to the rules of justice and the rights of the minor party, but by the superior force of an interested and overbearing majority." The "principal task of modern legislation," therefore, is the regulation of the various and conflicting interests.

Madison tended to dislike both factions and parties. In the twentieth century, parties have actually served to dilute faction and crass self-interest. Yet the Supreme Court has contributed to the decline of political parties, for example, in its rulings against patronage. Through the enactment and interpretation of election finance laws, Congress and the Court together have contributed to the rise of PACs, with their pernicious effect on American politics.

In its one-person, one-vote decisions (*Baker* v. *Carr* opening the door in 1962 and *Reynolds* v. *Sims* reaching the issue squarely in 1964), the Court has prevented the states from structuring their legislatures so as to protect competing interests. Dissenting justices such as John Marshall Harlan complained that the Court's majority were writing their own notions of political theory into the Constitution. But an egalitarian, population-based reading of the Fourteenth Amendment prevailed.

With institutional evolution from Madison's time to our own, the search for ways to mute the ills of faction—more precisely, to protect minorities from the heavy hand of majorities—has turned more and more to the courts. In 1938, in the famous fourth footnote in *United States* v. *Carolene Products*, Justice Stone called for a heightened judicial role in protecting First Amendment freedoms, the political process, and racial, ethnic, and religious minorities.

Spurred by the example set in *Brown* v. *Board of Education* (1954), federal judges, both trial and appellate, have become increasingly active in articulating substantive rights and fashioning remedies to redress grievances, especially those lodged by racial minorities or other groups commanding less influence in the political arena. Through a process of "selective" incorporation, the Supreme Court has applied most of the provisions of the Bill of

Rights to the states by way of the Fourteenth Amendment. State courts, too, have been active. In cases involving constitutional objections to economic regulation (an arena in which the Supreme Court since 1937 has taken a largely hands-off attitude), state courts have proved willing to enquire into the realities of preference and overreaching that often characterize laws restricting access to trades and professions. The abuses that Madison recognized—the darker side of faction—are still with us; what is different is the forum in which, two centuries after the Constitution's birth, the problems are more likely to be addressed.

HUMAN FACULTIES

A true son of the Enlightenment, Madison proclaimed (in *Federalist* No. 10) that the "first object of government" is the protection of human faculties. In his *Memorial and Remonstrance* of 1784, Madison declared that the "opinions of men, depending only on the evidence contemplated by their own minds, cannot follow the dictates of other men." His political theory securely anchored in concepts of natural rights, Madison espoused classical liberty interests, chief among them freedom of conscience and expression.

Insofar as they interpret such constitutional language as the First Amendment's guarantees of speech and press, the modern cases owe much to the political theory of Madison and his generation. Current cases, however, go well beyond Madisonian assumptions, ploughing ground not so evidently part of Madison's theoretical terrain. The classical limits enforced *political* freedom—central among them freedom of speech, press, and assembly—and were thought to promote civic virtue.

Today's individual liberty cases owe as much to John Stuart Mill as to Madison. The traditional rights have been enlarged to reach non-political contexts. Self-expression as a value takes equal place with civic virtue. It is by such process of enlargement that the First Amendment has been used to limit the reach of obscenity laws and, invoking free market assumptions, has been invoked to protect even commercial speech.

Owing even more to Mill than Madison are judicial opinions establishing new "privacy" and "autonomy" rights. Madison and his contempraries would hardly have thought in the terms articulated by such Supreme Court opinions as *Griswold* v. *Connecticut*, finding a "privacy" right to the use of contraceptives, and *Roe* v. *Wade*, holding that due process protects a woman's rights to an abortion. The modern autonomy cases clash with the state's interest in enforcing morals and thus chart ground more familiar to twentieth-century notions about the individual and the state than to those of the founders' age.

EDUCATION

Few individuals have pursued their own education more assiduously than did Madison. His single-minded attention to his Princeton studies, to the neglect of his own health, might not be an attractive example to today's college student, but the profit Madison derived from his voracious appetite for books and ideas is undeniable.

Madison drew an explicit link between liberty and learning. Writing to a friend in 1822, he asked, "What spectacle can be more edifying, or more seasonable, than that of Liberty and Learning, each leaning on the other for their mutual and surest support?" Imbued by the same spirit that led him to espouse Jefferson's Bill for the More General Diffusion of Knowledge, Madison declared that a "popular government, without popular information, or the means of acquiring it, is but a prologue to a farce or a tragedy, or perhaps both."

A general system of education, open to all classes and conditions of people, was slow in coming. Madison's hope was to see such a system established, and he looked to legislation, not to the Constitution (which nowhere mentions education). The notion that education is an entitlement—equated, in constitutional terms, with more traditional rights such as speech and religion—was the development of a later age.

The Supreme Court has refused the invitation to declare education a "fundamental" right under the Constitution. Thus, in *Rodriguez* v. *San Antonio School District* (1973), a majority of the justices ruled that the Fourteenth Amendment's equal protection clause did not require Texas to equalize expenditures among poor and wealthy school districts. Nevertheless, in a more oblique fashion, education has come to acquire many of the trappings of constitutional protection. In such decisions as those requiring desegregation of public schools and that holding that Texas could not refuse education to the children of illegal immigrants, the Court looked upon education as having a close connection to other rights.

Madison's state of Virginia has been more explicit. In drafting the commonwealth's present constitution (effective in 1971), Virginians placed education in the Declaration of Rights, alongside the rights deriving from George Mason's 1776 draft. Madison might be surprised to find education thus given constitutional status. But given his linking of education and freedom, he surely would approve.

RELIGIOUS FREEDOM

The road to the First Amendment was paved as much by Madison as by any of the founders. At the Virginia Convention of 1776, the youthful Madison thought Mason's language of toleration inadequate and enlarged the constitutional right to that of religious liberty. In 1784 Madison penned the *Memorial and Remonstrance against Religious Assessments.* In 1791, in the first Congress, he saw to the adoption of the First Amendment, with its twin guarantees of free exercise of religion and no establishment of religion.

In interpreting the First Amendment, the modern Supreme Court has placed direct reliance on Madison. The seminal case is *Everson* v. *Board of Education* (1947), in which the Court split sharply over the issue of a state's reimbursing Catholic parents for the expense of transporting their children to parochial schools. It is intriguing that both Justice Black, for the majority, and Justice Rutledge, in dissent, looked to Madison's *Memorial and Remonstrance* as a kind of legislative history giving meaning to the First Amendment. This reliance on Madison is especially striking when one considers that, unlike the *Federalist* essays, Madison's *Memorial and Remonstrance* was not addressed to the federal Constitution or its Bill of Rights (neither of which existed in 1784), but to an issue of public policy in Virginia.

The Warren Court added to the "wall of separation" between church and state in a series of decisions in the 1960s forbidding the reading of the Bible and the reciting of prayers in public schools. To the surprise of some Court-watchers, the Burger Court—in some respects a more conservative tribunal than was the Warren Court—has proved, in the religion cases, by and large even more separationist. Especially is this true in the "parochaid" cases, in which the court has struck down a wide range of devices by which state legislatures have sought to channel state aid to church-related private schools.

The spirit of Madison hovers over these modern cases. The more obvious Madisonian legacy lies in the majority opinions, separationist in thrust, which keep church and state well separated. One of the arguments in the parochaid cases—that allowing state aid to flow to church-related schools would bring about "political divisiveness," a bitter competition along sectarian lines for public funds—has distinctly Madisonian overtones, reminiscent of his concern about factions, especially religious factions.

The Court's accommodationists, those who would be more permissive of state aid that (if otherwise neutral) may have the indirect effect of aiding religion, might also invoke Madison. To the extent that a governmental program encourages pluralism in education, this might be argued to draw upon another thread in Madisonian thought, that which encourages a pluralistic society as diffusing the coercive power of the state.

The argument between the separationists and the accommodationists is by no means concluded. In two cases in 1984, the Court took an accommodationist tact in upholding Nebraska's paying a legislative chaplain and rejected a challenge to the public display of a crèche by the city of Pawtucket, Rhode Island. The next year, however, a majority of the justices reached separationist results in invalidating state and federal programs paying public employees to teach selected classes in parochial schools. The Court's opinions, and the sharp dissents are occasions for rereading Madison's *Memorial and Remonstrance.*

LIMITED GOVERNMENT

That government operates within a limited sphere was an assumption widely shared by a generation of thinkers nurtured on Lockean notions of compact theory and inalienable rights. The federal Constitution, drafted in the eighteenth century, reflects that century's notions about negative government. Constitutions drafted in the twentieth century—such as the charters of former colonies that became nations after World War II—reveal modern notions about positive government. The newer constitutions expressly recognize duties of government—claims such as social welfare (the right to a job, old age benefits, etc.).

On its face, the United States Constitution continues to stand in the eighteenth-century tradition of using a constitution to allocate governmental powers and to declare the limits on those powers. On such questions as distributing the burdens and benefits of the economy, the Constitution is largely silent.

The gap in practice between the United States Constitution and those of newer nations is perhaps less than one might suppose from a reading of the respective documents. Although the Constitution has not been amended to give explicit recognition to government's affirmative obligations, the courts, through judicial interpretation, have moved in that direction. Especially is this true of the federal district courts' use of their equity powers to undertake the reform of public institutions such as prisons and mental hospitals. Through institutional litigation, judges become managers and oversee obligations imposed upon states or localities to spend money to achieve results ordained by judicial opinions. This trend is distinctly modern (though it has vague roots in earlier cases such as nineteenth-century decisions involving municipal bankruptcies) and would no doubt bemuse Madison and his contemporaries.

A common theme runs through my treatment of the several issues here discussed: the enlarged role of the courts in the making of the constitutional system. At the time of the Constitution's adoption, the idea of judicial review had already begun to emerge. The concept had roots in provisions of colonial charters (for example, those requiring approval of colonial laws by the Privy Council in London) and in a few decisions of state courts predating the Constitution. The need for judicial review became more evident with the adoption of the Bill of Rights and the enactment (also in 1791) of the first Judiciary Act. Marshall made the concept explicit in *Marbury* v. *Madison* (1803).

In modern times the principle of judicial review has ripened into a broader claim—judicial supremacy. Faced with the challenge by Southern officials in the Little Rock School case, the Court proclaimed unmistakably that its reading of the Constitution is no mere law of the case, binding on parties to the litigation and on lower courts, but is in every sense the law of the land. When the modern Court invokes John Marshall's often quoted statement that it is the province of the Court "to say what the law is," the Court means that it has the final word.

Against this backdrop of a more active Supreme Court one can better understand the emergence of what may be called the "litigious society"—a trend to taking more and more disputes to courts for resolution. Among the phenomena associated with this urge to litigate are:

——a marked increase in the sheer volume of litigation (accompanied— perhaps encouraged?—by the number of American lawyers doubling in twenty years);

——courts being asked to solve problems formerly not taken to court (such as sports fans' complaints about a referee's calls);

——judges' growing willingness to declare rights, both substantive (such as rights of personal autonomy) and procedural (such as requirements of hearings by administrative agencies);

——courts' fashioning of more sweeping remedies (as happens in institutional reform cases), resulting in judges becoming managers and administrators;

——the emergence of "public" litigation (class actions seeking ongoing relief), in contrast to the more traditional lawsuit, in which one party sues another for limited relief (such as damages);

——judges' willingness to solve problems and to be policy-makers.

Madison, to be sure, liked to see problems solved. He shared with Jefferson a zeal for reform, although in Madison that instinct was strongly tempered by a pragmatist's search for the middle way. Had they been fellow citizens, Madison and England's Jeremy Bentham would have been admirable partners in addressing practical problems of the body politic.

Going to court to seek solutions to society's thorny problems is attractive to the reformer. Judges may be expected to hand down decrees unencumbered by the compromises and trade-offs of the political process. Judicial review is especially appropriate when used to protect minorities from discriminatory legislation or individuals from arbitrary or capricious governmental acts. Judicial review is, after all, meant to put limits on what majorities may do; that is the point of a bill of rights.

Restraining majorities, putting bounds on the actions of government— Madison would understand all that. But he believed equally in the separation of powers, in checks and balances, and in a republican form of government. Just because he believed that men were tempted to follow their base and selfish motives, this did not mean that he cared to put society's fortunes in the hands of some benevolent dictator. Distrust of human ambitions and designs did not undermine Madison's belief in self-government, in liberty under law.

Were Madison to return and while away a few hours reading modern Supreme Court opinions, he would likely turn his thoughtful mind to a central question of American constitutionalism—how to reconcile the tension between judicial review and our commitment to government in which policy is made by officials ultimately accountable to the people as electors. Since Madison himself cannot give us the advice we want, the next best measure is to take stock of his profound constitutional heritage. Whether it be mulling the power of judges, or thinking through some other question of public policy, we would do well to bring into the balance that nice mix of theory and practice, of past and present, of hope and caution, that characterizes the legacy of James Madison.

PART XII

The Challenge of Madison

Referring to the current conflicts over church and state against the backdrop of the Madisonian heritage, philosopher Paul Kurtz noted: "When the Bible is draped in the flag and used to support a political position, it is difficult for a politician or public figure to criticize it without fear of incurring the wrath of an intolerant public opinion. . . . Was Senator Barry Goldwater not correct when he observed: 'The uncompromising position of these groups is a divisive element that could tear apart the very spirit of our representative system if they gain in sufficient strength'?" This final essay by the most distinguished historian Henry Steele Commager offers profound comment on the Madisonian tradition against the backdrop of modern conditions.

Henry Steele Commager

Take Care of Me When I am Dead

Let me begin with a quotation from a document that is not as well known as it might be. I refer to the treaty that President Washington negotiated with Tripoli in 1796. Article 11 reads: "As the Government of the United States is not, in any sense, founded on the Christian Religion, it has, in itself, no character of enmity against the Laws, Religion or Tranquillity of Musselmen [Muslims]; and as the said United States have never entered into any war or act of hostility against any Mohametan nation, it is declared by the parties that no pretext arising from religious opinion shall ever produce an interruption of the harmony existing between the two countries."

That statement was, needless to say, technically correct. The American people were—and are—predominantly Christian, but the American government has no religious affiliation. That principle is, after all, written into the Constitution—not specifically in terms of Christianity, but in terms of any religion—see the concluding sentence of Article 6. It was reasserted in Article 1 of the Bill of Rights: Madison originally drafted that article to include prohibitions on the states, as well as on the Congress—a provision somewhat mysteriously lost in committees.

There is no doubt that in the revolutionary era the American people and the nation were religious in a score of ways: they acknowledged a divine order, an overruling providence, and so forth. We can go further. A common religion did flourish among Protestants, Catholics, Jews, and deists: we have come to call that a civil religion—a term not used at the time. I would describe it rather as a religion of morality and of virtue. Never was that allegiance put more eloquently than by the most distinguished deist of his

From *Free Inquiry* 3: no. 3 (Summer 1983). Copyright © 1983 by *Free Inquiry*. Reprinted by permission.

age. Listen to the simple and eloquent profession of faith in Jefferson's first inaugural:

> Kindly separated by nature and a wide ocean from the exterminating havoc of one-quarter of the globe, too high-minded to endure the degradations of the others, possessing a chosen country with room enough for our descendants to the thousandth and thousandth generation, enlightened by a benign religion, professed indeed and practiced in various forms, yet all of them inculcating honesty, truth, temperance, gratitude and the love of man, acknowledging and adoring an overruling providence which by all its dispensations proves that it delights in the happiness of man here and his greater happiness hereafter. . . .

Here is Jefferson's friend and rival, John Adams, writing to Mercy Warren whose history of the American Revolution explained American victory in terms of virtue. "Government," wrote Adams, "is only to be supported by pure religion or austere morals. Public virtue cannot exist in a nation without private virtue . . . There must be a positive passion for the public good, the public interest, the public honor, power, glory, established in the minds of the people, or there can be no republican government, or any real liberty."

This "civil" religion was not original with Americans—how could it be?—but accepted, or embraced, by the Enlightenment everywhere, it found perhaps more persuasive confirmation here than elsewhere on the globe—a conclusion put with characteristic succinctness by Thomas Paine: "The American is a new Adam in a new Paradise." It relied on reason as well as on faith, embraced mankind rather than the individual, and was ever conscious of the claims of posterity—a word that has all but disappeared from our vocabulary today. It did not reject Jesus or the Gospels but took from these—as with Jefferson's compilation of the life and morals of Jesus—what was universally valid. Its testaments, moral, philosophical, or political, celebrated virtue, happiness, equality in the sight of God and the law, justice, and life here rather than hereafter. It believed in one form of immortality—the immortality of *fame*—which was the spur: "Take care of me when I am dead," Jefferson wrote Madison; it was in a sense the *cri de coeur* of their generation.

The religion of virtue was put with characteristic simplicity by its most famous popularizer, Dr. Franklin, in his proposal for *The Art of Virtue:* (1) That virtuous men ought to league together to strengthen the interest of virtue in the whole world, and, so, to strengthen themselves in virtue. (2) That knowledge and learning are to be cultivated and ignorance dissipated. (3) That none but the virtuous are wise. (4) That men's perfection is virtue.

This too was the religion of the Enlightenment in Europe, where the *philosophes* of every nation adored wisdom and virtue. They adored it in China, which, as Leibniz said, should be the model for all Europe. They adored it in the South Seas, as we know from reading Diderot's Supplement to *Bougainville.* They adored it among the American Indians, and among the

American non-Indians, too, and a hundred men of letters rejoiced that the Americans were innocent, the Americans were virtuous, the Americans were uncontaminated by Old World vices. America, Turgot concluded, was "the hope of the human race." It was a sentiment with which most Americans agreed.

This was the essence, the quintessence, of the American civil religion. "It is a sublime truth that a bold unequivocal virtue is the best handmaiden to ambition," wrote Washington, and in his Inaugural address he observed that "there is no truth more thoroughly established than that there exists in the economy and course of nature an indissoluble union between virtue and happiness." And when Jefferson paid tribute to Madison it was because "with his consummate powers were united a pure and spotless virtue."

I must resist the temptation to elaborate on a theme that is inexhaustible. Turn rather to the other character that American religion presented—and still presents. For even before the triumph of independence American religion (or religion in America) confessed a split personality. Far more widespread and more popular than enlightenment was fundamentalism. The great awakening antedated the American enlightenment. The great revival of 1803 came while Jefferson was in the White House, and revivals of the camp meeting variety persisted well after Jeffersonian enlightenment was succeeded by Jacksonian romanticism. The fundamentalism of that age, like the fundamentalism of ours, emphasized private, not public virtue; private not universal salvation; and, most passionately, private rather than public sin. It was this fundamentalist faith that found expression in so many of the state constitutions—constitutions setting up, in effect, a state church, requiring overt displays of orthodoxy and disqualifying heretics from the exercise of political rights. All this is familiar enough.

What is astonishing is that popular fundamentalism had so little effect on actual politics. The constitutional limitations on office-holding by nonbelievers had no impact on Franklin's tenure as president of Pennsylvania's executive council. Jefferson, who drafted the statute of religious freedom of Virginia, closed the divinity departments at William and Mary College, befriended Tom Paine, and excluded religion, and not the clergy, from the new State University of Virginia, was not denied any office that he asked for by his fellow Virginians, or by his fellow Americans. He was execrated by the New England clergy, but as early as 1804 he carried every state in New England except Connecticut. Or consider the fate of the great Dr. Priestley, theologian, historian, moral philosopher and natural philosopher, discoverer of oxygen, and founder of Unitarianism. He supported the French Revolution and entered the lists against Edmund Burke. A Birmingham mob destroyed his library and his laboratory and he sought refuge in the United States. When this notorious radical and infidel sailed into New York harbor the bells of all the churches tolled a welcome, Governor Clinton sailed out to greet him, three states invited him to settle in their domains, the University of Pennsylvania offered him a professorship in chemistry, and Jefferson tried to lure him to Virginia.

As president, Jefferson refused to follow his predecessors in designating a day for thanksgiving, as he refused to permit publicly paid chaplains in the houses of Congress or in the armed services. Madison endorsed the Jeffersonian principle, but did not see fit to reverse the precedents of the 1790s, though, as he wrote, he "was always careful to make the proclamations indiscriminate and merely recommendatory."

Philosophically—if that is the *mot juste*—the fundamentalism of the great revivals of the eighteenth century and that of the Moral Majority today is much the same. Both are obsessed with private sin rather than with public vice, both place great significance on public and ceremonial displays of religious devotion, both appeal to emotion rather than reason. But the contrasts—though not so ostentatious—are even more significant. The fundamentalism of the Jeffersonian era, as I have noted, did not attempt to impose its standards on society as a whole, did not punish liberals or deists for their heresies, and did not—with a good many exceptions, to be sure—seek to write their own dogmas into law.

Even where the two evangelical crusades are similar there is a difference in kind. Thus, while both confess a preoccupation, even an obsession, with private vice, it is the Moral Majority that seeks to invoke not just the public opinion but state and national government to punish it. Thus obsessed with whatever excites prurient interest or lascivious thoughts, the Moral Majority calls for censorship of books, films, and television. (Needless to say, this demand does not extend to censorshp of whatever excites thoughts of hatred, pride, ambition, corruption, contempt, envy, or avarice—the sins that most concerned the Founding Fathers.) They invoke the arm of the state to impose the death penalty for violence but have no word or rebuke for atrocities like Operation Phoenix, which took some twenty-five thousand lives, or dropping seven million tons of bombs on Vietnam. They have much to say about the wickedness of limiting posterity whether by birth control or abortion, but little to say about the kind of world children will be born into, or about the wanton destruction of their rightful inheritance of natural resources. They are outraged by injustices in totalitarian nations ("evil empires," President Reagan called them), but did not raise their voices against injustices to blacks and Hispanics in the American south in the fifties and sixties. Their indignation at Iran's seizure of hostages was limitless, but they have not joined those who demand justice to the 104,000 Japanese imprisoned for four years during World War II. They profess to believe in equality in the eyes of God but are undisturbed by gross inequalities in their own society.

How explain the crusade for the subversion of the constitutional guarantees of the separation of church and state and its support by those in the highest places.

First, the increasing number and complexity of those problems that glare upon us from every quarter of the horizon and the ever-present threat to the end of man and of life on earth—a threat too immense to grasp—leads almost inevitably to a retreat to those problems of simple personal morality that men and women can understand, and to which they have, so they believe, answers—answers authenticated by God himself. They intone once again with Henry Lyte, "Change and decay in all about I see, O Thou who changest not abide with me."

Second, connected with this, helpless to understand or cope with immense evils, they turn with relief to those evils that are familiar, that have long been recognized as reprehensible, and that can be dealt with simply and without misgivings, and whose frustration, or punishment, provides not only reassurance but the sense of victory over evil.

Third, government itself has increasingly ignored or repudiated morality in law and in politics, so that the people have become insensitive and calloused to public corruption, unable or unwilling to be outraged by it or to visit it with punishment. Remember Justice Brandeis's warning in the first wiretapping case (*Olmsted* v. *U.S.*, 277 U.S. 438, 1928)?

> Decency, security and liberty alike demand that government officials be subjected to the same rules of conduct that are commands to the citizens. In a government of laws the existence of the government will be imperiled if it fails to observe the law scrupulously. Our government is the potent, the omnipresent teacher. For good or for ill, it teaches the whole people by its example. Crime is contagious. If the government becomes a law-breaker, it breeds contempt for law. It invites every man to become a law unto himself. It invites anarchy.

Finally, politically active religious and moral groups have found a new way of circumventing the constitutional prohibition of any religious test as qualification for any office of trust under the United States. In the past that prohibition has been pretty generally respected, but we are confronted now with concerted efforts to bypass it by the simple device of injecting religious issues and charges, into campaigns by fixing on candidates who do not support prayers in school or oppose abortion with sufficient vigor, the stigma of religious heresy, in short, by a religious intimidation that functions like a religious disqualification.

Jefferson addressed himself to this problem in his memorable bill for establishing religious freedom:

> The proscribing of any citizen as unworthy of the public confidence by laying upon him an incapacity of being called to offices of trust and emoluments, unless he profess to renounce this or that religious opinion is depriving him of those privileges and advantages to which . . . he has a natural right . . . and that the opinions of men are not the objects of civil government or under its jurisdiction, that to suffer the civil magistrate to intrude his power into the field of opinion . . . destroys all religious liberty. . . .

336 James Madison On Religious Liberty

A quarter-century after smarting under the attacks upon him by the New England clergy, he returned to this theme in words that have a contemporary application. "We ought with one heart and one hand to hew down the dangerous efforts of those who would seduce the public opinion to substitute itself into that tyranny over religious faith which the laws have so justly abdicated. For this reason were my opinions not up to the standards of those who arrogate the right of questioning them, I would not countenance that arrogance by descending to an explanation" (1803).

Surely if our courts can interpret the prohibition of a religious "establishment" to forbid a state to provide free textbooks to parochial schools, or to concoct even a nondenominational prayer, it should have the ingenuity to nullify attempts by churches or other organizations to impose religious qualifications for successful candidacy for offices that are constitutionally free of such qualifications.

As Jefferson said to Madison, so Madison may be saying to us over the arch of time: "Take care of me when I am dead."

Contributors

ROBERT S. ALLEY — Professor of Humanities, University of Richmond. Author of *So Help Me God: Religion and the Presidency, Wilson to Nixon* and *Revolt Against the Faithful.*

JOHN W. BAKER — Attorney. Until his death in December, 1984, Associate Executive Director, and Director of Research, The Baptist Joint Committee on Public Affairs, Washington.

DANIEL J. BOORSTIN — Librarian of Congress. Author of numerous critically acclaimed volumes including *The Discoverers* and *The Americans.*

HENRY STEELE COMMAGER — Professor of History, Amherst College. Prolific author of books on American history, including *The Empire of Reason* and *Freedom, Loyalty, Dissent.*

DONALD L. DRAKEMAN — Attorney in New Jersey and currently a Ph.D. candidate in religion at Princeton University. His scholarly area of interest is religion and law in America.

SAM J. ERVIN, JR. — Former United States Senator (D) from North Carolina. Best known for his role in the Watergate hearings, he was a staunch advocate of First Amendment rights.

ROBERT HOLSWORTH — Associate Professor of Political Science, Virginia Commonwealth University. Author of *Public Interest, Liberalism and the Crisis of Affluence* and *American Politics and Everyday Life.*

A. E. DICK HOWARD — White Burkett Miller Professor of Law and Public Affairs, University of Virginia. Author of *the Road from Runnymeade: Magna Carta and Constitutionalism in America.* He served for two years as law clerk to Justice Hugo Black.

ROBISON B. JAMES — Professor of Religion, University of Richmond. Former delegate (1976-1983) in the Virginia General Assembly.

W. K. JORDAN — Late Professor of History, Harvard University. Former President, Radcliffe College. Author of *The Development of Religious Toleration in England*, 4 volumes.

RALPH L. KETCHAM — Professor of Political Science, Syracuse University. Author of *James Madison: A Biography*.

ZELOTES FULLER — American Universalist of the early nineteenth century.

DUMAS MALONE — Former Professor of History at Columbia University, Yale University, and the University of Virginia. Celebrated author of the sterling multi-volume biography *Jefferson and His Time*.

RICHARD B. MORRIS — Gouverneur Morris Emeritus Professor of History, Columbia University. Author of thirty books on American history, including *John Jay: The Making of a Revolutionary*.

PAUL C. NAGEL — Director of the Virginia Historical Society. Formerly a professor of constitutional history. Author of *Descent From Glory.*.

MICHAEL NOVAK — Resident Scholar, American Enterprise Institute. Syndicated columnist and author of *The Rise of the Unmeltable Ethnics* and *Choosing Our King*.

ROBERT A. RUTLAND — Professor of History, University of Virginia. Editor-in-chief of *The Papers of James Madison*. Author of *The Birth of the Bill of Rights.*

MARVIN K. SINGLETON — Formerly Walter Perry Johnson Scholar in Law, School of Law, University of California. Author of *H. L. Mencken and the American Mercury.*.

LOWELL P. WEICKER, JR. — United States Senator (R) from the state of Connecticut. He led the fight against the school prayer advocates in 1984.

JOHN F. WILSON — Collard Professor of Religion, Princeton University. Author and editor of several books on American religious history and public religion, he is working on an interpretation of the church-state issue in American culture.